STRIKE SWIFTLY!

STRIKE SWIFTLY!

THE
70TH TANK BATTALION

FROM NORTH AFRICA TO
NORMANDY TO GERMANY

MARVIN JENSEN

PRESIDIO

In memory of my parents, Lawrence and Ann Jensen

Copyright © 1997 by Marvin G. Jensen

Published by Presidio Press
505 B San Marin Drive, Suite 300
Novato, CA 94945-1340

Library of Congress Cataloging-in-Publication Data

Jenson, Marvin G.
    Strike swiftly! : the 70th Tank Battalion from North Africa to Normandy to Germany / Marvin G. Jensen.
        p.   cm.
    Includes bibliographical references.
    ISBN 0-89141-610-2 (hardcover)
    1. United States. Army. Tank Battalion, 70th—History. 2. World War, 1939–1945—Regimental histories—United States. I. Title. II. Title: Strike swiftly, the seventieth Tank Battalion from North Africa to Normandy to Germany
D769.306 70th.J46   1997
940.54'1273—dc21   96-50273
                                          CIP

All photos from author's collection unless otherwise noted.

Printed in the United States of America

Contents

Foreword

I recently had the honor of being invited to speak at a reunion of the 70th Tank Battalion Association (World War II veterans) and the 70th Heavy Tank Battalion Association (Korean war veterans) in September 1996. As I stood at the podium and looked out at the seated veterans, their families, and their friends, I felt so inadequate. How could I stand there and talk to *them* about the army? Most of these men had seen months of combat, many had been wounded, some several times. I was nervous, but made it through my presentation all right, ultimately strengthened by the presence of these fine, brave men.

The 70th Tank Battalion's history in World War II is one of the most remarkable stories in the annals of military history. Marvin Jensen, a veteran of the 70th, compellingly describes the men, their machines, and the incredible stories of combat in eight major campaigns in the European theater of World War II. Starting in July 1940, the first battalion of the newly created armored force was added to the rolls of the United States Army. Fifty-six years, three wars, and sixteen campaigns later, the 70th Armor continues to actively serve its country. The story of those first tankers is found within these pages. It is the story of courage, of the capabilities of the human spirit, and the bond between men forged in battle. Through North Africa, Sicily, Normandy, and Germany, the tankers of the 70th fought against Hitler's Panzers. Outgunned and outarmored, they prevailed to achieve victory over the evil that threatened to cover the world. One hundred and sixty-one men of the battalion paid the supreme price for freedom.

The story of the 70th continued after World War II. Robert Baker, a young 1st lieutenant of C Company, led the breakout from Pusan in the Korean War and was the first to link up with MacArthur outside Inchon in 1950. Every tank in B Company was destroyed at Unsan, the survivors fought south on foot through thousands of Chinese to reach U. N. lines. Forty-seven soldiers died, more than 500 were wounded by the end of 1951. Finally, in 1991, the 2d and 4th battalions of the 70th found themselves in Saudi Arabia. On the 24th of February they, as part of the First Armored Division, crossed the border into Iraq. Eighty-nine hours and 255 kilometers later the war was over. In this last war, the 70th lost no one. The weapons and technology have changed, but it is still the men in the tanks that fight the wars. The Sherman dozer tanks that came ashore during D-Day are far removed from the mineplow-equipped MIA1s that smashed the Iraqi defenses in the Gulf War. But the soldiers are the same.

Currently, there is only one battalion of the 70th Armor on active duty, the 2d Battalion. Assigned to Fort Riley, Kansas, the regimental flag hands proudly at its headquarters. Twenty-two streamers, signifying sixteen campaigns, four Presidential unit citations, and two foreign decorations for valor fly from its staff. The 70th, not surprisingly, is recognized as the most decorated armor unit in the military of the United States.

Six hundred and thirty five soldiers carry on the traditions begun fifty-six years ago. On organization day, 15 July, the soldiers stand in formation and listen as the history of the regiment is read. The men talk proudly about "their" tanks at Normandy, Taegu, The Huertgen Forest, and Safwari. On 6 June of each year a wreath is laid at the "Rock" in front of the battalion's headquarters in memory of those who fell at Utah beach in 1944. The traditions continue, lest we forget.

Today, the 2d Battalion is organized as a heavy tank battalion—fifty-eight MIA1 main battle tanks make up its striking power. Four tank companies supported by a headquarters company are prepared to go anywhere, at anytime, to accomplish any mission.

Scott L. Downing
1st Lieutenant, Armor
Regimental Historian
70th Armor Regiment
United States Army

Preface

This is the story of what men of the 70th Tank Battalion saw and did. Most contributions are from interviews and conversations conducted from the summer of 1990 to September 1993. A few men submitted written accounts. Although their recollections go back fifty years, most are as fresh and vital as if the events occurred yesterday, for this was a pivotal and traumatic period of their lives. Some declined to comment. Whatever their reasons, they remain inviolate.

The journals of Charles Myers and John Ahearn date from the time. So do my letters, which fortunately my mother kept. Other original source material was used for particulars on where, when, and what happened. For the actions involving C Company in French Morocco, the official after-action reports of the company commander were useful. So were the reports of the battalion commander and the C Company commander in Sicily. A clerk from B Company kept a daily unofficial journal beginning in Sicily, with the only lapse in England, continuing again from D day until the end of the war. This daily journal was unearthed at the National Archives. Joseph Nesbit served as the C Company clerk through the war. He had access to other reports, which he retained and sent to me.

The History of the 70th Tank Battalion was of particular and special value. This unpublished history was produced by the 70th Tank Battalion Association in 1950, a time close to the events. It provided a good basis for understanding what happened and where, and for accounts of many of the incidents used in the narrative.

In writing this book, I have a dual role. I participated in many of the events, but I write as a historian. The term *participated* is used advisedly. I was a cook and never experienced combat in the way tankers did. There was a special confraternity among tankers that I, for one, never sought to enter. It would have been unseemly to do so. In Normandy, for example, tankers would often leave the bivouac at dawn and return at dusk. It was likely someone I knew would be killed or wounded, yet I never dared ask how.

This is not to derogate what I and others did in support of the combat elements. Everyone had a duty to perform. Together we made the battalion function. So although the focus is on the fighting, I have also tried to make this a complete story of the battalion. We were all men of the 70th, and proud of it.

As much as possible, I let the men involved tell their story. My task, as I see it, is to piece it all together to make it a story of one tank battalion. It is not a history of World War II, although the record of the 70th encompasses about as much of the European war as any small American unit could. The men of the 70th deserve more recognition than they have received. Posterity should know of it. This is the obligation I feel. Soon our voices will be silent. It has to be done now.

My decision to undertake this labor of love occurred long after retirement from teaching. Since the end of the war, my life evolved around family, friends, and the academic world. Yet never for a moment was my war experience forgotten. Then, in 1989, my old buddy Paul Gaul mailed a letter urging me to attend the annual unit reunion to be held in Canton, Ohio. I did, and what I saw and felt was so moving that I was quickly drawn back into what had been the greatest single experience of my life. "Before this evening is over, Jensen, you will be crying like a baby," Paul Gaul told me at the banquet. He was referring to the Ceremony of the Flames. One man from each company lit candles for our dead comrades. Gaul was right.

The esprit de corps of the 70th lives on at these reunions, now including an extended family of wives and children. Since the first reunion in 1948, not a single year has passed without one. This speaks volumes about the 70th and of the men who forged a lifelong comradeship.

There were many good outfits that served the nation well. Each has earned its place in history. So has the 70th. It was one of the best. During the postwar period, only units with outstanding war records were selected to remain in the army as part of the school system. The 70th was selected as the outstanding tank battalion and assigned to Fort Knox, "The Home of Armor."

In the Korean war the 70th Heavy Tank Battalion added more battle streamers to the battalion flag. So did the 70th Armored Regiment in Desert Storm, the war against Iraq, bringing the total number of streamers to 21, the most for a tank unit in the Unites States Army.

The traditions established during World War II were ably carried on. A new 70th remained active until 1992. Let us hope that in a world of humanity at peace there will never be a need for it to be reactivated.

The list of people who helped me most in preparing this book is found in the bibliography. My gratitude extends to Norman and Natalie Friend. Without them, the road would have been far more difficult, if not impossible.

Michael Tansey was instrumental in getting me going after a halting start, and he read and edited the entire manuscript. Richard Tansey provided guidance in both style and content. Roland Lee read the manuscript and made needed corrections. Ridley Virdeh and Elizabeth Waldo also read it and gave me the viewpoint of an intelligent, attentive readers from a younger generation. Charles Tansey offered good advice and constant encouragement. Richard Waldo, Erich David, and Bill Grinager all provided much-needed technical support. Elizabeth Waldo produced the computer maps at Graphics Plus, San Jose, California.

The following is offered to assist the reader unaccustomed to terms used in the book regarding military organization:

In North Africa and Sicily, the 70th was a light tank battalion, with three tank companies, each with three platoons of five tanks, plus command tanks. Light tanks had crews of four men. From England and on as a standard tank battalion, the 70th had three medium tank companies, and one light tank company, all with three platoons of five tanks. Mediums (Shermans) had crews of five. In all campaigns the battalion had a headquarters company, a service company, and a medical detachment.

The 70th was attached to infantry divisions, each of which had three regiments with three battalions per regiment. In the chain of command, infantry divisions were under the command of a corps, and a corps under the command of an army.

Introduction

This is a soldiers' story of a remarkable tank battalion in World War II. What the men of the 70th Tank Battalion achieved exemplifies the American spirit and the American tradition of civilian soldiers coming forward during dire national need.

These soldiers were ordinary, average, common citizens—common in the sense that they were undistinguished in peacetime occupation, social position, economic advantage, or education. These were the soldiers I served with, and whose testimony I record in this book. Working together they performed uncommonly well in the war. And when the work they had to do was finished, they returned to the peacetime concerns they had left behind, without making any claim to exceptional privilege or reward. The prevailing attitude as I heard it expressed in their own words was far from vainglorious. It was like that in the statement of an American soldier from another time and place.

> I reflected that armies are made up of average people, and that no more would be demanded of me than the general run of people could accomplish . . . Don't call me Hero. I trust I did my duty as a soldier respectably, and did nothing remarkable.

These are the statements of a Union soldier in the Civil War, three times wounded in battle, twice almost fatally. The attitude and tone are those of the great tradition of the American civilian soldier. It was not an unusual statement then, and, from the testimony of the men of the 70th Tank Battalion, it is not unusual now.

We have in our history, wisely I think, been wary of a large standing army. This means that we as citizens have to fight our big wars. Our small peacetime army keeps the guns cleaned and ready for civilians to use when needed. When war happened, relatively few trained soldiers provided the core for an army later consisting primarily of civilians.

The 70th was a perfect example. It was formed in peacetime from regular army infantry, but before being chosen for the earliest combat in the European war, most of its ranks were filled by civilians. Regular army soldiers taught incoming volunteers and draftees the ways of the army. Together they built a unit that was distinctive from the outset.

This was because the 70th was the *first* independent tank battalion in the U.S. Army and was initially designated as the *only* tank battalion controlled by Army General Headquarters (GHQ). The very highest commanders knew of the 70th in its training period and its worth throughout the war. True to its historic destiny, the battalion was first in many ways, and by its accomplishments it showed just how well the American traditional system of building military units could work.

Some elements of the 70th fought in eight campaigns, more than any other U.S. independent tank battalion in World War II. As an independent tank battalion, the 70th would be attached to infantry divisions and be under their command. Most people think of tank warfare in World War II in terms of thrusts by massed armor. Many great battles in Europe, however, were slugging matches, fought by infantry with support from a tank battalion such as the 70th.

Casualty figures in the battalion were so high that the 70th was referred to as the "Purple Heart Battalion." However, despite casualties and despite being in action from the beginning until the end, the men of the 70th never cracked. The unit never became cautious or wavered when called upon for tough assignments.

Why did these men fight so long and so well? Was it simply because they had a job to do and they did it? Or was there perhaps a deeper motivation?

Revisionist historians of World War II might claim that they fought with neither conviction nor commitment but because they were forced to, either by superiors or out of fear and desperation, merely to stay alive. Yet these were young men nurtured and reared in a democratic society. Did they discard all they had known and believed when they became soldiers? Did they fight with less conviction than young Germans reaching adulthood in a ruthless, militaristic-and racially oriented regime preaching what amounted to a murderous religion?

The common men who became uncommon tankers of the 70th were, on the other hand, free of ideological compulsions, but they defeated their enemy with a spirited determination that must have arisen from deep, shared convictions. The revisionist view ignores the fact that in the danger and horror of combat there could be, and was, high courage widely manifest, cool decision, judicious command, skillful maneuver, and technical control. These men were not driven by terror or ideological obsessions and automatic response, but as free men they respected as well as they could in war human decency even though it was their obligation to kill the enemy. They were convinced that their cause was just, and they defended it successfully because they themselves created during their campaigns fraternal loyalty, esprit de corps, and the communal sense of indomitable prowess. These qualities, more and more deeply ingrained by recurring feats of arms, inspired the whole unit to act together with conspicuous courage and recognized distinction. The men of the 70th Tank Battalion fulfilled the hopes, and more than met the expectations, of a free society that puts its trust in the uncommon valor of its common soldiers.

1
Beginnings

> Our meager U.S. Army tank tactics manuals had become obsolete by the German blitzkrieg in Europe, so we relearned modern tank warfare, being on the ground floor, so to speak.
>
> —Michael Varhol, Adjutant
> 70th Tank Battalion[1]

A heavily guarded convoy sailed past Long Island on January 9, 1942. Suddenly one of the ships blew up, torpedoed by a German U-boat while still within sight of shore. The convoy sailed on toward its target, the French island of Martinique in the West Indies. On board the ships were the U.S. 1st Infantry Division, the 1st Marine Raider Battalion, and the 70th Tank Battalion. Thirty-two days after Pearl Harbor, and only twenty nine-days after Germany and Italy declared war on the United States, the 70th was already on the move.

Part of Historic Change

Why was the 70th chosen for this early mission? Undoubtedly, the high command of the U.S. Army knew that the unit was combat ready and would fit the needs. In fact, the 70th was probably the *only* tank battalion combat ready for this amphibious operation. It was logical to pair the 70th with the 1st Infantry Division since they had trained together in making landings and in tank-infantry coordination.

The United States had been late in recognizing tanks as a key in modern ground warfare. It was not until the German *blitzkriegs* of 1939 and 1940 that action was taken. German mechanized columns led by tanks, with close coordination between air and ground units, changed the whole concept of war. Country after country fell before the Nazi onslaught. Finally, on July 15, 1940, less than a month after Paris fell and France capitulated, the United States created an armored force, consisting of the 1st and 2d Armored Divisions and the 70th Tank Battalion. The 70th was an "independent tank battalion," a designation that determined the role it would play in the war. It was to provide tank support for infantry divisions and be under their command, as was the case in the move toward Martinique. Armored divisions, on the other hand, controlled their own infantry while fighting as a division.

Whether infantry control of tanks attached to them extended to tactical use was a matter left to be resolved on the battlefield. Tankers knew best the capabilities of tanks and how best to help infantry. Yet in upper echelons, infantrymen outranked tankers. There was a potential for difficulty. Later in this narrative, instances of tank misuse will be related. So will the general pattern of good infantry-tank cooperation.

The new armored force was an attempt to incorporate two views of the use of tanks. One was similar to the German model with large numbers of tanks utilizing firepower and mobility along with mechanized infantry to penetrate deep in long thrusts. The other held that infantry was still the principal ground arm, and the function of tanks was to provide close support. This latter view was official doctrine in the decades after World War I as infantry officers controlled the army. These differences on the use of tanks continued, affecting the types of tanks to be designed and produced.

For close support, light tanks were thought sufficient. Their machine guns and 37mm cannon would be effective at the point of attack. Speed and mobility were realized by using small cannon and armor thick enough to deflect only small-arms fire. Since antitank guns were considered the master of the tank, it seemed pointless to add weight with thick armor.[2] In 1939 as a consequence, the United States produced 325 light tanks and 6 mediums. Even the new armored divisions in 1940 had two regiments of light tanks and one of mediums. The 70th originally was designated a medium tank battalion, but only light tanks were available. In 1941 the United States produced 2,591 light tanks and 1,461 mediums. In that year the 70th was redesignated a light tank battalion. By 1942 the trend was toward mediums, with 14,049 produced as compared to 10,947 lights. Then, each armored division was to have two regiments of mediums and one of lights. In 1943 tank battalions became "standard," with three medium tank companies and one light, and tank production changed accordingly. The 70th remained a light tank battalion until late 1943.

It might be noted that low tank production into 1940 was reflective of American society at the time. The United States had been isolationist and antiwar for two decades, and the Great Depression lasted until World War II. Tanks, even lights, were costly to design and produce. The refrain in the 1930s was: "Tanks are tanks, and tanks are dear. There will be no tanks again this year."[3]

Both infantry and armored uses of tanks were employed during the European war. Infantry with tank support, as provided by the 70th, was essential in invasions and fought prolonged battles in terrain ill suited for tanks. Armored divisions did make long thrusts when the terrain and situation were suitable. They also were involved in invasions and most of the more static and prolonged battles. In cases of need, a battalion of tanks from an armored division might be attached to an infantry division. At such times they resembled an independent tank battalion.

Destined to Be in the Center of Events

These were the conditions and times in which the historic 70th was born, a year and a half before Pearl Harbor. Because of the unique circumstances surrounding its creation, it was made the first GHQ tank battalion. The 70th was, in fact, a laboratory in which tank training and tactics in support of infantry were worked out. The battalion was on the "ground floor."

At first stationed at Fort Meade, Maryland, the 70th, and its progress, was watched by the highest officers in the Army Ground Forces in nearby Washington, D.C. This would have both future and immediate implications. During the war top commanders often showed that they knew of the 70th, entrusting it with many important missions. At the beginning, it meant that 70th commanders were given an unusual opportunity to build the kind of battalion that GHQ wanted.

The Commanders

Choice of commanders, therefore, was extremely important. Lieutenant Colonel Stephen Henry was commander when the 67th Infantry (medium tanks) was redesignated the 70th Tank Battalion. His role, however, was only organizational. Once that was accomplished, Henry moved to the Armored Force Headquarters at Fort Knox, later achieving the rank of major general.

Two men were particularly important in building the character of the 70th in their own image. Lieutenant Colonel Thomas N. Stark assumed command ten days after activation, July 25, 1940, and guided the unit until March 25, 1942. Stark was an old line infantry officer with considerable World War I experience. He was a strict disciplinarian and an able leader.

Stark was replaced by Lt. Col. John C. Welborn, a West Point graduate, who headed the 70th until after the liberation of Paris in August 1944. Welborn was the commander most men remember. Above all others, he is credited by his men for maintaining the high esprit de corps that exists to this day. Building on Stark's organization, Welborn would firmly and irrevocably put his stamp on the 70th. He would lead the 70th in battle, the only way a unit can prove itself. Welborn was relentless in seeing to it that the men of the 70th were kept sharp, disciplined, and ready to perform at the peak of efficiency at all times. This regimen began during the early days of training and never ceased. If there was a respite during the war, training schedules were soon put in place.

Origins in Regular Army Infantry

Another significant element in building this extraordinary unit was that it alone among independent tank battalions had its origins in regular army infantry. Floyd West was present at the creation. He had enlisted in the army in 1924, and in 1940 was a platoon sergeant in the 34th Infantry Regiment. West's account of the first organizational changes testify to the woeful state of affairs in the peacetime army. "We were on maneuvers in Louisiana and Tennessee when the 1st Battalion was designated a medium tank unit and for training purposes the 2d Battalion antitank. After the maneuvers we were sent to Fort Meade, which for years had been a tank post. There, we from the 34th were intermingled with tankers from the 67th in what was now the 70th Tank Battalion."

Everything was new. "We started from zero. There were no precedents or guidelines for organizing and training a GHQ tank battalion. While we were called a medium tank unit, there were none available so we trained in light tanks. We had to learn everything about them, starting with mechanics, then how to drive and operate a tank. It took quite a time to learn it all."

With the Selective Service Act of September 1940, draftees and volunteers entered the army in large numbers. Again, the 70th was in a favored position. It already had a solid core of soldiers who knew the military, its ways, its discipline, and its structure. Noncommissioned officers (noncoms) have throughout history been the solid basis of any unit in any army. That was certainly the case in the 70th. According to Floyd West, the noncoms who came with him from the 34th Infantry were the finest he had seen in his sixteen years of service. Michael Varhol agrees. "Regulars at the beginning helped instill military knowledge, patriotism, and of course, esprit de corps."

Atlee Wampler was one of the first reserve officers to arrive. He served as A Company commander in Tunisia and then as battalion operations officer in Sicily before being sent to teach tank tactics at the Armored Force School. When asked why the 70th was so closely knit, he answered: "The officers took care of the men, and the men took care of the officers. The officers saw to it to get the best for the men they possibly could, be it food, shelter, or equipment. The men did the best they could with what they had, and that was largely due to the noncoms. The first sergeants, staff sergeants, and buck sergeants maintained the discipline. The officers did too, but the noncoms were there all the time, seeing to it that the men worked well together, kept their guns clean, their feet dry, and so on."

Helping Each Other in the Peacetime Army and Later

Floyd West provides another insight on why the high esprit de corps of the 70th originated in the core of regular army soldiers. The peacetime army, he reminds us, was treated like an orphan. Civilian society usually paid little heed to it, and military appropriations were minimal. Out of necessity, soldiers had to band together in comradeship. "There was a feeling that we had to take care of ourselves, with a sense of family in a unit. This was transferred to the 70th more than to any other unit I later served in during the war or after." (West served in many units during his more than thirty years in the army. He retired as a major.)

West was first sergeant in a company commanded by then Capt. John Welborn at Fort Meade. "Welborn didn't want to see any soldier in his outfit go hurting. While still in peacetime, we passed around a collection sheet on payday. Perhaps Sergeant so-and-so's wife was sick, or Private so-and-so's child needed something. The rest of the company would contribute a half a buck or a buck each, whatever could be spared, to help out the family of a buddy." Welborn favored this, and West, as his first sergeant, got involved. "Once, I recall, Welborn asked me about the gambling. I told him I hadn't seen any. He wanted to protect the losers. We always had some slickers around, and he was afraid some family men would lose the little bit they had. They wanted to increase their purse for their families, and these slickers would take it from them, so we had to protect them as far as possible."

Frank Gross enlisted in the army in 1939. He spent four years as an enlisted man before being made a warrant officer. "Late in 1940, we were in the pit of what was called the 1000 inch range at Fort Meade, Maryland, firing water-cooled model 1917 machine guns. If you became an expert machine gunner, you received 'shooting pay' of $5 per month. To a $21 per month private, that $5 seemed like a million bucks."

In the impecunious regular army, a company fund was essential. West relates that this fund "was derived in part from donations given by parents of men in the unit. Also, the PX offered credit, as did the movie house, the tailors, and other services. We would collect from the men and when we paid their bills were given a percentage which went into the company fund. Contributions also came from the Military Motion Picture Association and the PX Association. The company fund was intended primarily for the recreation of the men and to supplement the food."

Alvin Woods became a member of B Company in 1942 at Fort Bragg, North Carolina. He had lied about his age and enlisted in the army when he was only seventeen. "The 70th Tank Battalion was just like a home to me. The men were superb; you couldn't have asked for better men to be with anywhere else in the U.S. Army. I fell in love with the whole system, being a farm boy from Mississippi who didn't know anything and a young kid of seventeen. The older people in B Company just seemed to take us youngsters under their wings and took care of us. They showed us what the military was all about. I am very grateful for that."

Woods went on to serve more than thirty years. "I took paratroop training, then flight school, ending up flying helicopters and fixed-wing aircraft. Many of my later years were in Special Forces, the Green Berets, and I had three tours in Vietnam. Through all those years, my mind would always go back to the 70th. I never found the cohesion or the comradeship or the discipline in any of the other units that I found in the 70th. It was just outstanding, the best I ever served in, and I served in a lot of very good ones."

Molding a Superior Unit

Just prior to the arrival of draftees and volunteer enlisted men in late 1940 came the first group of thirty reserve officers, among them Michael Varhol and Atlee Wampler. These reserve officers replaced nearly all the regular officers who were transferred back to infantry units. Lieutenant Colonel Stark had begun to put the pieces in place. He had the noncoms who would train the new enlisted men. To lead them would be officers of his choice.

Soon graduates from officer candidate school (OCS) would fill remaining vacancies. Again, because of its origins in the regular army, the 70th would obtain the best officers available. Varhol explains how it happened. It seems his sergeant major was a jolly Irishman named Raymond Riley, a World War I veteran with twenty-five years of service. Early one morning at Fort Meade, Riley showed Varhol an item in a newspaper reporting that FDR's son Elliott had been given the first direct commission as a captain. Riley asked Varhol for a pass so he could go to the War Department and apply. A direct commission in those days was an unheard of thing, so Varhol told Riley, "Sure, lotsa luck!"

The next morning Riley was waiting for Varhol to arrive to show him a copy of his appointment as a captain with assignment to the Armored School at Fort Knox. Varhol explains: "It was a payback by acting adjutant general A. P. Sullivan, who as a second lieutenant had been taught the *Manual of the Saber* by Riley. At Fort Knox, Riley organized the first OCS battalion and wrote me a letter saying as a payback to the 70th he would personally screen all our officer requisitions and send us the cream of the crop in leadership, for as he always said, 'Leaders win when the going gets tough.'"

According to Varhol the first twelve leaders Riley (who ultimately became lieutenant colonel) sent were excellent. The next thirteen who arrived somewhat later were equally good. "We were ecstatic. West Point couldn't produce better leaders . . . Assignments were based on education, occupation, training, physical condition, personality, desire, as well as our requirements. All these gentlemen were six feet tall. They were all athletes. They were all intelligent men who had been to college."

Most of these early arrivals stayed with the 70th throughout the war, such as John Ahearn and Franklin Anderson, both fine civilian officers of which we will hear much later in this narrative.

Good as these fresh graduates from OCS and activated reserve officers were, West recalls, "They knew absolutely nothing about the army, so we had to train them just like recruits in the way the army did things, such as military discipline." Once, a group of about ten came in on a weekend. West relates: "Welborn told me to take them down to the Quartermaster to give them a chance to buy their ornaments, and so on. This one new officer said he didn't want those gold bars and other stuff, he wanted stripes like I wore as a first sergeant. He was all put out about it. I must say, though, that with help and training most of them turned out to do a pretty good job."

The First Draftees

On November 30, 1940, the first Selective Service personnel (draftees) arrived at the 70th in Fort Meade. The old army would never be the same. Civilians would constitute the bulk of every unit. Still, Lieutenant Colonel Stark would find a way to get the men he wanted and weed out the misfits.

Carl Rambo tells of one way the process worked. "I was drafted in Pennsylvania where I was employed, rather than Tennessee, my home state. From Pittsburgh, our group was sent to Fort Meade where they weeded us out. The commander, Colonel Stark, had some weight with the commandant of Fort Meade whom he apparently knew well." Only seventy-five of a far larger group were sent to the

70th. "Every one of us were high school graduates, and all had a trade. They went big on heavy equipment operators, of which I was one, having worked for a construction company driving big 'cats.'" (Carl Rambo served with the 70th from April 1941 until the end of the war, and rose in rank from private to lieutenant.)

The fact that all the draftees were high school graduates was significant. A far smaller percentage of American males had graduated during those years as compared to subsequent eras. It meant that an early screening process had taken place.

Floyd West asserted, "Later on, they took anyone who was warm. The screening became haphazard. It was my experience that the illiterate and uneducated should have been left at home. They couldn't remember anything or learn anything and couldn't work together. They were always dependent on others. In a closely knit unit such as a tank crew, each member must rely on all others. The 70th was fortunate that in its early days, good, reliable people formed the basis of the organization."

Bob Connors was another of the first draftees to join the 70th. His recollections add a bit of flavor to what it was like to be drafted in 1940. "I was in a group of thirty young men from the Philadelphia area who came by train from the 30th Street station and unloaded at Odenton, Maryland. Our group of draftees and volunteers were among the first to come from our area." The sergeant who took them from the Schuylkill Arsenal to the train station handed Connors a manila folder containing all of their papers and told him he was now in charge. "I vividly remember hearing my mother, who was there to see me off, say, 'Look at that. He's only been in the army for a couple of hours and already he is in charge.' I appreciated her confidence, but in my own mind, I knew the reason for the sergeant's action. I was over six foot four and the biggest man in the group." (Yet motherly instincts were valid in this case. Connors rose in rank to colonel.)

On their arrival at Fort Meade, Connors and his charges slept in brick barracks the first night. He thought the army was not bad. This was a nice, comfortable place to be. However, this feeling did not last long since all new arrivals were assigned to squad tents. The tents had a canvas top and about three-foot-high boards all around the sides and a stove in the middle for heat. We slept on cots. During our stay in these tents, we went through the coldest and most severe winter that Maryland ever had. I don't remember when we went to the brick buildings, but it was probably after basic training. The move made us happy."

The "Networking" System Aids the 70th

The best graduates of OCS came to the 70th as a payback to his old unit by Raymond Riley. Lieutenant Colonel Stark, as a friend of the Fort Meade commandant, got to choose the draftees he wanted. They are examples of the "network" in operation. Between the wars, the peacetime regular army was small. Everyone in a unit knew everyone else. Beyond individual units, most officers had served with one another sometime during their careers. Thus was created a networking system that included the top brass in the War Department.

A significant example is that of Lt. Col. John C. Welborn. Not only was he a West Point graduate, so was his father, Col. Ira Welborn, commander of all tank forces within the United States in 1919. Among his officers was the young Dwight D. Eisenhower. Tradition was lacking in American tank forces, but, if it existed anywhere, it was present in the 70th. John Welborn had been in the army all his life and knew most of the officers in the network, as did Colonel Stark. General Patton knew of the 70th and selected it to be part of the Western Task Force he commanded in Operation Torch, and later for the Sicilian campaign. General Bradley sent the 70th to England to train for the invasion of Normandy, where it would be in the spearhead at Utah Beach. General Theodore Roosevelt, Jr., son of the president, knew the 70th from its early training with the 1st Infantry Division. He and Welborn were good friends. The 70th thought of him as "our general"; he thought of the 70th as "his boys."

Even President Roosevelt had contact with the 70th. Michael Varhol relates: "When FDR came to visit the 70th on September 30, 1940, Stark, the 70th commander, had us officers drawn up in a straight line in front of the post flagpole where he told us he would lead FDR from his car when he arrived to shake hands with each of us. The press had done a perfect cover-up for political vitality. No one knew FDR could not walk."

Training as Soldiers and Tankers

During its formative period, the 70th had more control of training operations than would be possible in units formed later. This gave commanders and noncoms another advantage in molding their kind of unit. Everything begins with training. Carl Rambo remembers that he and his group "got basic training in the 70th. In B Company there were twenty-seven too many noncoms because they had just reorganized. Everyone who made a false move got busted, and man, those noncoms worked us to death. I was in the army eighteen months before I made private first class, and nobody around got ratings since they were all filled. We came up the slow, hard way. We didn't even have tanks at first, so I was trained as an infantryman. When we got tanks, all of our training was turned toward them."

Actually, all army basic training has infantry roots. The first things recruits must learn are to instinctively obey commands and to act together as a team. It has been so since the advent of organized warfare, which began with infantry. When people operate as a team, control can be maintained, and control is the opposite of panic.

The fact that all of the original men and most early arrivals had training in the infantry was obviously ideal for a tank unit that would spend the war working with infantry. During the Tennessee maneuvers in June 1941, and with the 1st Infantry Division from August until December 2, 1941, cooperation between infantry and armor was emphasized. Tactics were developed on how tanks could best help infantry and how infantry could help tanks. For survival as well as progress, each arm needed the other.

Before tactics, however, everything about a tank had to be mastered. What were the capabilities of a particular type and model? How steep an incline could be negotiated? Under what conditions could a sharp turn be made without throwing a track? How is a track put back on? Light tank crews were often responsible for turning tracks over to expose less worn rubber pads on the reverse side.

Further, every duty in a tank had to be learned. Coordination was essential among all members of a crew as well as among individual tanks. Each man in a crew had to be ready to do a different function at any time. With casualties in battle, changes were frequent. A light tank had a crew of four: tank commander and gunner/loader in the turret, driver and assistant driver/bow gunner in positions below. A medium tank had five crewmen: commander, gunner, and loader in the turret and driver and assistant driver/bow gunner below. Usually, new men became assistant drivers or loaders. A driver often became tank commander. All crewmen were given thorough training in tank driving and practice sighting and firing the 37mm gun on a light tank and later the 75mm of a medium tank. Although the sight on the gun was more precise, a good gunner could eyeball a target with good results. Gunnery, however, took experience, which is why a top gunner was not moved often from his position, even to be elevated in rank.

Specialized Training

In January 1941, A Company was sent to Indiantown Gap, Pennsylvania, to qualify all personnel in gunnery and tank tactics and to test equipment. One of the men involved was Frank Gross. "We spent the better part of a month living in unfinished barracks. Workmen were there every day constructing the camp. Some of us lived in buildings without windows and no heat. It was freezing cold, with about three feet of snow." They were using light tanks, firing the 37mm and all machine guns. "On this particular model tank, there were two .30-caliber machine guns on the sponson that were fired by solenoid switches on the driver's level. To aim the guns, the driver had to pull the levers to raise or lower the nose of the tank. This we found to be ridiculous. The guy in the turret aiming the 37mm was suddenly thrown off target. Well, our experience and reporting helped, because a change was soon made and the problem corrected."

Early in 1941, a number of officers and men were sent to the Armored Force School in Fort Knox, Kentucky. Instruction was given in gunnery, radio, mechanics, and personnel work, with officers also learning tank tactics. On their return to the battalion, these officers and men would then impart knowledge gained to others. The battalion also engaged in tests of antitank weapons with the newly formed 93d Antitank Battalion. Tactical employment of antitank weapons was studied, to the benefit of both the 70th and the 93d.

Beginning in June 1941, A Company participated with the 1st Infantry Division in amphibious training, the first ever by a tank unit.

Frank Gross recalls: "We would load up in the New York Port of Embarkation, the tanks on freighters, the troops on the transport SS *Joseph T. Dickman*. The landings were made off New River, North Carolina, with the Marines acting as defending troops while we were the invaders. Landings were repeated, each time with a different element of the 1st Division." On the last of these exercises a submarine scare caused them to scoot back to the New York Port and then to Fort Devens, Massachusetts, where they were based. "With continuing sub threats, further training was canceled. This was in early December. I know because we were in Fort Devens at the time of Pearl Harbor."

Amphibious training had everything to do with the fact that the 70th as an independent tank battalion would support infantry on invasions. Landing beaches throughout the war had to be taken and held by infantry.

Pearl Harbor

Sunday, December 7, 1941, was unseasonably warm. Bob Connors and several friends from the Philadelphia area decided to go from Fort Meade into nearby Washington, D.C., to see a professional football game between the Eagles and the Redskins. "We didn't have any free tickets, but intended to walk in after the first quarter was over. We had done this a couple of times before, and since we were in uniform, no one bothered us about tickets." Prior to going to the stadium, Connors and his friends were killing time walking around Washington. "We walked in front of the Japanese Embassy and could see them burning papers of some sort in large trash cans on their lawn. We wondered why but didn't give it much thought. It wasn't too long after this that the MPs rounded us up and told us to report back to camp. It was then that we heard about the bombing at Pearl. I think it was that same afternoon when the 70th sent a company or platoon of tanks to guard the White House."

For Connors and two close friends, their year of service had been completed. They were scheduled to be discharged from the army on Monday, December 8. That morning, the three men reported to company headquarters to see then Captain Welborn. "He looked at our group and said, 'Here are your discharges' and then proceeded to tear them up in front of us, saying, 'You won't get these now!' We found out later from the company clerk that they were blank sheets of paper, since he didn't have all the necessary forms available . . . I finally got my discharge in April 1946, and that doesn't say much for my being in the army, supposedly for just one year."

That same day, December 8, Lieutenant Colonel Stark assembled the battalion in the post theater at Fort Meade and delivered a forceful message. The United States was at war. This was no longer a peacetime army. The colonel assured the men that, because of their training, they would perform with distinction in battle. "Now," he said, "we must prepare for combat with a new vigor."[4]

The new vigor and the shape of things to come was clearly indicated in a letter to the Armored Force Liaison Office dated December 23, 1941, and signed by Brig. Gen. Mark W. Clark, then deputy chief of staff. He wrote that the 70th "will have immediate priority pertaining to such items as the necessary 37mm guns (tank), machine guns and other weapons. Steps should be taken to ensure that all such equipment is on hand in the unit *within one week.*"[5]

Vital Missions Soon After Pearl Harbor

When General Clark said one week, he meant it, or nearly so. On January 4, 1942, the 70th less C Company was alerted for an imminent combat mission. Combat elements of the battalion moved by train to the Brooklyn Naval Base. It was only a month after Pearl Harbor, and the 70th was headed for combat somewhere.

"Before loading," Michael Varhol remembers, "we were told of the navy's strict rules—no booze on navy ships at any time! About midnight the first night at sea, a well-boozed Brig. Gen. Teddy Roosevelt divulged that he had visited Secretary [of War] Frank Knox the previous week who had told him our navy had been devastated [at Pearl Harbor] with seventeen battleships hit, several sunk, and many severely damaged."

This was the mission to Martinique with the 1st Infantry Division and the 1st Marine Raider Battalion noted at the beginning of this chapter. Martinique, strategically vital to hemispheric defense, was now in the hands of the pro-Nazi Vichy French government. Sitting on an airfield were forty P-40 fighter planes that the United States earlier had sold to the French. According to 70th staff officer Michael

Varhol, the mission of the convoy was to capture these planes before they could raise havoc in the region. "Our convoy circled Martinique, at which point Vichy Governor-General Roberte saw the handwriting on the wall." Diplomatic negotiations then obviated the need for military action. When it was canceled after circling Martinique, all combat elements made what in effect was a practice amphibious landing near Norfolk, Virginia, before returning by train to Fort Meade.

C Company was detached and left on February 12 for Iceland, where it was redesignated the 10th Light Tank Company. Americans replaced British forces who had been on the island to prevent a German invasion since early in the European hostilities. The 10th Light Tank Company took over British-built Camp White Heather, a few miles inland from Reykjavik. Iceland was vital in Atlantic crossings with the harbor at Reykjavik and an air base at Keflavik. It was also strategically located as a transshipment point for material going to the USSR on the northern route.

New officers and men were brought in to re-form C Company, with men from other companies providing the core and stability. This was done with hardly a missed step.

Fine Tuning for Combat at Fort Bragg

It had to be, for soon the War Department needed the combat-ready 70th to conduct amphibious training with another infantry division, this time the 9th. On March 11, 1942, the battalion moved to spacious Fort Bragg and training commenced. It was here that John Welborn became battalion commander. Events were moving rapidly, and Welborn knew there was little time until the 70th would be involved in another mission. On a hot day in May, he "ordered and led a forced march of five miles to determine the physical condition of the officers and enlisted men. A good number . . . could not keep up the pace through ankle deep sandy trails and dropped out . . . exhausted. As a direct result of this experience, elimination by transfer of physically unfit personnel was accomplished."[6]

Shifts in personnel continued. In August, the 70th was ordered to provide a cadre for a new tank battalion, the 746th. Six officers and 135 enlisted men were accordingly sent to Camp Rucker, Alabama.

Although this was a tribute to the effectiveness of the 70th, all those chosen for the cadre were reluctant to leave. (Bob Connors was among them. He still belongs to the 70th Association.)

Despite the fact that this transfer occurred less than two months before A Company sailed for North Africa, and despite the fact that, along with a new C Company, about half of the combat elements were affected, the organization and training of the battalion were so solid that it was quickly made ready for battle.

On September 4, General Patton addressed the 9th Infantry Division and the 70th at Fort Bragg. Frank Gross recalls: "There was a podium built, about six feet high, and General Patton got up on it. There were ladies in the background. When Patton saw them he indicated what he had to say was for the ears of the combat troops, so he would not be offended if the ladies chose to leave. Nobody moved. He said, 'Oh, well, here we go!' It was his 'blood and guts' speech."

Patton told the assembled troops they would soon have the privilege of striking the first blow against Nazi-held territory, and that they and their modern equipment would be "irresistible." The reason he was giving this speech, the general said, "was to let you know that you are not going in to take casualties, but to kill the enemy. Attack them, cut their guts out with your bayonets."

Lawrence Krumwiede in C Company was suitably impressed. "I felt that we were pretty well equipped and trained, and that we were finally going somewhere." Indeed they were. Soon the modern equipment arrived in the form of new M-5 light tanks. The men loved them. They had twin Cadillac engines, hydromatic transmissions, and gun stabilizers. The M-5 was speedy and maneuverable, and the 37mm could be fired on the run.

Next the three line companies were moved to bivouac areas apart from other units on the vast confines of Fort Bragg. Here, as Lawrence Krumwiede reports, "Tanks were caulked and made watertight. The snorkels were added and we were taught how to break them away after landing." (Two snorkels, or shrouds, extended well above the waterline. One enabled air to get to the crew and to the engine, and the other was for exhaust. Once on land, they had to be removed. More air was needed for the engine to function normally.)

One reason for secluding the companies was security. Yet, Krumwiede says, it was lax. "We would go back to Headquarters Company for showers and crap games. In spite of security, we were able to make a few trips to Fayetteville. That was until the Sunday morning when the whole company answered roll call, but only a few guys were present and accounted for." The following day almost everyone was stripped of his chevrons or had promotions canceled. "Captain Edwards [C Company commander] announced that we could fight the war as privates, and *I did*. I answered for Fusco and Rzegocki of my crew and a few others. Sergeant Joe Farkas had given me a set of his stripes, so I gave them back to him and we had a good laugh. There had not been a roll call the Sunday before, and I had busted my tail making it back in the early morning hours. If there had been a roll call, I'm sure someone would have answered for me."

Slipping Away From Fort Bragg

On September 17, 1942, A Company slipped away in the dead of night and boarded a train. It was done so secretly that no one in the other companies knew they had left until the next morning. Nor did anyone have the slightest inkling at the time that A Company would be engaged in operations so different from the rest of the battalion that it would be nine months before reunification.

When the train came to a stop, A Company was in Fort Dix, New Jersey. Posted in latrines, in dayrooms, and wherever men sit or stand were warnings that "Loose lips sink ships." Some men grumbled, "Who the hell am I going to tell. I can't even go to the john without being watched." Still, there wasn't a man in A Company who didn't take the warning seriously. Fort Dix was a staging area for the New York Port of Embarkation.

C Company and two platoons of B Company left Fort Bragg on October 19. Lawrence Krumwiede stood guard on the train carrying C Company. "I had a bad holster, so I tucked the .45 caliber in my belt. A chaplain on board joked, 'I'll bet you're from Chicago,' since I was toting a gun like a gangster. I told him, no, I'm from Cicero, but my tank is named Chicago. When we got to Norfolk, the tanks were loaded on USS *Susan B. Anthony*, USS *Henry T. Allen*, and USS *Clymer*. Our platoon was aboard USS *Susan B. Anthony*."

The men were kept busy with work details and orientations, but Krumwiede was intent on a bit of last-minute pleasure before leaving the States. "It was easy to get off the ship to visit the Port Cafe. We would put class A uniforms on under our coveralls, pick up a case of rations, and walk off the ship. We would duck the case of rations and coveralls in the warehouse until we were ready to board the ship again."

C Company and the 1st and 2d Platoons of B Company sailed for all of one day before stopping for one last "dress rehearsal." Repeated landings were practiced at Solomons Island in Chesapeake Bay. Fully ladened with combat gear, troops scrambled down nets onto landing craft. Tanks, guns, and trucks were lowered onto lighters in the dead of night, everything being accomplished in a strict blackout.

Destinations Unknown

The pattern of how the 70th would fight the war had been established prior to departure for the first combat mission. In support of infantry, each company would be assigned to a regiment and would rarely see one another in battle. Even platoons within a company could normally be in a different action. So the 70th went off to war as companies and platoons, all on different ships. The battalion commander and his staff remained at Fort Bragg with the remainder of the battalion. Line company commanders were in charge, taking and executing orders from infantry officers. Yet, no one ever forgot they were men of the 70th. Esprit de corps remained high, and the men were well trained and in top physical condition. Soon they would be in combat. Where it would be was still unknown. Their destinations would be revealed in due course, after each ship was well out to sea.

2
The Invasion of North Africa

On the ship going to North Africa, I tried to figure out how I could fight this war honorably and stay alive. I thought about this a lot on that trip. . . .

—Carl Rambo
B Company tanker

A Company sailed after midnight on September 26, 1942. As the convoy silently maneuvered out of New York harbor, George Brookstein stood at the rail and, even in complete darkness, could pick out familiar places. Brookstein was from Brooklyn and, as the A Company liaison corporal, was on the ship carrying the headquarters section. They had been on invasion maneuvers before, but everything about their recent moves was different. This was the real thing, Brookstein thought. "The fellows I knew in the 70th were all good, brave Americans. They knew the Nazis were terrible people and that our cause was just. If the Nazis invaded England, and if England fell, what about Canada?" At that time, German subs were sinking American ships right off our shores. "I was very patriotic and thought I lived a happy life before the war. I lived in New York, the nation's biggest city, and I was an American. I was brought up with all the patriotism my people could teach. Where we were going I did not know, but I couldn't have been with a finer group of men." All of Brookstein's circle of close friends had been civilians only months before. "We represented America. We came from cities, farms, and towns across the country. Marszalek was Polish, Tortorello Italian, Mueller German, and I was Jewish. It didn't matter if you were Irish Catholic or Scandinavian Lutheran, we were all in this together."

A few days out the ships joined a larger convoy off the coast of Nova Scotia and headed out to sea. Finally, the men of A Company learned they were heading for the British Isles. This was a dangerous crossing. George Brookstein recalls early in the voyage, "seeing destroyers drop depth charges. All army personnel were told to go below. We did, but Stanley Marzalek, Tony Tortorello, and I snuck back up to the deck. We watched two torpedoes coming toward us. Using the most profane language imaginable, we nonetheless seemed to accept our fate." (Marzalek was killed on D day in Normandy, Tortorello a few days later.) Miraculously, the torpedoes missed the ship.

According to Winston Churchill, more than 100 German U-boats were active in these waters at the time. The battle of the Atlantic was at its height. In November, Allied losses were the highest in the entire war.[1] Yet with extra protection provided by British and American naval and air forces, the convoy made it to safety after a ten-day voyage. The three tank platoons landed at Belfast, Northern Ireland, on October 6, the headquarters section at Greenock, Scotland. On October 15, all of A Company boarded the same ships in which they crossed the Atlantic and sailed to Inveraray, Scotland. There, for ten days the company participated in combined operations maneuvers as part of Combat Team 39 of the 9th Infantry Division. Land, sea, and air forces from the United States and Britain were involved. Whatever this was building up to was big, very big.

These massive forces, including A Company, began to move on October 26. Ships in many convoys maneuvered into assigned positions. Those carrying men and equipment making the initial assault were in the lead. A Company was naturally near the front of the line. Once at sea, the men were told of their destination. It was Algiers.

They were part of Operation Torch, the invasion and conquest of French North Africa. The landings in Algeria were mounted from Britain because the objective was far into the Mediterranean. After subduing French resistance around Oran and Algiers, plans called for the taking of Tunisia, the ultimate objective of Torch. These operations would require larger land, sea, and air forces than the United States could then supply. Further, the British were more experienced in the war, particularly in this area; thus the need for a combined Anglo-American effort and maneuvers under joint command. It was, of course, only the first of many such Allied efforts.

The Long Voyage of B and C Companies

On October 19, nearly a month after the A Company departure from New York, C Company and two platoons of B Company boarded ships at Hampton Roads and Norfolk, Virginia. They were headed for French Morocco, each company in support of one regiment of the 9th Infantry Division. Mounting this invasion from the United States was the biggest amphibious effort the nation had ever attempted, and it took superb planning and execution by both the navy and army. The voyage took more than two weeks, a long time for soldiers unaccustomed to the constant motion of a ship at sea.

Tanker Lawrence Krumwiede of C Company was on board USS *Susan B. Anthony*. "After dry runs at Solomons Island, everyone was glad to get under way. The invasion money that was issued soon found its way into never-ending crap games. It wasn't until a pamphlet on North Africa was passed out that we knew our destination." The men were kept busy with orientations and weapons classes. "Here was where we first saw a bazooka, the newest weapon. It was to be used against enemy tanks on the invasion. Hell, some of the guys in the 60th Infantry Regiment [of the 9th Infantry Division] were fresh out of basic training. One of them while cleaning his rifle triggered off a shot in the hold. The slug lodged in a bulkhead. Fortunately no one was injured."

Susan B. Anthony developed water problems, and all mess kits were washed in salt water. "Everyone on board had dysentery and there were long lines to the sick bay and the heads. Soldiers hung over the rails, threw up on the decks and ladders." The trip was far from uneventful. "The smoking lamp was out for several days while the ship dropped to the rear of the convoy to pump gasoline over the side because of a leak. Thousands of gallons were pumped into the sea while we were at the rear of the convoy, at the mercy of enemy submarines. We resumed our place in the convoy, then ran into heavy seas. A couple of our tanks broke loose in the hold. It took hours to secure them. Thanks to our sailors they were kept from going through the hull of the ship."

Joseph Nesbit, a C Company clerk, was on a merchant marine vessel with several other 70th men. "The ship was loaded with trucks carrying gasoline and ammunition. It was quite a large convoy, which because of the submarine threat changed directions every five minutes. There were many times when the sub chasers fired depth charges." Nesbit's work area was in the ship purser's office, a pleasant place. "Where I slept, though, was not so good. Or rather where I tried to sleep. My bunk was in the bow of the ship, right next to the anchors, which kept me awake by constantly banging against the side of the ship. I remember one night the anchor came loose and hit the side of the ship with a loud bang. The fellow in the bunk next to mine sat straight up and said, 'My God, we've been torpedoed!' I guess I was too naive to be scared."

As the men of B Company sailed toward their first combat, most pondered not only what it would be like, but also how they would react. In the quote at the beginning of this chapter, Carl Rambo, at the time a tank driver, tried to figure out how he could fight this war honorably and stay alive. "I thought about this a lot on that trip, and the only thing I could think of was to obey all orders and to tend to my own business." (Elsewhere in this narrative he will be quoted to show times when he didn't "tend to his own business," resulting in greater than usual risk.)

A Company en Route to Algiers

At the same time that B and C Companies were sailing toward French Morocco, A Company left the United Kingdom for Algiers on board the same ships that carried them across the Atlantic: USS *Chase,* USS *Stone,* USS *Leedstown,* and USS *Exceller.* The 2d Platoon, Lieutenant Schmiess, and twenty-nine men were on USS *Stone* together with the 2d Battalion, 39th Infantry Regiment, 9th Infantry Division.

Early on November 7, after twelve days at sea, Francis Ross, a member of the 2d Platoon, recalls: "We were at General Quarters when I heard a loud explosion and felt the ship veer. Pretty soon the call came over the loudspeaker, 'All troops stand by.'" *Stone* had been hit by the enemy. "Somehow the captain turned the ship around and away from the convoy, which in any case was moving away from us. Next came the call for 'All troops to lifeboat stations, ready to abandon ship.' We tankers ran to our tanks, pulled off machine guns, and put them in lifeboats." *Stone* lay dead in the water, 150 miles from Algiers, its propeller and rudder inoperative.

A small British corvette, HMS *Sprey*, was left behind to stand guard as the rest of the convoy sailed on to complete its mission. A tug was immediately dispatched from Gibraltar but would not arrive for at least twenty-four hours. Two British destroyers on their way to help expected to reach *Stone* two hours after dark, a matter of nearly fifteen hours. Until then, the only protection was *Sprey*. If the enemy knew of the hit or if the ship was spotted by an Axis airplane, surface ship, or submarine, *Stone* wouldn't have had a chance. All on board realized that they were sitting ducks. Radio contact was out of the question as that would have given away their position. All that could be done had been done. The only hope was that the enemy was focused elsewhere. Yet, according to Ross, there was no panic. "Everyone was busy, and everything was orderly." For troops who had until then not been fired upon in anger and were unused to the sea, such behavior in the circumstances was extraordinary.

Sometime in the afternoon, Maj. Walter Oates, the 2d Battalion commander, convinced the captain of *Stone* to allow him to board about 700 infantrymen on their landing craft and set out for Algiers, escorted by *Sprey*. If they waited until nearly dark, the risk would be minimal. The two British destroyers were to arrive in about two hours. Although A Company tanks could not be taken, at least part of Combat Team 39 might get to the beach in time for the invasion.

So off they went, in landing craft not designed for such a sea voyage. One after another broke down. Early the next day all troops were taken on board *Sprey*, and eventually the landing craft had to be scuttled. It was not until the morning of November 9 that *Sprey* put the troops ashore at Algiers. By then French resistance had ended. The troops had missed the invasion, but at least their ordeal was over.

For those left on *Stone*, including the 2d Platoon of A Company, the fearful waiting continued. Probably not very reassuring was the fact that sufficient boats and life rafts remained on board in case they were sunk in an attack. The two tank lighters on the ship were lowered to serve as rescue craft if needed, and two remaining landing craft were positioned in the water on both sides of the ship to serve as makeshift antisubmarine screens.

Some anxiety was lifted when the two British destroyers, HMS *Velox* and HMS *Wishart,* arrived on schedule. In the darkness, the British captains were wary. Ross reported that one of the destroyers challenged *Stone.* After two loud shouts by megaphone demanding identification, *Stone* answered, and the destroyers came to the ship. According to Ross, one British captain suggested half the personnel be put on each destroyer, preparatory to scuttling *Stone.* This the captain of *Stone* refused to do. Towlines were tried but to no avail. Sometime during the night Ross heard planes circling and saw flares dropped.

At daybreak on November 8, the British tug, *St. Day,* reached the scene. Every possible combination of towing was attempted. Nothing worked well, but through superb seamanship, patience, and cool calculation, USS *Stone* was brought to an anchor off Algiers at 1030 on November 11, 1942. The 2d Platoon of A Company for the first time in sixteen days stood on dry land. They, too, had missed the invasion.

In his official naval history of World War II, S. E. Morison states that there were no casualties[2]. Francis Ross, however, remembers at least six people being buried at sea. Morison believes *Stone* was probably hit by a bomb from an Axis plane. Ross thinks it was a torpedo from a submarine. He saw the damage after arriving in Algiers. There was a huge gap aft, with the propeller sitting up in the air. Franklin Anderson also saw *Stone* in Algiers and concluded the explosion was from below, not above.

The First American Expeditionary Force

All three 70th companies were members of the United States Expeditionary Forces in North Africa, the first in World War II. Most of the men had not known their destination or their mission until given the pamphlet on North Africa, which Lawrence Krumwiede noted previously.

The pamphlet began with the statement: "Your present journey will be taking you to new parts of the world where the people, their customs and manner of living and geography of the country will be, for the majority of us, completely strange and foreign. Furthermore, our welcome by the inhabitants of Morocco, Algeria, and Tunis *is not known at this time.*" Although British troops, ships, and planes were essential, the pamphlet continued, "It was the wish of the president that the first blow in this assault should be primarily American. The name of the United States will stand for freedom to millions of Frenchmen as it does to all the people of Europe . . . This operation has been decided on as the quickest way to strike at one of the enemy's vulnerable points, and millions of Frenchmen are going to see the point, no matter what their Nazified government tries to tell them."

Germany had occupied half of France, but not French North Africa, which was controlled by the pro-German Vichy French government. It was a "vulnerable point." French resistance was not expected to be more than "token." Yet, no one knew for sure, and assault troops were primed to go in with guns blazing. Vigorous diplomatic efforts had been conducted before and after the landings to gain the support of the French not loyal to Vichy.

B Company at Safi

For the evening meal on November 7, 1942, the navy served steak and French fries, along with copious quantities of ketchup. The men of the 1st and 2d Platoons of B Company, and of the 1st and 2d Battalions of the 47th Infantry Regiment, 9th Infantry Division, wolfed down the feast, though with noticeably little good-humored chatter. Not that the atmosphere was somber, but after all, they were facing their first battle in a matter of hours.

Their objective was to seize the port, to secure it and its approaches. This would be done by infantry with the support of B Company in light tanks. The reason Safi was chosen was because it was the only deepwater port in the area. Here medium tanks could be landed off the ships that had carried them across the ocean. Once on shore, these tanks would be in position to march on a good road to Casablanca, 140 miles to the north. This fabled city was the key to the whole operation in French Morocco, but it was too well fortified for a direct assault.

There was a French garrison of about 1,000 men at Safi. Since it was not known if they would fight, surprise was essential. Debarkation began in total darkness. Heavily laden infantrymen climbed down nets into waiting lighters. The surf was tricky, making the task more difficult. Harder by far was lifting sixteen-ton light tanks into lighters in the black of night as the ship tossed and turned. It was accomplished with little delay. Training exercises in the States were worthwhile after all.

Carl Rambo believes that the B Company tanks and crews were loaded onto lighters about eight miles out, at 0400 on November 8. "I think I was the first one over the rail, but we were all ready to go. They gave us some seasick pills for the trip in, but they were very quick to pick them up if we hadn't used them. I don't think they were seasick pills at all, but probably tranquilizers. Whatever they were, I didn't need them. I didn't have a fear in the world. We were really primed." There were some big guns on a fortress that fired a few rounds before the U.S. Navy blew them away. The only resistance was from a French Foreign Legion outfit. "They were tough and hadn't got the word that Americans were coming. A few Frenchmen were killed, but the first guy I saw killed was an American infantryman who had a very loud mouth. He had been bragging that they wouldn't get him, and the poor guy lasted only a few minutes. We were going up a hill and I saw him in a street, blood running from him."

Private Paul Elinsky from Brooklyn carried an American flag ashore. It was thought to be the first one raised in North Africa. By daybreak most of Safi was in American hands, and at noon only the walled barracks held out. They fell at 1530. Everything was pretty much on schedule as medium tanks were unloaded and soon began to form a column ready to drive on Casablanca. This was delayed due to a threat of French forces hurrying to the scene from Marrakech. A strong U.S. force was sent to halt the French and did so after a skirmish. Carrier-based U.S. planes also bombed Marrakech airfield and strafed the French column heading toward Safi. That pretty much ended the fighting.

B Company suffered no casualties, and now was put in place as part of the 47th Regimental Combat Team (RCT) of the 9th Division to protect Safi and the rear of the medium tank column, separate from the battalion, that started for Casablanca.

Casablanca Is Captured

These tanks were to be part of a coordinated attack on Casablanca with the 3d Infantry Division, which landed at Fedala, only eighteen miles north of Casablanca. Here, the landing of men and supplies was delayed due to the high surf and the inexperience of American forces, causing the drive on Casablanca to be postponed for a day. Also standing in the way of American success were the shore batteries in and around Casablanca and a substantial French fleet, including the unfinished battleship *Jean Bart*. A fierce naval battle at Casablanca was waged for nearly three days.

United States infantry units moved to the outskirts of Casablanca the night of November 10. General Patton scheduled a coordinated attack for the next morning. The medium tanks from Safi were in place, as were infantry and artillery elements. Naval ships were to begin a bombardment at 0600, and carrier-based planes were to bomb at the same hour.

At 0420, Patton was awakened with the news that the French were surrendering elsewhere in French Morocco. His staff wanted to call off the scheduled attack, but Patton would not. "It was too late," he wrote, "besides, it is bad to change plans."[3] Nonetheless, the hour of attack was changed until 0730. At 0640, the French asked for a cease-fire. Casablanca was saved from further destruction and was occupied, the great harbor ready within hours to receive Allied shipping.

C Company at Mehdia–Port Lyautey

Lawrence Krumwiede enjoyed the feast the navy served on *Susan B. Anthony* the day before landings were to begin. "It was like a Thanksgiving meal, and we all wondered when we would ever have one like that again. For many it was their last meal. That night we sailed close enough to shore to see lights and hear music at Rabat."

As at Safi, U.S. troops did not expect to do much fighting. The word went around the ships in the convoy that they were to be welcomed by "brass bands," as one sergeant put it.[4] Certainly, the French had ample time to distribute band instruments and sheet music. A French steamer had seen the convoy at anchor and signaled "Be aware. Alert on shore for 0500." So surprise was not an advantage.

Neither was darkness, because debarking men and equipment took longer than planned in the heavy surf. (Heavy seas plagued other landings as well and nearly led to a diversion of the Western Task Force to Gibraltar.)

Krumwiede tells of the uncertainty and confusion that existed. "I never knew who was in charge or where we were to land until years later when I learned that Gen. Lucian Truscott was in command . . . and that he had to find the five transports and that he personally had to climb the cargo nets of each ship to coordinate the landings and the assault on Port Lyautey." After their tanks were loaded onto assault boats the crews scrambled down the cargo nets. The assault boats circled the ships until it was almost light. "The ship to ship radios were not working and we waited for orders to make our landings. Lights in town were on and our naval guns were pounding Port Lyautey installations."

About 0630 the assault boats headed for shore. "French Deoitine fighter planes strafed and dropped a series of bombs on the assault boats. We came upon two of the boats that had been hit and swamped. It was my first look at death of our own troops. I thought, if this is token resistance, what the hell is a real all-out war like?"[5]

On the way in, Sgt. Herbert Hankins became the first 70th casualty of the war when he fell off the landing craft carrying his vehicle to shore. He was swept out to sea in the high surf and drowned. One tank was swamped during the landing, drowning the four-man crew consisting of Sergeant Wrenn, T-5 (technician fifth grade) Ford, and Privates Hackeworth and Schonman.

Another tank commanded by Sgt. Jack Lovell barely reached the beach when something went wrong. Exhaust fumes came pouring into the tank. Lovell thinks it was because of the waterproofing. "My driver and bow gunner passed out. The driver had his foot tromping on the accelerator and with the engine in automatic drive our tank spun around, and we were going full blast back into the ocean. The water was above the lower hatches and over most of the turret before it killed the engine and we stopped. I climbed down to the lower level and got both the driver and bow gunner out and up to the open hatch in the turret, where I gave them artificial respiration. I saved both of their lives myself."

Luckily a navy ship saw him trying to revive these men and sent "a couple of guys in a small boat to pick us up. The driver and bow gunner were sent to a hospital ship and never came back to the company, though I heard they were alright. I hurt my foot in getting the two out, but it would have been a lot worse if the navy hadn't seen us. I don't know what would have happened."

The objective of the landings was the airfield at Port Lyautey. As the only all-weather airport in French Morocco, it was vital for air operations in securing the entire region. Plans were to take it on November 8, the day of the landings. It proved to be a formidable task. Aside from the high surf, French resistance was greater than elsewhere in Torch, and topographical features made operations complex.

Due to a navigational error, C Company was put ashore in the wrong place, causing a three-mile detour and more delay. Lawrence Krumwiede was in platoon leader Lt. Raymond Herbert's tank. "We got rid of the snorkel and formed up on the base of the bluffs." They had landed at Mehdia Plage (a beach resort) and moved slightly inland. "We saw infantry escorting a number of women taken from a bathhouse to a safe place. A French officer was captured by a GI who was hurrying him along with a bayonet. We just waited out the rest of the day. Our position was safe, but we felt useless."

Landing delays allowed a French armored column and two battalions of infantry time to reach the southern sector from Rabat. A small force of seven 2d Armored Division light tanks under Lieutenant Colonel Semmes was sent to hold them back. This they did, and well-directed U.S. naval gunfire forced the French to withdraw. Yet, by nightfall on November 8, no American unit was close to attaining its objective.

The First 70th Tank Knocked Out in Action

At daybreak on November 9, C Company tanks commanded by Lieutenant Herbert were sent to help Semmes's forces stem the French drive from Rabat. Lawrence Krumwiede recalls: "We found a way our tanks could travel. As we got inland we saw Arabs working in the fields and some little boys shepherding their flocks of goats and sheep. The kids asked for cigarettes and preferred Lucky

Strikes." French artillery came in as they neared the target area. "It was our first action where we could actually see the enemy and shoot to kill. We overran several machine gun nests, knocking them out. As we approached the 'Cactus Village' our command tank was on the point [leading]." Enemy Renault tanks were camouflaged in the huts in the village. "I saw tracers coming out of the huts and fired at them with HE shells. We took a hit on the front slope plate, knocking out the driver's periscope. We made several hits and saw one hit on a Renault as it backed out of a defilade position [protected from enemy fire]. Its turret swung free and it stopped dead in its tracks."

Almost immediately, Krumwiede recalls, their tank was hit by an antitank gun. "I didn't know I was hit but was paralyzed from the waist down. I figured it was from concussion and kept firing the guns as best I could." The tank was instantly in flames. "I shouted over the intercom that we were on fire and to get the hell out. I tried to get out of the seat and nothing happened. I pulled my goggles down because of the fire. When I looked down I could see my legs were all twisted around, one under the seat." His clothes were on fire. "I knew I had to get out of there, and I heard Lieutenant Herbert scream when he got hit as he got out of the turret. I reached down and picked up my legs by holding the pant legs, got them straightened out enough to pull myself up onto the back of the seat and got my legs on the seat. Then I knew I would have to get out of the turret and off the tank in a hurry." Krumwiede knew he would not be able to jump and would just have to fall off. "I thought about the radio spring antenna and made sure I would grab it to break my fall. When I hit the ground I blanked out for a moment, but crawled to the shell hole where Fusco, Rzegocki, and Lieutenant Herbert were lying."

All four were wounded. "Rzegocki had a really bad hip wound that he got when he exited through the lower hatch. Lieutenant Herbert had been shot through the leg when he got out. Fusco had some shrapnel wounds but was able to apply tourniquets to my legs and help all of us. We lay in the shell hole, which was a small depression in the sand. We were getting machine-gun fire from the village." An Arab came running toward them. "I was about to shoot when I saw it was a frantic old lady, so I waved her to the rear where I knew our company was located. I was having a lot of bad thoughts. All I could remember was World War I veterans on Chicago street corners selling apples and pencils. I thought that's what I'll be doing, because by the looks of my legs I thought I'd lose both of them. I knew that unless we could get out of there I'd bleed to death."

Krumwiede saw Corporal Eck, a crewman from another tank, sneaking along in the cactus. "I fired a shot and hollered at him. He saw us and motioned that he'd be back. He did come back with Felix Beard, Clyde Reynolds, and Robert Newman. They rolled me onto a blanket and pulled me along the ground as they crawled back to the rear. I don't know how they got Matt Rzegocki or Lieutenant Herbert back. Newman and Fusco covered the rescue with machine-gun fire, Fusco despite his serious wounds." All the men carrying out the rescue were awarded Silver Stars. "They got us back to where they could load us on a tank. At the rally position Captain Edwards took my .45 out of my hand and all the skin from my right hand and wrist covered the gun."

All were too badly wounded to be transferred to another vehicle, so they continued on the back of the tank. "We hung on till we got back to the beach area where the navy had set up aid stations. I was given something for pain and blood plasma. I was in good hands, but enemy fighter planes were raising hell so I asked the navy medics to move me off the road. It was really only a wagon track road that the local fishermen used to get to the beach. They moved me off the road and shortly thereafter the road was strafed."

Later in a hospital in Swannanoa, North Carolina, Krumwiede met an infantryman, Earl Le Beau, who had been on the road lying on a stretcher. "He said a burst went through the stretcher up to his crotch and stopped, then began again above his head. It was strange that we'd meet after going through the same strafing."

As the day wore on, the medics became increasingly concerned about the more seriously wounded. "I heard them talking about some of us not making it if we didn't get to the hospital ship. The surf was running so high it was difficult to get a boat off the beach. It continued until later that night when they had to make a decision to move us out to a ship. A naval doctor asked me if I wanted to try, that it was necessary but dangerous. I wanted to go, so they loaded a number of us into a boat." The surf was running fifteen to seventeen feet high. "Sailors turned all the power on, and the engines on our boat burned up. They had all the men they could muster trying to get us out to sea. They pushed until exhausted. Luckily, a boat that was out of the surf shot us a line to help tow our boat. The boat was swamped with seawater, and we were soaked. Finally we were out to sea."

Lieutenant Commander Judson Milspaugh, a doctor, took them to USS *John Penn*. "Alongside the ship our boat was lifted up parallel to the deck. Transferring stretchers to the deck on the rocking ship was perilous. They almost dropped Rzegocki into the sea. A couple of sailors held the boat away from the ship until Matt could be pulled up to the deck."

Krumwiede was taken to the officers' mess, where medics cut off his clothes and cleaned him. "My legs were put in casts and I was moved into the sick bay. The ship sailed into Casablanca harbor. The sailors raised me up to a porthole so I could see the scuttled French battleship *Jean Bart*."

Krumwiede lost track of time and could recall only certain things that happened. "I know some sniper shot through the porthole in the sick bay and the bullet ricocheted around, but no one was hurt. I recall Dr. Judson Milspaugh telling me that my right leg would have to be removed. He was the kindest and gentlest doctor, and he promised not to take both of my legs off." Krumwiede remembers a "bird colonel" visiting him aboard ship. "He brought me a French rifle, a helmet, and a few thousand francs. He told me he had seen the action we were in. He sure made me feel that it wasn't in vain. We were told we were returning to the USA as soon as *John Penn* was unloaded. One day I awoke in the officers' quarters above deck. I could hear a record of Bing Crosby singing 'I'm Dreaming of a White Christmas.'" [6]

Further C Company Action

Lieutenant Herbert's tank was hit on November 9. He and all of his gallant crew were out of the war within minutes, some crippled for life. The action in which they were involved was soon over. The French tank column from Rabat was removed as a threat to the American forces driving toward the airport. The French Renault tanks

were no match for the U.S. M-5 light tanks. Although both fired
37mm guns, the Renaults were antiquated, with thinner armor and
a less powerful engine.

At 1445, C Company was shifted to the southwest sector in the
hope that, with their support, infantrymen from the 60th RCT might
reach the airport by nightfall. "All roads being under artillery fire,
C Company proceeded northwest cross country to designated meeting place. En route . . . encountered two companies of enemy infantry approaching 1st Battalion, 60th Combat Team from the rear
and on observing our tanks, enemy ran without opposition."[7]

The timely arrival of C Company along with well-directed fire from
the 60th Field Artillery (FA) Battalion had broken up a French counterattack. Naval gunfire and bombing by sea-based planes then
cleared the way to the airport. Error and misfortune again intervened. The American front was not properly marked with identification panels. C Company "received . . . two bombing attacks by a
U.S. naval seaplane."[8] These attacks were followed by artillery fire
from an unidentified source. The resulting disorganization delayed
preparations for the attack until darkness was too near to begin a
tank-infantry action. C Company moved into a defensive position for
the night.

Although tanks rarely operated at night, infantry could and did.
The 1st Battalion of the 60th RCT set out for the airport around midnight. They were supposed to bypass the town of Port Lyautey, but
in the darkness they veered toward it. Encountering a machine-gun
outpost that they thought was guarding the approach to the airport,
the battalion divided into three parts for the final push. The main
group at 0430 arrived at a blacked-out building that they assumed
was the airfield barracks. The structure was stealthily surrounded,
and all exits were covered by machine guns. The Americans rushed
in, yelling at the occupants to surrender, which they did—after
putting down their wineglasses. It was a cafe, not a barracks. All the
occupants were taken prisoner and another 100 people rounded up.[9]
That a cafe was open at 0430 and doing business in the middle of an
ongoing battle demonstrates either the correct priorities of colonial
Frenchmen or that many were not serious about fighting Americans,
or both.

Shortly after dawn, the French commander in that area saw no reason to continue fighting. But only those under his command surrendered, whereas other French units did not. Therefore, when C Company and fifty-five infantrymen started at daybreak for the airport, they met some opposition. C Company tanks accounted for four French antitank guns and twenty-eight machine guns. By about 1100 on November 10, they were on the western edge of the airport.

The Airport Is Taken

Other American units were converging on the airport from other directions and by other means. They joined the 1st Battalion and C Company around noon. A French relief column from Meknes was broken up by naval gunfire. Only a French Foreign Legion unit continued to fight on the afternoon of the tenth. At 2200 the French commander for the region asked to meet the American commander. With a French bugler repeatedly blowing the cease-fire call, U.S. Major Hamilton of General Truscott's staff came to the C Company command tank and by radio arranged for both commanders to meet at the gate of a medieval Portuguese fort called the Kasba at 0800 the next morning, November 11, 1942. The fighting was over.

C Company Headquarters Element

The C Company headquarters element landed at Port Lyautey early on November 10. Joseph Nesbit, the company clerk, remembers: "I stashed my field desk on the back end of a load of gasoline and hitched a ride on the truck. It was very tricky to lift a two-and-a-half-ton truck and drop it in a lighter. It was around midnight and the surf was so bad that they decided to go up the river and land on a bank. For the first time I was really scared. I was more afraid of drowning than being hit by gunfire. We made it ashore, then waited around for quite a while until they told us that the airport was secure and we were to proceed there."

Cecil Nash was Nesbit's assistant during the fighting for the airport. On the evening of the armistice, he was detailed to go by truck to the port at Mehdia to pick up the barracks bags belonging to all of the men in the company. "There were a lot of bags, because every man had two. This was an easy way to get personal supplies to the combat zone. At the port there were some Arabs working, the first I had seen. It was dusk, and their skins were dark. They were hooded and wore strange garb, and I was scared. That tells you something about who I was at the time—just a small-town midwestern boy, a long way from home, and among people I couldn't talk to and didn't understand, as they jabbered away in Arabic."

Shortly thereafter, Nesbit and Nash set up their company clerk's office in Mehdia Plage. Nash says, "All of the people had left except one family. We picked out the vacant house we wanted and moved in, occupying it for about a month. These were summer homes in pleasant surroundings, much like you would see at an American beach area. Since it was November and into December, it was quite cold at night. But it was fine, right on the beach, and the house was pretty good."

A Bivouac in a Cork Forest

A few days after the end of hostilities, B Company left Safi to rejoin C Company. On the way, the company paused in Casablanca long enough to take part in a grand victory parade in which the B Company tanks were erroneously listed as being part of Ernie Harmon's 2d Armored Division.

The two companies shared the same bivouac area in a cork forest near Port Lyautey. They were together to celebrate Christmas and the New Year. "Somehow my friend Cecil Nash got hold of a bottle of champagne for New Year's Eve," Joseph Nesbit remembers. "When we opened it in our pup tent most of it blew onto the ceiling. What a mess!"

This was to have been a treat after drinking the red wine of the region, which B Company tanker Ed Gossler says was purchased at a winery near the Spanish Moroccan border, in five-gallon water cans. These, he recalls, were fine times. They ate huge, good-tasting oranges and had marvelous, long-lasting bonfires, burning cork stripped from local trees.

A Chilling Spy Adventure

Once again the 70th was called on for an important assignment. C Company and an attachment of assault guns from Headquarters Company moved to the Spanish Moroccan border. Their mission was to be in position to delay any attack by Spanish forces; in the event of an attack, they were to alert the 9th Infantry Division at Port Lyautey. A bivouac was established on the outskirts of a small town at the base of a mountain. There were only two roads leading through mountain passes. A single tank and one assault gun were dispatched to form roadblocks across each road.

"Border traffic was checked and an attempt was made to weed out any suspicious characters who might be engaged in espionage . . . Civilian trade was allowed to cross the border. CIC [counterintelligence] men stationed in town disguised themselves as laborers and mingled with the townspeople. One CIC man thus disguised was assigned to each truck with a French driver that crossed into Spanish Morocco. Spanish troop movements were reported on."[10]

After two weeks of this chilling adventure, C Company and the assault guns were relieved and returned to the cork forest near Port Lyautey.

Meanwhile, in Algiers

The day of the cease-fire, the 2d Platoon of A Company finally landed in Algiers, after sixteen days on USS *Stone*. They had missed the invasion, but they had been in far greater peril on board the stricken ship than had the rest of the company, which landed on time. This was because the landings in and around Algiers were met with almost no resistance from the French. Diplomatic preparation and the activity of the anti-Vichy French "underground" had been highly successful. By nightfall on November 8, a cease-fire was declared in Algiers. This was extended to become a general armistice effective in all of the Torch area at the eleventh hour of the eleventh day of the eleventh month—precisely the same timing that ended World War I in 1918.

Germany viewed the French failure to fully defend her North African possessions as a violation of the 1940 treaty that ended the conflict between Germany and France. Therefore, they occupied all of France. German and Italian troops began arriving in Tunisia, and Algeria was considered fair game for bombing.

At 1640 on November 8, German bombers made their first attack on Algiers. The main targets were Allied ships anchored near the landing beaches and in Algiers Bay. The ship most heavily damaged was USS *Leedstown,* on which the 3d Platoon of A Company had arrived. No company casualties were suffered, but much equipment was lost. "Doc" Shechner, battalion medical officer assigned to A Company, had to abandon ship without his belongings, most conspicuous of which were his pants. He was able to borrow a pair from a friend on shore.[11] The next day, November 9, *Leedstown* was sunk. A Company had narrowly escaped disaster on not one but two ships.

The company now moved inland to guard Blida Airport, and on November 21 established a bivouac in Ecole Ville de Birmandreis. The school was situated in Parc d'Hydra, on the outskirts of Algiers. The war was never far away, however, as the German bombing continued for several weeks. Enemy targets now extended to troop concentrations. This is shown in the following notations in the official history as kept by A Company commander, Capt. Ralph Lennon.

November 20. Bombed by enemy.

November 21. Enemy bombardment.

November 24. Air raids.

November 25. Found automatic pencil "booby trap" just 25 yards from kitchen truck.

November 26. Put on alert against enemy paratroopers and low-level bombing.

A Company Enjoys a Pleasant Stay in Algiers

For nearly a month, A Company enjoyed light duty in most pleasant surroundings. During this time, George Brookstein made friends with a French family. "We made no attempt to isolate ourselves in the lovely park where we lived in a school. Many people, both young and old, would come to look at us and mingle with their American liberators. One was a young, very attractive girl who kept looking at me. When I went over to her, she asked, 'Etes vous Juif?' I said, 'Yes, I am.' She became quite excited and went home to tell her parents. On her return, she asked if I could please come to her home for dinner. I was delighted to accept with thanks."

Brookstein didn't know how she could tell he was Jewish, but somehow she did. From then on until the end of their stay, he had numerous meals and evenings with the Colon Adad family. They owned a little grocery store and had a small home, warm and comfortable. "Paulette was about sixteen at the time and had two older brothers who lived at home. They all treated me very well and seemed to enjoy my presence. I guess Paulette became sort of infatuated with me and I made the mistake of giving her a little gold football that I had been awarded when I played high school football in Brooklyn. I knew nothing could come of our relationship. She was so young, and I knew the war was a long way from over." They were never alone, but always chaperoned either by her mother or one of the brothers. "The most that ever happened was once when she kissed me on the cheek. On many occasions she played the piano for me, the classical music I loved, such as Bach, Beethoven, and Shubert. That sort of got to me."

All in the family spoke some English, and Brookstein was interested in improving the little French he had picked up by studying language books available on board ship during the two sea voyages. Paulette was particularly helpful, and, before the company left for Tunisia, Brookstein was able to at least make his needs known in French.

Paulette's two brothers had been in the Algiers anti-Vichy "underground." They were arrested the day of the landings and were about to be executed when their lives were saved by the cease-fire. Being colonial French and Jewish, this family was naturally loyal to the France that existed prior to the establishment of the pro-German government at Vichy. They would have known of the way the hated *milice* (Vichy police) rounded up Jews for shipment to concentration and death camps. Information on the Vichy record of anti-Semitism would easily have been known in Algeria, part of metropolitan France, and especially in the capital city.

After A Company left Algiers, Brookstein carried on a correspondence with Paulette and the Adad family. He never saw any of them again, but he remembers the interlude as one of the good experiences during the war.

The Rest of the Battalion Sails

As the three tank companies plus assault gun, mortar, and medical attachments sailed off to do battle in the Torch landings, the rest of the battalion stayed on at Fort Bragg until January 1, 1943. They then moved to Fort Dix, New Jersey, where they waited for orders to go overseas. Rumors persisted that A, B, and C Companies had all suffered terrible losses in the landings. Other rumors—these true—circulated about the heavy losses Allied shipping was encountering on the North Atlantic.

In this atmosphere, men such as Charles Myers boarded the Grace Lines ship *Santa Rosa* on January 13, 1943, at Staten Island, New York. Myers kept a journal during the voyage. In it he writes poignant and moving passages of his farewells to his parents and to his future wife, Edythe. "I got by Dad with a shaking of hands and a gulp in my throat and an ache in my heart. Masculine pride (dammit) in each of us, I am sure of myself, prevented me from rushing into his arms and laying my head on his shoulder as I did when I was twelve years old."

Myers's mother was different. "She was brave. I tried to be but failed miserably, for when I kissed her, her eyes were dry but she had tears rolling down her left cheek from my own eyes . . . I kissed her and ran because I knew if I stayed I would be bawling like a baby. I left with one statement: 'Ma you'll never know how much I love you nor how much I truly thank you for all you have done for me.' She said, 'Charles, don't . . .' and I ran because I could not take it."

To Edythe he wrote: "Thought of you a lot today . . . especially while I was alone under a blanket of darkness. The ships are really running 'blacked out.' Not a light showing on any of them. Maybe it was the moon—maybe it was the knowledge that it will be a long time if ever I see you again and if I do see you what will be the conditions? Will I be whole? Will you be married? How much will I have changed?"

Myers was a prolific reader. He reread *Lost Horizon* by James Hilton in one day during the voyage and found it very enjoyable and timely. "Remember that passage: 'Dark ages, such as the world has never known, will destroy the culture of the entire world.' My hope is that a place, too difficult to find or considered too minor to bomb, will survive and from there shall lead the world out of barbarism to peace and culture. This I believe to be the mission of Shangri-La."

Myers finds a parallel in that President Roosevelt told the world the planes led by General Doolittle that bombed Japan came from Shangri-La. Then Myers adds, "America with its easygoing ways, tho' maybe rough and tarnished, still had a better life, before the war, than any of her enemies and allies. If this nation could instill her tolerance, democracy, charity, and faith to all the world upon the outcome of this war, then the world would really have been blessed by this war."

Charles Myers wondered if he would ever return, whether he would be whole, or if the woman he loved would be there waiting. Yet, as he went off to fight, there was no doubt in his mind that his nation's cause was right.

The sea was heavy on the twelve-day crossing. Myers notes that many men became seasick, though he did not. In fact, besides being a regular for both meals every day, he records eating a large amount of candy.

John Ahearn also kept a journal, and as a second lieutenant his recollections reflect the privileges of rank. "The dining room still stirs pleasant comfortable feelings in my stomach. *Santa Rosa* was well stocked, and we had choices for all meals. The chefs were wonderful and everything was prepared well. Again in the evenings loads of sandwiches and coffee sated our salty appetites."

Toward the end of the voyage, Ahearn decided to have ingrown toenails surgically removed. "I had suffered from them since the age of about fifteen but they were really bad during OCS. I would return from hikes with my boots full of blood and was afraid I would be washed out because of them. Finally during the sea voyage the battalion surgeon, Dr. Wisnefski, said we should do something about them." Wisnefski wanted his medical detachment to watch, so they all gathered around while the ingrown toenails were swiftly cut out. Although the operation was successful, Ahearn suffered excruciating pain for several weeks as he carried out his duties after landing. (The tragic irony is that on D day in Normandy, John Ahearn lost both feet when he stepped on a mine.)

When *Santa Rosa* docked at Casablanca on January 29, 1943, all components of the 70th had at last reached North Africa. They had sailed at different times on different ships and had arrived in different places. Although they were on the same continent, the men

of the battalion would still not come together until A Company rejoined it after the close of the Tunisian campaign.

Casablanca

Casablanca was a strange and fascinating place to begin a foreign
adventure. After setting up their bivouac on the outskirts of the city,
John Ahearn and some fellow officers started to walk to a nearby hotel. It was a pitch black night, suddenly made ominous by what they
took to be an apparition appearing out of nowhere. Scared out of
their collective wits, one of the group retained enough sense to flash
a light. Revealed was a giant Moroccan engulfed in a great coat pointing to a cigarette dangling from his mouth. The figure gesticulated
wildly to make himself understood. All he wanted was a match.

The next day Ahearn was in a group of officers granted permission to visit Casablanca. "We immediately hailed a horse and carriage
and galloped into the heart of the city. The sultan's palace was really
beautiful. A good-sized park contained numerous buildings of
Moslem design . . . The gardens were very picturesque and meticu-
lously cared for; numerous fountains decorated the landscape and
the buildings were rich in splendor." (The historic Casablanca Conference had just finished. Some of the meetings were in the sultan's
palace.)

Francis Synder was at the time with battalion maintenance. "I was
one of a few people who stayed in Casablanca several days to retrieve
our belongings when they came onto the dock. Every night, somebody had to stand guard to keep Arabs from stealing everything. The
way we stood guard was interesting. They gave us ammo for our rifles, then locked us in boxcars. If it caught fire, you were one dead
GI." Synder's story gives truth to the expression common at the time:
"There are two ways to do things—the right way and the army way."

The rest of those who had shipped with the battalion sections
boarded a train for Port Lyautey. On arriving they learned of the five
C Company men who had lost their lives at Mehdia–Port Lyautey.
Lieutenant John Ahearn had known them all: Hankins, Wrenn, Ford,
Hackeworth, Schonman. "Their faces, features, and characteristics
still are very vivid to me. Tragically, I learned that both Ford and
Hackeworth had become fathers while on the journey across." Han-
kins had been in Ahearn's platoon. "I visited Sergeant Hankins's

grave with my platoon. He was buried in the military cemetery high on a hill alongside the French fort guarding the city of Port Lyautey." (Men who had lost their lives in wars through the centuries must have been buried in the medieval Kasba.)

The Move to Tlemcen

The 70th (less A Company) was still attached to the 9th Infantry Division and moved with them for Tlemcen, Algeria, on February 4, a journey of nearly 500 miles. Cecil Nash recalls: "We traveled in old boxcars, sleeping head to foot."

John Ahearn was part of the advance party sent in a road convoy to establish bivouac areas. "It was a long trip . . . and a damned cold one in open jeeps as we went through the picturesque Atlas Mountains. The first evening we encamped in an open field in the center of a town. All night long we were serenaded by singing from a crowd in the hills outside of town." There had been a marriage a few days before and the party was still going on. "You could see the lights steadily blinking in the hills. The singing was more like a monastic chant . . . wailing would be a more descriptive term." The last leg of the trip, along the Oujda-Tlemcen road, Ahearn describes as truly beautiful. "One little spot captured my fancy. It was just a small place at the bend in the road but it was an enthrallingly exquisite scene." It reminded him of a biblical picture he had seen as a child, with Bethlehem the representation of the beautiful, the peaceful, the hopeful beacon of truth and good. The scene was complete even to lambs innocently grazing on a hillside.

As a major rail and road center about seventy miles southwest of Oran, Tlemcen was a convenient place to reorganize and stage troops moving from Casablanca and French Morocco to the Tunisian front. The 34th Infantry Division had paused in Tlemcen, and now, in early February, it was the 9th. Because of this movement of large numbers of men and equipment, the situation was in flux and impermanent.

Freezing and Snowbound in Algeria

The 70th first bivouacked at a racetrack, but when that proved too small, the 9th Division assigned an area high on a hill outside Tlemcen. It might have looked good on a map, but for the 70th the site was a disaster. John Ahearn remembers that the location was on bar-ren, sloping terrain cut by a road miles from nowhere. "Bivouacs were established, vehicles stationed on the perimeter, tents dug in, and the inevitable personal and vehicular cleaning began. Life was mis-erable with rainy, dark days and cold, freezing nights." Colonel Wel-born and his staff haunted division headquarters asking to be as-signed elsewhere. "Then the snows came, heavy and fast. The battalion became completely mired and helpless. Tanks and half-tracks could not budge safely. The heavy snows engulfed everything. Tents collapsed under their burden. The temperature dropped dur-ing the day to zero, lower during the night." There was no shelter anywhere. "Everyone wore all the clothing they had and huddled in their tents endeavoring to escape the cold gales. At night they slept with all their clothes on, shared their blankets, and huddled together in pathetic attempts to keep warm. Fires unfortunately were against security regulations. Men emerged from their miserable shelters only at chow times, struggling to the kitchens for the only food available, hot coffee and C rations. Some men did not report. Investigation dis-closed a good deal of sickness."

One of the men who emerged from his miserable shelter only at chow times was Walter "Bad Eye" Waszyn, a B Company me-chanic. "We were cold, and did it ever snow. About three feet came down in no time." Two of his buddies, Sabo and Keller, had spot-ted a farmhouse over a hill, and one morning they walked down to see if they could get something to eat. "They stayed all day, got soused on wine, and came back with about five gallons of wine and about five dozen eggs. On the way back they stole a huge frying pan someplace. They brought the stuff into the four-man tent I had pitched. Sabo broke the eggs in a pan and started to scramble them. He was so drunk he just poured salt on them. No one but Sabo could eat them, but he swallowed the whole batch, washed down with wine. The rest of us drank the wine, but just watched him eat, as hungry as we were."

The only plausible explanation for the choice of this site is that the 9th Division staff thought it was only for a short time and were preoccupied with their move to Tunisia. It was at this time that Rom-mel was breaking through the Kasserine Pass in Tunisia. Elements of the 9th, particularly its artillery, were being rushed to the scene. Whatever the reason, the 9th paid no heed to Colonel Welborn's entreaties. It was one time his influence was useless.

Assigned a Politically Sensitive Task

Furthermore, the 70th was not going with the 9th to Tunisia. When this decision was made is not known. The 70th had been attached to the 9th all the way back to Fort Bragg, and together they had been involved in the Torch landings. However, A Company of the 70th was already in Tunisia providing tank support for French infantry. To detach them from the French for return to the 70th and the 9th would have been both militarily and politically unsound.

Welborn was called to higher headquarters in Oran and was told that the battalion would be the only combat unit in the area. It was to operate the railhead and hospital and make preparations to operate a training school for cadres of French officers and noncoms on the M-5 tank.[12]

These were important tasks, and politically sensitive. France had again become an ally but had no modern tanks. They now had to rely completely on American-built tanks and on training in them by Americans. The 70th was the logical choice. They had been involved in tank training from the beginning and had provided cadres for other tank units. The French would be trained by the best!

The Caserne Bideaux

The moment the 9th left Tlemcen, John Ahearn records, "We came out of the hills, dirty, disheveled, but joyous." Their new billet was in the Caserne Bideaux, an imposing building designed as the architectural embodiment of French colonial power. The might of empire, however, never established dominion over hordes of bedbugs. This according to Joseph Nesbit, who remembers them well. The company kitchens were set up in the stables formerly used by the 2d Algerian Cavalry. After each rainfall the brick paving exuded an unmistakable odor of horses and horses' deposits. Yet the pleasure-pain principle was in full operation. Compared to the experience in the hills, this was like a luxury hotel.

Not the food, however; especially not at first when the 70th stopped drawing rations from the 9th Division and the new alignment was tenuous. Joseph Nesbit, some forty-eight years later, still gets indigestion thinking about Spam and Vienna sausage. Camel was served once, but the men made it known that they would smoke them but not eat them again. For breakfast, the men often faced powdered eggs, which at least would stick to the ribs, or almost anywhere else for that matter. Hotcakes swimming in a watery syrup was also a great way to start a day.

"Bad Eye" Waszyn recalls that French enlisted men present for tank instruction at first shared 70th mess facilities. "The first batch of students tasted the lemonade we were being served. They began to jabber in French and make wild gestures with their arms and hands. Whatever else they did I don't know, but starting the next day they had wine at meals. The French brought in their own rations. Once a horse-drawn cart came through the main gate with a skinned goat on the floorboards. 'Doc' Wisnefski took one look at it and ordered: 'Bury it!'"

Louis Rizzo in battalion supply had to travel around a good deal. "Once at an army supply dump I saw a guy who handled frozen beef. I knew everybody in our outfit was sick and tired of canned meat, so I asked him what he would take for four boxes of beef the next time I came by. He said a tanker combat jacket like the one I was wearing. Well, I had extra jackets, so the next time we made the deal. One box for each company. We all had the first fresh beef we had tasted in five months. It was made into beef stew, but it was beef."

Life improved in March when the 70th became attached to the VI Corps. PX supplies became available, a telephone exchange was installed, and frozen meat and butter were delivered once a week by refrigerated truck. [13]

Life and Duty in Tlemcen

Also arriving was a platoon of VI Corps MPs, thus relieving the 70th of performing police duties. When they had them, Frank Gross recalls, intrigues between the French and the Arabs were a constant source of trouble. "One particular night, I was sergeant of the guard and was told by Captain McLanahan to post sentries around a restaurant where it was believed trouble was brewing. We were armed with tommy guns and .45s. Well, absolutely nothing happened, at least nothing apparent on the outside. But we were ready to storm that damned place, and sure had the firepower to do it!"

Francis Snyder in maintenance says he "pulled patrol to make sure there was no trouble between GIs and French soldiers, who, by the way, were not given ammunition. I drove a half-track, mostly at night. We would take a sergeant from the French Foreign Legion with us, and when we encountered anything to check at night, he would yell out in French. Until he got an appropriate answer we didn't move in to check the situation."

When VI Corps MPs relieved the 70th of these onerous duties, at first they were viewed as a mixed blessing, but soon as totally negative. After all, Tlemcen was pretty much the 70th's town, and these MPs were not family, but rather they inhibited the men from freely pursuing available pleasures. The Casbah, for an example, was off limits. Frank Gross, after his police role was over, frequented the Casbah on occasion. "If caught, we were subject to arrest. We would go in there anyway, because it was a fascinating place, and we could get something to eat and drink. The MPs were really no problem in the Casbah. Young Arab kids for very little money would guide us through narrow, twisting streets, and away from any patrol that might be around."

There were also approved places to go, including a French movie house and another house more frequently visited. This other house had to be licensed. Floyd West, as battalion sergeant major, was involved in the process. "Captain Varhol and I took an enlisted man with us who spoke French and went out prospecting for a house of prostitution that we could license. Here I was, a strict Baptist, visiting one house of prostitution after the other, biting my lip all the time. It turned out that the enlisted man spoke Cajun French and couldn't understand any of the madams we interviewed. Captain Varhol did speak a little French, though, and we finally selected several houses that were given a license."

According to Francis Snyder, "We regularly patrolled the 'beauty parlors' at night. I remember that I had a tommy gun, and that we got to know the madams pretty well. They wouldn't give us anything free except for a couple of drinks. Everything else cost!" Presumably the women in the house were French. If not, the advice in the pamphlet on North Africa to stay clear of native women was being officially ignored.

Three nightspots had been approved for enlisted men: Chez Pepico, better known as "The Bucket of Blood," La Belle Rose, and La Favorite. About all that could be purchased was Algerian wine, fondly referred to as *l'encre* (ink).

Officers obviously had a wider selection of places to drink. John Ahearn loved a "wonderful Hotel Transatlantique where we would go on evenings and weekends. Here was my first exposure to Brandy Alexander. The hotel had a beautiful garden and a pleasant little bar."

He has described Tlemcen as a walled city with much history. Through the centuries it must have been an important merchant and market city on a caravan route, as well as a military center. "The city had wide cobblestone boulevards, with narrow streets of shopkeepers, lovely squares, native quarters, and sidewalk cafes." It was, as Ahearn has indicated, very much a colonial French city. "Moroccan troops were stationed there, as was a unit of Spahia Cavalry. This was a very colorful unit, especially in full dress uniform with their headdress and sabers, mounted on Arabian horses. From adjacent towns, a number of French Foreign Legionnaires would drift into the city on weekends, as would French paratroopers, and some of our own paratroopers. So on weekends, in the cafes and bistros, it was a great time meeting with all these people, talking, singing songs, et cetera."

It was in Tlemcen that Capt. Harry Volk, one of Ahearn's closest buddies, met his future wife, Paulette. She was twenty at the time, the daughter of a French army officer stationed there. Ahearn remembers that shortly after they announced their engagement, "one of the hilarious things we had many laughs about was when Harry took Paulette out one Sunday afternoon. Harry had rented one of those donkey carts, and as they came down one of Tlemcen's tremendously large boulevards, we all hailed them. Harry was half in the bag, and soon was half in the cart as he leaned out with a bow and a wide sweep of his arm. It was a very funny sight."

The 70th became highly influential in Tlemcen. Lieutenant Colonel Welborn, as the highest ranking officer, became sort of a mayor, and Captain Varhol the provost marshal. Welborn received a great many invitations to attend dinner with both French and Arab townspeople. Not wishing to offend anyone or show favoritism, he declined them all.

Whether Colonel Welborn or anyone else in the 70th had much contact with Arab people is highly improbable. As has been recounted several times previously, encounters with native people were bewildering. After some experiences in Tlemcen, Floyd West asserts, the conclusion reached was that, "They would steal anything that wasn't tied down. As a consequence, gasoline cans and boxes of ammunition were smeared with bacon rind with which the Koran forbids contact."

West also related another example of cultural differences. Apparently some Arabs had seen American soldiers washing articles of clothing in gasoline. "On one exercise in the desert an Arab stole about four cans of gasoline. His wife was going to do her washing over a fire and burned up." (Arabs of later generations know all about oil and its by-products. Apparently they didn't then.)

Training French Cadres in U.S. Tanks

During the last week in March, the first of four classes of French officers and noncoms arrived for the two weeks of schooling in the operation of the M-5 light tank. They came from the enormous region stretching from Constantine in eastern Algeria to Dakar in French West Africa.

The first week of instruction was on the tank and its armament, including nomenclature and maintenance. During the second week, the French students drove the tank and fired the 37mm gun. This was done in the desert, some distance from Tlemcen. "We would go out for three days, bivouac in the desert," according to Cecil Nash, one of the instructors. "It was very cold at night in the desert, especially in March and April, so we would take a gallon can and bury it so the top was close to ground level. We would fill it with gasoline and light it. This would provide a little heat for a while, but your face got awfully dirty from the smoke of the burning gasoline."

John Ahearn said that the French were impressed with the M-5 light tank, "particularly its speed and acceleration. They also loved our communication system, and would get on the radio and talk back and forth with no apparent purpose other than sheer pleasure." All instruction of necessity was in English, translated by an indispensable French Captain Pinon, who soon became an honorary member of the 70th. Once teaching methods were worked out, the language barrier became less important.

The last class was in early May and consisted largely of men from Le Deuxieme Spahia d'Alger who had lived side by side with the 70th now for three months. With the conclusion of instruction, a grand joint American-French parade was held, and officers of the 70th were invited to a formal dinner given by French officers.[14] No mention is made of what enlisted men did, but a fair assumption is that French and Americans quaffed a few bottles of *l'encre* together, and no lemonade.

Some of the trained cadres became core elements in the French 2d Armored Division. The 70th would see them again during the liberation of Paris.

The Departure From Tlemcen

In late May, the 70th received orders to leave Tlemcen for the port of Arzew, just outside Oran. Malaria, that Mediterranean scourge, had made its appearance prior to departure. Atabrine was the prescribed drug, but after taking the first dose, half of the battalion became ill.

At Arzew, the bivouac was in an area appropriately named "mosquito hill," where malaria hit very hard. Frank Gross remembers many recurring cases among the men. "I never got it. I used the lotion they gave us to guard against mosquito bites, and I took the Atabrine and salt tablets as ordered. Also I must have been damned lucky."

The four months spent in Tlemcen had been good, and a longer stay than they had any reason to expect. A Company had been engaged in combat from December until just days before the rest of the battalion left for Arzew. Even when in Tlemcen, everyone knew that all of the 70th would be in combat before long. Arriving at a port on the Mediterranean was a sure sign that it would very soon.

3
The Tunisian Campaign

In Tunisia we were always on our own, always with somebody
higher above us. It was our little company against the world.

—Atlee Wampler, A Company
commander in Tunisia

One of Eisenhower's Biggest Disappointments

By November 5, 1942, General Rommel and the German Afrika
Korps were retreating rapidly westward from Egypt after their defeat
at El Alamein by the British Eighth Army under General Mont-
gomery. If Tunisia could be taken before Rommel arrived there, the
Axis would be driven from all of North Africa. Consequently, on
November 10 an Allied army under British General Anderson left
Algiers for Tunisia. The hope and plan was to move 450 miles and
capture Tunis within two weeks.

By the end of November, the advance was stopped. The Vichy government under the notorious Pierre Laval gave Germany permission
to send troops to Tunisia, a French protectorate. Although Allied
forces had numerical superiority, the mountainous terrain favored
the defense. Axis forces were able to establish a bridgehead protecting the key port cities of Tunis and Bizerte. The enemy also had
tactical air superiority with control of the only three all-weather air-
fields in the sector.

Then weather became a major factor. Heavy rains turned routes
of the Allied advance into seas of mud. For a month there was very
little movement. Hopes of capturing Tunis and Bizerte were quickly
dashed. All that could be done for the time being was to straighten
and connect scattered Allied lines, supply and reinforce positions in
both the north and the south, and wait for better weather. The wait
proved to be too long. Rommel would win the race. Eisenhower admitted that the failure to take Tunisia quickly was one of his greatest disappointments of the war.

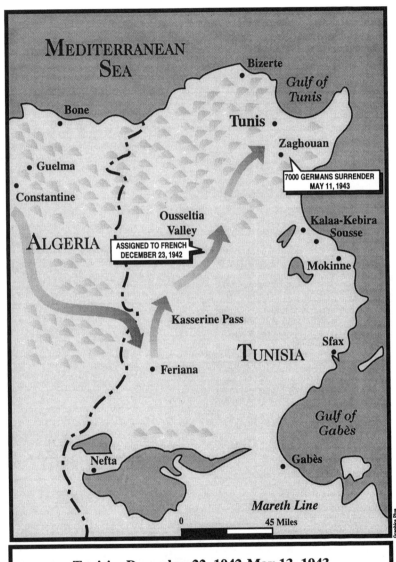

MEDITERRANEAN
SEA

Bizerte
Gulf of
Tunis

Bone

Tunis

Zaghouan

Guelma

7000 GERMANS SURRENDER
MAY 11, 1943

Constantine

Ousseltia
Valley

Kalaa-Kebira
Sousse

ALGERIA

ASSIGNED TO FRENCH
DECEMBER 23, 1942

Mokinne

Kasserine Pass

TUNISIA

Sfax

Feriana

Gulf of
Gabès

Nefta

Gabès

Mareth Line

0   45 Miles

Tunisia: December 22, 1942–May 13, 1943

A Company Arrives in Tunisia

As stated by Eisenhower, "The only flank protection in the south from Tebessa to Gafsa had been provided by scattered French irregulars reinforced and inspired by a small U.S. parachute detachment under the command of a gallant American, Col. Edson D. Raff."[1] Not mentioned by the general was that on December 22, Colonel Raff received support from other gallant Americans—A Company of the 70th. On that date, Captain Lennon, the present company commander, entered in the official historical record: "Moved in the rain from Tebessa to headquarters of Col. Raff at Feriana."[2] (In the Tunisian campaign, attached to A Company were elements of the mortar and assault gun platoons of Headquarters Company, a transportation platoon from Service Company, and a medical attachment headed by Capt. Isadore Shechner.)

With the end of the Allied offensive toward Bizerte and Tunis, the enemy could "concentrate his troops at will. It was unreasonable to assume that he would fail to realize our great weakness in the Tebessa region; it was likely that he would strike us a damaging blow unless we took prompt measures to prevent it."[3] Weakness and the piecemeal nature of Allied defensive positions in the region were obvious in the next entries of the A Company historical record.

December 23, 1942. Assigned to French task force. Reassigned to Tunisian task force.

December 26, 1942. Assigned to French corps. Moved from Feriana at 1715 to Fondouk el Okbi . . . arriving there at daybreak.

December 27, 1942. Came under enemy fire at Fondouk el Okbi. Three enlisted men wounded. Three enlisted men missing in action, seven vehicles mired in crossing river under fire. Assigned to the Algerian division.

December 27, 1942. Company commander reported to [French] Colonel Condroyer for duty at Pichon. Only other American troops here is one tank destroyer company from the 601st Tank Destroyer Battalion. Company went into bivouac at Pichon. Air raid by twelve JU 88s . . . near misses.

Supporting French Infantry in the Ousseltia Valley

A Company was now assigned to the French in the Ousseltia Valley. Here it would stay until close to the end of the Tunisian campaign. The zone of operations was generally in and around Pichon in the south, to Ousseltia roughly seventeen miles to the north, and to Kesra, about twelve miles west of Ousseltia. This was the central sector of the Allied line, and the fighting was for control of the important passes through the Western Dorsal chain of the Atlas Mountains. This control was a formidable task because the sector was still the weakest link in the Allied line.

French forces remained the principal component, and at first the only Allied support was A Company of the 70th and the company from the 601st Tank Destroyer Battalion. (Several British units would soon join.) Just eight miles west of Ousseltia lies the Kairouan Pass, and about ten miles south of Pichon the pass at Fondouk el Aouareb.

The Famed Afrika Korps Is Encountered

German pressure around these points was constant, and as early as December 29 by no less a force than the famed Afrika Korps. Rommel's forces had arrived in Tunisia. Their presence was established in a sharp encounter on that date. As described by Captain Lennon in his official account, an attack was made against a German strong point five miles northeast of Pichon. The A Company light tanks

> were supported by one platoon of Company A, 601st Tank Destroyer Battalion, and about fifty French infantrymen. The infantry was transported into the attack by two half-tracks and a two-and-a-half-ton truck. Attack preceded by a five-minute quick fire from two batteries of French .75s. The two-and-a-half-ton truck, which also contained four enlisted men of this company, was lost to enemy fire. The assault gun . . . with five enlisted men was lost to the enemy. Two tanks were put out of action by enemy antitank fire and were lost . . . The French infantry did not get into the action. Estimated enemy strength: about 200 Afrika Korps infantry, four antitank guns (47mm caliber) and one battery of mortars [known to be Afrika Korps by enemy dead and prisoners].

This was a terrible beating, the worst A Company suffered in the entire campaign. Franklin Anderson, then a lieutenant, notes that the assault gun, which was mounted on a half-track, should not have been in the column. "At the time it seemed to make sense, but there was really nothing it could do." Also, it was the last vehicle in line, and the Germans picked it off without tankers even knowing it. "The two tanks we lost had for some unaccountable reason veered off and approached a hill from the front where the antitank gun was concealed from view. We didn't know where they had gone because of our maintaining radio silence. This was also a mistake, and one we didn't make again. We were new to combat, and I guess were afraid of our radio communications being intercepted. This was our baptism of fire, and we were up against veterans. We learned from our mistakes, but it was a costly lesson."

A few days later, according to the historical record, the body of Pvt. Jewel W. Hagwood was recovered. He was buried next to Captain Steel of the tank destroyer company. Also found were the graves of three other A Company men: T-5 Oscar Osborne and Privates Russell J. Boucher and William M. George. They had been buried by the Germans who had put their dog tags in a bottle atop the graves with the note, in German, "Here lie three valorous American *panzer* soldiers who fell on 29 December 1942."[4]

British ack-ack guns went into position at Pichon on January 2, 1943. This is the first indication in the A Company record of a British unit in the French sector.

Using Light Tanks as Bait

The entry in the official record dated January 20 is startling and revealing. "Seven tanks used as bait to draw German tanks into range of A Company, 601st TDs and British 6-pound AT guns. Our tanks came under fire of medium and heavy German tanks and successfully carried out their mission fifteen miles northeast of Ousseltia."

What a damning indictment of the value of light tanks and indeed the value of tankers who rode in them! Only months before at Fort Bragg, these same tankers had been told by General Patton that they and their modern equipment would be irresistible. They had been schooled to be aggressive in attack. Yet here they had been used as nothing but bait, defenseless as they paraded in front of medium and heavy German tanks! How harrowing to actually invite Germans to fire their 75mm and 88mm guns on their thinly armored tanks with the certain knowledge that any hit would blow them to pieces!

This tactic had been successfully used by the British at El Alamein. Now it was successful again with the 70th. They got away with it this one time but never tried the gambit again. Later, in Europe, medium tanks were used to draw small-arms fire, but never again as bait for tanks and antitank guns.

Plugging Leaks in the Line

During this period, A Company seems to have been sort of a mechanized fire brigade sent to one incendiary situation after another in this thinly held Allied sector. The historical record notes on January 29 that seven tanks were sent to another danger point near Ousseltia by order of French General Deligne. On February 1 they were ordered north by U.S. General Roosevelt, and the same day moved again when a German attack from Fondouk to Pichon was expected. On February 8 they were with U.S. Combat Team 135, February 13 back again under General Roosevelt, and February 19 with the French XIX Corps as part of a holding force at Kesra.

Efforts were made to disguise weaknesses. Then-Lt. Franklin Anderson tells us that normally they would wipe out tank tracks so they couldn't be observed from the air. "During this period we would drive around a lot and leave the tracks.

"Most planes in the air were German, and we hoped they would report our presence. Also, Captain Lennon would move us around the Ousseltia Valley at night, making our presence known in place after place. Once, after Captain Wampler took command, we were on a roadway on the side of a mountain. We discovered the road went around and came back, so we drove our tanks around and around to show we had more than we had."

The Germans Attack Elsewhere

The entry in the official history on February 1 regarding an expected German attack from Fondouk to Pichon was an assessment of U.S. intelligence. It was a bad mistake. As Eisenhower records, it caused commanders to make faulty dispositions "although we had reconnaissance units in the Ousseltia Valley, near Fondouk, who insisted the Germans were not concentrating in that area."[5] Based on what happened, German intelligence was superior at that time, including, no doubt, knowledge that the attempt to hide weakness in the Ousseltia Valley was not worth exploiting. Instead, the Germans went after far larger game. General Von Arnim struck westward through the Eastern Dorsal Mountains at Faid Pass in one arm of a pincer while Rommel hit the southernmost point of the American sector at Gafsa with the other.

On February 13, Von Arnim met armored units of the U.S. II Corps at Sidi-bou-Zid and caught them in the open. German 88mm antitank guns and Mark V Panther and Mark VI Tiger tanks inflicted extremely heavy losses on II Corps. Outgunned and outarmored, American tanks, many of them Shermans, could do nothing. General Omar Bradley states that "more than ninety tanks were left burning on the valley floor."[6]

Tank Problems Revealed but Nothing Was Done

Ninety tanks! It had been one of the worst defeats in American military history. Yet, despite the lessons learned at Sidi-bou-Zid, the Sherman continued to be the American tank of choice, though badly outgunned and outarmored by German Panthers and Tigers. There had been earlier warnings of the need for heavier tanks to fight tanks. Germany, too, had made the mistake of relying on smaller tanks in invading the USSR in June 1941. Things went well until the Soviet thirty-two-ton T-34 and the fifty-two-ton KV1 began to control the battlefield. To counter them, Germany rushed the Panther from the drawing board to the battlefield, bugs and all. The Tiger, with an 88mm gun and heavy armor plating, was also rushed into production.

In the United States, meanwhile, debates continued between those holding differing points of view regarding the employment of tanks. More important was the insistence on durability and the avoidance of mechanical failure. "Perhaps the most vital clue to the American tank problem is that indefinable standard of tactical utility, reliability, and durability called 'battle worthiness'. . . time after time an alleged lack of quality resulted in not getting a heavier tank than the Sherman into action."[7]

What to do about heavier German tanks was a quandary. This was apparent in a change of tactics in Tunisia. Three battalions of artillery were to accompany one battalion of tanks. What a devastating indictment of our tanks! The United States also relied heavily on tank destroyers. By 1943 there were only thirteen fewer tank destroyer battalions than tank battalions. From then on there was a decline. Tank destroyers (TDs) proved useful throughout the war, but they were too thinly armored to go against German tanks at short range. They could not do what a heavier tank could have done.

No attempt was made to solve another major problem. American tanks simply burned up too fast. Tankers believed the major cause was the use of high-octane gasoline for fuel. Another was that armor was too thin to protect 75mm ammunition storage. Already in Tunisia, tankers pleaded with General Bradley to "replace these firetraps."[8] Shermans were called "Ronson Lighters" after a popular cigarette lighter that had an advertising slogan, "They light every time."

Not heeding lessons learned about tanks in Tunisia and producing a better armed and armored tank earlier was a major mistake. This decision might well have prolonged the war.

Despite Defeats, the Allied Position Improves

Rommel's offensive ended after his forces pushed through Kasserine Pass, so stoutly defended by American forces. He received word that British General Montgomery and his Eighth Army had reached the Mareth Line on the border between Libya and Tunisia. Ill with jaundice, Rommel made a decision uncharacteristic of him. He concluded that his offensive couldn't succeed and opted to return immediately to confront Montgomery before his own supplies ran out.

American forces had suffered several bruising defeats, but now Rommel's wide-ranging maneuvering was over. Eisenhower has written that, from the close of the Kasserine battle, the Allied position improved in a number of ways. Now, the U.S. II Corps with four divisions could concentrate around Tebessa and soon would link with Montgomery and the Eighth Army.[9] With a solid front forming an arc around German and Italian forces defending Bizerte and Tunis, the Allies could begin closing in, squeezing the enemy into a smaller and smaller area.

A Company During and After the Axis Offensive

During the Axis offensive, A Company held defensive positions near Maktar, about forty miles north of where German General Von Arnim drove for the pass at Sbiba. On February 21, one platoon made a reconnaissance three miles ahead of a French infantry battalion and encountered three German Mark IV tanks. After a brief engagement, the Mark IVs withdrew. On the twenty-third, an entry in the official history notes conditions near Maktar: "Mired two tanks in the mud and threw a track on another one. Terrain unsuitable for tank operations. British tank officer with six Churchills refused to make an attack over the same ground."

Churchill tanks were mediums, firing the equivalent of a 75mm gun. This entry was the first reference to a squadron of them under British Major Dow that supported the French and A Company until close to the end of the campaign.

Part of an International Combination

The international flavor of these operations was becoming pronounced. An example is in the official history of March 11.

Made attack in Ousseltia Valley with one squadron of Churchills under Major Dow and one battalion of 7th Moroccan infantry. American aircraft screened the attack. Ghoum protected our right flank. Our light tanks led the attack with tank-borne infantry. 2d Platoon made attack north of Ousseltia. 1st Platoon attacked SE of the village, and the 3d Platoon (with three platoons of Churchills) attacked Hill 506 on the Kairouan Road, east of Ousseltia. 1st Platoon took eleven German prisoners. One of our light tanks was put out of action by enemy fire. An unsuccessful attempt was made to recover this tank and our troops destroyed it with hand grenades to prevent its capture by the enemy. Attack jumped off at 1200 noon. We rallied at 1500 under artillery fire and returned to attack position at 1530. Enemy dive bombers came over valley while we were in rally position. After the show was over, sixteen Stukas and five JU 88s and two Messerschmitts came over and bombed their own front lines. French and British artillery supported the attack.

No casualties . . . returned to bivouac south of Kesra after dark.
Hard rain during night . . . Major Peterson . . . of the 34th Ordnance Company . . . left information that this company had
been attached to II Corps for administration and supply." [The
company remained under French command, however.]

The A Company Orphans

The attachment to II Corps for administration and supply continued only until the corps was shifted to the northernmost sector
west of Bizerte in the third week of April. Captain Atlee Wampler,
who replaced Captain Lennon as commander on March 30, recalls:
"General Patton helped me very considerably when he took over II
Corps. He was an armored officer in an infantry corps, and I was an
armored officer in a foreign army. We therefore had something in
common. Not that we were buddy-buddy, far from it, but he told his
staff to do what they could for me. They allowed me to draw fifteen
days' rations at a time, which was unheard of, one day's rations being the standard."

Other than that, rations were French or British. Franklin Anderson remembers: "The French would come to our area with a truck-
load of bread. A French soldier would hop up on the load and kick
off our allotment of loaves. This bread was so hard we were convinced
it was left over from World War I. We also got wine from them, probably Algerian, which was poured from a barrel into our five-gallon
water cans." He never recalls getting any meat from the French. "The
British rations seemed always to be large cans of tea, marmalade, biscuits, and sausages. The biscuits would take the enamel off your
teeth, and the sausages were precooked and in a fatty substance. I'm
pretty sure the British and French gave us the same rations they themselves were issued."

Obtaining supplies was a problem throughout the campaign.
This was true even during the period when the company was under
II Corps for supply and administration. The official company historical record notes for an attack on March 25, only eight tanks were
available out of the seventeen in the company, "the others having
been knocked out by the enemy or deadlined for repairs." The entry for April 5 states that five new tanks were received, but this was
the only indication of the replacement of lost tanks or those beyond

repair in the entire campaign. On January 24, the company received two half-tracks, two two-and-a-half-ton trucks, and one 75mm anti-tank gun as replacements. Again, that was the only entry for this type of equipment while in Tunisia.

Like forgotten orphans, the men scavenged anything that looked like a weapon. "A British 2-pounder AT gun, some grenades, and two camouflage nets were recovered from an abandoned ammo dump. Supply Sergeant Kelly returned from Elba Ksoum with rations and 'picked up' a new .50-caliber machine gun. These additions to the firepower . . . caused more celebration within the company than packages from home at that time, for an engagement could be lost for lack of a weapon—and when a weapon was lost in those days, a replacement was hard to find." [10]

George Brookstein recalls that replacements of men lost to the company seldom arrived. The official record supports his recollection. The only entry regarding replacements was made on April 10, near the end of the campaign. Yet the entry of December 27, 1942, has three enlisted men wounded and three missing in action, and that of December 29 notes seventeen men missing, with four later confirmed as killed. Based on the official record, therefore, A Company did not have its full complement of tanks until at least April 5, or of men until April 10, if indeed they had either.

Medical supplies were generally if not always adequate. Franklin Anderson reports that at one point "some men were getting scabs from scurvy due to a lack of vitamin C. When supply sergeant Kelly went back for some supplies, 'Doc' Schechner had him pick up vitamin C tablets and Atabrine. Actually, we must have been in terrific physical condition. In January and February it was cold as well as damp, but we got no trench foot. Later in the spring it was warm during the daytime but still cold at night. We always slept on the ground, but in bedrolls and in tents made out alright."

George Brookstein as the company liaison corporal was provided with a jeep and driver and traveled around on a variety of missions. On a number of occasions, Brookstein had the presence of mind and the wit to obtain fresh fruit, vegetables, and eggs to supplement the company diet. "I would go right into the center of a village with anything the guys could spare, and display my wares much like a native bazaar. I knew enough French to make barter deals. Getting eggs was best, but we also could use fruits and vegetables providing they were protected by a skin that could be removed. Otherwise we wouldn't eat them.

"Once we bought a small herd of sheep," Brookstein observes. "Mess sergeant Stumbaugh made a big batch of mutton stew, but the stench was so bad we really couldn't eat it. When we left that bivouac area we didn't know if there were mines or not so we drove the sheep ahead of us. Once clear, the sheep went off on their own."

Ghoumier and Senegalese

These young American provincials of A Company had found themselves fighting side by side with people previously known only in schoolbooks or from the pages of the *National Geographic*. Ghoumiers and Senegalese were among the more interesting. At least they were to Franklin Anderson. He recalls that both had their own language or dialect. "So of course did we and the French. Consequently, there was little coordination. Everybody did what they could and tried to follow the commands as given. The Senegalese were known as terrific night fighters. They would go off into the sunset on their own, and I'm sure kept the enemy on his guard all night. I was told they were paid for the number of ears they brought back."

Noteworthy was that the Ghoum system of organization was completely different from ours. "Instead of companies or battalions, they went by clan or family. When enough of them were killed, and they decided they'd had enough, that clan or family would simply leave and be replaced by another clan or family. Make no mistake, though, they were terrific fighters."

Although the men didn't get to know any of these native troops, Anderson says he and "Doc" Shechner were invited to have lunch with some of them once. "They served couscous and some kind of nonalcoholic beverage. They ate with their fingers, of course, and were very sociable. We had a good, interesting experience."

The One and Only Mortar

As mentioned before, this was an expanded company. Assigned to it was one of three squads in the mortar platoon. One squad meant one gun, an 81mm mortar, mounted on a half-track. Frank Suleski was a member of the squad. "We were pioneers in mounted mortars, firing over the rear end of a half-track. Our vehicle had a rail all around the top, which aside from the mortar had one .50-caliber machine gun and two .30-calibers. Our personal weapons were pistols, tommy guns, and rifles." In their first action in Tunisia, they moved too fast to use the mortar, but fired the machine guns. "We went by a civilian car used by French soldiers. All the doors were open and all occupants on the ground, dead. The only thing alive was a turkey tied to a long cord and standing alongside the bodies outside the car. Our damage was a bullet hole in the frying pan and one five-gallon water can riddled with bullets. We first used our mortar at Sauvagère Hue El Asel. A number of high-explosive mortar [shells] were fired until a German gun tried to zero in on us. They came close, but we moved and continued firing."

The Difficulties of Combat Under Foreign Command

One of the greatest difficulties A Company faced was in coordination with infantry they were to support. It is axiomatic that in military operations, teamwork is essential to success. Much of training has to do with developing teamwork and coordination within units, between units, and in command structures. When tanks and infantry work together, each must know what the other can and cannot do. They must protect the other, or both are endangered and objectives cannot be attained. Yet, in the Tunisian campaign, A Company almost always fought side by side with people who spoke a different language, had different military traditions, and had different cultural values. Often, the company would be under one command for a half day, a day, or a week, then be under a different command, in a different area. It happened time after time.

Michael Varhol, then the battalion adjutant in Tlemcen, stated what was learned later. "We did not know under what difficult conditions they were mistreated by the French commanders who stupidly wanted to use tanks as forward sentinels or pillboxes with no infantry protection. Also, when action was at hand, the first thought was to send the tanks forward with no real plan of action." Varhol believes that Captain Lennon was relieved for fighting for his company, "the

French sending a message that he was crazy. I must fault my close friend, Colonel Welborn, our commander, for losing close contact with A Company and completely trusting the French. In reality our men were orphaned. It is a fact that never once did our commander or anyone else from the 70th visit them in Tunisia. It is significant that no one thought about rotating any personnel from A Company for a rest, and to let others gain combat experience."

Captain Lennon was removed without any American investigation of any kind as to his leadership capabilities, but he later became a major. Apparently the change in command was a matter determined only by the French and Colonel Welborn, who, as Varhol indicates, trusted the judgment of the French. There is no evidence that Lt. (later Captain) Isadore Shechner, A Company medical officer, was consulted regarding Lennon's mental state. The A Company official historical record notes only that Captain Wampler assumed command on March 30 and joined the forward echelon the following day. Wampler certainly had time to discuss the situation with Lennon and make his own assessment. With the statement given by Varhol in mind, Wampler's recollections are revealing.

"Immediately upon assuming command, a French liaison officer came up to me and said I was to find a particular regimental headquarters to which we were to be attached for an action the next day. I didn't speak French too well at the time, but there was a Canadian in the company who could speak French. You could hardly understand his English, but anyway, between the two of us we could communicate." After some discussion about where the headquarters was located, the liaison officer agreed to take Wampler there. "We finally found the commanding colonel in a hole in the ground up near the front. The Canadian interpreter introduced me to him. After acknowledging the introduction, the colonel didn't say another word, and neither did I. Instead, the liaison officer talked about twenty minutes, waving his arms, pointing at a map, pointing at me, pointing to the regimental commander. He was speaking French so rapidly, the interpreter couldn't begin to keep up."

When he was at last finished, he turned to Wampler and ordered him to make an attack. "I said we don't even know where the attack position is! The liaison officer said he would lead us to it. Later, in the dark, we did arrive at the attack position. Suddenly it dawned on me that the liaison officer was telling the colonel what he thought we should do, and in effect, was commanding the company. At daylight, I could see that the plan of attack was the opposite of what I would have done."

The company managed to survive the attack, but after it was over Wampler went right back to the colonel with his interpreter and asked that this liaison officer be relieved. "You have never heard so much French as came out in response." Finally the colonel threatened to send Wampler back to Eisenhower. "I told him you can send me back to Washington if you want, but as long as I am commanding A Company of the 70th Tank Battalion, I am going to command it. We are equals, I am not up here to be your lackey. Understand this, we are equals and I want to be in on the planning of operations that concern my men. I will tell you what we can do to help you, and you tell me what you can do to help us. Only this way can our joint effort work."

From then on, Wampler used his own liaison, George Brookstein, and very quickly learned enough French to get by, though always making certain that he understood what was being said, even if that required several repetitions. "We got along well after that, and I was in on the plans." Very often this meant night reconnaissance on foot by Wampler and other A Company officers.

Atlee Wampler on Tank Tactics

Wampler asserts that in both light and medium tanks it was hard to identify and sight a target on the move. The gyrostabilizers on the big gun were only moderately successful. "When on the move and bouncing up and down, you were looking at the sky and then the ground. So we learned the hard way in Tunisia that we needed someone in position to fire, to cover other tanks when we moved." When working with infantry, a platoon of tanks was divided into two sections. "As one section moved forward, the other remained in a stationary position, what we called 'over-watch,' ready to provide covering fire if needed. When the first tanks stopped or found a defilade position [screened from enemy fire], they became the 'over-watch' and the other two tanks moved forward. They sort of leapfrogged. That was a tactic we developed in the 70th, and it came out of combat experience." (This tactic closely resembles infantry leapfrogging. Its application to tanks may well have come from infantry roots.)

Another tactic that came from experience was used to great advantage later at Barrafranca, Sicily. It came from the knowledge of how high guns on German tanks could be elevated. Wampler explains: "If high ground could be attained, even our light tanks could disable larger and more powerful German tanks. The keys to success were not to be wrong on how high our tanks had to be, and to be fast and accurate in gunnery. The capabilities of both your tanks and those of the enemy had to be known, and men had to attain a proficiency that could be relied upon."

Wampler reiterates the critical factor when working with infantry. "We moved with them, and there had to be coordination. Infantry could help tanks a lot, and we could help them. Once you got used to working with someone, things went better. But you had to work as a team. You couldn't have some high commander dictating what was to be done if he didn't know what he was talking about regarding tanks, or didn't know the immediate situation." The ability to learn from experience was serving the 70th well, and would continue to do so throughout the war.

However, the question of authority regarding the use of tanks was settled only because Wampler had forcefully taken a stand. The issue did not come up again with the French, but would with American infantry commanders in Normandy and later. It was a matter to be worked out in the field. Perhaps this was all that could have been done, for each situation was different. Generally the arrangement was satisfactory except, as Wampler asserts, when senior-ranked infantry officers ordered misuse of tanks.

Enemy Air Superiority

Only in the later stages of the campaign did the Allies gain control of the air. Until then, the safe assumption was that any plane was hostile. When George Brookstein and his jeep driver, Paul Jones, went anywhere in daylight, Brookstein would turn around to face the rear and watch for enemy aircraft. "On one trip an English lorry passed us. The men in it were laughing at us, thinking us over-cautious. We went about our business and on the way back saw the same lorry, which had been strafed by the enemy. We helped a doctor who was with them administering first aid. They had been hit on a stretch of this road that was known to be dangerous. There were open fields next to it, so vehicles could easily be spotted and there was no place to get cover. If attacked, about all you could do was run away from your vehicle."

The first time Brookstein saw a flight of about twenty-four "Flying Fortresses," he thought it was a vast armada. "That is how seldom we saw our own planes. I was so thrilled on seeing them I wrote a poem and dedicated it to our air force.

> In the fields of wheat I lay,
> admiring the warmth of a bright, golden day.
> High above, in the pale blue sky,
> the birds of Mars are passing by.
> Northward roaring as they go,
> inflicting havoc on our foe.
> To them our heroes whom we admire,
> the Boston, Fortress and Spitfire.

Encircling the Enemy

In the first weeks of April, the stage was set for the final act. Montgomery and the British Eighth Army would have the principal role by driving from the southeast toward Tunis. The British First Army, led by General Anderson, was to take Bizerte and seal off the northwest.

Patton and Bradley realized that American forces were being shunted aside to play a minor role and were furious. Bradley now conceived a plan to get II Corps involved. Eisenhower had asked the War Department for an additional 5,400 trucks, and in less than three weeks they were on hand—a remarkable feat. Bradley used them to shift the entire II Corps from the south to the north. By April 23, Americans were in position next to the Mediterranean, ready to drive on Bizerte. In the new alignment, the British First Army from just south of II Corps was to drive in a sweeping arc toward Tunis, first moving a little south, then east and northeast. Montgomery was to continue to drive on Tunis from the southeast.

The French XIX Corps, still south of the British First Army, and still including A Company, would link up with Montgomery and the British Eighth Army.

To do this the French Constantine Division and A Company had to break through a pass in the Eastern Dorsal Mountains. The move toward it began on April 8. Heavy enemy artillery bombardments and mountain terrain strewn with mines made progress difficult. On April 10, one A Company tank struck a mine, wounding two men and knocking out the tank. The same day in the same vicinity, French General Welbert, commander of the Constantine Division, was killed when his vehicle also hit a mine. Despite these obstacles, the pass on the Ousseltia-Kairouan road had to be taken, so the mightiest task force of which A Company was a part in the Tunisian campaign was formed under the command of British Major Dow. All available A Company tanks were involved, as was the squadron of British Churchills, accompanied by four batteries of French field artillery and some British ack-ack guns. With such concentrated firepower, stiff resistance must have been expected. One company of Moroccan Ghoum infantry riding on the Churchills were to be the holding force until additional infantry could be brought up. A Company was to lead the attack and to form the reconnaissance for the rest of the task force.

In the official history, Captain Wampler, in the command tank, described the battle.

Company was in assembly position at 0515. Movement of task force delayed two hours due to French failing to provide trucks to transport the company of Ghoums. Ordered to move toward objective at 0745. Distance from assembly position about twelve miles. Company moved through very difficult terrain and reached objective. Upon reaching the high ground 3,000 yards south of objective, and proceeding down north slope toward the pass, three tanks of 1st Platoon and command and staff tanks were fired on by three enemy antitank guns. Lieutenant Williams's tank was hit and caught fire at once. Crew evacuated tank under enemy smallarms fire. T-5 Paul R. Miller . . . came out of tank with clothes aflame. Private John B. Johnson . . . while under enemy fire, extinguished the flames. The crew then returned on foot to the rest of the company. Lieutenant Anderson's tank was hit but was not disabled. The three tanks of the 1st Platoon and the command tank withdrew to position on south slope of the ridge. Company extended and held position awaiting arrival of rest of force. Company came under artillery and mortar fire. Rest of force arrived and artillery opened fire on enemy gun emplacements. Churchill tanks made a small flanking movement to the right flank with a detail of Ghoums. Attack of Churchills unsuccessful due to terrain. However, Ghoums took 125 enemy prisoners. Terrain too difficult for any further tank attack, therefore a battalion of Ghoums were brought in from rear and attacked pass during the night.

According to George Brookstein, T-5 Paul Miller did not return with the rest of Lieutenant Williams's crew. Brookstein and Williams immediately went back to the burning tank and found Miller in a state of shock. Keeping low as German small-arms fire was still coming in, they dragged him to safety. Brookstein remembers this "because after Paul had pulled himself together, he went to the edge of a flat plateau surrounded by mountains and got down on his knees in prayer. He looked up into the heavens with tears rolling down his cheeks. This, of course, brought tears to my eyes."

A Company Breaks Out of the Ousseltia Valley

Although the terrain was too difficult for tank operations, the great firepower of the task force at the point of attack enabled the Ghoum infantry to proceed, with the pass taken that night. The way was now open to finally leave the Ousseltia Valley. On April 17, A Company drove fifty-two miles to Siliana, and on April 22 moved another forty-two miles to the area of Bon Arada. Here they became part of a *groupement blindé* (armored group) under the command of French General Le Couteaux.

Bizerte and Tunis Fall

General Bradley's U.S. II Corps (General Patton left II Corps on April 15 to return to Morrocco to plan the invasion of Sicily) jumped off on April 23. The terrain was rugged, and the enemy had months to prepare defensive positions. After nearly two weeks of fierce fighting, including that for Hill 609, the U.S. 34th Division and 1st Armored Division neared Bizerte. The enemy was forced to surrender the city on May 7. The honor of occupying Bizerte was given to the 9th Infantry Division, those old comrades of the 70th.

On April 22 the IX Corps of the British First Army began its offensive for Tunis in the area of Sebkretel Kourzia. Both the British and the enemy incurred heavy losses in the seesaw tank battle. While the British offensive stalled, the Axis headquarters was forced to shift most available mobile reserves to the area, and to expend irreplaceable supplies.

While this battle was in progress, on April 25 A Company reconnaissance contacted the right flank of the British IX Corps. Sebkretel Kourzia was just ten miles away. For the next ten days, the Allies kept applying pressure, with the enemy slowly giving ground, as noted in the official history. The company was bombed by enemy planes on April 26. Enemy artillery fire and more bombing continued through May 1. Company tanks were within sight of German lines and positions.

The French XIX Corps still including A Company now protected the right flank of a corridor through which British IX Corps tanks would strike out for Tunis. The British V Corps protected the left flank of the corridor. At dusk on May 5, the Allies began the biggest air attack in the Tunisian campaign.[11] The British IX Corps moved out on May 6, and Tunis was captured the next day. It fell so rapidly that the capital city escaped the destruction of the last-ditch stand Hitler had ordered.

Last Battles Involve A Company

In the south, however, the war continued until May 13. A larger proportion of Axis forces remained in this sector. In terrain well suited for defense, a large-scale evacuation was possible. Substantial numbers of enemy troops remained around Zaghouan and in the mountains between Zaghouan and Hammamet. True to its destiny to be in the front of events, A Company headed for Zaghouan on May 4 and was involved in the final battles until the last shot was fired. Artillery duels occurred on a daily basis as the *groupement blindé* moved steadily toward Zaghouan. The official history notes that ten French Valentine tanks (British made) were lost due to artillery and mines, and that two A Company men were wounded by artillery shells on May 8, and two more on May 10.

Thousands of the Enemy Surrender to A Company

Then, suddenly, the whole Axis front collapsed, and May 11, 1943, proved to be one of the most amazing days in the history of the 70th Tank Battalion. The entry in the official history for that day begins with orders from French General Le Couteaux to attack. At a junction on the Zaghouan-Reboa road, many prisoners were taken and Germans began destroying equipment. Very soon thereafter, company commander Wampler and Lieutenant Boatwright with the 3d Platoon took 1,500 Italian prisoners, complete with their trucks and weapons. The highest ranking officer was a major. The 2d Platoon, led by company executive officer Williams and Lieutenant Schmiess, took 90 German prisoners, including nine officers, one of whom was Col. Alfred Bauer, commander of German artillery in the area, presumably the very same that the day before had shelled the company. These prisoners were marched off to a nearby farm, "the German prisoners well disciplined, the Italians disorganized."

At about 1700, the French commander ordered A Company to attack Zaghouan. As Atlee Wampler recalls, "I told him we can't possibly attack Zaghouan; it's the strong point on the German line and we have only thirteen light tanks!" When the colonel insisted, Wampler said, "Well, we will try, but as soon as they start shooting, we may have to get the hell out of there because we won't stand a snowball's chance against them."

Despite his apprehension, Wampler gave the command to start for Zaghouan without infantry support. "As we came within a mile or two of the town, we saw a white flag being waved from the ditch. It was a German lieutenant. We were afraid they were going to pop up and start shooting so we paused. Anyway, they didn't, and the lieutenant came toward us. We didn't fully understand what he was saying so I sent word back for Lt. Stu Williams to come forward, as he spoke some German." Williams talked with the German lieutenant and told Wampler that the German commander wanted to surrender his whole force. "I told Stu that I didn't know what we could do, as it was now about 1830, but for him to go with the lieutenant and get details as to number, and so on. I told Stu, 'Go in our jeep and put the German lieutenant on the radiator, so if anybody starts shooting, he will get it first. If you are not back in an hour and a half, we're coming in to get you.'"

The next time Wampler saw Williams, he was in his jeep leading a German colonel sitting in the backseat of a big black Mercedes. "The colonel stepped out of the car resplendent in full dress uniform like he was going to a diplomatic reception. We were in the same combat fatigues we had been wearing for six weeks. Anyway, the colonel came down and surrendered to me. I took Stu aside and told him we couldn't handle this. It was too big for us. About this time the whole mountain started to explode. The Germans were destroying their ammunition, equipment, and so on. They were going to surrender to us whether we liked it or not."

By now it was about 2030 and getting dark, so Wampler told Williams to take the colonel back to the French, and to tell General Le Couteaux that they would have to take over the surrender. The company would proceed to Zaghouan, and the French should come there as soon as possible.

In Zaghouan headlights were turned on, as it was now completely dark. "The Germans came out of the mountains and into town in columns of squads, in perfect order. You can't believe how many Germans marched in. They kept coming and coming. All of them were singing, I suppose because the war was over for them and they were surrendering to Americans. When they found out they were to be turned over to the French, they became a bit despondent, but we couldn't consider handling so many." A small tank company had no food, equipment, or anything else to handle such a situation. "Hundreds were milling around the tanks. For once, I was happy about German discipline. They could have overpowered us in a minute. The French took over about 0100, so we had them for over three hours." German Colonel Becker unconditionally surrendered more than 7,000 members of the once-proud Hermann Goering Division to A Company of the 70th Tank Battalion.

George Brookstein was one of the men positioned on top of a tank manning a machine gun. "They were orderly and came around my tank and talked with me. I spoke to them in half English, half Yiddish. They wanted to surrender to us because we were the only American unit in the area."

Lieutenant Franklin Anderson remembers the German commander asking Wampler where the German troops should go. Wampler pointed to a field. "The Germans promptly proceeded to the field and we went to the end of it and posted guards. As few as we were, that was rather useless. Sort of like the biblical story of the sheep and the lion lying down together." Some Germans talked to Anderson in perfect English. "I had no fear at all. They were professional soldiers, and when they gave their word to surrender, they would abide by it. A few wanted to come with us and work in the kitchen. 'We will shine everything,' they said. Of course that wasn't possible. They all had to go with the French."

On May 11, 1943, A Company accepted the surrender of between 8,500 and 9,500 Germans and Italians.

The next day A Company was ordered to advance again. Captain Wampler and Lieutenant Williams were still busy with the German surrender, so Franklin Anderson led the company. "A jeep came along and told us to stop. A French colonel got out of the jeep and came over to my tank. In perfect English, he said he was a representative of General de Gaulle and that in the jeep was none other than General Giraud, who wanted to review our tanks. He asked if we would go to a field, which he pointed to, where there was room to line up our tanks."

Anderson said they would be honored. The tanks were moved into line, all 37mm guns at the same elevation. "We were dirty and disheveled, but the French party came right over. The colonel introduced me to General Giraud and we shook hands. With General Giraud in front and me and the colonel right behind, we proceeded down and back. Then the colonel gave a nice little talk about how much our efforts were appreciated. They certainly had heard of us, and that we had worked side by side with their troops. It was a true and genuine acknowledgment of what we had done."

On May 13, the company once again received orders to advance toward another known concentration of enemy forces. They did so with all hatches buttoned up, and all eyes on alert. This could be just the time some looney fanatic might choose to do and die for the führer or Il Duce. As recorded in the last entry of the official history: "Company ordered to advance to vicinity of Heuncher Djeradou with the mission of attacking and capturing any enemy in that position. As company reached objective, German and Italian soldiers surrendered by the thousands. Enemy surrendered so rapidly that company was overwhelmed. 210 vehicles captured intact; over 10,000 enemy prisoners taken, including two Italian colonels and several high-ranking German officers. Company turned over all prisoners and vehicles to French at 1500. Met forward elements of British Eighth Army at 1500. The end of the African campaign."

Another 10,000 men had surrendered to one light tank company! The highest estimate would approximate 20,000 in the last three days. Whatever the figure, these spectacles were absolutely incredible. Obviously, the surrender of many thousands of enemy soldiers to A Company had little to do with its undoubted prowess. More likely George Brookstein was closer to the truth when he said that the company was the only American unit in the area. Both Italians and Germans for a number of obvious reasons wanted to surrender to Americans, and not to the British or French.

A Company in the Tunisian Campaign

Nonetheless, there was poetic justice to it all. These men had been a lone company in a foreign army for much of the previous four to five months. Assigned to one command after the other, seldom receiving necessary supplies and replacements, eating French and British rations and only infrequently their own food, they tirelessly went on performing their duty in an exemplary way.

Eight men had lost their lives. Although the official record is not always clear, entries indicate at least nine were wounded and eleven missing in action. Since at full strength the company and attachments consisted of six officers and 128 enlisted men, the casualty rate was approximately 22 percent. Tankers, of course, were the majority of these losses.

They had been in the field 158 consecutive days, most of them on the line. Well into March, the weather was wet and cold. Finding a place to pitch a two-man pup tent was frequently impossible. The same clothes were worn day and night, often for weeks on end. Chances for baths were few and far between.

Fighting alongside troops speaking different languages and with different military traditions, the men of A Company learned to adapt and learned from early mistakes. Rather than fall apart in bickering and complaining, these men grew closer together in comradeship. Atlee Wampler was aware of this. "We were always on our own, always in a situation where somebody was higher above us. It was our little company against the world. Particularly when we were with the French. We knew we couldn't expect much from them because they didn't have anything to give us." Esprit de corps was higher at the end than it was at the beginning in Tunisia. The men of A Company kept their self-respect and maintained their integrity throughout difficult times.

In most American histories, biographies, and autobiographies, however, little attention is given to French operations, much less to one U.S. light tank company attached to them. So, in an ironic sense, it was the enemy who gave A Company a deserved honor by surrendering to them. This, of course, is not noted in most books on the campaign.

The French, however, were the best judges of the worth of A Company. They awarded twenty-five men with the croix de guerre, an exceptionally high percentage of the company. General Giraud, high commissioner of French North Africa, reviewed them in the field.

More honors were to come. A Company moved into Tunis, bivouacked as Franklin Anderson recalls, "in a lovely park. We had a chance to do some sight-seeing. I went to see the ruins of Carthage and saw the grand bazaar." George Brookstein remembers eating camel steak in restaurants during their stay of several weeks.

On May 20 there was a grand victory parade in Tunis. Representative contingents from most of the Allied units that had participated in the victory were there, as were the leaders. Eisenhower, his second in command, Lord Alexander, Patton, Bradley, Montgomery, Anderson, Giraud, Juin, and many others sat in the reviewing stands accepting the salute of the ground, air, and naval units as they marched or flew by.

At this symbolically important function, the French paid A Company the highest tribute—they made them the honor guard. Franklin Anderson will never forget it. "The parade was on the main boulevard, which was very wide and lined with palm trees. Two of our tanks were placed between each of these trees, stretching out from both sides of the reviewing stand. We were dressed in our class A uniforms, our tanks all shined up and positioned in an exact line with all 37mm guns at precisely the same elevation. My, we felt proud."

After the parade a French lieutenant whom Franklin Anderson had gotten to know well came over to greet him. "We had seen a good deal of each other earlier in the Ousseltia Valley. Once he had expressed admiration for a watch I was wearing, which among other features had a luminous dial. This was really something in those days, and very useful for an army officer. Well, I wrote to my wife, who bought one and sent it to me. By the time it arrived, we had gone off in different directions, so I put it in my tank. Now, after the parade, I went to my tank and got it and gave it to him. He was surprised and delighted at the watch, but more, because I had shown my appreciation for our friendship."

4
Sicily

These German tanks stayed on the road, and . . . we would run up to the crest of a hill, fire a shot or two, back off, then go right or left, run up again and fire . . . We never lost a tank and shot them up pretty good.

—Carl Rambo
B Company tank commander

At the Casablanca Conference in January 1943, Allied leaders decided to invade Sicily once the Tunisian campaign was successfully concluded. General Patton was selected to plan the American involvement, but as Winston Churchill has noted, "it was not until April that we could tell which troops were fit to take part."[1]

Still, with Patton in charge, it was a good bet he knew that the 70th would be "fit to take part." Patton insisted that the 1st Infantry Division—The Big Red One—be included for the landing at Gela and for the campaign. "I want those sons of bitches," he said.[2] When Patton's request was granted, the choice of the 70th to provide tank support was logical. After all, the 70th and the 1st had trained together and had shared the mission to Martinique.

A Company in June moved from Tunisia to rejoin the battalion at the port of Arzew, near Oran on the Algerian Mediterranean coast. The 70th was together as a unit for the first time since September 1942.

The Invasion of Sicily

With the assault forces landing at Gela was a 70th reconnaissance team consisting of two officers and ten enlisted men. Captain Atlee Wampler, who was in command, relates: "We were supposed to be with the 1st Division, but there was a mix-up due to heavy seas and we landed with the 1st Ranger Battalion. These were the famous

Darby's Rangers, who were instrumental in taking Gela." The mission involved preparing an assembly point for the 70th arriving on several different ships. "In our group of ten enlisted men were experienced sergeants from each company. The assembly point was to be in the 1st Division zone, but it didn't work out that way. A strong German counterattack separated us from the 1st Division for several days. The corridor to them was blocked. We couldn't get through."

One of the sergeants was Cecil Nash. "We landed at Gela in an LCI [landing craft infantry] and waded ashore through waist-high water. We had our musette bags on our backs and our rifles and .45s, and that was all." First they picked out a house on the waterfront as an assembly point for the reconnaissance group. "Here we met and slept for two nights. There was a lot of strafing for several days. While the enemy didn't have much airpower, they did have bases close by and our planes had to come from North Africa. We had a good vantage point to see the activity that was taking place in the air. A lot of our C-47s were being shot down, but what we didn't know was that our own trigger-happy people were doing the firing."[3] Nash's group found an Italian 20mm gun and about four or five rounds of ammunition. With this gun and their rifles, four men maintained an outpost guard on a culvert under a highway leading into Gela in case the enemy used this route for a counterattack.

The next day, Nash went into the center of Gela to try to find ammunition. "We couldn't do much with four or five rounds, or really with that one 20mm gun, for that matter. Anyway, I was trying to find ammo. German planes strafed the town, but it was easy to find safety behind buildings. While I was directly across from a headquarters building, two half-tracks roared up bristling with .50-caliber machine guns. They were protection for General Patton, who I saw leave his jeep and walk into the building. What we wouldn't have given for a couple of those .50 calibers!"

They moved from the waterfront house and set up a guard post at a road intersection in the eastern outskirts. "Somewhere in here we could see DUKWs with [amphibious load carriers, pronounced 'ducks'] landing supplies. This was the first time I had seen them. We were now in a wooded area where we found a mini one-man tank. I would guess it weighed about a ton and had one gun about the size of a .50 caliber. I think it was an Italian product. Two of us were there at the time and took turns driving it around for an hour or two until the engine stopped, probably because it was out of fuel."

One Snafu After Another

As the accounts of Wampler and Nash indicate, the landings around Gela were anything but smooth. A high sea made landings difficult, and high winds played havoc with airborne landings. Also apparent was that much still remained to be learned about invasions, as one snafu followed another. (snafu: situation normal, all fouled up. The expression originated during World War II, at which time a more colorful *F* word was used.) The main body of the 70th, as an example, arrived at Gela in bits and pieces for three days—July 13, 14, and 15. When the loading plan for the invasion of Sicily was prepared by the 1st Infantry Division, Michael Varhol of the battalion staff asserts: *"Our commander had no imput concerning any priorities he may have wanted.* On D+3 I waded ashore at Gela with Colonel Welborn and thirty-three others. Right behind us followed about fifty nurses from an evacuation hospital. What a mess!" The 70th commander had neither a jeep nor a radio. "So we knew nothing as we walked to the front lines. Colonel Welborn kept asking, 'Where in hell are our tanks?' In this fiasco, our combat elements did not land until D+4." By this time German counterattacks had been beaten back, and the crucial phase of the landings at Gela was over.

Lieutenant Colonel Welborn in the *Official 70th Tank Battalion Unit Journal* states that most companies reached the assembly point on July 14, but by 1600 "no vehicles had as yet arrived, making supply extremely difficult. Most of the combat echelon was in the bivouac by dark."

Snafus were everywhere. C Company clerk Joseph Nesbit landed on July 15, "We had a nice surprise on landing. Before we could get the trucks off, we had to unload all the gasoline and ammunition they had placed up front by the big doors." No planning down to the last detail. Francis Snyder, with the maintenance platoon of Service Company, also landed shortly after midnight on the fifteenth. He remembers: "We clambered down a net into a lighter that took us to shore. It was pitch black, but luckily all we had to carry was our musette bags and rifles." Barracks bags arrived later.

According to Welborn's official journal, by dusk of the fifteenth the strength of the battalion "in combat vehicles consisted of forty-five tanks, three assault guns, and three mortars on half-tracks . . . two kitchen trucks and other vehicles joined the battalion after dark, alleviating the supply problem . . . At 0800 orders were received for a contemplated attack in conjunction with the 26th Infantry [Regiment] on Barrafranca. The mission of the battalion was to seize and secure the high ground northwest of this town. The battalion was alerted for a movement north at 2300." [4] Despite all the mix-ups, confusion, and heavy German resistance, when the 70th was up to strength, it was ready to do battle within hours.

With Gela firmly in American hands, Axis forces moved back to form defensive positions in nearby mountainous terrain. Hence the need to get units such as the 70th quickly in place in support of the 26th Regiment, 1st Infantry Division.

The Two-Day Battle of Barrafranca

The need was urgent. About twenty miles north in the vicinity of Barrafranca a powerful German force, led by tanks, was preparing a counterattack. If they were not stopped, Gela and the entire beachhead could be threatened. John Ahearn commanded the assault gun platoon in Sicily. "I was called to a meeting at 0600 with all leaders of combat elements and the battalion staff. It was already daylight, so Lieutenant Jones and I thought it incongruous that we were all huddled in a big tent going over instructions using flashlights. There was plenty of light to see but I guess the staff had learned this somewhere or another. Of course this was the first battle experience for many of us, and the first the battalion was in as a complete unit."

The intelligence was that the Germans were coming down to drive the whole American army out to sea. "It was going to be a big tank attack. Sure enough, within an hour or so, we spotted a column of medium tanks (Mark IVs) coming down that road. This was accompanied by an extraordinary event." Prior to the German tanks arriving, the men of the 70th were subjected to their first barrage by *nebel-werfers*. "They were multiple rocket launchers, and, when they fired them, it sounded like railroad boxcars coming through the sky. Mind you, this was for many our first experience in combat, and, fortunately for us, they didn't have the range. Perhaps because they were so goddamned heavy, they were falling in front of us by maybe a couple of hundred yards." Infantrymen were hit, as they had moved out first. "I administered first aid to one infantryman. When they exploded, they broke into little pieces and were not an effective weapon. Psychologically, though, they scared the shit out of us."

Right after the *nebelwerfer* fire stopped, the column of German tanks came down. "Luckily for us, Welborn told us to deploy on this hill, including the assault guns, and the German tanks kept coming right down the road. Everybody was firing, the tanks with their 37mm and us with our 75mm assault gun. It was a very successful operation and we were excited about it."

As a sergeant in command of a tank in the 1st Platoon of B Company, Carl Rambo was in the midst of the action. "These German tanks stayed on a road and we ran up in the hills. B Company was on the left, and A Company on the right. We would run up to the crest of the hill, fire a shot or two, back off, then go to the right or left, run up again, and fire another shot. We never lost a tank and shot them up pretty good. Nobody even got hit, but some inexperienced drivers threw tracks off of their tanks in the hills." Rambo had learned his lesson way back at Fort Bragg. "You don't run a tank fast down a hill and make a turn unless you keep the power on. If you don't keep the power on the tracks, you throw them off."

Five Mark IVs were destroyed by the 70th; another four were stopped and then knocked out by accompanying artillery. Seven more retreated. Since the Mark IV was far more heavily armored and carried a 75mm as compared to a 37mm on our light tanks, victory required quick thinking and superb execution.

The tactic used was one that A Company developed in Tunisia. Atlee Wampler explains: "We found out the hard way that we could fire on larger German tanks if we attained a higher elevation. They could elevate their big guns only so much, and we had to estimate how much higher we had to be. Then we could shoot and run, shoot and run, before they could get their tanks sloped upward to raise their gun elevation. But we had better be right." It took perfect execution and exacting gunnery. "If we could hit the tracks of German tanks we could stop them, and if we could hit them in the rear where the engine was vulnerable, we could disable them or knock them out. But we had to be correct in estimating our necessary height advantage and fast and accurate in our firing."

Once the remaining Mark IVs retreated, the 70th aggressively pressed its advantage. Carl Rambo remembers waiting for the order to begin the attack. "We were looking at a bridge from up above where we had been shooting at the tanks. 'It's mined,' we were told, 'so don't cross it.'" Soon, they were ordered to attack Barrafranca. "We were going right down that road, with B Company in the lead, and the 1st Platoon first, with me on the point. I spoke up and said that we had been told not to cross that bridge because it was mined." Rambo was told the bridge was clear now. "I didn't believe them. Hell, no one was closer to the bridge than I, and nothing happened to clear it. Well, I told Glenn Griffin, my driver, to gun it. That's all we could do, go right over it, and if it blew, it might blow behind us. We got a good start and were probably making forty miles an hour over that sucker. Either it wasn't mined or the Germans didn't have time to blow it because nothing happened."

Rambo's orders were to turn left after the bridge, cross a field, and go up a hill. "We did, and the rest of B Company was following me. As we were going across that field, I heard an explosion. I looked around, and one of our tanks had hit a mine. Well, when one of our light tanks hit a mine on the left side, the driver was usually wounded or killed. When it hit on the right side, the assistant driver was the one." This mine ripped out the bottom of the tank, and no one was wounded. "In a minute there was another explosion as the tank on my right hit a mine. The rest of the company quit coming, but we went on to the top of the hill. I saw dirt bulging off on our left. It was an AP shell, so we stopped and backed off. I told Glenn, 'When we go up again, don't go to the same spot, go right or left, and when we get to the top of the hill, start zigzagging.'" These were well-grazed, smooth hills, long and rolling. "We went over the top and they took two more shots at us, which hit the ground. The next thing I saw was the German gun, which the gun crew had left. We had run them off!"

A little farther on Rambo spotted a German Tiger tank sitting in some woods. "Well, we sure didn't want to disturb him, so we swung around. Now we were jumping the terraces and got into an olive grove. We were supposed to have support but didn't, so we kept swinging around and got back in line." Our planes had blown Barrafranca to pieces. "We were easing our way through the town. I was toward the end of the column. I looked around and saw a German carrier of some kind. I wheeled my gun around and started shooting over the top of the rest of the column and bam, hit that carrier right in the fuel tank."

Corporal Frank Suleski was with the mortar platoon as he had been in Tunisia. "We were in position on a side hill and fired a large amount of high-explosive mortar shells. The battle was terrific with explosions, noise, fire, and smoke. As we changed our position, we were disabled by a close hit. Our half-track was saved by a tank that hooked on a cable and pulled us away to safety. Our maintenance had the half-track ready for use by morning."

Brigadier General Theodore Roosevelt, Jr.

The next day, July 17, the battle continued a few miles north of Barrafranca, along the road to Pietraperzia. Prior to the attack by the 1st Infantry supported by our tanks, the 70th bivouac areas were hit by air strikes, artillery, and *nebelwerfer* fire. Walter "Bad Eye" Waszyn was in B Company maintenance. Like John Ahearn and everybody else who ever heard these screaming meemies incoming, he can never forget the terror they created. This also was Waszyn's first combat, and he recalls: "The *nebelwerfer* fire absolutely froze us. Six shells coming at you at one time. We really bogged down and were thinking of getting the hell out of there when I looked around and saw General Roosevelt in our area. He must have been hit with a little liquor because he had no helmet on and had a cane that he was swinging. He waved it around and pointed to the Germans and said: 'Follow me, you sons of bitches, we're going after them.' I guess he saved the day, because we routed the Germans after settling down."

General Theodore Roosevelt, Jr., was much admired by the men of the 70th. George Brookstein, the A company liaison corporal, recalls an incident remarkably similar to that told by Waszyn. "I saw with my own eyes that some of our infantry panicked at Barrafranca. Then I saw General Roosevelt with his cane chasing them all back to the line. I got to know the general, his driver, and his liaison officer. I and my driver, Paul Jones, were often at headquarters when he was around our area. We would make some coffee and chat with him. He seemed to take a liking to me. I was five foot two and a half and for a time wore a red beard. Maybe that got his attention. By his actions and everything else, there is no doubt he considered the 70th his boys."

Although the general couldn't be everywhere, he has been placed at battalion headquarters around dawn of July 17. While he was conferring with 70th staff officers regarding the impending attack, German aircraft bombed the area. "The conferees started for a cave in the hillside. Lieutenant Hirsch got there first. He stepped back to allow General Roosevelt to enter, whereupon the general spoke those famous words: 'Go ahead, Lieutenant, there is no rank in a situation like this!'"[5]

The Enemy Retreats After Barrafranca

In the attack on July 17, the mountainous terrain forced our light tanks and the mediums attached to the 70th from the 753d Tank Battalion to stay on the road. This meant they could be easily observed by the enemy. The artillery barrage thrown at them was furious. Yet the attack was pressed. Buttoned up—hatches closed—the tankers ran the gauntlet of artillery shells until they were on top of the enemy, at which point German artillery ceased, since it would then fall on their own troops. Our tanks poured machine-gun fire on every possible enemy position, and immediately 1st Division infantry moved in. The enemy by now was in full retreat, but the 1st Platoon of C Company could continue to maintain contact. Northeast of Barrafranca they encountered an extensive mine field, which had to be bypassed. In doing so, "the tanks were exposed to heavy antitank fire. The first round hit the lead tank manned by Sergeant Kovacik, Corporals Silva and Roberts, and Private De Vita. With the rear track blown off, Corporal Roberts, the driver, attempted to maneuver the tank into a roadside ditch. The vehicle was hit by two more rounds. Out of control, it turned over in the ditch. As the crew abandoned the tank, it came under mortar and machine-gun fire. Silva pulled Kovacik out of the tank and together they extricated Roberts, who was entangled in the steering lever and driver's hatch. The three men crawled behind the tank for whatever protection could be found . . . In an attempt to climb out of the ditch to escape over a nearby hill, De Vita was severely wounded by machine-gun fire. Kovacik dragged the wounded man to safety. While administering first aid to De Vita, Kovacik was wounded. Silva then set out to find medical aid . . . Kovacik, despite his wounds, managed to drag De Vita farther away and out of range of enemy fire."[6]

Jack Lovell recalls a side note to this action. "Roberts, who was the driver, had some false teeth, I think it was a bridge, and they hurt him so he had tied them to a bar just in front of him. Well, when the tank was hit, he left without these teeth and was captured. I remember the Germans later sent a message to get the teeth to him, as he would need them in the POW camp." The teeth were retrieved and sent on to the Germans.

By noon of July 17, the 70th was at the Salso River. In the official battalion journal, an entry crisply noted: "Observation had disclosed that the enemy had hastily evacuated his positions in this vicinity." The field and the day had been won.

The Battle of Barrafranca in the History of the 70th

The battle of Barrafranca was a defining moment for the 70th. The battalion emerged with increased confidence in its ability. For the first time, it had fought as a unit, using tactics devised by its own men, and executed them with precision. Everything came together for the 70th in those two days. The *concept* of the 70th as a battalion had been firmly established in combat. Every member was proud of what he had done, a pride that grew stronger with each success.

On August 7, 1943, the following article appeared in *Stars & Stripes,* the official U.S. Army newspaper. Because the Sicilian campaign had not yet concluded, the 70th was not named as the unit.

LIGHT TANK OUTFITS LAY 'EM IN POCKETS,
by SSgt. Ralph Martin

WITH AMERICAN FORCES IN SICILY—In terrain best fitted for feet and mules a light tank outfit has been busy punching short, sharp jabs at the enemy lines, smashing through annoying machine gun nests and softening up tight pockets of

Jerry infantry. Their slogan is "We open closed pockets." They opened up a lot of them a few days ago in the Nicosia sector.

There were several pockets, southwest of town, that had held out two days. After some light tanks went in on a twenty-minute job of strafing the ditches, knocking out a lot of guns, the Germans were convinced their show was over. But these light tank boys aren't restricted to cleanup jobs. Quite often, they're the determining factor in an important battle like the one at Barrafranca.

The infantry was pushing forward fast, meeting little opposition, when suddenly sixteen Mark IVs rushed out of the flanking hill in a surprise attack to overrun our infantry. Immediately the light tanks raced up to within 1,000 yards of the Jerry Mark IVs and let loose at point-blank range. When the smoke cleared away, the Mark IV were seen heading fast in a different direction, with five of their number resting quite still, all burnt out and twisted, going nowhere.

This tactic isn't in the books. You don't throw a light tank armed only with a 37mm cannon and a few machine guns up against a heavily armed Mark IV. Especially not at 1,000-yard range. It takes guts plenty. But these tankmen know what the odds are. On occasion they have even stood up against the giant Mark Vs and they have gone in and knocked out German 88 guns too.

T-5 John Francis, Bristol, Rhode Island, wiped out two gun positions with the 37mm. To do that, you have to be young and crazy and come in damn close. For most of the outfit, sweeping up through Sicily, this has been their first fighting. But for one company, commanded by J. Stewart Williams, Long Island, New York, this is just an extension of the same stuff they did when they were attached to the French XIX Corps all through the Tunisian campaign. They fought twenty-eight separate engagements then in all kinds of terrain, against all kinds of odds. But they remember best such towns as Zaghouan, when seventeen tanks went in, without any infantry support, and came out with 7,000 prisoners.

Staff Sergeant Coy Parker, Beckley, West Virginia, remembers the night the tanks were advancing along a heavily shelled road when some wire crossed their radio wave and they heard somebody singing "Look Down, Look Down, That Lonesome Road." "For a few minutes nobody said anything," related Parker. "Everybody thought the other guy would think he had gone section 8. Then we all looked at each other and busted out laughing, with shells dropping all around us."

Parker is the guy who stopped his tank in a little town called Bompietro to examine a German half-track lying on the side of the road. As he got close to it, he noticed thirty German soldiers lying in a ditch, very comfortable. With his tommy gun he motioned for them to get up and they did. But when he looked aside the Heinies, unsportsmanlike, turned and tried to run for it. Parker used his tommy gun. Next of kin have been notified.[7]

Crossing the Salso River

Just as A Company had fought the Tunisian campaign apart from the battalion, now, late in the day of July 17, C Company was detached. For the remainder of the Sicilian campaign, it provided support for the 45th Infantry Division, which with the 1st formed the basis of II Corps, commanded by Gen. Omar Bradley.

The B Company journal was kept by the company clerk and was based in large part on the company commander's after-action reports. The entry for July 18 notes that a bridge over the Salso River "had been blown out and was covered by enemy fire. Five tanks overcame this obstacle by fording the river. They then attacked and drove back several companies of German infantry. This permitted the engineers to repair the bridge and move more troops forward."

In the action the company had one officer and nine enlisted men wounded. One tank was destroyed and two more were disabled but retrieved. A Company also crossed the Salso and fought in an action in which one man was wounded, one tank was destroyed, three more were disabled, and one half-track was disabled. It had been a costly day for the 70th, but again highly successful. B Company alone took 140 prisoners.

Driving North Through Mountains

After the Salso, the 70th (from now on less C Company) remained in support of the 1st Infantry Division and continued to drive north through the rugged terrain of central Sicily. Immediately to their left (west) was the 45th Infantry Division and C Company. To their right (east) were the British and Canadians, driving toward and west of Mount Etna. For the drive north, one company of Sherman mediums from the 753d Tank Battalion stayed with the 70th and the 1st Division. Both medium tanks and the battalion assault guns were armed with 75mm cannon.

Lieutenant John Ahearn commanded the assault guns, mounted on half-tracks. "We had four of them and they were used almost as a tank in Sicily. In fact, several times we were on point, if you can imagine that, as relatively unprotected as we were in half-tracks. In Sicily we were always road-bound, moving in a line, be it assault guns or tanks. The Germans, of course, had to do the same thing, but they were very effective in retreat. All they had to do was center their 88s on a crossroad and pick us off as we entered it."

Ahearn recalls a town where the Germans, upon leaving, could have moved to the left or to the right. "I ran across a priest who spoke no English and I spoke no Italian. He did speak French, however, and I had supplemented my high school learning of the language while in Tlemcen. The priest gladly told me where the Germans had gone and we pursued them. A day or so later, Welborn dispatched me and Lieutenant Volk to take my assault guns and his mortars to an area and fire on German positions. It was the first time both platoons had been used in unison, the purpose for which they were intended."

A group of five men from the mortar platoon were sent forward to direct the fire. "Volk and I knew they were on their way up a hill, and that the Germans were higher, so we deployed our guns at the base of the hill and began to fire over the heads of our guys on to the German positions. Subsequently, I had fears about this, wondering if our guys were farther up than we thought, and that perhaps we might have fired on them."

This fear of putting our own men in harm's way by "friendly fire" was constant during the war. In this case, however, it had not happened. Corporal Frank Suleski, one of the five men from the mortar platoon, has provided an account. "Staff Sergeant Wansink, Sergeant Arthur, Corporal Bauer, Corporal Dugan, and I went up to observe and ran into heavy fire. Sergeant Wansink was killed immediately. Corporal Dugan was wounded in the thigh. We were pinned down for about ten minutes. By then the Germans came right up to us and took us prisoner. I was wounded but able to carry Corporal Dugan about one hundred yards to some German medics, and they went to work on him immediately. Then they moved us back away from our own line. By now I had an end of the world feeling." Daniel Dugan died from his wounds while in German hands. Russell, Bauer, and Suleski became prisoners of war.[8]

C Company Meets Little Opposition

C Company was attached to the 45th Division for the period July 17–31. Most actions ended on July 25, however, and in those eight days of combat, very little opposition was encountered. Cecil Nash, a tank driver at the time, recounts that the 45th "would send out night patrols and in the morning we would move up. We were mostly up against Italians, and they were tired of war."

Daily entries in the C Company official record of events confirm Nash's judgment. On July 18, the tanks moved with infantry starting at 0100, and the town of Caltanissetta fell by 0800. Because tanks rarely moved at night, little or no opposition was expected, and none occurred. The next day C Company was the advance party. "The enemy has fled leaving many destroyed vehicles of obsolete type." On July 21, "Six enemy light tanks (Renaults) were encountered and destroyed." Renaults were also obsolete, used by Italians but not by Germans. On July 22 the company was again on point. "Enemy flees after destroying many vehicles, much food, and many thousands of gallons of fuel." Castelbuono was captured at 0400, again in darkness, and a prisoner of war camp was established, which already held over 600 prisoners.

Italians and Germans

Mussolini was removed from power by the Grand Council in the early morning hours of July 25, but it was apparent earlier that this was Germany's war, even though it was fought on Italian home territory. The 70th and the 1st Division were up against retreating German forces but, like C Company, saw themselves welcomed by Italians as liberators and not conquerors. Ahearn remembers an action well because it was in a sulphurous area. "The sulphur permeated the air. We went up a valley to a hill to see what was going on. It turned out to be kind of a dead-end, and I got out of my vehicle with only my .45 caliber. I walked to the top where there was a small building." As Ahearn proceeded toward it, a uniformed man popped out. "He could easily have killed me as I was totally surprised. He turned out to be an Italian soldier deserting his unit who ran to me and threw his arms around me in absolute joy. There was no doubt but that the Germans were the only ones fighting this war in Sicily."

Carl Rambo concurs. "In Sicily every day, the Germans would back off and leave some Italians out front. We didn't have a bit of trouble with them. I saw one of our tanks with one track in a ditch going around a bank and ran a four- or five-man Italian gun crew off without firing a shot. Every day, we would meet Italians, then go another mile or two and there were the Germans. They stopped us nearly every day, and the next day it was more of the same."

It is little wonder that, given obsolete equipment and put out in front to act as human shields and to draw fire, Italians surrendered at the earliest opportunity. Germans—even the Wehrmacht—had in this tactic shown themselves unworthy of respect, either by their foes or by their allies.

Rugged Fights at Alimena and Bompietro

On July 21 our intelligence learned of substantial enemy forces in the vicinity of Alimena and Bompietro. To counter it, the 1st Division formed a powerful task force around the 70th to be commanded by Lieutenant Colonel Welborn. In addition to the company of medium tanks from the 753d Tank Battalion, this task force had in it the 1st Engineer Battalion, the 26th Infantry Cannon Company, A Company of the 26th Infantry in trucks supplied by the 70th, the 1st Reconnaissance Troop, and observers from the 33d Field Artillery Battalion. With the 70th light tanks and assault guns on the point, this force rolled up the enemy and easily captured Alimena, taking many Italian prisoners and much materiel.

Twice in two days the enemy destroyed bridges over a ravine and a river. Even so, the advance continued. Approaching Bompietro, opposition stiffened. Carl Rambo recalls: "They were dropping those screaming meemies in on us. One came close enough to my tank to blow off the periscope. My driver couldn't see and ran off the road. The tank got hung up, one track straddled on a pipeline. Gas was pouring out so we had to bail out. As we did, I saw a stream of flaming gas. As soon as it hit the gasoline tank, the tank blew up. We were all out and got away, but the screaming meemies kept coming in."

The Germans made a strong counterattack on the morning of July 22 which caused some anxious moments until beaten off. During the heat of the attack, an A Company tank commanded by Lieutenant Lyons was hit by an antitank gun. "All of his crew were killed, but the explosion threw Lieutenant Lyons out of the turret to the ground, where he lay while the tank burned itself out. In the meantime a whole battalion of German infantry walked past the spot, thinking the lieutenant was dead. Early the next morning he regained consciousness and wandered along in a dazed condition until he reached the outposts of the 1st Infantry Division."[9]

John Ahearn recalls that his assault guns were with the tanks. "The counterattack drove us into some woods. There were a lot of infantry in there, and they hated to see us come in because we drew fire immediately. We had a vantage point very high looking down on a road. I was on this hill looking out at what faced us. Eighty-eights were firing at us, and I could actually see their puffs of smoke."

While Ahearn was surveying the field, a young captain came up and tapped him on the shoulder, saying the general would like to borrow his field glasses. "It turned out to be Gen. Omar Bradley. He took my glasses and I pointed out to him what was going on. Then the general said, and I can never forget it, perhaps in comparison to what Patton might have said, 'Well don't worry about it, son, we are going to bring up artillery and air. We won't send you off until things have been taken care of.' I have always had great admiration for Bradley, who deserves to be called the 'soldiers' soldier.'"

An air strike was called in, but our forces were too close to the enemy. In the resulting miscalculation, as Ahearn recalls, the planes "bombed and strafed the hell out of us. We were flying into ditches and all was confusion."

The Death of a Medical Officer

With the confusion, the advance on Bompietro was postponed until 1800. Just prior to the renewed attack, Ahearn deployed his assault guns in such a position that they could fire out to the flanks. "We had a pretty good idea of the enemy position, so we began to pump shells at them. While we didn't know precisely where they were, for psychological reasons if for no other, it was thought a good idea to throw in a lot of stuff. What happened was that the Germans were much closer than we believed. As a matter of fact, while I was standing there directing fire, the Germans got close enough to lob a grenade at us. I was not hit, but Sergeant Revell, who was about six feet from me, was seriously wounded in the back." Ahearn radioed for medical aid and administered a morphine Syrette and applied bandages. (Usually a frontline soldier had a ready morphine Syrette taped to his steel helmet.) "Though there were 1st Division aid people much closer to us, I was told one of our battalion medical officers was on the way and so I placed a guide at a road junction to direct him to the spot."

Then an unfortunate coincidence occurred. The guide was picked up by a medical half-track, which shortly came to the junction. Meanwhile, George Brookstein, the A Company liaison corporal, was at the battalion command post (CP). "A call came for medical help, and, my jeep being available, I was ordered to take Captain Flessa to a man who had been injured. While I always rode in the front with my driver, Captain Flessa insisted on this seat. We were supposed to meet a guide at a crossroad to be led to the casualty, but, when we got there, he wasn't around." Brookstein was an experienced liaison man, who knew how to read a map and had good instincts where to go. "When we didn't see the guide, I said, 'Jesus, somebody should have been here. We must be wrong and had better turn around.' At that instant we were fired upon by mortars and rifles. Captain Flessa was killed outright, shot through the head. I was hit in the hand as I zigzagged across the road to a ditch. I crawled several hundred yards until an ambulance came by and picked me up." Brookstein stayed at the aid station several days. "When I got back to the company, I found that Jones, my driver, was alright, but being with Captain Flessa when he was killed was something I'll never forget." (Sergeant Revell, the original casualty, survived but it is not known if he returned to the war.)

Bompietro Is Taken

The attack on Bompietro was preceded by an extremely heavy barrage by all divisional artillery plus 155mm cannon fire from II Corps. For thirty minutes shells rained in on high ground in and around Bompietro. A Company tanks then moved toward the town, firing on anything or anyone that moved. In the town, they met stiff resistance. Several tanks were knocked out, and the 26th Infantry Regiment suffered heavy casualties.

Once the town was secured, A Company moved to the northern approaches and established a defensive position. B Company provided supporting fire from positions southwest of the town, protecting the left flank, where enemy tanks had been reported. A Company of the 753d Tank Battalion, on the south, protected the right flank. By the end of the day, Bompietro was ours, but the cost was high. Six 70th men had been killed, and five wounded. Five 70th tanks had been disabled, along with another four Shermans of the 753d. It was a difficult fight against a strong enemy force. [10]

The Last Battle for the 70th

The route of advance swung eastward at Petralia. On July 23, Colonel Welborn was ordered by the 1st Division to send a force to secure two bridges over the Acqua Amara River and hold until our infantry could occupy the approaches. This was accomplished without opposition. Continuing to the east, the next objective was Nicosia.

Desperate to give their forces time to get to the coast, the enemy fought a retrograde action on high ground two miles southeast of Petralia. Late on the day of July 27, Colonel Welborn received an order to subdue them. The Germans had held on all day and were strong in mortars, antitank guns, and machine guns. Welborn designated B Company to take the lead, to be followed by the Sherman medium tanks and the assault gun and mortar platoons. With our infantry already there, such a powerful force was ready for a stiff fight. B Company left the bivouac at 2105, with orders to continue the attack until dark. [11]

Unfortunately, fighting continued after sundown with disastrous results for Carl Rambo and his crew. "We were told to go in, shoot everything, and come back out. It was quite dark, and we had no lights on. So we went in, everything ablaze. We were shooting; the

Germans were shooting; we could see their guns flashing. I was turned off the left of the road and shooting. The tank ahead of us stopped, so we stopped and we never should have."

Rambo remembers the action took place in big hills. "I could have gone around the tank that stopped ahead of me, but I saw the tank behind me hit and on fire, and around that time here came the other tanks back. We did not have two-way radios, only the platoon leader had that, so all we could do was receive."

The instant Rambo's tank stopped it was hit. "The tank shook, and I was told later that the projectile went through brass on the am- munition rack. The turret hatch was open, and I was blown through it. When I came to, my head was hanging down almost to the ground. I kicked loose and started looking for my crew. I ran to the front of the tank and the assistant driver was out. So was the gunner but he had fire all over him."

All of this was in a matter of seconds. Rambo looked for Glenn Griffin, the driver. "All I could see were his legs. He had turned around and tried to go out the top, then went right into the face of that fire and got it right there." Rambo grabbed the gunner, whose clothes were all aflame and pulled him into a ditch. "I heard the Ger- mans up overhead and took out my .45. My hand was burned raw. Well, our tanks came by, but I didn't dare go in front of one to stop them for fear they would shoot, so I ran in back of one and hollered until they stopped. We got my gunner on the back of this tank and got him out. Well, I ended up in a field hospital and they told me Lauderdale, my gunner, had died."

The next day Rambo was on a hospital ship headed for Oran. "My hand, arm, and face were burned. My ears were alright because of the rubber doughnuts on my helmet. When I stripped the burning clothes off the gunner, some fire went up my trouser legs. I had leg- gings on, so my legs weren't burned, but my knees were as was my back. I was alright but tender for a long time. I got back to Sicily in time to eat chow a time or two before we boarded a ship for England."

According to the B Company journal, in this battle two men were killed and five wounded, and three company tanks were totally de- stroyed by antitank guns. As Rambo states, "We didn't fight often af- ter dark, but I guess it was important to clean out the German strong point right away to keep them moving back." The brief but furious encounter took place less than fifteen miles from the northern coastal road.

C Company returned to the battalion on July 31. The bivouac area now was near Mistretta, conveniently close to a major road that joined the coastal road only five miles away.

This move was away from the 1st Division thrust toward Troina, which proved to be a bitterly fought battle lasting six days. In rugged mountains, German defenders had every advantage. East of Nicosia, as noted in the official journal, the 70th was ordered to reconnoiter for possible tank routes on the right of the division zone of action. None were found. For the 70th, combat in Sicily was over.

The Campaign in Summary

It took just thirteen days of actual combat for the 70th with the 1st and 45th to advance across central Sicily from Gela on the southern coast to the northern coastal area. The terrain was too mountainous for large-scale tank operations by either side. That, no doubt, was the reason the 70th with light tanks was chosen to support infantry that carried the major load. The medium tanks of the 753d were used effectively when circumstances allowed.

Being road-bound most of the time enabled the retreating enemy to zero in on roads and intersections, which he did masterfully. Enemy artillery, mortars, antitank guns, mines, and small-arms fire accounted for nearly all of the 70th losses in both men and materiel. While enemy air forces did infrequently bomb and strafe, the skies generally belonged to the Allies, a situation that was indispensable for victory.

The question of authority regarding the use of tanks did not arise in Sicily. This was because the 70th and the 1st Infantry Division knew one another from training and the Martinique mission. Of vital significance was the close personal relationship between Lieutenant Colonel Welborn and General Roosevelt. After not being consulted on the landing at Gela, Welborn was definitely in command in the field, including employment of the medium tanks of the 753d.

In the campaign eleven men were killed, at least forty wounded and four missing, of which three were prisoners of war. With a total of fifty-five casualties, the rate was roughly 10 percent of total battalion strength. Tank crews from the three line companies as always sustained by far the highest casualties, a rate of about 27 percent. Fifteen tanks were destroyed, 34 percent of the fifty-one from the three line companies. A number more were hit but were repaired.

Near but Far From War

As the 70th moved into their bivouac on a hilltop near Mistretta on August 1, they were strafed by enemy planes. The next day the planes were back, this time beaten off by machine-gun fire from tanks and half-tracks. The area had only recently been cleared of Germans. Or so it was thought. Alvin Woods discovered otherwise. Woods and his buddy Joe Trujillo, both B Company tankers,

wandered off a ways from the bivouac area. Joe said, "Let's go over to that house and see if we can get some bread." It would taste good after being on canned rations. He sat down by a little stream where some people were washing and tinkering around. I went over to the house, maybe a few hundred yards away. I didn't speak Italian, but I knew enough to ask for some bread. An elderly man and his wife let me inside, and I was making all kinds of motions indicating we wanted some bread to eat. I turned around as I heard a noise behind me, coming from another room. Lo and behold, there stood a German soldier, fully armed, fully uniformed with his helmet on. He was just there, and I thought, oh boy, my time has come! I figured I had better bluff it out, so I told him to come with me and gave a wave of the hand, which wasn't brave at all. Well it turned out he wanted to surrender, so I took his rifle. My God, he could have killed me a dozen times. We walked back toward the company area. When Joe saw us, he jumped about three feet in the air! First Sergeant Hall took over in the company area, and Sergeant Sharpless gave him something to eat. We had a lot of laughs about that. It was comical in a way. Nothing was dramatic about it, and certainly it was not heroic. Here was a German surrounded by the entire American army, and nobody had bothered to check that house.

I took his wallet from him. In it he had a picture of himself and two of his buddies, which I still have. It turned out that they had been in the Afrika Korps and had come over into Sicily before the big surrender in Tunisia.

Expecting More Combat

There was every expectation that the battalion would see more combat in Sicily. In fact, when Patton's drive along the northern coastal road was stalled at Santo Stefano di Camastra, only a few miles from Mistretta, the 45th Division was involved in some fierce fighting. For whatever reason, however, C Company was not reattached to the division it had recently supported.

The 70th as usual kept in fighting trim. Training of all sorts continued day after day. The 37mm tank guns were fired on a range, as were the 75mm assault guns. Small-arms firing was practiced by just about everyone, and equipment was made ready, as was the physical condition of the entire battalion.

According to the B Company journal, eighteen replacements arrived at the company and were trained to operate tanks on mountain roads. One new M5A1 tank arrived on August 17, and three more on August 20. The other companies also received replacements of men and equipment. Since the massive enemy withdrawal to the mainland concluded on the night of August 16 and 17, and on August 17 Messina was formally surrendered, the arrival of these new tanks seemed to indicate that the 70th was slated for action in Italy.

For the moment, however, everyone relaxed. Volleyball games were played, sometimes pitting company against company. A movie, *The Philadelphia Story*, starring Cary Grant, Katherine Hepburn, and James Stewart, was set up, canceled due to fog, and seen the next evening. On another evening, as recorded in the B Company journal, "The men are congregated around #16 tank listening to the news and the German propaganda program whose cast includes 'Sally,' who gives us a sexy lecture every once in a while." She honored the 70th by calling it a division rather than a battalion.

Malaria

At this time there was another round of malaria as bad as or worse than the men suffered in Africa. A number of men were hospitalized, including Francis Snyder, who had the complication of a bad case of the GIs" (diarrhea). "What I had recurred from time to time. When I got home, after the war, it was determined that I had amoebic dysentery in Sicily. I was finally cured over two years later in a VA hospital."

John Ahearn was hauled away in an ambulance on August 9. "I don't know if I neglected to take the Atabrine tablets we had been given starting in North Africa, but I came down with malaria. I was first sent to a field hospital, where a nurse and a doctor told me that General Patton had been there the day before and had slapped the hell out of some kid. They were still upset about it, and the whole place was buzzing about how outrageous Patton's behavior had been."

A Seaside Bivouac

On August 26, the 70th moved to a new bivouac area in an olive grove on a hillside overlooking the Mediterranean, four miles east of Termini Imerese. This rather delightful setting was about thirty miles along the coast from Palermo. Joseph Nesbit remembers, "Passes were issued to Palermo. We could swim in the sea, play baseball and touch football." Training schedules were maintained as usual. Everyone and everything was ready for battle.

Germans now openly occupied Italy and were fighting doggedly to make the Allies pay dearly for territory. The American landing at Salerno had gained a foothold, and the 45th Infantry Division was heavily engaged in the capture of Naples, which fell on October 1. Surely, the 1st Division and the 70th would soon be on their way.

They weren't, and, as summer passed into autumn, the 70th became more firmly ensconced at Termini Imerese. As at Tlemcen, this was too good to be true. The food was good in camp but better in Palermo. Wine was readily available, and the Sicilian people were very friendly.

The Big Move

On or about November 1, a group of ten junior officers left the battalion as an advance party. Within minutes everyone knew they had left. The question was where? Rumors, the lifeblood of army "bull sessions," abounded. It had to be Italy. "Why would we get new light tanks if it was not Italy?" When the rest of the battalion moved to a staging area west of Palermo on November 5 without their combat vehicles, the rumor mill went into overdrive.

John Ahearn was in the advance party. They sailed off in a U.S. Navy ship, and while at sea learned that their destination was England. "This ship had the best food I had during all my service. Thanksgiving dinner was wonderful. I kept the menu, and it is probably still somewhere among my souvenirs. We junior officers were for the first time separated from the higher battalion staff, so as a diversion we had a beard-growing contest."

As soon as they arrived in Liverpool, a higher-ranking officer who had preceded them ordered every beard shaved off. "'You had better,' he said, 'or the colonel will demote you.' I had been promoted to first lieutenant and moved from the assault gun platoon to become the executive officer of A Company under Stu Williams. I most certainly shaved off my beard, and so did everyone else."

On November 11, exactly one year from the day the French agreed to a cease-fire in Morocco and Algeria, the battalion sailed from Palermo on board the USS *Monterey*. The first day out, the men were told that it wasn't Italy after all!

5
England

When we were sent to England instead of Italy, most of us figured we would be in on the "Second Front" that everybody was talking about. Then when we trained in DDs, we knew damned well we would be in the first wave. This was confirmed at the invasion maneuvers.

—Ed Gossler
B Company tanker

When the USS *Monterey* sailed through the Straits of Gibraltar, it headed west and continued to do so for another seven days. Despite being told they were going to England, many of the men took the route to mean they were going home. "It was unbelievable the amount of money that was bet," Frank Gross remembers. Those betting on the United States reasoned or rationalized that as experienced tankers they were needed to train fresh troops. Realists, such as Gross, said, "How in the heck can they send a combat trained and bloodied unit home at this stage of the game?" (*Bloodied* is a quaint military term meaning that a unit has been tested on the battlefield.) Finally, Gross recalls, "We joined a very large naval convoy and changed direction to sail to the west coast of Ireland, past Scotland, and down the Irish Sea to Liverpool." The reason for the circuitous route was to stay in protected shipping lanes from the Mediterranean to the States until entering protected shipping lanes from the States to England. Up the coast of Spain and France would have been shorter but well within range of enemy naval and air bases.

They landed at Liverpool on November 28. While still on board ship, a marvelous Thanksgiving dinner was served. At about 0200, November 30, the battalion arrived at Ogbourne St. George, a British territorial army camp near Swindon.

A Cross-Channel Invasion

Americans had steadfastly held that the defeat of Germany by the most direct route was the way to end the war quickly. This meant a cross-channel invasion as early as possible. After the successful completion of the conquest of Sicily, building up for this invasion was given high priority.

The 70th, as an independent tank battalion, was chosen to be with the infantry in the initial assault, just as it had in both Torch and Sicily. According to Lt. Col. Henry Davidson, deputy to Welborn until late August 1944 but later the commander, the battalion was personally selected by General Bradley to travel hundreds of miles to England to be a leading element.[1]

The Former C Company Arrives From Iceland

Waiting for the 70th to arrive at Ogbourne St. George were old buddies from the States. When the battalion arrived, all enjoyed a second Thanksgiving dinner, as I know. I helped prepare it after arriving about a week before from Iceland. It was a reunion for some because C Company had been detached in February 1942 and sent to Iceland, where it was redesignated the 10th Light Tank Company. I joined the 10th in Iceland and moved with them to England.

Everything Had More Meaning in the 70th

Now, in England, I was assigned to B Company, and I learned immediately that the focus of my military career was far larger. I was now in a unit that had a sense of pride in its accomplishments. Everything seemed to have more meaning, more purpose than ever before. If one did his job, no matter what it was, the war would end victoriously. My optimism and willingness to accept my situation were apparent in a letter to my parents in early January 1944. "Just a brief note to let you know I'm well and happy. I have received little mail of late, and most of it quite old. Yet, any mail from you is welcome beyond expression. I know now that I'll never do much in the army by way of advancement as long as I remain in the kitchen, but here is where I belong and where I intend to stay. The news continues to be good.

The Russians are driving toward Berlin. I don't see how Germany

can hold out much longer. I certainly hope to be home this year or
early next year."

Medium and Light Tanks in the "Standard" Tank Battalion

The limited capability of light tanks had long been apparent. The
"standard" tank battalion, which the 70th became upon reaching
England, consisted of three medium tank companies and one light
tank company. Light tanks still had functions, such as reconnaissance, screening, and roadblocks.

Still not recognized were the limitations of the M-4 Sherman
medium tank. It was now more than two years since Germany started
producing heavily armored and armed tanks to fight the Soviet T-34
and KV1, and approaching a year since the American disaster at Sidi-
bou-Zid. Yet the Sherman remained the tank of choice. It was easy
to produce, and production lines were well established. In 1943 an
amazing 21,250 were turned out. This far exceeded the number of
Tigers and Panthers that Germany got to the battlefield.

What couldn't be done in tank against tank would apparently be
done by sheer number. At least so concluded General Bradley. "U.S.
superiority in numbers enabled us to surround the enemy in battle
and knock his tanks out from the flank. But this willingness to expend Shermans offered little comfort to crews who were forced to
expend themselves as well."[2]

Superiority in number was also on other minds. A news corre-
spondent with the 3d Armored Division noted late in the war that
captured German tankers seemed to have a stock joke, concluded
from the many times it was heard. "Von off our tanks iss besser zan
ten off yours, but you alvays haff elefen."[3] Yet, Bradley must have been
referring to operations by armored divisions. Independent tank battalions such as the 70th were still to be used in support of infantry.
Seldom would they be in situations in which large numbers of tanks
were engaged.

At the time in England, of course, the attributes of tanks was not
a fruitful subject of discussion by 70th tankers. Their job, as they saw
it, was to do the best they could with what they had. To them, the
Sherman felt good, with much more firepower and armor than the
light tank. Once they got used to it, confidence increased.

There was so much that had to be learned about the new medium tank that classes and training began immediately. One of the teachers was Owen Gavigan, who had joined the 70th in Sicily as a gunner. His stateside training had been in mediums. Yet Gavigan was only nineteen and until now just another member of a tank crew. Instructing seasoned veterans was a challenging experience. "It was alright, though," he affirms. "We were a small unit and used to helping each other. Much of what I taught had to do with aiming and firing the 75mm, the use of azimuth readings, triangulation, and so on. The tanks we got were brand new. It took a long time to get off the Cosmoline [an oil-based preservative]."

Cecil Nash, who had been a light tank driver in Sicily, found mediums more difficult to drive. "You had to be a little stronger. Sometimes when making a sharp turn you really had to pull back on the stick, and I was not big of stature. I actually had to stand on one foot to get the leverage to pull back hard on one stick while pressing the accelerator all the way down with the other foot." (*Sticks* were levers braking the tracks. Pulling both right and left with equal pressure would brake both tracks and stop the tank. Pulling one lever would slow down or stop the track on that side and the tank would turn in that direction.)

The medium tank was also much harder to shift than the M-5 light tank, which had hydromatic transmissions. "You really had to double-clutch the mediums, like you did the big trucks of that vintage. The light had twin Cadillac engines, the medium a powerful air-cooled airplane type of radial engine. Both the driver and assistant driver seats moved up and down in the medium, so we could drive with the hatch open or closed."

The 70th stayed at Ogbourne St. George for about two and a half months. Although this was a considerable length of time to be in one place, there was much to do to get ready for the big show everyone knew was coming. As was the policy in the 70th, each crew member had to learn the duties and functions of each position in a tank, ready to take over for a man wounded or killed. Much of this had been learned before, but for those new to medium tanks, practice was necessary. It was not long before the men recognized that the Sherman was a far more powerful weapon than was the light tank.

Reorganization

All the officers and men of the former 10th Light Tank Company from Iceland were assigned to various companies. There was a need for them, and more. Medium tanks had crews of five as compared to four in light tanks. A, B, and C Companies used medium tanks, with D the light tank company. Headquarters and Service Companies also expanded in size. A light tank battalion had 550 men; the 70th as a standard tank battalion had 750.

With one additional company, and with 200 additional men, there was a lot of shuffling of personnel. Walter Waszyn was transferred from B Company maintenance to perform the same duties in D Company. Frank Gross was promoted to warrant officer in charge of all clerks.[4]

In another case, John Ahearn, who had been commander of the assault gun platoon in Sicily, then executive officer of A Company, was now promoted to C Company commander. Upon assuming command, Ahearn learned that "noncoms were getting themselves comfortable and out of the elements by gathering in the first sergeant's warm office while their men had to suffer through the morning cold. Something had to be done, so I called in the first sergeant and told him who was in charge and to chase the noncoms back to their units. I did this immediately, and it was an important thing to do." Ahearn's task was to get his company ready for the invasion. He made an important first step.

Diversions in the Camp

Training schedules kept the battalion busy by day at Ogbourne St. George, but in the evening for those who didn't go into nearby Swindon or Marlborough, there were diversions in camp. There was the usual British NAAFI (Navy, Army, Air Force Institute, similar in some respects to U.S. Red Cross canteens). Here one could buy items such as tea, biscuits, sandwiches, and sometimes sausages. Called "bangers," these sausages were a wartime product that seemed to consist of about 80 percent meal and 20 percent meat, unlike the present variety enjoyed during a British breakfast. GIs named them "sawdust in battledress." Occasionally the NAAFI would sponsor a dance, with local girls trucked in and out. Frank Gross frequented the NAAFI more than most. For one thing, as a warrant officer he had more freedom of movement. For another, he liked tea. Most particularly, he liked the company. "Mrs. Smith was in charge of the section that served tea and snacks. She would call me on the telephone and invite me in for tea in the afternoon when the NAAFI was otherwise closed. I would sit with her and the eight regular serving girls enjoying tea and crumpets and much good conversation. We had a joyous time."

Apart from the NAAFI, camp life in England resembled that experienced in the States. Poker and crap games went on with about the same frequency, as did bull sessions. Some men even read books. Movies were provided and well attended. I wrote home on December 23, 1943: "I just got back from seeing the movie *Katina,* starring Sonja Henie and John Payne. It was a pretty good show and all movies are free. I go quite often. It is something to do . . . Life is as usual here—just doing our work and trying to find something to do in the evening, which we usually do."

I wrote of my new assignment as a cook in the officers' mess. "The only difference is that there are less men to feed and naturally the food can be prepared a little different. I am still baking and find the flour, sugar, and lard isn't the same as ours. It is hard to get used to, but I will in time. We will probably be busy for Xmas, since that occasion calls for a little extra."

Swindon in County Wiltshire

Bob Knoebel was a B Company tanker who had joined the 70th in Sicily as a replacement. "I loved England. I had a ball and was out almost every night."

Joseph Nesbit agrees. "I enjoyed the British Isles. It has so much history, and I liked the people very much. When we arrived, we all had a greenish tan from so much Atabrine and sun. We were quite a contrast to the fair-skinned English."

Almost everyone did appreciate Britain, and most of all Swindon. This was the first and really the only place men came to know the people, their customs, and their institutions. During the two and a half months in the vicinity, passes to Swindon were granted liberally. A truck was made available for transportation into the city and back to camp.

"England is a pretty country," I wrote to my family, "with rolling hills and valleys. The towns are picturesque, with their small houses with square roofs and funny chimneys, all in a neat row. In almost every town the church steeple towers above all. The streets are narrow, but the cars are small and have ample room." Swindon was a busy smaller city, the chief market and shopping town for that part of Wiltshire. Red brick and stone buildings seemed to predominate, both in "Old Town" and "New Town." I couldn't see a big difference between the two, thinking them both old and equally charming.

Meeting Brits

By the time the 70th arrived, much of the well-documented earlier animosity between GIs and their hosts had dissipated. Some still remained, particularly among male British "other ranks" who had strong American competition for the attention of British women. The problem with GIs, according to Brits, was that they were "overpaid, overfed, oversexed, and over here." Although this is often quoted, not as well-known is the GIs counter: "The Brits are underpaid, underfed, and under Eisenhower." Complaints by lower-rank British soldiers was understandable. American pay was approximately six times that of British counterparts. American uniforms were smart and better tailored. GIs also had an easygoing attitude and were to many women a fresh and novel change.[5]

Generally, the men of the 70th, as with other GIs, were treated warmly and were generous in giving hard-to-get items to people they met. I once handed an orange to a lad of about six, who had never seen one and didn't know what to do with it. Nor can anyone forget young British children asking, "Got any gum, chum?"

Especially for those men who had been in North Africa and Sicily for a year, being in Britain was the next best thing to home. If for no other reason, they could at least make themselves understood and understand most people they met. "Jeez," one GI was heard to say, "all deez foreigners speak English!" This they did, albeit with dialects, accents, and slang expressions that sometimes caused chuckles or utter consternation. "Why don't you knock me up?" was a favorite when said by a woman. (The British meaning was to call on someone.) Another was "Keep your pecker up," rather than "Keep your chin up"—to stay cheerful. A rubber meant an eraser to the British but not to Americans. A pair of them were called galoshes, not two erasers.

Numbers of 70th men were invited to Sunday dinner in homes around Swindon, often arranged through a church. Joseph Nesbit had such an experience and an even better one. He got a three-day pass and went by train to Scotland. "I visited the Nesbit House, a small castle that was the home of the Nesbit clan. It was being used as a barracks by Poles who had escaped from their occupied country and were training to go with Allied forces to the mainland of Europe. A gardener was in charge of the property. He showed me around and invited me in for tea and crumpets. What a thrill it was for me to be in my ancestral home!"

George Brookstein enjoyed Swindon the most. "The most important thing in my life happened there. I met my wife." Stella Brookstein has written that she was living with her family in London when the war started in 1939. "All schoolchildren were evacuated in order to preserve the younger generation. It was a haphazard affair. We were just tagged and put on trains, to God knows where. We were to write our parents later to tell them where we ended up. Since I was thirteen, I was saddled with my brother, who was five, and my cousin, who was also five. In effect, I became a mother at thirteen!" After six months things were fairly quiet, so Stella and her charges returned to London. "Then nightly bombing started. Every night we took public transport and traveled to subways in the West End of London. Sleeping in subways with thousands of people was a trial indeed. A relative heard of a place in Wiltshire called Swindon, which wasn't being bombed. We left our house in London to the care of an aunt and uncle and moved there for the duration." Her father got a job in Plessey's aircraft factory, and they started a happy life in Swindon. "My sister and I often went to Bradford Hall to dances. No liquor was served, but tea and those small English sandwiches with fish paste in them were available. There was usually a six piece band playing the latest Glenn Miller hits."

Bradford Hall was where George met Stella. "It was rather funny how it happened. The dance hall was on the second floor with a big flight of stairs leading up to it. I and my pal, Jack Richmond, a Jewish boy like me, were just leaving. I was at the foot of the stairs when

Jack at the top yelled down at me in a loud voice, 'Hey George, there's a Yid up here!' I went back up and saw this attractive young woman wearing a necklace with a Star of David on it.[6] She was talking with a female friend." George started a conversation with them, then asked Stella if she would like to dance a few more numbers. "She answered, 'Yes, I'd like to.' I walked her home later, and, while I wasn't invited in, we did arrange to meet at Bradford Hall to dance the next night."

From then on, he saw her almost every night. Even when the battalion moved to Barton Stacey, Brookstein managed to get back to see Stella frequently. Eventually he proposed marriage and Stella agreed. He was confident he would survive. In North Africa, Brookstein relates, "I didn't have that confidence. I had matured a lot in battle and in the companionship I had with my buddies. Well, I nearly didn't make it and was wounded late in the war. Right after V-E Day I got back to England and we were married in Swindon."

When I learned (during an interview in September 1990) that the Brooksteins had met in Bradford Hall, I was overjoyed. This was also my favorite place in "Old Town." I remember well singing and dancing the "hokey-pokey," and just singing the raucous "Roll me over, in the clover." I may even have danced with Stella or one of her friends.

Although George Brookstein had no trouble getting into Swindon nearly every night to see Stella, I had not been in the field, and, although passes were usually available, they were not always, especially not to a "new boy." Besides, getting a pass was cumbersome, because one had to go by truck and return according to someone else's schedule. Preferred was an unguarded route to the road where a local civilian bus ran. Not only was the way easy, but added was the thrill of doing something out of regulation. At any time, an MP might ask to be shown a pass.

After a number of successes, I was honored when a buddy asked to be shown the route. Naturally, this was the time to be caught red-handed. On reporting to the company commander the next morning, I was called a "damned roller skater" and confined to barracks for a week and given extra duty. Fortunately, "damned roller skater" was not official army terminology, so I was not stripped of my "good conduct" ribbon, and much later I rose to the rank of T-5.

Pubs and Beer

British pubs were the source of much pleasure, although Americans didn't understand the hours or much like the beer. The pubs closed at 2230, and at about 2200 a bell was sounded, followed by the announcement, "Time please! Time please!" Final orders then had to be placed at bar counters usually about three deep with anxious patrons. The beer was served too warm for American taste and seemed to plummet through the body like mercury. Consequently, GIs named it after an American fighter airplane, the P-38. "You drink one and pee 38." They were also heard to say, "Pour it back in the horse!"

Frank Gross frequented a charming old pub in Old Town. "On one of the first occasions there, I was sitting at the bar on a stool and had just ordered a pint of bitter when an RAF flight commander asked if he could join me. He did, and we immediately hit it off well, talking about many subjects, including the fact that when the American colonies separated from the mother country, England already had a very old history. One thing led to another, and on return visits I got accepted by the regulars in the pub, thanks to the RAF officer." Gross became part of a group that included husbands and wives, single men—all kinds of people. "One night I was watching a dart game, and a man walked over to me and asked if I wanted to play. He offered his personal darts and a few pointers. Well, the flight officer had told me that darts are a very precious possession, which owners keep for themselves. So I told the man, no, 'I wouldn't want to use your darts.' He said he would be honored. Naturally I accepted, and after that, I played darts all the time, with someone always offering to let me use theirs."

A Feud Between Paratroopers and Tankers

As previously noted, there was some animosity between lower-rank British soldiers and Americans. This was nothing, however, compared to the feud that took place while at Ogbourne St. George between U.S. tankers and U.S. paratroopers. It developed over which branch of the service had the right to blouse trouser ends over boots. Paratroopers claimed to be elite troops with a distinctive uniform, an important part of which were special boots shown to better advantage by a smart blousing of trouser ends over them. Tankers of the 70th with combat experience thought of themselves as even more elite. Indeed, they didn't have special boots, only the regularly issued GI shoes with a strap sewn on the top. But these looked more like real boots with bloused trousers. The undoubtedly correct version was that paratroopers started the feud by beating up on tankers when they had overwhelming numerical superiority. In one case, in blacked-out Swindon a tanker was helped onto a truck that he was told was going to Ogbourne St. George. It wasn't, and he was beaten and tossed out alongside a road in the middle of nowhere. To every action there was an opposite and equal reaction. Then, as quickly as it started, the feud stopped, which was a good thing because a few months later tankers from the 70th would be fighting side by side with these same 82d paratroopers.

London

A number of men went to London from Ogbourne St. George and later from Barton Stacey. Joseph Nesbit went twice. "On my first visit to London, my friend Cecil Nash and I experienced our first night-time bombing raid. We were fascinated with the searchlights, anti-aircraft fire, and barrage balloons. We were standing on the sidewalk watching the show when a bobby told us we had better get under cover because what goes up must come down. We sought an air raid shelter. I think we and the bobby were the only people on the street."

Cecil Nash spent "nine days in London on two forty-eight-hour passes and a five-day furlough. I had been lucky gambling so had all the money I needed. In fact, I had a suite of rooms in a very good hotel. Several guys came in to stay with me for short periods."

Gambling was great for the winners. Paul Gaul, who was in Iceland with me and who became the B Company commander's jeep driver, has told of being on guard one night at Ogbourne St. George. "Johnny Callahan and I were on together, and it happened to be payday night. Johnny wanted to start a blackjack game, which we did. Together we won something in the neighborhood of 800 British pounds, which was a hell of a lot of money. We tried to get a furlough or a pass to London, but couldn't. All we could get was an overnight pass to Swindon. When we got there, we bought some booze, met some women, and took off for London." Johnny and Gaul lived like kings for about a week. "We rented rooms and hired a taxicab for the whole time. We paid him what he made for a week and he was our personal driver, night and day. Did we ever have a great time! But oh, did we pay for it when we got back." They were brazen enough to wake up First Sergeant Hall to complain to him about not having a place to sleep. The sergeant informed them in a not entirely soothing manner, "'I don't give a damn if you sleep in a latrine, but you be in my office at 0600, polished and shined.' Needless to say, we were, and needless to say, we got court-martialled, with thirty days extra duty and two-thirds of my $21 pay for a month. We cleaned shit in the motor pool area, where the tanks came in all muddy. We dug ditches. We paid for that trip, Johnny and I. But it was all worth it, believe me! I never forgot that time in London, and I especially remembered it when I heard Johnny got killed on D day."

Monty Reviews the 70th

General Bernard Montgomery, hero of El Alamein, visited Ogbourne St. George and spoke to the 70th. Frank Gross remembers: "It was customary when a high-ranking British officer spoke to British troops for them to doff their hats. Well, we lined up on the parade ground, and he asked us to remove our helmets. There was a shuffle among our staff officers, almost to a point of embarrassment because we were trained never to take our hats off when under arms. So it was half on, half off and a sticky wicket there for a while. He asked us to break ranks and gather around him, which we did. He was short and had a cocky air about him."

A Sad Departure From Ogbourne St. George

February 16, 1944, was an unhappy day for the men of the 70th. They had liked their situation at Ogbourne St. George and Swindon, and now moved to Camp Barton Stacey, near Andover on the Salisbury Plain. More room was needed for tactical tank maneuvers, and the Salisbury Plain provided it, just as it had for armies dating back to Roman times. Immediately on arrival in the new area, the tank companies left for firing ranges in Wales. Crews in medium tanks had never fired the 75mm before. Much practice was needed.

C Company went off alone to the range at Castlemartin, near Pembroke, Wales. For John Ahearn, C Company commander, this presented an opportunity he did not waste. "We tried out our 75mm guns by firing them into the Irish Sea . . . Here I had a remarkable chance to establish rapport with the men. It was my first time with them separate from the rest of the units. I was being harassed by one of the staff officers with some silly orders, which I recognized as being so, as did the men. I told the men to forget about these orders, which they thought was great. They thought, here is a guy who will be a good company commander."

Cecil Nash, as a C Company tank driver, remembers something else about firing at the range in Wales. "We had several men injured from faulty shells. The shell casings were reused and some had cracks in them. The firing pin would hit and a little powder would leak out. This resulted in a flashback in the turret. Several men were burned. I was told that many of these casings had been used several times, repacked and reassembled." (Casings were retrieved and reused throughout the war. They were brass, and metal was in short supply, particularly copper.)

A and B Companies together went to the firing range near Pembroke for about ten days. I recall one Sunday afternoon when four or five of us began to walk along a surfaced road into Pembroke. It was a lovely day, and the Welsh countryside beautiful. After walking several miles, a road sign indicated that Pembroke was only one and a half miles farther. At least two more miles down the road was another sign pointing to Pembroke, still one and a half miles away. The men were undaunted yet puzzled; this was the only road, so the obvious choice was to continue. Fifteen minutes later, Pembroke came into view, and it was a delightful surprise. Located at the head of Milford Haven, it was picturesque and charming. None of us had seen anything quite like it before. A number of medieval buildings awaited inspection, with Pembroke Castle the highlight. Guidebook in hand, we Americans saw it all—turrets, walls, towers, the dungeon. This was history brought to life. The castle had been associated with King Henry VII. Seeing a real castle was a singular experience. This everyone agreed to as a few beers were quaffed before beginning our trek back to camp.

Francis Snyder was a truck driver with Service Company on detached service with A Company at Pembroke. One morning he was told to pick up the garbage and haul it to the dump. "I said I couldn't because the lieutenant had ordered me to go to Swansea and pick up a load of beer for the local NAAFI. Actually, this was a fib. The lieutenant hadn't told me. I was the one who had told the NAAFI that I could get the beer for them. So I drove to a brewery in Swansea where I was taken into a cave and given a pint of the best beer they had, not the P-38 stuff, but the real thing. They loaded the truck and I brought it back. Nobody was the wiser, and everybody was happy about getting the beer."

Secret Training in Great Yarmouth

Barely had A and B Companies returned to Barton Stacey when they moved on March 4 to Great Yarmouth to undergo highly secret training. The tanks were left at the camp, so the trip was easily made in one day, skirting the western suburbs of London en route. Great Yarmouth was a city of perhaps 50,000 located on the North Sea, about twenty miles from Norwich, an old fishing port that in peacetime was a popular seaside vacation center with many hotels.

I recall men from both companies filing into a hotel and going to assigned floors—those floors that remained, that is, because this ten or twelve story hotel had received a direct hit from a German bomb. The upper four or five floors were demolished and unsafe, with debris everywhere. Few windows remained intact, allowing cold March winds off the North Sea to air-condition the rooms. All furnishings had been removed, and with them nearly all reminders that this had been a hotel. Yet it didn't take long to sweep broken glass from the floor and put bedrolls in place, ready for use, three men to a room. Explorations revealed that along some blasted corridors, the sky was plainly visible through a gaping hole in the roof. Still, this was better than a bivouac entirely out of doors, and strangely offered a feeling of security on the theory that bombs, like lightning, are said to never strike twice in exactly the same place.

The DD Tank

Tankers in the two companies began secret training immediately in what they discovered were amphibious (DD) tanks. Three U.S. tank battalions had been selected for their use during the invasion of France. The 70th was naturally one, and naturally the first to be trained. Although there never had been any doubt that the battalion would be in on the upcoming big show, we now knew that it would be among the first to land. As Alvin Woods, who was in a B Company DD asserts, "They were designed for one mission, for one purpose, and that was to get from the LCT to shore. Once we were on shore, it had served its purpose."

The idea for amphibious tanks was British. In January 1944 Eisenhower and Bradley had seen trials of the DD and "were impressed by its potential as self-propelled instant artillery for the beaches. Three hundred had been ordered, and the first one hundred came to Liverpool ready for trials in the final exercises preceding D day."[7] A rubberized collapsible canvas collar was tightly attached to the body of a medium tank, just above the tracks. Bottles of compressed air were used to inflate vertical rubber columns. When this was done, the canvas, which was secured to the columns, rose upward forming a rectangular screen around the tank to a height slightly above the turret. The tank would become a makeshift boat, replete with that naval-sounding device—a bilge pump. It was driven by two brass propellers protruding out the rear below the waterline. The twin propellers were turned by the running tracks, hence the designation of the tank was DD, for duplex drive. These propellers could be rotated to steer the craft, and the tank had a tiller operated from outside the turret. When launched, the tank was completely below the waterline. The driver, with an extended periscope, could see where he was going, and so could the commander from his turret position.

The element of surprise was obviously most important. DDs could be dropped off LCTs 3,000 yards from shore to go in on their own power. Once on land, the canvas screen was to be dropped and the propellers raised; instantly the boat was a tank again, in position to deploy and start firing.

To keep the secret, the DDs were always kept under black shrouds. Tankers were told not to disclose the existence of DDs to anyone, even to other members of the battalion not directly involved. I remember asking my tanker buddies about the training and being told it was a military secret. No doubt complete silence was impossible, but with lives on the line, those who knew kept it to themselves, as I did when I eventually learned. All in all, secrecy was maintained amazingly well.

Then 1st Lt. Franklin Anderson had been sent ahead to Great Yarmouth from Barton Stacey as the battalion advance man. He saw to arrangements for bivouacs and participated in the preparation of training schedules. Anderson records that when the tankers arrived, the first exercise was to conquer the fear of being submersed in water.

"Hidden in the trees, surrounded by a high fence, and closely guarded was a large water tank, like the one at Groton, Connecticut, which is used for submarine training. A small group at a time, we went there not knowing what to expect. We were issued diving equipment, and shown how to put it on and use it. Next, we entered the tank, which was quite a set-up, all electrical and automatic." One by one, the men descended into the water, holding onto a ladder. "Upon reaching the bottom we walked across it and came up the ladder on the other side. Next, we were taught how to use a skirt to control the rate of ascent. If you pulled up on the skirt it would billow out and slow your ascent. The faster you brought it down, the faster you would go up." This part of the training was a simulated escape from a sunken DD. "In fact, they had a Valentine tank sitting on the bottom with water coming in with the same effect as if it had sunk. Some of our guys were not swimmers and more than a little apprehensive about going underwater and performing these procedures. Yet, the British instructors were very good, telling them you didn't have to be a swimmer, but just to stay calm and you will do all right."

Not one of the men dropped out. "They did just fine, descending, walking across, and controlling the ascent with the skirt. After that training we were brought to a pond on the edge of the North Sea where they had Valentine DD tanks. The Shermans didn't arrive until the time of 'Exercise Tiger.'" The security at this pond was very tight. "Here we learned how the DD worked and the procedure to operate them. In a day or two, we started to practice in them. The Valentines had only one propeller, and the gun was a 3-pounder.

"Much of our training using the DD was at night. During the day we would learn about them, what to do if they sank, and about getting to shore and converting back to a land tank. For nighttime use, on the back of the tank was a device something like a candelabra, with little lights." These were warning lights to avoid collisions. "We were also taught a new radio system which later became standard. (This was the Able, Baker, Charley, and so on) Incidentally, originally there was no 'over and out,' but for some reason people had a hard time just saying 'out' so someone added the 'over,' which worked." Until the arrival of Shermans everyone thought Valentines would be used. "That would have been a mess, having to change back into Shermans after D day . . . We got thirty-two Shermans in time for further training at Slapton Sands. They had twin propellers and the periscope was modified to make it higher."

Life Goes On in Great Yarmouth

A and B Companies were in Great Yarmouth for about ten days. It was the only time during the half-year stay in Britain that they lived in the middle of a city. Here they could see and experience first-hand some aspects of life in wartime England that they could not in a camp. As an old port city, the central section had the expected narrow, twisting streets and lanes. A major, more modern street connected the city center with a very long quay.

Out on a strand was a dance hall, which I visited several times. One night was particularly memorable. There was a sizeable crowd dancing to music in the Glenn Miller style. Late in the evening, perhaps around 2200, a placard was placed on a music stand positioned on the stage, which announced the approach of German planes. The people were amazing. They calmly danced on. The next placard was ominous, something like "Air raid alert!" Even then the dance number was not cut short. As the music stopped the floor was still packed with dancers. The third placard was accompanied by an announcement that an air raid was in progress and directions given to the nearest shelters. No one rushed. Everyone filed out, chatting pleasantly as they went.

I had never been in an air raid before, so rather than go to a shelter, I crossed the street to view the fascinating show taking place overhead. A German bomber was twisting and turning, darting and diving, attempting to escape from a number of searchlight beams. Ack-ack guns boom-boomed away, trying to hit the bomber that eventually escaped. Fairly close by, I could hear the ping of small bits of shrapnel from spent antiaircraft shells. So close, in fact, that a male English voice called out, "I say, Yank, you had better get under cover." This advice was so sound that I joined the voice standing in a deep entrance to a building. Soon the all clear sounded. Several people walked by saying "Not much of a show tonight!" It was to me. Thinking nothing could top it, I quickened my pace toward the bombed-out hotel, hunching my shoulders as cold March winds blew off the North Sea. How I marvelled at the people I had seen who refused to let a minor bombing raid interrupt their evening.

In Limbo at Barton Stacey

A and B Companies rejoined the battalion at Barton Stacey where training continued for another month. Everyone sensed that the invasion was not far off, but few talked about it. This was the lull before the storm. Adding to the feeling of being in limbo was that there was no nearby large town to provide diversions. A lucky few did get passes to London, but for most enlisted men the best offer was truck transportation to a nearby U.S. air base, where an enlisted men's club served real American draft beer. This was a real treat. On one occasion I was part of a group that came prepared. Just prior to closing, at which time the truck would leave, several members of the group stationed themselves outside an open window with five-gallon water cans that had been brought for the purpose. Compatriots inside bought as many beers as they could handle, and as fast as they could, handed them through the window to those outside. All this so that drinking could continue on the ride back to camp and after. It worked, but the beer was so stale the exploit was never repeated.

To the Devonshire Coast

In early April the line companies moved to staging areas at Torcross, near Torquay on the English Channel. En route, B Company paused for the better part of a day near Exeter. It was a Sunday, and a small group of friends and I had a chance to see the great gothic cathedral. The spring day was lovely, just right for a leisurely stroll through the beautifully green Devonshire countryside outside the city. How peaceful it was; a time to forget the war and the impending invasion.

Our group happened upon a charming country inn sitting alone on a tree-lined lane. It was during pub hours, but unfortunately, the publican had sold his allotment of beer. He offered instead what he termed "famous Devonshire apple cider." Famous or not, no one in the group had ever heard of it, but being thirsty we condescended to try what was assumed to be glorified apple juice. It proved to be not only thirst-quenching but rather good. The first round went down quickly, and another was ordered. Be careful, the publican warned, Devonshire cider is mighty potent. Ignoring his admonition, the second glass was quaffed, though admittedly not as easily as the first. By now, everyone in the group was reeling and with great difficulty someone slurred an order for a third. After the fourth, there was no fifth. In fact, someone suggested "let's stay here forever," and we nearly did.

In the staging areas preparations for the invasion began in earnest. At Torcross, A and B Companies received their thirty-two Sherman DD tanks. At nearby Lupton Camp, C Company soon inherited dozer tanks (with bulldozer type blades in front).

Here also was born the battalion emblem, which was stenciled on every vehicle. Joe Peckerwood was a turtle wearing tanker's goggles and helmet. The turtle stood upright on a globe and held a 75mm shell under the left arm. Across the chest was emblazoned *"Soixante Dix,"* which no doubt grew out of the association with the French in North Africa. Joe Peckerwood was an instant success.

Exercise Tiger

The 70th was now ready to participate in Exercise Tiger, designed as the culmination of all previous training. The upcoming invasion was to be simulated as close to the real thing as possible. An extensive area at Slapton Sands had been chosen for its similarity to the landing site at Utah Beach and to the hedgerow country behind it. The practice area had a lagoon just back of the beach, as did the Utah site. The one at Utah Beach "was a wide lagoon created when the Germans flooded the fields and marshlands. Only narrow causeways led from the beaches to the interior. If the Germans controlled . . . these causeways, our troops could easily be trapped and slaughtered."[8] This worried high commanders and was one reason for paratroop landings behind the beach to protect the seaborne landings. Utah Beach had not been in the original plans. It was added because of its close proximity to the base of the Cotentin Peninsula. The drive for Cherbourg could begin immediately; this port was necessary for the buildup of men and materiel.[9]

In the area in Devon where Exercise Tiger was held, residents of many villages had been evacuated, and extremely tight security was maintained. Every vehicle entering or leaving was carefully checked. An example of the tight security was demonstrated by Corporal Arlington, a gunner in a B Company tank. While on guard duty at a checkpoint, he challenged General Montgomery and demanded to see his papers. Arlington had recognized the general to be sure, but he was obeying orders to the letter. Montgomery commended him for his diligence.

A and B Companies moved into houses belonging to evacuees on April 10, and stayed in them until April 28, 1944. Tankers for the first time operated the DDs in the sea rather than in a quiet pond as at Great Yarmouth. Ed Gossler was a gunner in a B Company DD tank and recalls: "We would go out in the English Channel on board navy LCTs that held four tanks. They had to unload us very gently or we might have sunk. That was the reason for us having diving equipment and all that training in Great Yarmouth. In case we did sink, we were taught to wait until the tank filled up with water before escaping. That would give us time to get our air tanks operational, and so on. We made a lot of practice landings at Torcross, day after day."

To "sail" a thirty-two-ton tank and land on a hostile shore was, after all, a hazardous endeavor, to say the least. Every detail of the operation had to be learned, and in precious little time. Carl Rambo, commander of a DD during the invasion, recalls that he and Mike Jones, his driver, went over every operation the driver had to perform. "There were twenty-three steps, and we had them all listed in writing. This is what you do at this point. You do this, next you do this. We went over them again and again." All controls were near the driver. "Things like jacking up the screen, filling the struts with air, shutting off the air, checking to see that the struts were locked, because if they weren't, the screen would collapse. When the navy let the tank off the LCT, Mike had to lower the propellers and see that they were functioning properly." The driver had the major responsibility, so if he didn't do things right, Rambo concludes, the crew would be swimming. "Being trained, knowing what you are doing, and having a good crew means a lot, and we were well trained before going in on D day."

Francis Songer, then B Company commander, reports he used experience gained in practice landings at Slapton Sands to test the canvas skirts of DDs. Songer fired a machine gun at the waterline and determined that reinforcement was needed. He then scoured neighboring villages to obtain sail material, gut and other fishing line, needles, wax, and tar, using company fund money to purchase the items. He and some trusted noncoms completed the reinforcement.

One of the A Company DDs sank during a practice run. Because the sinking occurred only fifteen feet after launching, Sgt. Orris Johnson and his crew escaped unharmed. Navy crewmen on the LCT that launched the DD pulled them from the water and brought them to shore.

April 26 was the day of the practice landing and I, along with other B Company support troops, was allowed to view it from a hilltop a safe distance away. It was spectacular. Although naval guns did not plaster the beach as they would on the actual landings, the air force did fly over, dropping sacks of flour. Engineers came in first, followed immediately by the 70th DDs. Then came 8th Regiment infantry and C Company, some with dozer tanks using their blades to clear the beach and to burst through holes in the seawall made by engineers.

Exercise Tiger Becomes a Disaster

What I didn't see was that Exercise Tiger was a disaster. Live ammunition was used, and Americans killed hundreds of other Americans. Hundreds more died when enemy torpedo boats sank several LCTs in a convoy participating in the exercise. Troops knew about the torpedo boat attack at the time, but only that it had happened. Postwar critics have called Exercise Tiger a blunder. It cannot be denied that terrible mistakes were made that resulted in high loss of life. Estimates vary but approach 1,000 dead, far more than at the actual landings at Utah Beach. Neither can it be denied that a realistic practice was necessary. The invasion of France was the largest and most complex in history, involving forces of many nations operating under joint command. Much needed to be learned, and much was learned. For the 70th the exercise was highly successful, not only because it suffered no loss of life. Crews for the first time "sailed" their DDs to shore. Coordination between tanks and other units was more firmly developed.

Secrecy was obviously necessary at the time. If the enemy came to know that this was a practice invasion, they might have been able to deduce the location of the "Utah" site. Also there was a fear that some of the dead or wounded were "bigots," the code name for individuals privy to the invasion plans. If they or their bodies were carrying the plans with them, surprise was no longer an advantage. Secrecy at the time was one thing however, but the whole fiasco was hushed up for decades, the deserved focus of much postwar criticism.[10]

Practice in Blowing Holes in the Seawall

Many other things were learned at Slapton Sands. One was how to deal with "Hitler's Westwall" at Utah Beach. Engineers were to blow holes in it. 70th dozer tanks were then to enlarge these holes for regular medium tanks to go through. With the 70th involved in this operation, Colonel Welborn designated Lt. Franklin Anderson to be battalion liaison with the engineers. "With me were two 70th men who had a radio so large it was in two sections. Both were waterproofed, and each man carried one section. We were sent to a training area on the coast. Here I was assigned to a combat engineer assault squad. There were maybe six teams of about six men each. These teams had 'bangalore torpedoes,' which were long tubes or shafts that could be extended out and had explosives on the end. The combat engineers also had spare explosives taped across their chests on assault jackets."

Anderson and the radio operators were issued the same kind of assault jacket, though they did not have explosives taped to their bodies. "I soon learned the reason for the bangalore torpedoes and all the explosives. Our main mission was to blow holes in the seawall in certain places so our tanks could go through. This meant we were to be the first on the beach. My job, as a tank officer, was to pick the places to blow. I knew what a tank could do and couldn't do, and I was to select places where a tank could not only go through but also could operate on the other side of the seawall." The 70th radiomen were to be in contact with the tanks to direct them where to go. "There was also a naval officer on our team with two radiomen. He was to radio the navy warships to tell them when to cease fire so we could go to the seawall and do our job. It was obvious we not only had a dangerous mission, but a vital one. General Roosevelt came to our training site, probably to emphasize our importance in the plans."

General Roosevelt had been transferred from the 1st Infantry Division to the 4th Infantry Division. It was at his strong suggestion that the 70th became attached to the 4th. He is reputed to have said that the untested 4th Division would need the battle-experienced 70th more than would the tested 1st Division, although the 4th and the 70th had not trained together until the invasion maneuvers. Tactics and the ever-present matter of authority on the use of tanks would again have to be worked out in the field. Recognizing the need for a tank officer such as Lieutenant Anderson to assess where tanks could best operate around the seawall was, nonetheless, a good beginning to the relationship.

Another possible way to create holes in the seawall was to have tanks blast away at it. John Ahearn tells of an experiment. High commanders ordered a steel platform welded onto conventional tanks to hold a rocket launcher. "We were told to take some of our tanks down to the beach. Several British generals were there, along with higher American officers, including Welborn. We were ordered to fire rockets at a cement wall. Most were duds, and those that exploded barely made a dent. Welborn very quickly told one of our guys to fire a 75mm AP, which did all the rocket was supposed to do and didn't. That was the end of the rocket experiment."

Cecil Nash, who drove one of the experimental tanks, said: "Thank God for Welborn's quick action. The rocket launcher used in the experiment made it impossible to escape through the turret hatch if the tank got hit. The three guys in the turret would have to get out through the lower hatches or through the bottom escape hatch, which was worthless in emergencies. Shermans could burn up in seconds."

No Training in the Hedgerows

The training area was selected in part because there were hedgerows inland from the beach area. Yet no training took place in how to fight in terrain dominated by them, this despite the fact that the 4th Infantry Division and the 70th were by then firmly attached to each other. All training was for the invasion. Infantry and tanks had no opportunity to work on coordination or tactics in hedgerow country or anywhere else.

Last-Minute Tension and Changes at Lupton Camp

There were other things complicating John Ahearn's life during the pressure-packed weeks before the invasion. C Company was with the battalion at Lupton Camp, a few miles from Slapton Sands where A and B Companies were busy training in DDs. Ahearn was the only line company commander there. "I don't know where D Company was—and the battalion staff were besieging me with directives. They were bothering the hell out of me. For an example, I remember a directive that the men were to take down their pinup pictures of Hollywood stars like Betty Grable, because someone thought them too much of a distraction. How amazing! That one really pissed me off, but I stayed cool about it and let it pass, which it did."

Another perplexing order came through at this time. "Nick Corrado was a very good friend to all of us, a wonderful guy, very handsome and extremely charming. Nick was purportedly being used by some higher ranks to obtain hard-to-get items and to make certain arrangements. I don't know what his job was other than that, but anyway we all loved to be around him. About two weeks before the invasion, he came to me on a Sunday and said, 'John, I'm going to be assigned to a tank, and I don't know the first thing about it. Will you help me?" So Ahearn and Corrado spent hours in a hurry-up session on tanks that particular Sunday. "Of course, he went to Europe in a tank and didn't make it."

The next thing Ahearn couldn't do anything about. "I had seventeen tanks in my company, and now they gave me eight in addition that had dozer blades welded onto them. These dozer tanks were to help engineers clear the beach and bust through the seawall. This was all well and good, but it was only weeks before the invasion, and where in the hell was I going to get the personnel?" Ahearn had his crews all set, and they were experienced in working together. "Now, weeks before combat, I had to break them all up to have at least some experienced men in each tank, especially as commanders and gunners. Twenty-four engineers were assigned to me who had never been in a tank before. Finally, one tank was to stay back, so I ended up with twenty-four under my command. I put three engineers in each dozer as drivers, bow gunners, and loaders. Weeks before the invasion! That's the way they did things in the army."

Lt. John Ahearn Plans the C Company Invasion

An even more perplexing thing was about to happen. Ahearn was told one day to join a big meeting, conducted by Col. James Van Fleet, who headed the 8th Regiment of the 4th Infantry Division. "I was there, a first lieutenant, outranked by everyone else. The colonel proceeded to talk about what we were going to do, the broad sweep of things. I was a greenhorn and had never participated in these grand designs before, these critiques, these plans. One thing that came across to me was that Van Fleet was talking in language familiar to me, namely in football terms. That struck me!"

At the close of the meeting, a 70th staff officer told Ahearn to go to a certain dock and meet a British officer who would be in charge of the LCTs on which his company tanks would cross the Channel. "I was told that I and this British officer, also a lieutenant, were to plan our part of the invasion of France!" Ahearn and his executive officer, also a lieutenant, met the British lieutenant, who had with him two junior lieutenants. How ludicrous, Ahearn recalls thinking, that the greatest invasion in all of history was about to take place, and here were five lieutenants meeting each other for the first time, casually planning their operations! On the other hand, who could better plan their specific operation than those involved? "We had been assigned to British LCTs, which had been around quite a while. They could take five tanks, but for our purposes we decided to put three tanks on each of eight vessels. We might have to fire on the way in, so we would place one dozer in the middle and two regular tanks on each side, which then could fire laterally if necessary."

Ahearn's responsibilities as a company commander were staggering in these final weeks and days. "I had a lot of new youngsters. One was a great kid named Owen Gavigan, who I think was barely nineteen. I made him a tank commander, and he proved to be a good one. Fortunately, the only guys who needed training were the engineers. We did have time for some training, sufficient, I felt, to carry out our duties."

Something happened that still disturbs Ahearn today, fifty years later. "One of the men who had been with us all along and who was an excellent driver had reported ill. I had been told that he probably was not ill but was trying to get out of this thing. I was told he was in the medical tent, and I went down to drag this guy out. I told him how much I needed him, that he was a good man who couldn't easily be replaced. He said he was ill with some respiratory ailment, which I thought didn't sound terribly serious. He did come along and did alright, but the whole episode really bothered me."

A Second Looey and the Big Brass

Lieutenant Franklin Anderson was scheduled to be on the beach before the first wave, so Lieutenant Colonel Welborn wanted him to attend a high-level meeting. Lieutenants never ask superior officers why; all he knew was that he was to be ready when the colonel came to pick him up. "We went in the colonel's jeep to a Nissen hut that was loaded with brass. Generals were there, as was Colonel Van Fleet and other colonels. Then there was me, a second looey. I recall Colonel Van Fleet going over the landing, making sure everyone knew about all the different operations. I was sitting there like a church mouse. They were talking about air saturation, the naval bombardment, and how they could control it." Every now and then somebody would look around and see that solitary second looey and wonder why he was present. "I was getting smaller and smaller. Finally one officer talked about all the smoke that would be there and how we couldn't know what weather conditions might be on the day; it might be foggy or raining. One officer said we might use Verey pistols (green or red signal flares). That was when Colonel Welborn stood up and said we should not rely on Verey pistols. With all the explosions and smoke, they might not be visible or distinct." Another officer then stood up and said that since Welborn was a man with combat experience, his advice carried weight. "Welborn went on to say that you can't set up an invasion and depend on it working the way it was planned. That was not the way it happens. Things go wrong, the unexpected occurs. You must innovate, expedite, do what is best under the circumstances. You must know where you are and what you are doing. Then, perhaps, other things will fall into place. Get up the beach and get off it. Use your head. So Welborn told them this, and they listened. I felt pretty good about being there with him."

"I'll See You on the Beaches"

For a few weeks in early May, the battalion was together again at Lupton Camp. General Roosevelt visited the bivouac. He made it known by his presence that he still thought of the men of the 70th as "his boys," and the feeling was reciprocated.

On May 13, everyone polished shoes, belts, and anything else demanding attention, and put on class A uniforms. Marching to what served as the parade ground, the battalion was formed in the formal military manner. Major General J. Lawton Collins, commander of VII Corps, conducted a review, then presented the Legion of Merit to Lieutenant Colonel Welborn. The Silver Star was presented to Lieutenant Oakland, Lieutenant Miller, and Private Silva. Sergeant Suranic of B Company received the Purple Heart. [11]

I found all of this most impressive and felt great pride in being a part of it. Even when "Lightning Joe" Collins said, "I'll see you on the beaches," I thought the general meant me, though I really knew as a cook he didn't. In the middle of May the service elements of the 70th, including me, moved to Poole to await the outcome of the invasion.

The combat elements became one of thousands of units making final preparations in "sausage camps" situated near ports of embarkation on the Channel coast. Six months of training had been shaped for the invasion. Lieutenant Colonel Welborn had seen to it that the battalion would be ready. He was confident that line company commanders had prepared well, and in this he was justified. At the "go" signal, the men of the 70th would be off to meet the enemy, and whatever fate had in store for them.

6
The Utah Beach Landings and Beachhead

I was on deck . . . [of an LCT returning to England with wounded from Utah Beach]. Everything had been hazy as I was in shock, but now I realized I had lost both my legs, and I began to cry. I was soothed by a navy corpsman.

—John Ahearn
C Company commander.

On the eve of D day, the senior army Catholic chaplain held a huge outdoor field mass for 5,000 troops near Dartmouth. Michael Varhol attended. "He extended general absolution to all because he said for many this may be their final church service. I received Holy Communion along with one of my best friends, a big Irish lieutenant named Tom Tighe from Detroit. Leaving the mass area Tighe remarked, 'Mike, I know you have faith and will not laugh at me, but I would like to give you something that could save your life in the upcoming invasion.' I said, 'Tom, I can use all the help I can get; what do you want to give me?' He opened his wallet, giving me a small piece of paper on which was printed a prayer to Saint Joseph." Tighe told Varhol his father had given him this because all the men in his World War I company carried it through the big battles in France and all returned safely without a scratch. "I put it in my thin wallet, which contained only my ID and a few scrip-type French francs we had exchanged dollars for."

The 70th Tank Battalion assault forces made ready to board LCTs. Some of the men had made the invasions of North Africa and Sicily, but this one, they knew, would be far different. This was against Hitler's formidable "Westwall," prepared by Rommel himself. Officers of the 70th attended meetings at 4th Division headquarters going over last-minute details. A and B Companies were to land their DD tanks in the first wave at H hour. C Company, with five additional dozer tanks, was to land at H hour plus 15 minutes. All three medium tank companies were to provide continuous support for the 1st and

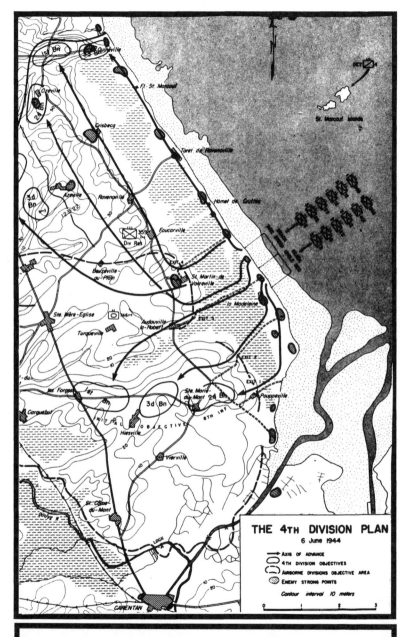

Landing at Utah Beach with 4th Infantry Division

2d Battalions of the 8th Infantry Regiment. The initial objective was to secure Utah Beach, go through holes blasted in the seawall by combat engineers, and control the exits so that follow-up troops could get beyond areas inundated by the Germans. D Company in light tanks was to land H plus 260 minutes and support the 101st Airborne Division, which would be inland a few miles after landing by parachute and in gliders in the early morning hours.

June 2, 1944, LCTs Are Boarded

In southern England, staging areas were close to ports of embarkation. During the last few days, most 70th enlisted men scoured their camps for rations, cigarettes—anything that might prove useful and could be stored aboard already crowded tanks. In B Company, according to its journal, Private Shepherd made the biggest haul, but it would not fit into a tank. The 100-pound sack of potatoes was therefore transformed into French fries.

On June 2, the men tested their assault gas masks in a gas chamber. In the evening, the medium tank crews boarded LCTs. A and B Companies, with sixteen tanks each, were on eight LCTs, four tanks per craft. C Company, with twenty-one tanks including five dozers, was on seven LCTs, two regular tanks and one dozer on five of the craft and three regular tanks on the other two.

The headquarters section boarded LCTs at Dartmouth, which served as the gathering point for all 70th assault units. All units stayed on board at anchor the remainder of June 2 and the entire day of June 3, finally moving into line in heavy seas on June 4.

Major Michael Varhol as battalion adjutant was with the assault forces. "Who can ever forget our travel to the great unknown—Festung Europa, especially the . . . sight of our leaving Dartmouth, England, in full daylight for a Top Secret voyage to the invasion, and the ironic festive farewell being afforded our sea armada by the usually staid, but obviously grateful populace living along the shoreline who were waving Union Jacks, bedsheets, and even occasionally Old Glory. I never dreamed that that very night severe storms would force us to limp back into the dismal port of Portland."

The invasion was scheduled for June 5, but the storms caused a postponement. For an additional twenty-four hours, the men of the

70th were told to "hang tough." The invasion was still on. Eisenhower made the decision to "go" at 2145 the night of June 4. The English Channel was still nearly impassable, but a slight break in the weather had been predicted. Upward of 4,000 ships and more than 2,000 smaller craft now had to get into line to assault five beaches at the right place, at the right time, and in the right order.

As they started sailing again on June 5, Major Varhol remembers passing two seagoing tugs towing huge barges filled with hundreds of 155mm shells. "Atop the shells were perched six glum-looking black soldiers wearing Mae Wests and steel helmets. Never having seen black soldiers in a combat situation before, we chuckled insanely in bewilderment at this potential major explosion just waiting to happen. Then the more serious thought occurred to me that the world may never know what a great sacrifice these men were making despite their lack of full democracy at home."

For the men of the 70th assault groups, the voyage was a frightful experience. Even before heading for France, they had been aboard for up to eighty-two hours and still had ten more to go. The flat-bottomed LCTs constantly rolled and pitched. Many men were terribly seasick, some for two or three days without respite. According to the B Company journal, "10 in 1" rations were aboard each tank but largely went untouched.

Lieutenant Franklin Anderson and two 70th radiomen along with combat engineers were on a ship rather than an LCT. Anderson was below deck in the terrible weather. "I had been assigned to one of those six high hammocks that never stopped swaying back and forth. A lieutenant from the 4th Division came by and saw that I was from the 70th. He said he knew some officers in the 70th and asked who else was here. I told him only me and two radiomen. He said, 'Wait here,' and went into a door along a passageway. Soon he returned and said, 'General Roosevelt wants to see you.'" Anderson wondered what he had done now.

"I walked into this cabin, and there was General Roosevelt propped up on his bunk reading a book. He looked up and asked me, 'Well, how is Colonel Welborn?' I told him fine, but that I hadn't seen him for some time as I was attached to combat engineers. 'Oh, that's right,' he said, 'you're the one I saw.' Then he asked where I was staying. I told him in one of those hammocks. He turned to his aide and told him to have another cot brought in. I was to stay with him, he said."

Well, a lieutenant does not say no, only thank-you, to a general, so Anderson stayed in that little cabin with General Roosevelt and his aide for two nights. "I became good friends with the lieutenant and saw him several times later, but General Roosevelt, of course, died from a heart attack while we were still in Normandy. He really liked the 70th and was a good friend of Welborn's."

Major Varhol spent his time standing on the rocking LCT deck or sitting on his hard half-track seat, for there were no cots. "I was groggy with seasickness despite having taken anti-seasick pills. The only rations consumed for two days were cans of self-heating, rather repulsive, British-made kidney stew with the odor of urine." By now he couldn't wait to set foot on dry land, even if held by the enemy. "As we wondered if the invasion was on for real, our answer came about 0145 when the expected 378 paratrooper-carrying C-47 aircraft plus their many escorts droned overhead at low altitude, about 600 feet up, flying in an easterly direction toward which we were heading."

During the seemingly endless hours before the assault, John Ahearn spent as much time as possible with his men. Since tank crews had been changed only a short time before, he felt a steady, reassuring hand was needed. But as the final run approached, Ahearn thought he had better get some sleep to ready himself for the vital role he as company commander would play in a few hours. "I went below deck and tried to sleep but couldn't, so I pulled out a little book I had been intending to read about my home city, *A Tree Grows in Brooklyn*. I read it in three or four hours, but never could go to sleep."

As a company commander Ahearn had been issued an escape map in case he was captured. Printed on a silk cloth, 24 by 24 inches, it was a map of all of France. Delineated were German coastal defense zones from Holland to the Spanish border; patrol areas along the Pyrenees; another coastal defense zone on the French southern coast; patrol areas along the French eastern border, past Switzerland, and along the French-German border; and the former occupied and unoccupied zones in France. Ahearn rolled the silk map tightly and stuck it into a boot so that it could not be seen.

He went up on deck again about 0300, and by now there was a good deal of activity. Patrol boats were moving around, getting in line for the final run at the beach. "One of them pulled abreast of us, and British navy Lieutenant Hart—the one with whom I planned our part of the invasion—was shouting through a megaphone to the patrol boat commander regarding our position in the line. About fifteen minutes before dawn our planes came over to bomb the beach defenses, and the big guns of our warships opened fire. We could see the flashes, hear the roar of the cannon, and hear the shells as they passed over us."

The men of B Company were also on deck watching the great show, as the whole horizon was filled with the flashes of the naval bombardment. "About 0530 they gave us the word to make preparations for launching. While the tank engines were warming up and the DDs made correct, the men filtered into the ship's galley for a last cup of hot java. At 0626 the Air Corps presented us with a very fine show and in a very few minutes left the beaches in chaos. Heavy clouds of black and gray smoke hung low over the once well-fortified pillboxes. We disembarked at 0630 despite heavy seas."[1]

Lieutenant Franklin Anderson and the two radiomen landed pretty much on schedule with the combat engineers. It was H hour minus 3 minutes. "We were the first going up the beach. Leaving the landing craft, I was in water going high up on my chest, but I really didn't feel it, wanting to get going and keep going. Fortunately we all made it. Of course German shells were coming in, and a lot of our guys hit the dirt. I told them not to worry about those you hear, worry about those you don't hear. I thought about what I had to do and started up a long, shallow beach toward the seawall."

Before reaching it Anderson was hit in the leg. "I looked down and saw it bleeding. It was what we called a through and through. There wasn't much pain so I kept going and was able to do my job by hobbling around. We blew one hole in the seawall, but I wasn't able to continue. After the bleeding stopped, the area around the wound got hard and swollen, and soon the leg got stiff." A medic came by to give him aid. "He said for me to take my watches off. I told him I was hit in the leg, not the arm, and the watches were staying on. I had two on, my own and one Colonel Welborn had earlier told supply to issue to me. This made sense, given the job I had to do. At least one had to be working. At any rate, the medic said I had been hit with shrapnel and bandaged the wound. Later in the day, I was evacuated back to England."

All sixteen B Company DDs were launched at about 1,500 yards, according to company commander Francis Songer, who gave the launch order. Ed Gossler was a gunner in one of the DDs. "It was a funny feeling because we knew a third of our tank was underwater. All of us but the driver were outside the tank when we got in the water in case it went down. We were also wearing these diving apparatuses. Once we got in the water, we had only one way to go, and that was for shore. I don't recall anyone being panicky or anything. We were trained well enough that we figured we could get to shore alright and once there we could establish a beachhead." In the tank there was even less room than usual to move around. "It was crowded with our special diving gear and newly issued gas masks, plus extra rations. We were very fortunate that we landed at Utah Beach. It was more level than the guys had at Omaha. Also, the air and naval support was tremendous." All sixteen B Company DDs made it ashore. "I understand that other DD battalions lost most of theirs at Omaha, where the water was rougher. It's hard to say if we had better navy people to unload us, or if we had better training. I do know we were well trained and the navy was terrific." [2]

"D day was quite an exciting day," Carl Rambo recollected. He commanded a B Company DD tank that was on the lead LCT. "Only the guide boat was ahead of us. I was on the same LCT as both Songer and our platoon leader. Around the middle of the night I flopped down on the deck and took a nap. I must have been tired because I went right to sleep." When he woke up things were happening. "Just about dawn, two engine bombers came over and they really saturated that beach. Germans were shooting at them, and one plane must have been hit in the gas tank as fire was belching out of the bomb bay before it blew apart. Parts of it were all around us."

Rambo agrees that the LCT crew got their "DDs into the water nice and easy. We had only fourteen inches of freeboard so a wave of two feet could have swamped us." He reports that the B Company DDs moved toward the beach pretty much in a line. "That's better than fanning out in case of artillery, especially since we could move only four miles an hour in the water."

Rambo reports: "Just before we left our LCT, an A Company LCT hit a mine. It was parallel to us and about a hundred yards off on our right, and maybe not that far. I saw tanks blown fifty to a hundred feet in the air. They tumbled as if they were flipped matchboxes. The LCT was broken in two."

Other reports confirm that the craft broke in two upon hitting a large mine. The four DDs and all personnel were thrown into the sea. "Staff sergeant Glenn Gibson landed about seventy-five yards from the wreckage of the LCT. The forward section of the landing craft had been sunk, but the stern half was still afloat. He swam to it and climbed aboard." Sergeant Gibson attempted to disentangle a navy enlisted man who was injured and caught in the door of the pilot's compartment. "The stern half then capsized, taking the navy man with it but throwing Gibson into the sea for a second time. He climbed upon a portion of the wreckage and was taken aboard an American LCT about twenty minutes later."[3] Nineteen of twenty tankers died. Only Gibson and two or three navy men survived.

George Brookstein had a number of close friends who were killed on that A Company LCT. Among them was Stanley Marszalek. Gibson later told Brookstein that Marszalek's last words were: "Boy are we going to give them hell!"

Dozer Tanks Prove Their Worth

Although the DDs were scheduled to be the first tanks ashore, the C Company dozer tank commanded by Owen Gavigan actually had that distinction. Gavigan was a nineteen-year-old who still had the rank of private first class because Lieutenant Ahearn had promoted him just prior to the invasion. As the Allied naval bombardment eased and the doors of the LCT lowered, Gavigan kept his eye on Ahearn, whose tank was to the left rear. "Ahearn gave me an arm signal to move out, and as he did so, I was surprised to see a smile on his face. We drove off into about seven or eight feet of water. While we were on land in a few seconds, I was a little concerned because, though I grew up on the shore of Lake Michigan, I had never learned how to swim."[4]

Next off was Ahearn's tank, followed by the other regular tank. These two tanks moved on, leaving Gavigan's tank alone in the immediate area. Gavigan went to work using the dozer blade to remove obstacles from the water and the beach. "The Germans had used things such as logs and triangular iron pieces welded together to delay the passage of vehicles.

"The Germans were doing a lot of firing, but right in the midst of it a jeep named 'Rough Rider' came to my tank. It was General Roosevelt." The ironic thought ran through Gavigan's mind that here was the oldest and most senior officer then on the beach giving orders to the youngest and most junior tank commander.

Roosevelt directed Gavigan to the left to where the seawall hadn't been blown by the engineers. "The general told me to fire a couple of rounds of 75mm at it. I did, and we made a hole in the wall, then enlarged it with our dozer. Then he ordered me to go farther left and fire on a gun emplacement that was shelling ships and boats heading for shore."

C Company dozer tanks that landed were under the command of Lieutenant Riley. Like Gavigan, other tank commanders immediately began their assigned duties of clearing the beach of obstacles and enlarging holes in the seawall. The idea of using tanks instead of regular bulldozers proved successful. Tanks provided the protection and firepower needed in the situation. When the beach was secure, supporting elements, supplies, and equipment, including bulldozers, quickly landed. Dozer tanks then were available for use as needed beyond the seawall.

Right after leaving the beach, Gavigan relates, "General Roosevelt again came to my tank and directed me to push stalled vehicles off a causeway through an inundated area. Troops and supplies were coming in fast and were bottlenecked on the beach."

Regular C Company Tanks in Action

John Ahearn commends the British lieutenant commanding the LCT he was on for a masterful job. "He got us to about eight feet from the beach," Ahearn relates. "We had shrouds and waterproofing, and, while we went under a bit, we were immediately on shore."

Tony Zampiello was Ahearn's tank driver. "When we went off the ramp I could see land on my left. Well, now we were under about eight feet of water, at least my hatch was, so all I could see was water. I kept going left, and Ahearn on the intercom kept saying, 'Right, Tony, right, right!' So I turned right, and we were on dry land. I had been turned around because of being underwater, but Ahearn could see, and anyway, I trusted his judgment."

Rockets were being fired, and there was a lot going on. "I saw a boat lying on its side, with a couple of guys standing on it waiting to be rescued. I got out of the tank to take off the shroud. It was like a ventilating duct and came off easily by removing a couple of pins. While outside I took a quick leak. Boy, did I have to go. I was so scared. But, I got right back in, and we drove off." The shroud kept water from the engine compartment. It had to be removed once on land for the engine to function properly.

In another C Company tank, Cecil Nash was the driver. When their LCT hit bottom, an enemy shell hit the ramp as it was being lowered for debarkation. "No damage was done I guess, as we were told to move off. The first off was the dozer, which took a scoop of sand off the bottom. My tank was next and I went off with an open driver's hatch, even though we were a number of yards from the beach. We took some water, but went on to the beach and opened the drain cocks to let the water out. At that time I got out and pulled the pins to drop the shroud. We were not drawing enemy fire at that time and were soon off the beach."

The first task of these regular C Company tanks, according to company commander John Ahearn, was to take care of the lateral defenses of the beach and to support A and B Companies. "I immediately saw that they weren't there, that in effect we were the assaulting unit. Also, all of my tanks weren't in. I had only about twelve tanks. (I learned later that two LCTs had trouble and returned to England.) That wasn't all, because it was obvious to me that we weren't landing in the designated places. I had all the maps, knew where the obstacles were located, and so on. I knew I had to do something and luckily saw General Roosevelt." Ahearn told him what the problem was, that they were in a new area of the beach. "I asked him what I should do and if there were any new orders. He said, 'No, carry out your previous orders, continue with your mission, do what has to be done.' So I radioed my exec, Lieutenant Yeoman, and told him to take half the tanks and proceed to the right, and I took the other half and went to the left."

Ahearn led his little task force of six tanks along the seawall looking for an opening. "I was very conscious that we had to get inland swiftly. General Barton had told us this, and Colonel Van Fleet had emphasized the same thing. The first break in the wall was kind of a gate, and at it was an object I had never seen before." It resembled a miniature tank, and Ahearn thought it probably was a mine. "I knew my mission was to get beyond the wall, so I didn't fire at it and proceeded through with no problem. Years later I learned that the Germans had remote controls for these objects, called 'Little Goliaths' [or Beetles], and they were filled with about 180 pounds of TNT. For some reason this one was not operative, the wires were cut or something. It is interesting to conjecture what might have happened, either if it had worked or if I fired on it."

Controlling the Causeways

Despite the loss of nineteen men killed and four tanks on the LCT that hit the mine, A Company under the command of Capt. J. Stewart Williams supported infantry in protecting causeways through inundated areas. Incoming waves of troops were then able to move farther inland. Two more A Company men, Sgt. John Callahan and Pvt. Lewis Saray, were killed soon after leaving the beach.

B Company had the least trouble. The first thing Ed Gossler saw after landing was "fifteen or twenty Germans coming out of a bombed-out pillbox. The air and naval bombardment had been right on target."

Carl Rambo's DD landed just after that of B Company commander Songer. "We dropped our screen and headed for the seawall. Engineers were there carrying fifty pounds of TNT on their backs. It was in a block, about the size of a farmer's salt block. They made a pyramid of them against the seawall and set it off, blowing out a big hole. One of our dozers was there moving concrete around. While it was working, I did a crazy thing and got out of my tank to help a wounded infantryman. He was nearly dead and I couldn't do anything for him. I never should have gotten out of my tank." This violated Rambo's own rule to tend to his own business, which was to take his tank through the wall.

He followed company commander Songer, who was leading. Continues Rambo: "We went over chunks of concrete in the hole and onto a causeway that went through a flooded swamp. Songer crossed a little culvert that was mined and blown. His tank got hung up for a little bit. My engine had started missing so we could barely move in low gear. Songer radioed me to bring my tank in, but I told him if I do I'll choke the area because I didn't have any power and would get hung up." Despite waterproofing, water had apparently reached the ignition system of Rambo's tank during the landing.

He pulled his tank off the side of the causeway, and the rest of the company tanks passed them. "I and the crew jerked the engine compartment open. We couldn't spot the trouble and tried turning the engine over, but there was nothing we could do. So there I was on this narrow exit and here came the whole damned army right behind me. My tank was nearly in the water and they were going around the other side. Some engineer came by and said to get that tank out of here, but I said it won't move. He said he would move it and called in a bulldozer." The tank was pushed into the water. "This was the thing to do at that point. Well, that took me out of action. We just sat there waiting in case a mechanic could help, but that was hopeless. We cut the DD screen off just in case and threw the two air bottles outside. Coming by were infantrymen who thought the air bottles were bombs, so we would kick them and say, 'See, they won't hurt you.' We had a lot of fun with that, but that is all the fun we had."

Now Rambo violated his rule again. "I did another damned fool thing and decided to go back to the beach and get me another tank. One of the guys said, 'What are you going to do even if you find a tank?' I told him I'll just jump in and drive off!" The landings were still going on, and German planes were coming in. American planes had white stripes painted underneath as identification. "So the krauts painted white stripes on theirs. Just a few of them got away with that trick, but it led to some confusion.

"One of our P-47s came in and our own antiaircraft blasted the hell out of it. The pilot bailed out, and I'll be damned if they didn't shoot at him with machine guns. Well, the next thing here came that damned burning plane so straight at me that I jumped up from the ditch I was in and ran across the road to another ditch." The plane crashed about 100 feet from him. "I damned near got killed. There was no way I was going to get another tank, and of course I didn't."

The War Is Over for John Ahearn

After the C Company tanks led by Ahearn moved to the other side of the seawall, they proceeded down parallel to the wall and the beach until reaching a road. "Our infantry were on the road, and I saw a concrete emplacement [Beau Guillot] that could threaten them, so I ordered my tanks to fire on it. As we fired, a number of German soldiers came out with their hands up. At least they wore German uniforms. They turned out not to be regular Werhmacht, but rather impressed East Europeans who had been put on the seawall by Rommel. They were not about to stand and fight for the fuhrer, so in the face of our strength . . . they quickly surrendered."

Ahearn got out of his tank to take them prisoner. "I was within maybe 150 yards of them and they started yelling 'Achtung Minen.' I realized I was in a minefield, so I returned to my tank and motioned for them to come forward. They did, without stepping on any mines. I, of course, could not hold them, so I turned them over to the infantry." Ahearn later reflected that by warning him, these prisoners demonstrated the humanity of man.

Ahearn continued south, parallel to the beach. They came to a crossroad with one road going inland on exit 1. Ahearn decided not to go on it but to stay with his mission to take care of the left flank. "I was not sure where the Germans were, or if they were around, and I was ahead of the infantry. We were now among hedgerows and the road narrowed down to a trail hardly wide enough for a tank. Shortly, the tank hit a mine, and the front left bogie blew. The track was misplaced, and we were inoperative. I don't recall if I radioed or hustled back to Lt. Tighe, who had been following me, but I told him to proceed inland on exit 1 toward Pouppeville, and that I would catch up with him later."

He told his crew to set up machine guns and stay on the alert. "They also began to heat water for coffee and open rations. Mind you, they hadn't eaten for some time and were naturally hungry."

Ahearn began to reconnoiter the area on foot. "I started out walking, very cautiously. I maybe had gone 100 yards when I heard people yelling 'Help!' I looked out in a field and saw two or three infantrymen, or more likely they were paratroopers. From this point and on, my memory is a little obscure." As he remembers, Ahearn was going to get as close to these wounded men as possible and got up on top of a hedgerow about six feet high and densely thatched. "It was very difficult to move through. So I proceeded slowly and cautiously. I knew there were mines. I knew it was dangerous. In my attempt to get as close to them as possible, I gingerly stepped over a small hedgerow. I was standing there, wondering what the hell I was going to do now, and Puff! What had happened was that I was standing on a defective S-mine."

Normally, Ahearn explains, these mines detonate with about six pounds of pressure and should have exploded when his foot first came down. "This one exploded and got both feet instead of one. Of course I was knocked unconscious and rolled up against the hedgerow. I don't know how long I was there, but as soon as I was conscious I started yelling for help. Zampiello and Beard came for me. After this, everything was very hazy but was in the affidavit Zampiello and Beard gave Major Varhol twenty days after the event." (The affidavit was for the Congressional Medal of Honor.)

Tony Zampiello remembers driving the tank down that narrow road and hearing Lieutenant Ahearn give the command to turn left. Zampiello through his periscope had seen barbed wire and a sign *"Achtung Minen,"* so he asked Ahearn over the intercom, "Did you say left, sir?" Ahearn said, "Yes, left, Tony." So, Zampiello has related, "I turned left and that was when we hit the mine. I jumped out, which was the natural thing to do. When I did, I saw that the left side of the tank was gone. I started to cry, and John asked me if I was hurt. I said, no, I was OK, but it hurt me to lose my tank. I had named it 'California Bomb,' because I came from Pasadena. I was in a strange country, and I guess I must have been shocked by the suddenness of what happened." Very quickly Zampiello was alright. "The lieutenant took his side arm and said he was going on foot reconnaissance. There was firing all over the place. He was gone only three or four minutes when I heard an explosion and then I heard him calling, 'Zamp! Zamp!' I grabbed the gunner, Felix Beard, and we ran down to where he was. We didn't think about mines or booby traps but just ran as fast as we could. When we got to him both his feet were blown apart."

Ahearn was not a small man. Picking him up and making their way through a hedgerow must have required superhuman strength. "We carried him to the tank, and I was surprised we didn't get blown up. There must have been mines all over the place. We radioed the medics, but none came for two or three hours." The long delay was because the medics were busy elsewhere, as Ahearn had advanced far beyond the infantry. The whole crew went with the medics to the evacuation center, which, Zampiello vividly recalls, "seemed a long way away. John wanted me to carry his map case and tanker's helmet, which I did. Captain Kreckler [70th staff officer] was at the aid station. John didn't want me to leave, but the captain said I couldn't do anything more for him. He took us back to headquarters in a jeep. We never did go back to the tank, even though all our stuff was in it. We didn't want to go near it or the place where John was hit."

Tony Zampiello and Felix Beard were awarded the Silver Star for their actions in rescuing Ahearn. Note that for Beard this was his second Silver Star. Beard had helped extricate Lawrence Krumwiede and other wounded men from danger after their tank was hit at Port Lyautey, French Morocco, on November 9, 1942.

The war was over for John Ahearn, but not the trauma. "Thank God there was a field hospital there, fully operative, within six or seven hours of the landing. They operated on me that night—it was still D day—operated on only one leg because I was so critical they decided not to do both. They prepared me for return to England, but here was my reading: the last flight of the Luftwaffe came over, I'd say three to six planes." Ahearn and a number of other badly wounded were out on stretchers waiting to be transported by jeep to LCTs that would take them to England. "The Luftwaffe came over and strafed us! That was the most helpless feeling I had during my service. I was caught in the woods in Sicily when someone began sniping at me, but this was far, far worse. I subsequently learned that this attack was the dying gasp of the Luftwaffe against the landings." As medics readied them for boarding an LCT, one of them blew up! "So we didn't get out that day but had to wait until the following morning. I was on deck, and all I had on me were my dogtags, a dirty T-shirt, and a pair of shorts, though I don't think I even had those. Everything had been hazy as I was in shock, but now I realized I had lost both my legs. It was a very traumatic moment, and I began to cry. I was soothed by a navy corpsman."

Engineers recovered Ahearn's tank three weeks later. In their report it was noted that about 1,100 mines had been found in the immediate area. (Approximately 15,000 were removed from the Utah Beach area.)

The Exemplary Efforts of John Ahearn

The devotion and loyalty of Ahearn's crew speaks volumes about him as a soldier, as a leader, and as a man. Barely conscious, he thought about his map case and tanker's helmet. These were attributes that identified him for what he was—a company commander of tankers on D day in France.

John Ahearn made indispensable contributions to success at Utah Beach.[5] He carried out his mission of protecting the left flank of the 4th Division, led his six tanks quickly through the seawall, subdued the gun emplacement, Beau Guillot, which controlled access to exit 2, took prisoner the soldiers operating this strong point, sent Lieutenant Tighe to Pouppeville where contact with the 101st Airborne and the 4th Infantry Division was established, and moved farther south than any other vehicle in the sector. For all these actions and his attempt to rescue wounded comrades, John Ahearn was awarded the Distinguished Service Cross. Fifty years later, Ahearn stated almost laconically, "I lost both my limbs, of course, but maneuver rather well, I think, on them."

Inland Beyond Inundated Areas

Just beyond the inundated area the hedgerows began. Owen Gavigan says, "We were unprepared for them but immediately began using the dozer blade to get through these hedgerows. We did this for the rest of the day. My driver, remember, was an engineer temporarily assigned to us. It was really thanks to him that we were able to get through."

Gavigan's tank came upon American gliders that had landed in the early morning darkness. "It was a sight to behold. I saw gliders that were nothing but a pile of matchsticks, gliders with wings torn off, gliders flipped upside down, gliders with jeeps sticking out of them. I had the driver stop to see if we could help the wounded. Unfortunately there were far more fatalities than wounded. We pulled out one dead 'bird colonel.' It was a very dramatic experience."

The fact that beyond the inundated areas American paratroopers and not Germans were in control was a matter of supreme importance. Despite heavy losses, the paratroopers had done their job. Without them, the whole venture could well have gone either way.

D Company Links Up With the 101st Airborne

D Company, commanded by Capt. Gordon Brodie, landed their light tanks on schedule, H hour plus 260 minutes. Sergeant Jack Lovell, a tank commander, recalls, "Our tanks were modified so we could go into five or six feet of water, but it turned out we didn't go in that deep and drove up an embankment to the beach. It took us maybe fifteen minutes and we were ready to go. The first job our platoon had been assigned was to protect General Collins. Since he wasn't around, we joined the rest of the company in the assembly area and took off to link up with the 101st Airborne." This was a dangerous mission, as the tanks went into areas not yet firmly under American control. The 101st had landed by parachute and glider during the early morning darkness and was "broken up in small groups. While able to hold their own against enemy pressure, they were encountering great difficulty in consolidating and making contact with one another."[6] D Company found large elements of the 101st, and by the end of the day enough consolidation had taken place to allow for an attack in the morning, D+1.

The Prayer to St. Joseph and Michael Varhol

Among the battalion staff that landed soon after H hour was adjutant Michael Varhol.

When we were approaching the Normandy beach at daybreak, the most poignant remembrance was the terrible noise of the battleship *Nevada*'s 16-inch guns as we sailed nearby, and the explosions of the aerial half-ton bombs, the bursting rockets, smoke, and the smell of gunpowder everywhere. Suddenly, floating in the water right in front of our LCT was a dead redheaded American infantryman with his full pack still strapped to his back. Moments later when my half-track landed on the sandy beach, I was standing in the open turret looking for the blasted hole in the seawall so we could egress the beach. There was considerable incoming artillery, and men were falling on the beach and not rising again. Unexpectedly, an enemy cannon shell, probably an 88mm, exploded in the air at arm's length to my right. Shell fragments ricocheted throughout the inside around my men, tearing metal, though no one was injured, just scared. The next incoming burst sank the LCT from which we had just departed, and the two Royal Navy lieutenants who had guided us to the invasion were swimming shoreward as we sped inland very fast. I was the only one who knew why we may have been spared and I never told my men my secret. Before I could find Tom Tighe on the battlefield to thank him for giving me the prayer to St. Joseph, he had been killed in action.

On the Beach With Truckloads of Gasoline and Ammunition

Another dangerous assignment was performed by often overlooked men—the truck drivers and their partners from Service Company of the 70th. One was Francis Snyder, who affirms that they landed on schedule, at about 1100, or H hour plus 290 minutes. "I had a mechanic with me, Sergeant Ungurean, who was called 'Meathead.' They were still shelling the beach when the doors of the LCT went down and I drove off. The water came up to the top of the hood, but I had it in low gear and accelerated and got on the beach without any problem. We didn't even get our feet wet. My first reaction with the load we had was to get the hell off the beach and away from those shells. Our truck was filled with both gas and ammunition." They had two rows of five-gallon cans of gas and 37mm shells for the D Company light tanks, packed in a cloverleaf shape. "I don't think we had room for .30 caliber.

"It wasn't very far to the wall, and the traction was good, so we were through fast. We dropped the first load in the battalion supply area, and then went back to the beach for another load. In fact, all day we went back and forth. We didn't get to the tanks until that night, when we dropped off C rations, gas, and ammo."

D Day Objectives Reached

By nightfall, the three medium tank companies in support of the 8th Infantry Regiment, 4th Infantry Division had reached assigned objectives. A Company with the 1st Battalion was in the vicinity of Turqueville; B Company and the 2d Battalion reached Pouppeville; C Company with the 3d Battalion was in position just south of B Company. After dark, the three companies and elements of the battalion forward echelon moved a short distance to an assembly area near St. Hubert, northeast of Ste. Marie du Mont. D Company remained under the control of the 101st Airborne Division. The beachhead had been established. Now it had to be maintained and expanded.

Expanding the Beachhead

Most of the action involving the 70th on D+1 was concerned with the destruction of scattered enemy positions within the perimeter of the beachhead. The 82d and 101st Airborne Divisions had pocketed sizable enemy forces but had insufficient strength to reduce them. Elements of the 70th, therefore, worked with these divisions while other units supported the 8th Infantry Regiment. The Germans still threatened the beachhead, particularly in a narrow salient extending close to the beach and blocking the important Carentan–Ste. Mère Eglise road. The task of the 8th and supporting 70th tanks was to reduce this salient, clean up pockets of resistance, and organize for a push inland in strength.

B Company, which had been committed until 2300 on D day, moved to a new assembly area at 0800 on D+1. "Everyone took off the D day beard and mirrored up," according to the company journal. In point of fact, most beards by then probably dated to June 2, when the men boarded LCTs. At any rate, the men seemed to want to look sharp for battle, starting at 1445 in support of the 8th Infantry. They continued in combat until midnight around Ste. Mère Eglise, with the hardest fight occurring north of the town.

C Company was this day operating close to B Company. As Cecil Nash remembers, his tank commander, Sgt. Ben Griffin, went to a meeting in the morning and came back with an 82d Airborne officer. Elements of the 82d were in Ste. Mère Eglise, and this officer had come through minefields to get help. "Sergeant Griffin volunteered to take him in the turret of our tank. At the edge of the town, we had to stop until the 82d cleared the road of mines they had laid. We were the first tank in Ste. Mère Eglise, and as we drove in, there was a sharp left turn at a crossroads. Our treads must have left black marks on the road because my foot was never off the accelerator. We went to 82d headquarters, and were they ever ecstatic at seeing an American tank!" They had been cut off for more than twenty-four hours since they came in by parachute and gliders. "We radioed back for the rest of our platoon to come in. Somehow, they missed the sharp left turn and went straight on until they ran into an 88mm dual-purpose gun. Two of our tanks were knocked out, several men killed, and others taken prisoner. Our platoon was pretty decimated." One of the men killed was Lt. Tom Tighe.

Private Henry Zbikowski was also in C Company. In the vicinity of Ste. Mère Eglise that day,

his platoon was attacking a line of German infantry entrenched in a field when his tank hit a mine. Thus immobilized, the tank became a target for the enemy's guns and it was no safe place for the crew. So, out they jumped into a nearby ditch, and just in time—because Jerry's 88 zeroed in on the tank. Henry and the rest of the crew were taken prisoner. Of the crew, Henry was the only one not wearing chevrons. The sergeants and corporals were whisked away and Henry remained with his hands behind his neck as the fight continued. In this position Henry stood for almost an hour until things got too hot for Jerry. The American troops were attacking now, and Jerry needed every man he could muster, even prisoners. The commanding officer . . . directed Henry to carry ammunition to the German gunners . . . across no-man's-land. The officer, who spoke fluent English, showed him how to carry four ammo boxes strung across the shoulder and warned him that if he stopped he would be shot on the spot . . . In four hours he made twenty trips, always under the watchful eye of a Jerry detailed to follow Henry in his sights. When Jerry's 88s were knocked out, the Germans offered to surrender to the Americans. As the Germans came out with their hands in the air, Henry began to collect his pay—time and a half for overtime. All in all, he collected about $40, a German watch, a shirt, and a luger. From the German CO he collected all he thought he owed him—a boot in the officer's pants! [7]

Operating with the 101st Airborne, D Company tank commander Sgt. Jack Lovell remembers on D+1 going down a narrow road with a steep embankment on both sides. "There were a lot of dead paratroopers hanging in their chutes in the trees. The krauts had set up antitank guns and machine guns in the hedgerows and had pulled dead American bodies on the road. We couldn't get out of our tanks to drag them off and were out in front of the infantry, so they couldn't either. This held us up, and we actually had to pull back." It was a fitful night with little sleep for Lovell and his group. "That night our naval guns really shelled the krauts, so the next day we could move forward again. If it wasn't for the navy we might have been pushed right back into the water. We have got to thank the navy for what they did at Utah."

Told that D Company was nearly out of gas and ammunition, Francis Snyder was detailed to lead other trucks to company headquarters. "I and Sergeant Ungurean were given a map and told where to go, but these maps didn't always have everything on them, and it was quite a distance away. When we got to the general area, we saw some 101st Airborne soldiers and asked them if they knew where the light tank headquarters was located. They told us we had better get the hell out of there, 'because the krauts were following you down the road with mortar fire.' Then we heard the Pop Pop Pop and turned our truck around." The problem was that the Germans had counterattacked and closed the road. "When it was clear, we started back to where the other trucks were waiting. We had no communications and were out on our own. Soon we came across some German corpses and knew live Germans were not far away. Our trucks had an opening in the roof where a .50-caliber machine gun was mounted. 'Meathead' had that gun loaded and was standing up ready to fire. Well, we made it OK and eventually were able to get the supplies to D Company, but that was sure a frightening time."

On June 8, D+2, German resistance was expected to be serious, since by then his reinforcements could have arrived. Such apprehension, however, is not apparent in the B Company journal. Most of the day "was spent in resting and personal cleanliness. Left Ste. Mère Eglise at 1600 and engaged the enemy at 1730 in the vicinity of Azeville, supporting the 22d Infantry. The company advanced in line formation with A and C Companies in support. Disengaged enemy at 2200, went into assembly area at Ste. Mère Eglise."

The lodgment area had been extended sufficiently for the 4th, supported by the 70th, to begin their advance on Cherbourg. The capture of this vital port was the principal reason for invading at Utah Beach, close to the base of the Cotentin Peninsula.

The Price of a "Piece of Cake"

The landings had been a grueling physical and emotional experience for the men of the 70th. They had been on board LCTs in stormy weather for more than three and a half days and fought until close to midnight after reaching shore.

Utah Beach, with causeways through inundated areas, had caused much preinvasion apprehension. It proved to be, as General Bradley put it, a "piece of cake." Omaha, on the other hand, was a nightmare that haunted him the rest of his life.

As comparatively easy as Utah Beach was, its cost to the 70th was high, due primarily to the A Company LCT that was sunk. Nineteen men lost their lives in that disaster, and three more died in fighting during the day. An additional seven were killed the following day, D+1. Many more were wounded both days, John Ahearn among the most seriously. 70th losses on D day were the largest for any single day in the war, but many days and weeks saw tougher fighting.

Among them were those in the hedgerow country, beginning the next day, without any respite.

The American high command again selected the 70th for a difficult assignment and the 70th again proved worthy. For its efforts in the landings and expanding the beachhead, the 70th was awarded a Presidential Unit Citation.

7
The Capture of Cherbourg

I have had a hard time after the war making anyone who was not there understand how hard the fighting was in the hedgerows, which sure as hell wasn't tank country.

—Clarence McNamee
B Company tanker

Upon leaving the beach area, the 70th was in the *bocage* country of Normandy and would stay in it for about two months. Here would be some of the hardest fighting of the entire war. The 70th, as always, did what was expected of it and more. Losses were high, but the battalion proved its ability to work at close quarters with infantry for sustained periods and in country ill suited for tank warfare.

The Battle Scene

Bocage by definition means woodland, and indeed in Normandy are groves of trees, woods, and large forested areas. Numerous streams and rivers run through valleys formed between steep hills. What made the fighting so difficult, however, were the hedgerows. These were large earthen banks, three to six feet high and encrusted with dense shrubbery or bushes and trees that brought the total height to as high as ten to twelve feet. Some were centuries old, dating from the end of the medieval manorial system and the advent of small, independent farmers who owned their own fields. Hedgerows served as fences, delineating each farmer's field from that of his neighbor. In Normandy there were countless numbers of these little fields, roughly 150 by 100 yards, dominating the entire Cotentin Peninsula and extending eastward another fifty miles. Leading to and around them were dirt paths and roads, often sunk below the level of the surrounding fields due to many decades of use. Somewhat wider roads connected hundreds of villages. Small farmers in France,

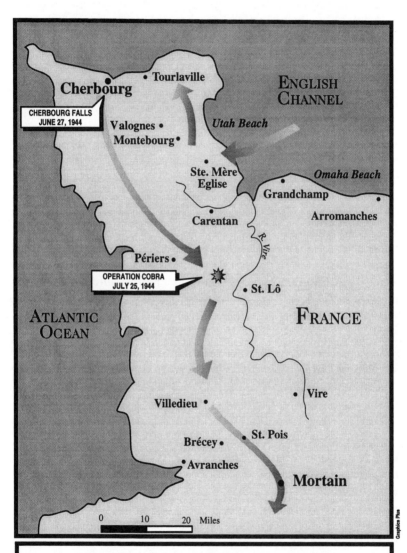

Normandy: June 6, 1944-August 13, 1944

as with most of Europe, lived in these villages, working their fields by day. In almost all villages there was a church, its steeple towering above the surrounding countryside, a perfect place for the enemy to observe Allied movements.

In military terms, everything about the hedgerow country favored the defense, and the Germans used it well. "They disposed their defenses throughout the disorderly maze of copses, woods, and hedgerows, thus making them unprofitable targets for artillery and air." [1]

Not only was Allied superiority in air and artillery minimized, so was the superior numbers in armor. For tanks, each hedgerow often was a death trap, with antitank guns or heavy German tanks easily concealed. When an Allied tank entered a field, it became a choice target at close range. A German *panzerfaust* rocket launcher fired at fifty yards could knock out an Allied tank with one well-placed shot, particularly on the tracks or the engine in the rear. If a projectile hit a tank squarely, Lt. Raiford Blackstone submits, "It could stick to the armor and by some chemical action penetrate and spew molten metal inside." A *panzerfaust* was twice as powerful as the American bazooka; although later in the war the gap was narrowed somewhat. Mines also proved effective against both vehicles and infantry.

On the ground, "Military doctrine generally holds that an offensive superiority of at least three to one is required to defeat a well-placed defender. In Normandy, the Germans found they could accept a ratio of nearly five to one." [2]

Some strategists such as British General Sir Alan Brooke warned in planning the cross-Channel attack (Overlord) that the *bocage* was the wrong place to fight. [3] Yet if Allied top brass had studied the Norman *bocage*, they kept it to themselves and did nothing to prepare units for what they would encounter. As noted earlier, the 70th and the 4th trained together only for the invasion. Dozer tank commander Owen Gavigan has reported that the first hedgerow he came to on D day was a surprise.

Because of the terrain, conventional "set-piece" battles were virtually impossible, with little opportunity for maneuver. Instead, the campaign "turned into a series of vicious, smaller unit actions, a classic confrontation at close quarters with no holds barred." [4] Success or failure in these slugfests depended upon the ability to take and *hold* ground. Taking ground required close cooperation between infantry and tanks as well as all other elements. At nightfall, tanks were almost always withdrawn. It took infantry to occupy ground taken in daylight.

In Normandy independent tank battalions, such as the 70th, that were part of the organization and in training with an integral part of infantry operations worked better than more mechanized and larger armored units, such as armored divisions.

The Dogged Drive for Cherbourg Begins

The drive for Cherbourg began in the vicinity of Ste. Mère Eglise. Most days were long, adding fatigue to the stress tankers faced. Often, they were up at dawn, returning to the bivouac or assembly area after dark, which in June and July meant 2100 or 2200. Clarence Mc-Namee recalls: "Between attacks, we might sit in the tanks and sleep, not because we wanted to, but because we were so tired." Examples of long days can be seen in the B Company journal for June 8 and 9. On the eighth, the tanks did not disengage the enemy until 2200 and returned only as far as the assembly area. By 0430 the next day, they had already left, engaging the enemy at 1000 in support of the 22d Infantry Regiment and returning to the bivouac in the early evening.

The battle was for the town of Azeville, which did not fall until June 11. At night, the men unrolled their bedrolls on the ground, and weather permitting slept next to their tanks, sleeping under the tanks when it rained. Meals were frequently eaten on the run, K rations, or C, or 10 in 1 (one meal for ten men) were carried on the tanks.

Meals were eaten under the tanks if artillery or mortar rounds came in on the bivouac area. Owen Gavigan described one such barrage a few days after D day. "We came under mortar attack and the whole crew got under our tank to eat. Tankers always carried rations in the tank. We ate a lot better than the infantry, which is why they followed us around, I guess. Well, we opened up a box of 10 in 1. These rations had jam, biscuits, candy bars, canned meats, and soup. The meats and soup cans had little tabs you pulled, which instantly heated the contents." This time they started on strawberry jam and hard biscuits. "One mortar shell hit pretty near. It shook some dirt on the bottom of the tank right into the jam, wrecking our supper. There was maybe about two feet of clearance under the tank, so the dirt didn't have far to fall."

Working With the 4th Infantry Division

With rare exceptions from D day until the end of the war, the 70th provided close tank support for the 4th Infantry Division. (On the Eisenhower jacket I wore when I arrived home after the war, a 70th patch is on one upper arm, a 4th Division "ivy leaf" patch on the other.) Matching the battle-experienced 70th with the inexperienced but well-trained 4th proved to be a wise decision. The more they worked together, the better it was.

As Ed Gossler reports, "There was one infantry captain who always asked for our platoon. When we saw him coming it always meant more combat. He knew the platoon, and we knew him." Trust and confidence in one another had been established.

Clarence McNamee, an observant enlisted man, has called the relationship between the 4th and the 70th "a perfect fit. Infantry would say what they wanted, but control was really jointly between our platoon leader and an infantry officer." They agreed that tanks should work alongside infantry—"in conjunction, not out in front, not behind. But every time we got with another outfit, they wanted us out in front by ourselves. This was no good for them or for us, and particularly not for us. You had to have infantry with you to keep *panzerfaust* men and others off you. If not, you could be a sitting duck. A *panzerfaust* man tried to hit you in the rear or the side. They couldn't knock you out head on."

How close infantry should be to tanks was another matter. Infantrymen were ambivalent about having tanks around. They needed them for protection from small-arms fire and for their firepower. Yet infantry also knew that tanks drew artillery and antitank fire. They were noisy, gave off smoke, and were choice targets since they could control the battlefield. Infantrymen were safer when walking separately, so if they rode on the back of a tank, they would dismount when close to the enemy.

Developing an Attack

Planning an attack would usually take place at an infantry head-quarters, normally at the regimental level. The 70th staff officers would be in attendance, as would a company commander. Maps showing checkpoints had overlays that a liaison corporal would use to produce the required number for the platoon leaders.

If changes were necessary, or there was an urgent need for an attack, hand-delivered messages were sent from infantry headquarters. One such (found in the National Archives) will illustrate the procedure. L. Sgt means liaison sergeant, C. G. commanding general.

Message
26 June, '44
To: C. O. 70th Tk. Bn.

Send liaison officer to the 22nd Inf. at once to plan for the use of tanks during their attack today. Report the number of tanks available for use w/the 22nd Inf. and # of tanks you recommend to be used. Report to be sent back with L. Sgt at once.

C. G. 4th Div.

In this message the line of authority is clear. It is from a superior officer to one subordinate to him.

Decisions by Platoon Leaders and Company Commanders

Planning involving the 70th staff would be general in nature, with tactics worked out by company commanders or platoon leaders. That was the pattern, according to Franklin Anderson, an officer who had a great variety of duties. "When in battle as a company commander, I dealt with infantry people in the field, not with higher infantry commanders or our own battalion staff. They wanted to know what was going on, to be sure, but quick decisions were made on the spot by those in the heat of action."

Unfortunately, the casualty rate of both infantry and tank platoon leaders was exceedingly high. The 70th platoon leaders were often in the high-risk position of leading an attack. One tanker who became a truck driver was regularly assigned to bring new officers to the front and to pick up their dead bodies for appropriate delivery. He has been quoted as saying: "I haul 'em up in the daytime and haul 'em back at night." This meant that replacement infantry and tank officers had to develop relationships quickly. Difficulties did arise, particularly as far as the 70th was concerned, with infantry officers who did not know what tanks could and could not do.

According to Carl Rambo, "At times we could be assigned to an infantry battalion and some second lieutenant of infantry tried to tell us what to do. Sometimes that was a problem. I have been told more than once to take our tanks and go down a road until we drew fire. Now, you didn't do that unless in open country. Some did, but they aren't alive. You have to see what is ahead or have infantry spot a gun around the corner, or another tank."

Replacing officers at the vital platoon level where the action took place highlights a problem that existed throughout the war. There was no way to prepare a replacement officer for combat, because although good training was essential, combat was an experience like no other. These young officers at the platoon level had to assume command immediately, responding to orders coming down from higher headquarters.

Leaders of the 70th were acutely aware of the problem and kept a close eye on incoming replacement officers. Raiford Blackstone, himself a replacement officer, and a good one, estimates that the 70th reclassified about 50 percent of incoming officers. "The 70th would brook no failure." Later, after Normandy, a number of proven sergeants were promoted by battlefield commissions.

Knocked Out of Two Tanks Within Minutes

Every battle had unique circumstances requiring different tactics and different methods of operation. Bob Knoebel provides an example of an engagement with a number of exceptions to usual practices. Knoebel was a B Company gunner in platoon leader Kirkpatrick's tank during the battle for Montebourg. "It was late in the day and we had been fighting since early morning. They must have been trying to make a breakthrough because the whole company was racing down a road. I remember hearing Colonel Welborn on the radio saying 'faster, faster'!" Knoebel believes Welborn was talking with Songer, who was in his company command tank #17.

So the entire company was involved, and the battalion commander was directing the flow of battle, with the company commander in the heat of action.

The next thing Knoebel remembers is that an 88mm antitank shell hit their tank. "We were going from one side of the road to the other, and our tank was instantly on fire. In fact, I glanced in back of me and the flames were already up in the air, just that quick." Platoon leader Kirkpatrick's tank was out in front, ahead of infantry and in single file, making it an easy target.

The crew bailed out. Knoebel went headfirst, sliding down the front slope plate. "I and Lieutenant Kirkpatrick landed together right alongside the tank. We looked up and saw a German standing maybe twenty yards away, pointing his rifle at us. He put another round in the chamber so he must have fired either at me or the lieutenant. He motioned for us to put our hands in the air, which we did, and stood up." The German soldier motioned for Knoebel and Kirkpatrick to come to him. "But we didn't. We saw the next tank coming down the road, and without any signal between us, we both started running back toward it. I looked over to our left and saw the 88 antitank gun that got us. There were a bunch of Germans waving for us to come over to them. You know, we had been told that the Germans wanted to take prisoners, and this proved it because they could have shot us anytime." The Americans kept running straight down the road. "When we got so far—and this is the way you can think—we figured that they know we are not coming over to them and they will now shoot. So, we both hit the ditch at precisely the same time, and, as we did, the Germans opened up on us with a machine gun." Neither man was hit. "Like I say, it's amazing how fast you can think and communicate. We started running at the same time and hit the ditch at the same time, without saying a word about what we were going to do. Then, we started running again at the same time and got to the other tank." The lieutenant told the tank commander to get out, as he would assume command. "Kirkpatrick got in this second tank, which started forward and went a very short distance to a crossroad, and just like that got knocked out."

Knoebel continued down the road until he saw a tank from Headquarters Company commanded by Lieutenant Corrado. "He told me to get in his tank, and as I did Colonel Welborn's tank came alongside and the colonel told Lieutenant Corrado to go around the back and try to get the antitank gun." Again they were ahead of the infantry. "We started across this field and got hit with five *panzerfaust* shells. So the second tank I was in got knocked out, and now I'm wounded. We bailed out, and I was in the ditch with Lieutenant Corrado, who was also wounded. The krauts let us lay in the ditch for a while, then just came over to get us. Corrado really helped me. He was hit in the upper part of his body, and I was hit on the bottom. Germans took us to their first aid station, where Lieutenant Kirkpatrick and the driver from his second tank came in."

Both Knoebel and Kirkpatrick had been in two tanks that had been knocked out within minutes. Both had been wounded, and both taken prisoner. "Well, they moved us back a couple of times. Lieutenant Corrado was with me for a while, but when we got back to a bigger aid station or perhaps a field hospital, we got split up. The Germans told me later he died, but I don't know how." [5]

Lieutenant Corrado was the friend whom John Ahearn had trained in a tank on a Sunday in England just prior to the invasion. His death, however, was not due to a lack of training. His tank was hit because he was ahead of infantry support.

Lieutenant Kirkpatrick's actions certainly were commendable. He could easily have ordered the next tank to go to the strong enemy position at the crossroad, but he chose to command the dangerous mission himself. (Were his actions unusual? He is not included in the list of higher awards and decorations.)

The objective must have been important and needed to be taken quickly for Lieutenant Colonel Welborn to be present. Officers at his level usually commanded from a less forward position for better control over the entire unit. With their knowledge of secret information, they should never fall into enemy hands. Welborn was with tanks in action on other occasions as well, another reason he was so admired and trusted by his men.

More Tanks Were Needed

Attaching a single tank battalion to an infantry division was insufficient, because the infantry needed more tanks. And when the tank battalion sustained losses on the line day after day for prolonged periods, as happened in Normandy, companies and platoons were almost always understrength. The ratio of tanks to infantry did not allow companies or platoons to be alternated as frequently on the line and in reserve as was the case with infantry units.

At one time or another all 70th companies worked with all three regiments of the 4th. A Company tended to operate with the 8th Infantry Regiment more than any other, B Company the 12th, and C Company the 22d. D Company was used by all, depending on the situation.

All three medium tank companies were normally involved in different actions, as were the three individual platoons of a given company. Usually, a platoon of five tanks plus a dozer worked with a battalion or a company of infantry. Sometimes even a platoon was split, in which case they likely were supporting a company. Many times there were single tank missions conducted at the request of an infantry officer or noncom who would be with the tank directing it to the target.

Shermans Against German Panthers and Tigers

Although the Germans had limited numbers of tanks available in the American sector, the 70th encountered them constantly. The largest number of German tanks were Mark IVs, later models with additional armor and a more powerful 75mm. However, the tanks that 70th tankers feared most in direct confrontation were Tigers and Panthers.

Often no more than one Tiger or Panther was seen at a time, but even if a 70th unit had numerical superiority, the best course of action was avoidance if possible. These two types were built to fight other tanks, and Shermans were not. Yet in Normandy, Shermans had to do just that when Germans on the defensive let them come to them as their tanks sat behind hedgerows. The huge Tiger was not as maneuverable as the Sherman, but in Normandy it didn't have to be.

As combat veteran Carl Rambo put it, "We wouldn't take on their tanks too much. Most of them got us going in. When you attacked them in the bushes [trees], somebody was waitin' on you. How many times a tank shot at me, I have no idea."

Cecil Nash concluded the power of the main gun was more important than armor thickness. The Tiger and Panther exceeded the Sherman in both.

Nash was the driver in Ben Griffin's tank that he believes was the only 70th tank to duel one on one with a Tiger and win. "We fired and hit him with shot after shot. Then the Tiger moved forward and again we hit him time after time. Finally, after thirty rounds, the Tiger burst into flames. We got it! During all of this, the Tiger had fired three rounds at us; one of them I saw land about fifty feet in front."

The Tiger was on a sunken road and couldn't elevate its gun to get Griffin's tank in his sights. "If he could have, he may have gotten us, though he would have had only one shot because we could have easily backed over the crest of a hill and gotten away fast." A day or two later Griffin had a chance to examine the burnt-out Tiger. "An AP round had hit on the downslope of the gun shield where armor is only about one-half inch thick. It must have been a lucky shot because our 75mm wouldn't penetrate either the front slope plate or the sides of the turret. We were firing HE in case we did penetrate with an AP, which we did. But it took a favorable position and a lucky shot to do it!"

Clarence McNamee tells of coming around a corner in a Norman village. "To our surprise we were face to face with a Tiger less than a block away. He didn't know we were there, so his 88 was slung around at a 70 degree angle. We got off six rounds before he could get his gun around. Our gun was electrically traversed and was faster than that on a Tiger." (The Tiger turret traverse was driven by the gearbox. If the tank was stopped, the turret had to be traversed by hand.) "By the time the Tiger was ready to fire, we were back around the corner on a sunken road. You could go only seven miles an hour in reverse, but we got out of it. We would have felt a whole lot better if we had the 88. It was the finest gun of the war. We had a peashooter 75 with a low charge and were elevating at 200 yards while the Germans were shooting flat trajectory at about 1,000 yards. Our six shots bounced off that Tiger like tennis balls. They didn't worry him one bit."

The Panther was generally considered an overall better tank than the Tiger. It was more maneuverable and less susceptible to breakdowns. The Panther's high-velocity 75mm round could penetrate thicker armor at greater distance than the Tiger's 88, though of course the 88 overall did more damage. The Panther's 75mm high velocity was due to a long barrel with extended rifling and a comparatively large amount of powder in tapered shells with broad bases.

The Workhorse and Reliable Sherman

Although the Sherman was badly overmatched by Tigers and Panthers and had a number of other faults, it was a real workhorse capable of doing most of what it was asked to do.

It was adaptable as in the DD and dozer and was easy to handle, maneuverable, fast, and durable. Ease in handling was essential in armies of conscripts of varying nationalities. Although maneuverability and speed could not be fully utilized in Normandy, they could in open country when tanks and not infantry set the pace.

Durability was a must since tanks had to be shipped across the Atlantic and then reach the front, which thankfully was ever more distant from ports. Once in combat, tankers had to rely on their tank; frequent breakdowns could not be tolerated, with repair difficult at best. The Sherman could travel greater distances and be in service for more hours than any comparable tank of any nation in the war.

Dozer Tanks in the Hedgerows

Cecil Nash believes that dozers have been underrated in value and in Normandy were of critical importance. With one dozer per platoon they enabled 70th tanks to go cross-country more easily than could German tanks.

Fortunately, as noted before, it was discovered as early as D day that dozers could be used to make holes in hedgerows for assault tanks to go through. The assignment of engineers to dozers for the landings proved to be beneficial. Dozer tank commander Owen Gavigan recalls: "On D day my driver was one of the engineers. By the second hedgerow he had figured out that we should approach obliquely rather than head on." He thinks it was about D+3 when the best method was learned. "The driver had to do it. All I could do was to say where to push through. Depending on the size of the hedgerow and the bushes or trees, we elevated the blade and pushed out the top third of the hedgerow, then lowered for the next third and the last third. If we went in from the bottom, the tank could tip up in the rear despite weighing nearly thirty-five tons."

The 70th also used the "Rhino" attachment—pointed metal bars welded on the front of a Sherman to make "teeth" that sliced through hedgerows—but the dozer worked better.

Certainly the dozer was more versatile. Before Owen Gavigan's tank was hit on June 13, "We pushed vehicles off the road and helped clear roads. In some hedgerow fields, we were the only tank. Once when this happened, we used our blade to scrape up enough soil to build an earthen cover for infantry until they could get enough supporting fire to advance. This took some time, but luckily we confronted only small-arms fire."

One misguided use of the dozer resulted in a horrifying experience for Gavigan. "We had just returned to the bivouac after some hard fighting in the hedgerows. The platoon leader ordered me to have my crew mount up and to take my tank down a narrow road. His tank was right behind mine, but no other tank was with us nor was any infantry." In the same area where they had fought a short time before, Gavigan was instructed to turn into a driveway leading to a two-story house. "Germans were holed up in the house, so I was told to fire at it with both HE and AP. We did, but flushed no one out. Then I was ordered to ram the building with the dozer blade. The house was made of stone and we could barely scratch the surface." Gavigan was then told to take his tank to the back of the building. "Around the corner in the back of the house were maybe fifteen or twenty German bicycle troops. They immediately raised their hands to surrender. I stopped the tank and radioed the lieutenant to tell him they were in my path so I couldn't go forward. His tank was now also in back of the house and just yards behind my tank so I couldn't go in reverse either." The Germans were trapped between the house and a low but thickly thatched hedgerow. Gavigan told the platoon leader he could not go forward. "The order was repeated: Go forward! I suppose he was concerned that there might be a *panzerfaust* in the hedgerow or the house and that to have both tanks back out would have been precarious. Anyway, he ordered me forward. I told my driver to inch forward to give the Germans time to get out of the way."

Although Gavigan doesn't know if any Germans were crushed by the tracks of his tank, the thought of it has caused him nightmares for fifty years. Only seven years ago was he able to tell people closest to him of the horrible incident. It has been on his mind and soul far more than his own crippling wound.

On the day Gavigan was severely wounded, they had made four holes in a hedgerow and were halfway through the fifth. "A shell came in and cut the hydraulic line that raised the blade on the dozer. When released, the blade fell of its own weight, so we were at an angle and couldn't move. Then another shell came in and knocked off one track. Now we were really a sitting duck. I was hit when another shell came in. I passed out and woke up on the beach. Fortunately a jeep pulling a trailer that had delivered a load of ammo had happened by."[6]

Every day or two, one of the battalion's nine dozers would be knocked out. Gavigan states: "We made a lot of noise when working on a hedgerow. The Germans also could see the trees or bushes moving, so they had plenty of warning where we were and what we were doing." Clarence McNamee recalls that he was asked to volunteer for dozer work, but he told them he wasn't about to commit suicide. "I could be ordered to go into one, but I would not volunteer. Guys were taking offers of ratings to go into dozers, but they seldom got them." They were dead or wounded before the ratings went through. "On the first or second day, bam, they were hit. The dozer would stick its nose through a hedgerow, and there was an 88 looking right at it. Depending on the situation, the krauts would let tanks go through and shoot them up, or not let the dozer go entirely through but shoot it right in the hole and plug it up."

A Cook's Tour Begins
During the invasion and the tough fighting that followed, kitchen crews and other service personnel were safe in England. They now sailed to rejoin their various companies. All elements made it to company bivouacs on June 16 except the B Company kitchen crew, which

arrived a day late. It hadn't been planned that way. Many elements were on the same LST and landed in France at the same time and in the same place.

In the beginning things went fine as the kitchen truck moved through about three feet of water for perhaps ten yards and up the sandy beach. I felt a surge of excitement as I saw the bewildering activity all around. Ships were scurrying about, pouring men and supplies onto newly won French soil.

Behind the beach the long column of vehicles turned inland onto a narrow temporary road, pointed at the middle of a murky swamp. A sense of foreboding began to press down upon the plucky kitchen crew as the pace slowed to a crawl. If the column didn't move faster, Mohnshine would be driving at dusk, and he was halfblind in broad daylight. He had been assigned to the kitchen truck to prevent harm to anyone important. To the right was a small wooded area. In it was a broken and twisted glider, one wing pointed skyward like a fantastic hat. A coastal fog began to move in, and with dusk descending rapidly the convoy halted more frequently.

The sound of artillery grew distinct. Some damned fool was directing the unprotected kitchen truck toward it, somewhere on the nether side of the swamp. White tape was stretched on bushes and stakes to indicate the edge of the "road" on both sides. "Shit, a lot of good that damned tape is going to do. Mohnshine can't see more than four feet, and that tape is at least five!"

Mohnshine proved them right. The truck lurched ahead, then all six wheels unnaturally moved sideways and slid helplessly into slimy French mud. Mohnshine frantically raced the engine, shifting from low to reverse and back again and again. The wheels churned wildly, digging deeper in the mire until the truck was sloped at a decided angle. Mohnshine turned off the engine and with mess sergeant Baird came back to join the group. "We're stuck," Baird announced in his usual obnoxious way.

Everyone stood, apathetically watching the vehicles of the convoy emerge out of the gloom, chugging inexorably around and past the truck until they were seen or heard no more. A cold, callous wind blew in from the English Channel. In spite of the season, everyone was thoroughly chilled. It was also long past chow time, and hungry cooks were reduced to eating cold K rations like common soldiers. As a pale and unfriendly moon rose, bedrolls (commonly called "fart-sacks") were made ready, and six men tried unsuccessfully to find warmth and comfort on an incline in the crowded truck. Fatigue led to fitful sleep.

It was disturbed around midnight by a crackle of twigs in the bushes beyond the white tape. Six heads popped up as one, each counting silently. "Christ! We are all here, so who in the hell is out there?" In a moment the springs of the truck creaked under someone's shifted weight. It was Mohnshine picking his way over bodies, holding a Thompson submachine gun in his right hand. Mohnshine jumped to the muddy ground and crouched down, the Thompson in position to fire at the unseen enemy. With two steps he was out of sight, though not out of sound. Crash! Mohnshine's feet went out from under him as he slid into a hole filled with water. When he reappeared, wet and muddy, he had a sheepish grin on his face. "Gimme a clip," he muttered hoarsely. He had gone out without ammunition!

Stifled laughter broke the tension as the absurdity of the situation became apparent to all. Mohnshine was patted on the back for his courageous effort, and this time sleep was more restful. The original "crackling" was caused only by the wind.

The next morning a jeep and a truck came to extricate the stricken vehicle. After unhitching the trailer and attaching a tow rope, it pulled our truck onto the road with comparative ease. We arrived at the B Company bivouac near Ste. Mère Eglise around noon. This was a place no rational man would choose to be, yet we all felt good about arriving because this was where we were supposed to be. Soon what had been on everyone's mind would be known— who in the company had been killed or wounded? I, like the rest of the kitchen crew, knew them all.

B Company moved into position to attack near Montebourg the next day. The new bivouac was in a wooded area. After setting up the kitchen tent and moving in the three field stoves, the crew was relaxing with a cup of coffee and enjoying free combat zone cigarettes when an enemy artillery shell whooshed overhead. Being the combat rookie of the crew, I must have shuddered because one of the veterans said, "Don't worry, Jensen, when you hear it, it's long gone.

When you don't, you're already in trouble." Not finding the statement terribly reassuring, I felt a fear-induced necessity to head for the woods and water a bit of French soil. Turning around a large tree, I looked down in horror at a dead German soldier lying where I was about to step. Immediately my eyes locked on his face. How gray his skin was, only slightly lighter than his field uniform. His eyes were open, cold and unmoving, like marbles that boys shoot in a game. Feeling it was indecent to stare, I tried to move away but couldn't.

Gravely, I reported my find to my kitchen crew buddies. One of them casually said, "Yeah, they leave dead Jerries around, but somebody picks up our own dead fast. It's supposed to be good for morale, I guess." Perhaps so, but I have never forgotten my first direct encounter with war. It didn't raise *my* morale.

The Fight for Montebourg

The fight for Montebourg from June 12 through 19 was hard and critical. It was a key location because it lay on the main regional highway to Cherbourg. The Germans had reinforced Montebourg, determined to hold it at all costs. Another fourteen 70th men died and Lt. Francis Songer, commander of B Company, received his second wound in six days, this one requiring evacuation to England. Since Ahearn of C Company was wounded on D day, two of the four line companies lost commanders in six days. It was a time for testing esprit de corps. Rather than wilt, the 70th was proving its worth.

B Company in support of the infantry cut eastward to the coast to reduce enemy resistance at Quinéville. This eliminated the threat of an attack on our flank and reduced German coastal artillery, which had since D day made the unloading of men and supplies at Utah Beach hazardous. For one day B Company worked with an outfit the 70th knew well—all the way back to Fort Bragg and the invasion of French North Africa—the 39th Infantry Regiment, 9th Division.

"By the 19th, after a saturation bombing attack by our air force and a coordinated attack by the ground forces, Montebourg fell—a pile of smoking ruins. The battalion moved through the still-smoking debris into position to continue the attack northeast of Montebourg, through Valognes." [7]

A Valuable Lesson

Lieutenant Herman Finkelstein was now B Company commander, like Songer a courageous soldier and superb leader. I recall being part of a small group of men in his presence on a day German artillery was really coming in. The lieutenant was explaining how good our chances were of not being hit. He paused at the end of a sentence, then calmly said, "And, if you fellows get captured, with names like Jensen, Teglas, Sharpless, or Stimson, nothing will happen to you. If I were to be captured, with a name like Finkelstein, you can imagine what the Germans would do to me." This gentle reminder of what the Nazis were doing to Jews in Europe was needed. The army, officially, did nothing to enlighten soldiers on what later was called the Holocaust.

A Prisoner of War Compound

In the area above Montebourg there was a temporary prisoner of war compound. Set up in an empty field, it was surrounded by barbed wire with sentries posted around the periphery. The division between men from the Wehrmacht and those from the SS was interesting. Though the SS constituted no more than one-quarter of the total, they had ample space in about half of the limited area, whereas the Wehrmacht soldiers were jammed together in the other half. What I saw became more significant to me after the war. It was then thoroughly documented that the Wehrmacht had no love for the SS, reciprocated by the Nazi soldiers. The SS was the military arm of the Nazi Party (called the Waffen SS) and was outside the military traditions of the army. They were the ideologues who were responsible for many mass murders. During the war, especially near the end, the 70th and other units encountered fanatical SS, loyal to the führer and to the Nazi cause.

No Time Out Due to Rain

On June 19, the worst storm in more than forty years hit Normandy. It raged for three days, during which some 800 Allied ships were beached or lost, a far larger number than that due to German naval and air activity during the invasion and since. A Mulberry artificial harbor in the American sector was demolished. (Mulberries consisted in large part of enormous concrete piers constructed in Britain and towed across the Channel. The idea was to allow beaches to function as ports.) The loss of supplies was so great that it interfered seriously with the buildup of Allied strength in Normandy.

The rain and wind made conditions unbearable for the men in the field. The winds made it impossible to erect tents. Artillery continued unabated on both sides. To keep safe and dry, most men slept in or under tanks. Sleeping in a tank, however, meant assuming and retaining an S position in the turret, on a cold steel floor. I tried it but found that tankers were correct. Under the tank was better. The favored position was in the middle of the tank, away from the water that gathered quickly in the trough made by the tank tracks in the sodden earth, and away from the rain blown in by the wind. Sleeping bags shed some water, but the clothing worn and usually slept in did not. It rained day and night on friend and foe alike, democratically soaking everyone, irrespective of rank.

Little cooking was done, but coffee was always on hand. The kitchen did heat canned rations and served meals to those in the bivouac area. Food soon became a watery soup before men could consume it. Rain not only fell directly into messkits but ran down steel helmets and into them as well.

Cherbourg Is Taken After Hard Fighting

Rain or no rain, the fighting was intense as Germans fought hard to hold Cherbourg. Tourlaville fell to the 4th Division and the 70th on June 24. By then the rain had subsided.

A Company was attacking on a line about twelve miles east of Cherbourg. Sergeant Lawrence Oren (KIA July 9, 1944) was in command of the lead tank. "He had advanced rapidly over an open stretch of terrain only to find that the sea lay before him. The tank had hardly halted when a shell burst landed some fifteen feet away. To the amazement of the crew, they found that a German gunboat had taken them under fire. Sergeant Oren fired three rounds at the vessel and moved his tank back under a protected position, dismounted, and directed fire from the tanks at five enemy 'get-away' boats." In the meantime the crew radioed to the battalion CP, and in less than fifteen minutes American bombers took over the attack. "This could well be the only incident in the war where tanks engaged German naval vessels."[8]

At 2300, July 25, the 1st and 3d Platoons of B Company were returning from the outskirts of Cherbourg when company commander Finkelstein's tank was disabled by mechanical failure. "The entire crew evacuated under heavy enemy artillery and sniper fire. At the bivouac we sweated them out but in the early morning they strolled safely back home. The company's tanks were the first in Cherbourg."[9]

Cherbourg fell on June 26, after a good deal of street fighting. Cecil Nash called it "hairy—because any window could have a machine gun or a *panzerfaust* behind it, and we were going along searching, moving slowly."

Large enemy shore installations still held out in the Cherbourg area, shelling B Company tanks on June 27. The highlight of the day was when Sergeants Newell and Fischel captured the commander of an enemy garrison who ordered his troops to surrender. Newell confiscated his automobile and later presented it to First Sergeant Hall.

Cherbourg with its excellent harbor was a prime objective in the planning for Overlord. Taking the city in three weeks was a job well done, given the dogged German resistance in the hedgerows all the way up the Cotentin Peninsula. As Americans approached the outskirts, Hitler had a plane load of Iron Crosses flown in on a special flight. The commander, General Schlieben, distributed them wholesale. On June 22, Hitler ordered Cherbourg troops to "defend the last bunker" and leave the harbor in ruins. "The German people and the whole world is watching."[10] The German defenders obeyed their leader. The port was not in operation for most of the Normandy campaign.

The Importance of Discipline and Experience
The men of the 70th had the discipline to be prepared for battle, down to the last detail. Mechanics made certain that tanks could be depended upon. Crews ensured that spare machine-gun barrels were in place, the main gun was in alignment, ammunition was ready, and all communication systems were reliable.

Unit cohesion came from discipline and experience. Albert Pachella noted, "You never had to look back to see if you were being covered. If it was called for, you always were. 70th men were dependable. They knew what was to be done and they did it."

Carl Rambo had two campaigns under his belt before the invasion and Normandy. He tells of an incident that shows the value of battlefield experience, and of the need for infantry warning of what was ahead. "Five of our tanks were fanned out in support of infantry against a machine-gun nest. We were throwing in a tremendous amount of fire—HE, machine-gun, saturating for the infantry. Yet right in the face of all our blasting came this German machine-gun fire. Bullets started bouncing off my tank that sounded like hail on a tin roof." Rambo realized a ground-mount machine-gun crew couldn't take the kind of fire that had been pouring in, so he radioed the other tanks. "I said that machine-gun fire has got to be coming from a tank, and he is suckering us in. I told them to be careful and not to move. About that time an infantryman ran across the field to me and said there was a German tank coming around behind me. I again called the others on the radio and told them to hold, 'I'm going back and see what's around the corner.'"

Rambo moved his tank under some trees where he could see around the corner. "The German tank was sitting close by, and I was really zeroed in on him. There sat an infantry colonel with a 57 ground mount set up—pulled by a tractor. He said, 'Get that tank back up there, what are you doing?' I said, 'Colonel, one of your men ran up and told me there was a tank around this corner, and I'm waitin' on him right here.' He said, 'You get back up there, and I'll take care of that tank right here.'" Rambo looked at him and his woefully inadequate gun. "'Colonel,' I told him, 'you better get that lil' ol' gun and get back out of the way, cause you're fixin' to get killed. I don't know if I can stop that tank or not, but I'm going to try!' Anyway, I jumped back in the tank and waited a long time, but nothing happened. After a while, we got pulled back, and I never heard any more from that colonel."

Rambo's plan was to fire some smoke and lay an AP at his tracks, then some more smoke. "We couldn't have been more than 100 yards from him. I had a good gunner and could have hit pretty close to where we aimed. Of course even if we immobilized him by hitting the tracks, he could still shoot us up, so the only hope was to keep him from moving and blind him with smoke, then get the hell out of there fast!"

Experienced tankers were well aware of how quickly tanks would draw fire when they started up. This was due not only to the noise, as Carl Rambo asserts, but "when you cranked up a tank, smoke billowed out of it. So when we were sitting out there in the hedgerows waiting for something to happen, waiting for a German attack or one of ours, well if you waited for hours, then cranked up, smoke came out and you were in trouble. So we would let the engines sit there and chug, chug, chug for minutes, or even for three or four hours. Then when we stepped on it there was no smoke to give away our position. But this clogged up all eighteen spark plugs." Sometimes they could barely get back to the bivouac. "You had to have a new set of spark plugs. The company maintenance guys raised hell. They had to put in spark plugs at night, maybe in five tanks. They wouldn't run worth a cuss!"

Young Men in a Man's War

Young men have always filled the front ranks in war. Many military terms are French from the age of Louis XIV. One is infantry—*enfant*, the young. This was certainly true in the 70th. Owen Gavigan commanded a tank at nineteen. Bob Knoebel was nineteen when he was knocked out of two tanks within minutes and spent time as a prisoner of war in a German hospital. He admits, "I joined the army when I was seventeen. I lied and told them I was eighteen. I just wanted to go in the army. Everything in 1943 was about the war—the propaganda, the John Wayne movies. All my friends wanted to be part of it, so I quit high school to join."

Ed Gossler was twenty. "There was very little room in our tanks, and, with all the stress associated with battle, they had to use young people who would do it. As a rule, older people wouldn't." That is except officers, some aged twenty-five years or older.

The Danger, Stress, and Fatigue of Tank Combat

As Gossler reports, part of the terrible mental and physical stress was being cooped up in a small space. "Sometimes we were under fire all day, unable to get out. There were times when we used our steel helmets for everything except to pee in. For that we could use an empty 75mm shell casing."

Frank Ciaravella joined the 70th a week after D day as a replacement. "I reported first to Service Company, which would hold people from line companies who had lost their tanks.

They would be there until tanks became available. During my brief period there, the people who had ridden in tanks in combat told us stories about how the escape hatch at the bottom was useless, how 88s would go in one side and come out the other, how tanks would burn almost like paper."

Ciaravella had been to tank mechanics' school and was sent to the 70th with a tank mechanic's rating. "Having heard those tankers' stories, when I reported to B Company platoon leader Lieutenant Townsend, he asked what I did. I eagerly told him I was a tank mechanic. He said, good, go over to #2 tank. I did and met the crew. Mike Jones, the driver, couldn't remember my name and couldn't pronounce it when he did. Jones had been in Sicily and dubbed me with the name 'Paisan.' From that day I was 'Paisan' and my last name didn't matter. Replacements usually became assistant drivers or loaders (cannoneers) because they are the easiest to learn. I became a loader."

In all tanks, men were subjected to a terrible pounding on their human senses and sensibilities. Ciaravella describes the concentration of actions and the sounds and smells in a medium tank. "The driver and bow gunner/assistant driver sat at their positions on the lower level, driver on the left. Each had a hatch. Both wore earphones to receive commands on the intercom from the tank commander." The driver had to be in constant communication with the tank commander and alert to what was going on. "Earphones did muffle the sound of the tank's powerful engine and of the tracks as they moved along, but only a little as tanks are noisy, even more so inside. There was the staccato of the .30-caliber machine gun when the bow gunner was firing. The shell casings dropped to the steel floor beside his feet on the inside, adding to the noise."

Three men were in the turret. "The tank commander and the gunner were to the right of the 75mm and the main hatch was close to them. There was no hatch for the loader, who was positioned to the left of the big gun. Going cross-country, the loader was susceptible to motion sickness. He couldn't see very much, didn't have a hatch, and was at the top of the tank. It would sway back and forth, up and down. You could feel like you were seasick." The tank commander stood in back of the gunner. "He got commands on the radio from outside—'faster, faster'—and barked commands to the driver. To the gunner he would command, for example, HE—traverse left—up five degrees. The gunner yelled HE to the loader. The loader loaded the HE shell into the tube and, to make certain it was in tight, slammed it home with the palm of his right hand—slam, bang—as the breech-block closed automatically." When the 75mm was fired, there was a tremendous boom. "Then came the clang of the instant recoil, and the empty casing was ejected, making a loud clattering sound as it hit the steel floor. As the next shell was being loaded, the gunner moved his foot from the solenoid button on the floor, which fired the 75mm, to the one that fired the .30-caliber machine gun. This machine gun was fired coaxially with the 75, so aside from its use as a gun, it helped the gunner aim the 75, with every fifth .30-caliber being a tracer bullet."

The .30-caliber rattled away, dumping hot empty shell casings on the steel floor while the loader slammed home the next 75mm. "When the action was hot and heavy, 75mm and .30-caliber shell casings piled up on the floor. These were hot when ejected, so in the summer it became quite hot inside the tank. Then there was smoke from the burned powder, which had a noxious, acrid odor, and when you fired fast this quickly accumulated." There was a small ventilator, but the smoke cleared only when the hatch was opened. "This smoke constantly gave me terrible headaches. While all of these loud noises were hammering on your head, and you could hardly breathe, you were so busy you could not think of anything else, but danger and excitement were always present."

Vulnerability Behind Armor Plating

German high-velocity shells did not bounce off the Sherman like tennis balls. A disadvantage of this tank was that the turret was too high and easy to hit. The three men in the turret were therefore at a higher risk than the driver and bow gunner positioned below. On most models there was only a single hatch in the turret whereas the driver and bow gunner each had one, closer to the ground.

Men in the turret were also at greater risk of being burned since fires reached them first. The rear of a tank, where the engine was located, had the least armor. When a shell hit it, the resulting fire would quickly reach the gasoline tank positioned slightly forward of the engine where the back deck joined the turret. This was the most likely cause of fire, although the gasoline could be hit by a shell penetrating the side armor.

If a shell came through a Sherman on the left front side, it could hit the storage area for the ammunition. All ammunition and gasoline would then explode, and none of the crew would survive. Frank Ciaravella recalls seeing a tank where this had happened. "The force of the explosion was so great that the entire turret was blown askew and tilted, and with the gun that meant something like thirteen tons." (Armor plates were added to reinforce the sides outside the ammunition and gasoline storage areas. These were known as problem areas, but the armor thickness was still insufficient.)

Dangers When Exposed

When hurriedly bailing out of a burning tank, the tankers were exposed to enemy fire. Even if not burning, a tank just knocked out was an easy target. As Clarence McNamee tells it: "I was a good buddy with Don Calderari. He was an Englishman who attended an American university and volunteered for duty in our army. Calderari was an accomplished musician who played an accordion. At night he often played for us in the dark, songs that soldiers knew, songs that were popular." McNamee was in a different tank but was in plain view of what happened. "I saw him jump out when his tank was hit. He ran around behind it, which was the wrong thing to do, because if they hit it once, they sure as hell could hit it again, plus the risk of gasoline exploding and burning." Calderari squatted down behind the tank. "An 88 came in on the tracks and took his head right off his shoulders. It was sickening. While killing became second nature, this was a friend. He had played his accordion for us just the night before. You couldn't dwell on it for long, but it made you sick at the time."

In any wooded area, there were a lot of snipers in trees. It was, therefore, advisable to stay buttoned up (hatches closed). This was not usually done, however, because vision with the naked eye was always better and with wider range than through a periscope. Personal safety was sacrificed for the good of the crew or simply for better execution. Many men were hit by snipers, especially tank commanders such as Pat Curry of B Company, who was extremely lucky. According to Ed Gossler, Curry was standing in the turret when "a sniper's bullet went right through his steel helmet without touching him. He took it home with him and had it on display in his bar in Brooklyn." (I can confirm this, having visited Curry's bar several times in 1954.)

Gossler also tells of another time in Normandy when his platoon stopped what they thought was some distance from the Germans. Sergeant Donald Papke "was standing on the back of his tank, sort of leaning against the turret. A sniper fired and hit him in the side. It didn't look too bad, but the bullet must have hit a vital part. We lifted him off the tank and put him on a jeep with a medic who was going to take him back. He died, but I don't know if it was from the wound. I heard that an artillery shell hit the jeep. But we found out where that sniper was, and I can tell you that he didn't last long. We left him hanging in that tree."

A Respite From War

In Cherbourg, Paul Gaul says, "We had overrun a German headquarters, and Pro [Provaznik], Hammersmith, and I were in the main building. Since I was supposedly an explosives expert, my job was to look for booby-traps, but along with Pro and George I was also looking for goodies—booze, money, gold, whatever. Pro found a box that I had just pissed on. He said this looks like a paybox. I said don't touch the damned thing, it might be booby-trapped. Pro said to hell with it and opened it. The damned thing was full of French currency as I recall." Pro got to send most of it home through army channels. "He was a lucky guy." Provaznik gave $100 to the company fund and was rumored to have promised several people a Nash automobile after the war.

With Cherbourg firmly in American hands on June 27, the 70th enjoyed about a week of well-deserved and much-needed rest. In B Company a good bivouac was set up, and maintenance and reorganization were carried out. Everything was fine except for days of rain. On July 1, mess sergeant Baird took the kitchen truck and Corporal Belgarde to purchase a "beef." They found one for $40, and the French farmer helped kill it and dress it at his farm. They also brought back onions and potatoes.

The next day, after a good breakfast, church services were held at 1045. "For the noon meal we had very delicious fried steak, whole grain corn, new potatoes, green peas, cream gravy, and coffee. We had Colonel Welborn, Majors Davidson and McKericher, and Captain Williams as our guests. Major General Barton also visited the company and spoke to several tank crews about past and future operations. In the evening we enjoyed some of Sergeant Baird's luscious hamburgers."[11]

General Barton was the commander of the 4th Infantry Division. The menu, as recorded in the journal, sounds grand. Most likely it was, since most of the men had not had anything remotely like it for more than a month. After a steady diet of canned beef stew or frankfurters and beans, any fresh meat would have tasted good.

Having been in the immediate surroundings, however, I know of some particulars. The whole grain corn and peas were the plain old canned version. The cream gravy was doubtless some concoction made with canned milk, perhaps added to flour browned in the grease used to fry the meat. The meat was called beef, though cow would be more accurate. Normandy is known for its dairy industry, not for herds of beef cattle, especially not after four years of German occupation. The meat was certainly fresh, having been aged for nearly a half day. What the journal calls steak was as tender as tankers' boots. Providing steak for about 150 men, this French cow must have had a remarkable anatomy. The hamburger was undoubtedly better, but I have forgotten if a meat grinder was part of field kitchen equipment. The meal was memorable enough to be described in detail in the journal so it must have been appreciated, and, after all these men had been through, that was all that mattered.

During this respite, the men had a chance to bathe, wash clothing, get haircuts from the company barber, play a little softball, and even see a movie in the battalion area. In a letter home I noted that the movie was *Crazy Horse,* starring Ole Oleson and Chic Johnson. Six new howitzers arrived for the assault gun platoon in Headquarters Company. Battalion maintenance installed new engines in tanks that needed them.

A Job Well Done

Major General Barton, commander of the 4th Infantry Division, issued a Commendation for Meritorious Service to the 70th and other attached units for the drive to and the capture of Cherbourg. The general wrote: "The price of our victory has been felt by many and the supreme *sacrifice* has been made by many of our comrades. The success of our mission has been heralded the world over and has brought chaos and annihilation to a part of the German Army. Our record speaks for itself and we are proud of it."

Given the difficulty of fighting in the hedgerows and the skill and determination of the Germans in using them to their advantage, taking Cherbourg in three weeks was indeed a job well done. Among the units involved on the ground, the 4th and the 70th had borne their share of the burden. They had been in the line constantly, going from hedgerow to hedgerow.

The 4th and the 70th had developed respect for each other, in a relationship that would serve them both well for the remainder of the Normandy campaign and to the end of the war.

8
Breakthrough and Victory in Normandy

There was total destruction. Germans were dead, without a mark on them, killed by concussion.

—Cecil Nash
C Company tanker

The Slugging Match for Control of the St. Lô–Périers Road

During the drive for Cherbourg, several American divisions cut across the base of the Cotentin Peninsula and sealed it off to the Germans. After the fall of Cherbourg, the forces that captured it moved south to that line. The 4th and the 70th now occupied positions only twenty miles from those held a month before.

As General Bradley has written: "The necessity for a very concentrated punch became apparent as soon as we established our beachhead because the German resistance was very tough. There were days when we wouldn't move, other days when, if we gained a thousand yards, we were doing pretty well . . ." Bradley candidly admitted underestimating the difficulties of fighting in hedgerow country in the planning phase. "Remember we were fighting in the so-called *bocage* country, and you can't appreciate that country until you have seen it. I hadn't visualized it at all, as much as I had studied photographs and maps before I went in."[1]

Bradley's concentrated punch was to be a great "carpet bombing" to be followed by a massive thrust by tanks and infantry through a hole created in the German defensive lines. Bradley chose an area of heavy German concentration to the west of St. Lô. A prominent road from St. Lô to Périers ran straight for a number of miles. He believed this would enable bombing crews flying parallel to it to sight the target area, thus reducing the risk of bombing our own troops.

Clearing Germans from the area west and north of the St. Lô–Périers road, therefore, became a necessity for the plan to work. This

180

meant more fighting in the *bocage* and hedgerow country, but that could not be avoided. "I said I didn't want to stand up and slug, but I also said that at one time we are going to have to do it, and this is it," Bradley told his aide, Chester Hansen. "While in this *bocage*, canalized by swamps, we can do nothing else. No room for maneuver, we've got to stand here and slug it out with him. Afterwards we can make the breakthrough and run deep."[2]

As usual, the 70th was in the midst of this slugging match. On July 6, VII Corps commander General Collins put the 4th into the line. It was by now considered one of the best infantry divisions and "all too literally 'blooded,' since it had suffered 5,400 casualties since D day . . ."[3]

This front had been static during the fight for Cherbourg, giving the enemy ample time to prepare. "This country will be well remembered for the advance made yard by yard, through the worst terrain possible. Part of the countryside was swampy and flooded. The hedgerows had been reinforced; gun positions were well fortified with communication trenches. The few roads through the swamps had been well covered by artillery and antitank weapons zeroed in on all approaches."[4]

A Two Day Battle for One Hedgerow

On July 6, one month after D day, the fighting was ferocious. Frank Ciaravella was the loader in Sgt. Carl Rambo's tank during a battle for a hedgerow field. Both men have given independent accounts of the action. Tanks from a unit other than the 70th had been badly mauled the day before. Ciaravella's account:

> We were given an assignment to go out to a hedgerow where the Germans had a strong defensive position. Our whole platoon and the dozer tank were involved. When we were approaching the area, we passed tanks from some other outfit that were still smoldering. That didn't bode well for our mission. We got to the hedgerow, and the dozer tank punched one hole through, backed out, and punched another hole through near the corner of the hedgerow. Our five tanks entered the field, and as soon as we were all in the Germans opened up and all

hell broke loose. Over the radio we heard 'so and so got hit, back up, go right, go left, there's the 88, another tank got hit.' I looked through my periscope and saw a tank that had been hit, and somebody leaped from the top hatch. I mean he put his hands on the two open halves of the hatch and literally sprang forward and reached the ground. There were reports on the radio that our men were being machine-gunned as they tried to escape from their tanks. Our tank got hit. We were firing. There was a lot of noise, a lot of fumes. The radio kept squawking. Sergeant Rambo, our tank commander, was ordering move here, move there. People were excited. Four of our tanks were burning. We got hit twice on the turret but the shells bounced off. Then we were hit on the slope plate, where the side and the slope plate meet, and the shell went through, gouging out a small hole. We carried about eighty-five rounds of 75mm ammo, and we kept firing while in motion. We fired every round of HE we had and somehow managed to get out of the field without more damage. Only our tank and one more got back . . . It was about midday in early July, so it was hot as hell in that tank, in more ways than one. We still used that tank, but it was a conversation piece with that hole in it. The hole was about three-quarters of an inch wide, and we could see daylight through it.

Rambo's account:

We had a new platoon leader and I guess he had been told the German location. The dozer went up and punched a hole in the hedgerow and he backed out. We were firing like crazy, and this officer gave us the order to go. I said hold up a minute until we get some more ammo up ready to fire, but he said no, we have to go—follow me. He stuck his nose through that hole and the Germans were zeroed in on him. Hit, the whole crew bailed out. The Germans were just across the field in the next hedgerow, so close we could see them. So we started playing our machine-gun fire right over that hedgerow, shooting just over their heads, keeping them down, and throwing in HEs too.

Shortly, the platoon sergeant said he was going in to pick up that crew that had bailed out, and I said, 'Don't do it, they're going to get you. Wait, and we'll work around to the right.' Well, he went anyway, and right away the Germans put one through his gas tank and the tank was ablaze. That crew bailed out. Now we had ten men on the ground. It was time for us to move.

I told my driver to move right or left, I don't remember, and an 88 came in. Mine was one of those old sharp square-cornered tanks, and the 88 shell hit and cut the corner off. From the assistant driver's side you could see daylight. If we had been inches away, it would have come right in and out through the back. I kept backing off, but didn't go over this hedgerow. A crew member of the second tank hit ran to me, and the platoon sergeant got into my tank, and they got him in the fleshy part of the leg as he was getting in. #4 was already knocked out and #5 was near me. We decided we had to get out of there.

The dozer tank turned to go out, and when he did they caught him on the right side and fire came out the top. The tank commander tried to get out but dropped back in. No one else got out. The only way for us to get out was behind them, and we went and they didn't get us. We broke out into this field, and my tank and #5 had our turrets turned backward and were firing, dodging all the time. We got back of another hedgerow. The maddest I ever got during the war was now. The 2d Platoon was sitting in behind us. I switched from the 1st Platoon channel to the 2d Platoon channel on my radio and called the platoon leader and told him we needed some help. He said, 'What's the matter, is the mud too deep up there?' I said no, it will dry real quick, we have four tanks on fire and I've been hit. I hung up, and that was the last time I spoke to him. He was later killed. Everybody in the 2d Platoon must have heard what I said.

Later in the afternoon they took the rest of the company and had dive bombers plaster the area. We didn't learn until then that a German Tiger tank was dug in. Nothing but his turret was sticking out, so there was no way for us to get him. We hadn't gone in properly prepared, properly instructed. They didn't tell us what happened the day before. It was a strong point, and they knew exactly where to go, because the lieutenant had the dozer punch a hole through the hedgerow straight in front of the German position. Jerry was on a little higher ground and could see over the hedgerow. But they could have softened that place with artillery or planes. They went back in the afternoon and got it with no trouble.

Rambo was known as a warrior, a courageous leader. "But, I believed in running when you had to, live today and fight tomorrow, rather than stay and lose every tank." Four out of six tanks were knocked out in about ten minutes. Five men were dead, another five wounded.

All in a Tanker's Lifetime

Private Carl Hallstrom was the loader in a B Company tank waiting for the order to attack. "We were all set; conversation lagged. Somebody would ask for a light or for the time, but most of us were silent." It was a hot day, and with the tension Hallstrom was sweating profusely. "Over the radio, a voice said, 'Move out.' The gunner asked one more time if the gun was in working order. I gave him a nod and we were on our way. I was looking out of my periscope when I saw #1 tank, which was in the lead, burst into flames." Five men bailed out and jumped for the cover of a ditch just below a hedgerow. "Our own infantry was about four hedgerows behind. Jerry was shooting at the five men from over the top of the hedgerow, so we sprayed the hedge with our machine gun. The tank commander spoke to the driver over the intercom. 'Pull up behind #1 so that those five men can use us for cover.' 'If we go up there, we'll get knocked off,' said the driver. 'Let's go anyway,' said the commander. We made it OK and the five men crowded behind our tank."

As they slowly backed off, Hallstrom through his periscope saw a bright flash spurt from the hedge. "It seemed like a ball of fire was hurtling toward us. Then the flames were roaring all about my body, licking at my face. I pushed the hatch open and dove out. I reached the ground ten feet below in one leap and started running. I believe my legs were in motion before I reached the ground." The Germans were only thirty yards away and firing at them. "I don't know how they missed us. Bullets were kicking up dust all around us. Once I glanced back over my shoulder at the tank we had left. Flames were leaping from the hatches, and the ammunition inside was exploding with tracers from the machine-gun ammunition shooting out of the hatches."

Hallstrom ran for about 125 yards right in front of the German line. Panting with fear and physical exertion, he dove into a swamp. "As I lay there, dirt from machine-gun bullets sifted down from the mound above my head and went down my neck. I had reached a place of comparative safety. The only escape was through an old drainpipe to my rear. It was small but I made it through, only to find three more just beyond. I got through two of them and into a ditch that was between me and the last pipe." He started to enter it but a dead GI blocked his passage. "Then I noticed I was not alone with my troubles. A couple of feet away lay a GI wounded in his leg. I helped him up, and together we made it across the field. While passing a burning tank, I said to him, 'Don't worry fella, God is with us.' He nodded, and together we stumbled across an open space. We reached a ditch safely, and I left him there with some doughboys. Soon I was rejoined by the rest of my crew. Together we made it back to the assembly area."[5]

The Slugging Match Continues

Casualties were so heavy that replacements arrived in unusually large numbers. B Company alone received two officers and twenty-three enlisted men on July 10—the equivalent of five tank crews. A few days before, Sergeants Whitaker and Rambo had taken over as platoon leaders due to the shortage of officers. When new officers arrived, both became platoon sergeants.[6]

The new men were put into tanks and went immediately into action. One poor soul was Rambo's bow gunner during the hedgerow battle described previously. Rambo recalls: "All of our guns were firing except the bow gun, so the driver hollered over to him to fire. The new kid said, 'I can't.' The driver said, 'Why not?' and the kid

said, 'I don't want to give our position away.' The driver told him it
was alright, the Germans know we are here. We had a lot of fun about
that later." Another replacement in B Company, according to the
journal, lasted only two days before being "relieved and hospitalized
from combat exhaustion."

Of the nine dozer tanks in the medium line companies, at least
one was now being knocked out almost daily. With fewer access roads
to hedgerow fields, dozers were being used in just about every action.
B Company lost two in five days before Private Harmon found a dove
wounded in a wing. He took it aboard his dozer as a good luck charm.
His tank was not hit, and B Company losses were cut in half—with
two dozers lost in the next ten days and no casualties.

Movement was again from hedgerow to hedgerow, with mines in
most fields. Paul Gaul, driving B Company commander Finkelstein
in his jeep, entered a hedgerow field. "We got to the middle, and
tank #13 came through alright, but tank #14 hit a mine right where
we and #13 had just passed. Finkelstein said, 'Gaul, There are mines
in here, check it out.' I did, and sure enough, we were right in the
middle of a minefield." Provaznik, Hammersmith, and Gaul pulled
out teller mines with telephone wire until they worked their way
back out. "I told a medic over near the entrance to be careful, there
are a lot of mines in here. The place is full of them. They had a little aid station there. About a half hour later, boom! The damn guy
had driven his jeep in there, hit a mine, and was killed along with
two other guys."

German night air raids were more frequent in this sector. The German command would have felt the pressure and hit back in any way
they could. The air was pretty much denied them by day, but at night
quick raids were possible. Potential bivouacs were limited in number, and enemy observers could guess the location of where noisy
tanks started in the morning and returned at night. They came un-
comfortably close, both with artillery and antipersonnel bombs
dropped from planes flying at low altitude.

Everyone was kept in a jittery state, alert from dark until daylight,
as the B Company journal notes. "Mess Sergeant Baird removed a
dud antipersonnel bomb from near the kitchen truck by deft handling of two small twigs." An unforgettable sound was that of Ger-

man bombers as they passed overhead, particularly in the silence of night. It was a pulsating rhythm as contrasted to the steady hum of our bombers, which were not flying at low altitude over front lines. Bombers passing over at night were most likely German. If the sound was "va-rum, va-rum," it was definite.

Operation Cobra: The St. Lô Bombing

After more than two weeks of this bloody fighting, the 4th and the 70th were close to St. Lô. In this area I had an opportunity to witness American airpower in action. Positioned on a hill, I could see P-47s peel off from a formation, dive on the target, pull up, turn, and dive again. One after another they bombed and strafed German concentrations. They timed their runs perfectly, crisscrossing as one group flew away to be replaced by another. It was exhilarating to watch and gave me satisfaction and reassurance. Although not saying so, this is what I meant when I wrote home: "I know Fritzie is as scared as I am, and I'll bet he's hunting a hole."

That demonstration was nothing compared to the famous bombing along the St. Lô–Périers road. Code-named Cobra, and commonly called the St. Lô bombing, this was the greatest tactical use of bombers until that time. In the American alignment, the 4th was moved to the center of the line.[7] Again, the 70th was called upon for an important mission—to help exploit the hole the bombing was to make in the German lines.

A day or two before the scheduled bombing, B Company moved into a bivouac area on the slope of a hill, facing the target area about four to five miles away. Shelter halves were set up, forming a small tent for two men. Shortly before dark, it seems that a two-and-a-half-ton truck loaded with five-gallon cans of gasoline arrived at a nearby tank bivouac. The driver reputedly announced his arrival by shouting out "Gas!" Within minutes the order reached B Company to put on gas masks. Stimson—my tentmate—and I dutifully obeyed. In a tent a few yards away was heard a gasping for air and a cry in panic: "Christ, they got me!" The suffocating man's tentmate muttered in a tone of disgust: "My god, you forgot to push the button in!" That apparently did the trick, for nothing more was heard from that tent. Shells designed to test the air for the presence of gas were shot up,

with negative results. Rumor had it that the gas scare spread to German lines, though as usual no one could verify it.

The bombing had been scheduled for July 24. Operations were
canceled due to inclement weather, but not before some 1,600
bombers took off. Though an attempt was made to recall them, they
continued on and dropped 700 tons of bombs on the target area. It
was a disaster. Twenty-five U.S. soldiers were killed and another 131
wounded as bombs fell on our own lines.

Bomb runs were perpendicular to the road, not parallel as Bradley
believed had been agreed upon. The air chiefs said no, that was never
the agreement. To fly parallel to the target would decrease its depth,
and therefore decrease time over the target. Bradley decided that further postponement could not be tolerated and ordered the bombing for the next day, July 25. [8]

From a position in the B Company bivouac, my mates and I had
a good view of the spectacular show taking place overhead. The
schedule was: twenty minutes 350 fighter-bombers; one hour 1,800
heavy bombers; twenty minutes 350 fighter-bombers (at this point,
assault units were to move to their departure lines); forty-five minutes 396 medium bombers (1,000 artillery guns also fired). On and
on the planes came, dropping their bombs from low altitude, then
turning quickly and disappearing over the horizon. They came in
what seemed an endless line stretching back farther than the eye
could see. It was an amazing display of might, and I was happy they
were not B-2s. (Be too damned bad if they aren't ours!)

Cecil Nash was now a tank commander in C Company. During
the bombing, "We had large pink-colored panels on the back deck
of our tanks. These were for identification so plane crews would
know where to bomb, and especially where not to. What a sight it
was to see the sky filled with our planes for what must have been two
or three hours. Soon after the bombing stopped we jumped off in
attack and went a mile or two with very little opposition." They then
had to use the dozer tank to make a spot to cross a swampy area.
"Our platoon went across this makeshift road and came to a large
field of maybe forty or fifty acres. The dozer tank broke through the
hedgerow and spotted about four German tanks in the next field.
Our platoon leader immediately called for a rapid 'strategic withdrawal,' but somehow I didn't get the message right away on my ra-

dio. I was on the right flank protecting the rest of the platoon and was intently watching that road, not knowing the rest of the platoon had withdrawn."

Nash radioed the leader that he was still in place. He was told to come back, and fast! "We made a tight U-turn to go back the way we came. On the narrow road the dozer had made, my driver, Al Orner, was a little too much to the right and we went into the quagmire, very much stuck. We had to evacuate and start back on foot. The platoon leader told me that they were going to stay in place and for me to take my crew back to the bivouac area." This was about a four mile walk. "Later in the evening we went back up to retrieve our tank. After cleaning up some spilled gasoline we were soon on our way."

"Planes Came Over Like a Conveyor Belt"

The view from the other side has been superbly expressed by Gen. Fritz Bayerlein of the German Panzer Lehr Division.

It was hell . . . The planes kept coming overhead like a conveyor belt, and the bomb carpets came down, now ahead, now on the right, now on the left . . . The fields were burning and smoldering. The bomb carpets unrolled in great rectangles . . . My front lines looked like a landscape on the moon, and at least 70 percent of my personnel were out of action—dead, wounded, crazed, or numbed. All of my frontline tanks were knocked out. Late in the afternoon, the American ground forces began filtering in. I had organized my last reserves to meet them—not over fifteen tanks, most of them from repair shops. The roads were practically impassable . . . We could do nothing but retreat. Marshal von Kluge sent word that the line along the St. Lô–Périers road must be held at all costs. It was already broken. But a new SS tank battalion was coming in with sixty tanks to drive to the Vire River and cut off the Americans. They arrived—five tanks, not sixty. [9]

Bombs Fell on Our Own Lines

What General Bayerlein did not see, nor did those safe in 70th bivouacs, was the now well-publicized horrendous mistake made in the second bombing. It was far worse than the first. Thousands of bombs fell on our own lines. The margin for error was obviously too small, and it was smaller still when bombardiers aimed at smoke from previous drops that was blown into our own lines by the wind.

Although they were in the target area, the 8th Infantry Regiment and A Company of the 70th suffered comparatively few casualties. One A Company tank was hit, but "Lieutenant Bauer dismounted from his tank, ran to the blazing tank, extricated the men, and led his platoon into an attack upon enemy positions. One of the tanks broke through a hedgerow into the field beyond. There it paused long enough for an infantryman to run alongside and ask for a shovel attached to the deck of the tank." The tank, in breaking through the hedgerow, had buried an infantryman in a ditch on the far side. "The tank crew hooked the tank to a tree that had been pushed over and pulled it out of the way. They then hastened to dig out the 'dough' who was uninjured except that he was pretty badly shaken up. As the 'doughboy' started back for an aid station, an enemy artillery shell exploded nearby, killing the man who had just a moment before cheated death."[10]

The Breakthrough

As 70th tankers moved into enemy lines, they saw what to General Bayerlein resembled a landscape of the moon. The ground was churned up, trees felled, dead birds and livestock everywhere about. Cecil Nash commanded one of the tanks. "We were going through where the bombs had fallen. There was total destruction. Germans were dead, without a mark on them, killed from concussion. A lot were completely immobilized and easily taken prisoner."

Despite the havoc, German resistance was at first stout in the 70th's sector. The shock experienced by frontline troops being hit by "friendly fire" and the fact that the ground, roads, and paths were full of craters produced little immediate gain. At the end of the day, 70th positions were consolidated only about 2,000 yards south of the St. Lô–Périers road. Movement was better the next day. The B Company journal records that fighting continued around the St. Lô–Périers road, but that the new bivouac was four miles distant— not four hedgerows.

By July 27, three days after the bombing, the Germans were in retreat. B Company could not move intact because the roads were so crowded by advancing American units. German vehicles, including tanks, were now more than ever forced to stay on roadways, easy targets for fighter-bombers. Pushing destroyed vehicles off roads became the main function for dozer tanks.

Although the tactical use of bombers in Cobra has been criticized by some since the war, prior to the bombing there was a stalemate in the hedgerows and considerable movement after. There seems no reason not to take General Bayerlein at his word. All the Germans could do was retreat. As General Bradley has written, "Slowly it came to me that Cobra had not failed. It had succeeded; we had broken through."[11]

General Patton's Third Army was now able to thrust into Brittany. There was movement along the entire American line. The next big action for the 70th was on August 1 at Villedieu, about twenty-five air miles from St. Lô. Because Villedieu was a major road center and a key to the sector, German resistance stiffened. All three medium tank companies were committed, each supporting an infantry regiment. D Company had one platoon of its light tanks attached to each medium tank company, acting as screening forces to cover the flanks. B Company and infantry pushed into Villedieu late in the afternoon. During the day's action, A Company lost two tanks, with two men killed and several injured.

On August 5 at St. Pois on the Sée River, the three medium companies again encountered considerable opposition. "In these days of close fighting, the enemy was getting desperate and was using tanks, mortars, and heavy artillery to throw back our advance. Four enemy tanks were destroyed—one by Capt. Gordon Brodie, commanding officer of A Company, who fired . . . as the German gunner was bringing his gun into position to fire a round into Brodie's tank. The captain and his crew had just broken into a field and surprised the enemy tank crew."[12]

Although the fighting could still be described as close, its character had changed appreciably. Now the Germans were defending road and rail centers. Gains were measured in miles, not hedgerow by hedgerow.

For its actions after the bombing, the 70th was awarded a Commendation for Meritorious Service by General Barton, commander of the 4th. It read in part: "The 70th Tank Battalion advanced rapidly in conjunction with the 8th Infantry and delivered devastating and accurate fire on enemy positions, destroying numerous strong points and aiding greatly in the advance of friendly ground troops."[13]

A Respite—Short for B Company

Only pockets of resistance remained in the sector after St. Pois was taken, and there was every indication that the battalion was going to enjoy a well-deserved rest. B Company purchased another cow (or "beef," as the journal insists). This time Lieutenant De Villiers served as interpreter for mess sergeant Baird. Whether due to the lieutenant's rank or the weight of the cow or local economic conditions, this one cost $35 compared to the $40 paid five weeks earlier. (Purchasing a cow must have meant scouring the countryside to find a farmer with a live one for sale. In areas where a battle had been fought, livestock could not be cared for and were killed by shellfire in substantial numbers. No one who was near the front can forget seeing these dead animals, their bloated bodies emitting a ghastly stench, their legs often pointed skyward, as though making a futile accusation.)

A USO show was presented in the battalion area on August 6, which most of the men attended. From the B Company journal, "Despite the long walk, many attended both shows at 1600 and 1900." In addition to the show, a Red Cross doughnut clubmobile visited the area. Seeing American women close-up was a great thrill. Seeing any woman close-up would have been. Most men hadn't seen one since leaving England two months before.

I wrote several letters to my family at this time, filled with thoughts of home. I stressed the fact that every advance got me closer to Berlin and to St. Paul. A letter dated August 1, 1944, reflects my optimism after the breakthrough. "I suppose you people back home are as thrilled with the news as we are over here! We believe that this war is going into the last lap. I sure hope it's true."

A Sudden Return to Action

It wasn't true. B Company tankers were attending classes in the battalion area until 1000, August 7, when they were called back to the company bivouac and alerted to move. As Carl Rambo describes the events: "We hadn't been paid for weeks. This one day we were paid and had the day off. We cleaned guns, got fed, and all of a sudden they yelled—'Go!—Throw everything together and move out!' They had done this before, I think to see what we would do. Everybody was relaxing, some sleeping. We had tied our tents to our tanks, so we cut the ropes and jumped into our tanks. I think we were on the road in three or four minutes." At 1800 the 1st Platoon left, followed by the 2d and 3d Platoons at 1900. The rest of B Company, led by company commander Lt. Francis Songer, back after being hospitalized in England, left at 1940. According to the journal, it was a "most tedious" road march of eighteen miles, arriving in the vicinity of Le Pointon at 0400.

The Battle of Mortain

The reason for the hurry-up call and the unusual road march was that the Germans were mounting a counterattack to cut off Patton's Third Army in the Mortain-Avranches sector. All their available forces were summoned for this last desperate attempt to hold back the Allied advance. Much depended on American forces holding at Mortain, because Bradley kept his divisions moving south. One reason he could do so, according to historian Russell Weigley, "was the availability of the excellent General Barton and his 4th Division."[14] Also, it can be assumed, the availability of the excellent Lieutenant Colonel Welborn and his 70th Tank Battalion, for we were part and parcel of the successes of the 4th.

In the battle of Mortain, the 30th Division bore the brunt of the burden, with the 22d Infantry Regiment and B Company of the 70th protecting a flank. The other two 70th medium tank companies were in reserve, and D Company maintained roadblocks.

The German attack began on the night of August 6–7. On the ninth, the three platoons of B Company arrived in the area. Carl Rambo recalls that one platoon would drop off, then another. "The 1st Platoon kept going . . . [until] we could see the [artillery] fire, which was solid. When we pulled up, the fire was everywhere in an arc in front of us. There was a lot of infantry around, and they were really getting shot up. We pulled into a field, put our tanks in a ring, and got them camouflaged. All we could do was sit there and let them shell us for several days. They blew that earth all to pieces, but never did scratch a one of us."

This was where Lieutenant Blackstone came up to take over the platoon. Rambo thought him "a pitiful sight, steel helmet jammed down over his head, bags slung over him, and I thought, good God, they have sent me another one. But he ended up doing a good job."

Paul Gaul's assessment of Blackstone was the same. "As the old man's jeep driver, one of my duties was to pick up replacement officers, and I picked up a lot of them, believe me. One stands out in my memory. I went to some 'rep'l depot' and there was a skinny little guy, looked no wider than a toothpick, his helmet looking bigger than his head. This was Lieutenant Blackstone. He turned out to be a hell of a good officer."

Blackstone remembers: "On first reaching battalion headquarters, I met Colonel Welborn, Captain Brodie, and Lieutenant Songer. After a while, Songer, who commanded B Company, turned to Brodie, CO of A Company, and said, 'You take the tall skinny one, and I'll take the little guy.' The tall one was Lieutenant Bidwell, and I was five foot five and a half inches and weighed 130 pounds. Lieutenant Songer and his jeep driver, Paul Gaul, delivered me to the 1st Platoon, which I was to lead. It was temporarily under the command of Sgt. Carl Rambo. As we left the B Company bivouac, we passed over two roads that were strewn with burned-out German and American tanks, trucks, half-tracks, and jeeps . . . Mainly they were German, evidence of a terrific battle that had just taken place. In the end, we could not go all the way to the 1st Platoon by jeep, so Lieutenant Songer and I walked across fields and hedgerows to where it was located."

German artillery was coming in, so most men were inside their tanks. "The crews had been under so much stress that they were tired, anxious, and, to some extent, jittery. Sometimes they would not or could not leave their tanks, even to answer calls of nature, instead choosing to use empty shell casings, at least for urinating."

Welcome to the war, Lieutenant. Mortain was probably not the best place to start, or to undertake the daunting task of assuming command of a battle-hardened platoon. Fortunately, Blackstone asserts, "I met a very fine platoon sergeant in Carl Rambo. He had been in North Africa and Sicily, had landed on D day, and had been all the way through Normandy. We also had in the twenty-three other men in the 1st Platoon very capable drivers, assistant drivers, loaders, and gunners. All were fine, capable men. There was no outward sign that I was being put to the test by these men, but I'm sure the test was there anyway."

Blackstone was clean shaven, fresh faced, small in stature, and an officer new to the company. "While no one challenged me, and while no one offered any opposition to anything I wanted done, I'm sure all platoon members watched me very carefully to see how I would perform. Fortunately, I didn't have to do anything of an outstanding nature, so in due time I am reasonably sure they accepted me as a platoon leader."

Blackstone is an unassuming man. Keys to his undoubted success were his ability to lead while simultaneously learning from experienced men in his platoon.

"That Tank Was Hit, But Man, It Just Drove Off!"

B Company was on the line for three days and three nights, never returning to the bivouac area. The platoons were so widely scattered that no contact was possible between them. The 22d Regiment and B Company were protecting the flank of the 30th Infantry Division and plugging holes in the line. Also, none of the three platoons moved very much, nor were they in a coordinated attack.

The 1st Platoon, according to Carl Rambo, sat there for two days, then got orders to move, but only one or two fields up. "We were bearing across and finally I picked up a German tank sitting sideways to me. I told my gunner to 'hit him low.' We threw about three rounds into the belly, and smoke rolled out of that tank. I said, 'We got him,' and there was so much to shoot at, so much going on, that we turned away, firing as fast as we could. Our gun got so hot that when we threw a shell in, it jammed. The gunner and the loader tried to jerk it back out but pulled the casing off the shell." Powder poured down into the turret. "So all we could fire were the .30 calibers, which we did. Finally we went back, and Sergeant Hampton asked me why we quit shooting that tank. I said, hell, we had him on fire. He said, man, that thing just drove off!"

Tanks carried a ramrod with a cone on the end of it to loosen jammed shells. Rambo says it was used as soon as possible. "Our gunner got out of the tank and put the ramrod in the barrel and gently tapped the jammed projectile until it loosened. The cone end didn't touch the detonator, so we could tap the casing and get it out. We cleaned the barrel and were ready to go. We had fired AP, then threw in HEs, so it was an HE that jammed."

Infantry Were Lying All Over the Place

Clarence Jay was the driver of tank #5 at Mortain. "My tank commander told me to pull through a hedgerow so we could pick up the fellows who had abandoned their tank that had just been hit. I asked him, 'Do you know what you're doing?' He told me 'Do what I tell you to do.' So we pulled through the hedgerow, and we took one right through the gas tank." The tank exploded in flames. Jay got out and behind the hedgerow intent on going back to where they started into the field. "There were infantry lying all over the place. This one infantry guy was hurting pretty bad, so I took him under my arm and dragged him back with me. I knew there was a big sluice under a road that if we could crawl through we would be in pretty good shape. But when we got back to the sluice, it was full of people. So he took out his wallet and showed me a picture of his wife and kids. He said, 'If I don't make it, see that they get this.' I told him, 'Don't worry, you'll make it. We'll go over the top of the road.'" They did, and Jay managed to get the man to the medics. "I gave him back his wallet and left. I don't know whether he made it or not."

Allied Air Supremacy

The next morning Jay was back as driver in another tank. "We pulled into a double hedgerow, and as soon as we did I saw a German Tiger and I quickly backed off. I heard some airplanes coming. They were two of ours, and they came right down and knocked out that Tiger and another one that I hadn't seen. Knocked those tanks right outta there."

Allied air supremacy was, of course, vital to success in Normandy and throughout the remainder of the war. Air-ground coordination improved with experience. Carl Rambo remembers that in Normandy identification panels were tied to the back deck of tanks. A waterproof material had a color on one side, a different color on the other, each to be displayed according to the color code of the day. Also, a bright light with about three colors, which was plugged into the tank electrical system, flashed to aircraft overhead, again showing the color code of the day.

A Humbling Experience

As usual, little information reached the company bivouac, although we knew the fighting was hard. Never before had all three platoons been on the line for so long without at least one returning. On the third day, the cooks were told that one platoon was going to pull back a distance from the line and would be in position to receive chow. I was told it was my turn to go up, so with containers full of hot food and coffee, I jumped into a jeep with my good buddy, Paul Gaul.

Stories of the ferocious battle being waged were reinforced by every burned-out vehicle I saw, and there were many. The road was narrow and unsurfaced, but good. The fact that we saw not one single live person and encountered no moving vehicles added to the feeling of being alone in an unprotected jeep. Gaul and I had known each other since our days in Iceland. Our usual banter was missing as a sense of foreboding and danger enveloped us both. The terrain was hilly, with more trees than seen earlier. Although there were fewer hedgerows, they were still prominent features of the landscape. All of this was seen through eyes that darted from side to side, then straight ahead. Gaul had been on this road before, so his hunched position and intensity in trying to reach the destination as fast as he could added immeasurably to my already high level of anxiety.

The tanks were parked in a field just off the road with little apparent attempt at concealment. That was encouraging. Perhaps the front was not just beyond the next hillock. Some of the men were seated on the ground; others leaned against their tanks. A few had flopped down, using their steel helmet as a pillow. All had a few days' beard and looked exhausted. After a laconic greeting, each held out his mess kit to be filled. No one bitched about the food. No comment was made about what they had been through, nor did I ask—that for a noncombatant would have been a violation. Although all were buddies and friends, the confraternity of men who fought and died together was special and always respected.

They appreciated the food, whatever it was, bolted it, and asked for seconds. The sound of artillery occasionally broke the silence, but no one paid any heed. It was part of the atmosphere. Each of the twenty-five men gave his mess kit a cursory cleaning with water from the two five-gallon cans brought for that purpose. Most men lit cigarettes, and with a second cup of coffee sat on the ground, back against the tracks and bogie wheels of tanks. Within a half hour, Gaul and I reloaded the jeep for the return trip.

The way back seemed shorter. However insignificant our mission, it was accomplished. Some sustenance was provided to brave men, not only in the food, but by the fact that it had been brought. For a few moments, these tankers had contact with people outside their tight circle of death and destruction. There was again little conversation between Gaul and me, although on the return this was not due so much to fear and apprehension. At least for me, it was because I was meditating on what I had seen. The eyes and drawn faces revealed what the tankers had not said. Soon, they would return to the same hell, while I was retreating to relative safety. It was a humbling experience.

Bivouacs Are Bombed

Ironically, as happened on this one occasion, Gaul and I were safer away from the bivouac than we would have been if we had been in it. The Luftwaffe ventured forth on a rare daylight raid, and bombs fell on the B Company bivouac area. T-5 Kovach was killed by shrapnel while seeking shelter under the maintenance half-track. First Sergeant Hall was nearly covered by dirt in his foxhole and had to be extricated by T-4 Kneebone.[15] After the end of the bombing, the bivouac moved.

German air activity increased during the battle of Mortain. Mostly at night, "the enemy sent over groups of planes to drop antipersonnel bombs. C Company took a beating from these planes, losing most of its kitchen force. B Company and A Company were also hit at this time and suffered casualties. The bombs were mean, about the size of a 40mm mortar shell, and were seemingly shoveled out by the bushel . . . over the target area." [16]

Dealing With Fear

Individuals deal with fear and stress differently. Most men in the 70th managed to climb back into tanks day after day through campaign after campaign. Carl Rambo, a warrior by any definition, admitted to fear. "I have been so scared my mouth was dry and I couldn't wet my lips. But you stand it." Even he probably could not explain how "you stand it."

Combat veterans such as Rambo were aware of their role. "I usually had younger men with me, so I felt I had to get in and go. I have had some [men] break down in the bivouac or assembly point, but not ever when we were in action."

Some tankers did break down, more than were realized. Ed Gossler tells of a tank driver who took off. "We never saw him again. Our assistant driver had to take over. The 4th Infantry wanted us to go to help the Signal Corps, who were laying wire and getting sniper fire. One of the Signal guys came into our tank as the bow gunner. Well, we went up and shot the snipers out of the trees, and, as usual, our tank drew artillery fire. When we got back to the assembly area, the Signal Corps guy jumped out of the tank and said, 'I'll never get in one of them damned things again.'"

According to Clarence McNamee, the driver deserted right after the St. Lô bombing. "He was caught and brought back to our army area and court-martialled, found guilty, and sent to a federal pen in the States. Some time after, he wrote someone that he was out of prison and dishonorably discharged before we ever got home. Some of the guys were just boiling mad when they heard the story." But, Mc-Namee adds, fear is a powerful emotion, and you had every reason to be in fear for your life. "No one could have been more scared than Gene Mayberry, but no one made more attacks than he did. He made every one of them in mortal fear, probably peed in his pants every time, but he never failed to make an attack. Mayberry was one of the best gunners we had, wet pants or dry. I had great respect for him."

McNamee was put into a tank in Normandy and saw what one crew was doing. "About the time the platoon was ready to go into attack, the driver reported that his tank wouldn't fire up, that his magneto was bad. The tank commander was a coconspirator and reported to the platoon leader that they couldn't go." McNamee couldn't and wouldn't do this, so he was able to transfer to a different tank. "Every tank operated as part of a team, and when they pulled this it was like the platoon going in with one finger short. But I want to emphasize that this was an exceptional incident. The esprit de corps of the 70th was so high, I know of no other case of a crew that cut and run and left their buddies."

Very few shirked their duties with gambits like this. Others did not fit and were transferred, officers and men alike, but most made it. Many wounded and hospitalized could have had easy duty elsewhere when recuperated, yet they volunteered to come back to their units. One was Francis Songer; another was Bob Knoebel. To him the only relevant question was, "Whom do you trust?" Knowing who can be trusted was the essence of comradeship in war.

Seeking Help From a Higher Power

There were few atheists in the front ranks, as men sought help from a higher power. Frank Ciaravella, who ended the war as a tank commander, made as many attacks as anyone in the battalion after joining about a week after D day. "I never was hit and was praying all the time."

At a church service the night before an expected big battle, I was one who accepted the chaplain's offer to write a brief letter to the folks at home. The letter, dated June 25, 1944, was sent via V mail.

Dear Mrs. Jensen,

Yesterday I saw your son at the church services we held in France. I am his chaplain and can tell you he is getting along fine. We have church at odd times and in peculiar places. For instance, our service last night was in a gully and the men sat on the sides. We often have services through the week for those who cannot attend on Sunday.

If you wish to write to me, do so at the above address. I shall be happy to hear from you.

Blessings on all of you at home.

Sincerely,
C. A. Arrington, Chaplain

On the Consumption of Alcohol

"Dutch Courage," alcohol to take off the edges of fear, was of course used in the 70th. Excessive drinking, however, did not occur. 70th tankers chose the time to drink with some discretion. Ed Gossler describes one such time. "Those in charge seemed to be debating whether or not to make an attack. We went up in the morning and were pulled back. In the afternoon the whole 2d Platoon went up again and waited. Finally the word came that there would be no attack. We waited and waited some more for orders to return to the bivouac. A few of us from my tank crew decided to investigate some nearby buildings." They found gallons of Calvados. "It must have been 180 proof and was in big jugs. We were busy drinking the stuff and pouring it into smaller bottles when all of sudden we heard our tanks start up and drive off. We had enough to drink by that time, but not enough to deaden our senses to the trouble we were in. The only thing to do was to start walking down the road we came in on. We knew that was away from the front, but we didn't have the foggiest notion of the location of our bivouac."

Luckily, a 4th Division jeep came by and took them back. "When we got to the company, our tank commander had already turned us in as absent. We had to report to company commander Songer. He said he would like to court-martial us but had no replacements. He also knew that money meant nothing, so a fine would be useless. All he could do was confine us to our tank—not the area, the tank! Of course we most likely went out the next morning. We almost always did. So the whole thing was forgotten."

Officers did not have to rely exclusively on unaged Calvados, which was all that was left after years of German occupation. Lieutenant Raiford Blackstone remembers his arrival in B Company. "When we reached the bivouac, First Sergeant Hall waved at a place in the field where I was to pitch my tent. A half hour later he came back and said, 'Give me $11.85.' I wasn't about to argue with the first sergeant, so I gave it to him. He then placed a burlap bag on the ground, saying this was the company officer's rations." Blackstone hadn't a clue what this was all about. "I looked in the bag and counted six bottles of Scotch whiskey and three bottles of gin. I later learned of an arrangement with the British government whereby every American officer bought a bottle of Scotch and a half bottle of gin per month at very low prices, which $1.31 per bottle was, even at that time."

Most drinking was done in bivouac areas. The 70th was too well disciplined to allow it to interfere with operations. Moreover, tank crews relied on one another. It would have been inconceivable that anyone would endanger his buddies by being incapacitated in action or that a crew would countenance having such a man on board.

The End of the Normandy Campaign

Four B Company men were wounded on August 10, and the next day another four when tank #11 was hit by antitank fire. All three platoons remained in place until returning to the company bivouac at 1030 on August 13. The terrible three-day fight in the battle of Mortain, for the tankers involved, was some of the hardest combat of the war.

The battalion stayed in reserve for a few days as Allied armies encircled the enemy. On August 16, only fifteen miles separated American forces at Argentan from the British and Canadians at Falaise. This was the famous Falaise Gap, through which thousands of Germans escaped eastward. The gap was sealed on August 19. In the Falaise Pocket alone, some 10,000 German soldiers died and an estimated 50,000 were taken prisoner. It was a devastating defeat for the enemy.

Mortain was the last battle in Normandy for the 70th. The unit had participated in the campaign from the beginning until victory was assured. The cost had been high. Ninety-four men were killed, and many more were wounded. On August 15, Lieutenant Colonel Welborn announced that the 70th had been awarded a Presidential Unit Citation for actions on D day and in enlarging the beachhead. I wrote home: "Our battalion received a Presidential Citation for gallantry in action against the enemy. We all got blue ribbons framed in gold. It is worn on the right side to make it stand out more. We are one of five outfits to receive the citation in the United States Army. I am justly proud."

B Company celebrated on August 15, as did all the companies. Another cow was purchased and served as "steak for all." A Red Cross clubmobile again dispensed coffee and doughnuts. Booze mysteriously appeared, and, according to the journal, officers and men alike "partied into the wee hours of the morning."

Headlines for Patton and the Third Army

Headlines and news stories eagerly told of the exploits of Gen. George Patton and the Third Army. I recall that in B Company these stories received something of a mixed response. To be sure, the Third was cheered on. What they were doing was certainly the stuff of headlines, and every mile gained was a mile closer to home. On the other hand, from the invasion and on for the next two months, our tankers battled in country decidedly unsuited for tank warfare. All this time, Patton and his armored divisions remained in Britain. Now, when the country was open, news stories made it appear that Patton was doing in days what masses of Allied forces couldn't do in two months. It seemed unfair, as we felt that our tankers were like unsung heroes of a football line who made long gaining offensive plays possible.

The long gainer executed by the Third Army that most directly affected the 70th was from Le Mans to Argentan. Without it, the encirclement of Germans in the Falaise Pocket would not have been complete. Other elements of Patton's army raced east and south, taking Chartres and Orléans, and these drives, too, would have much to do with 70th operations.

Biding Time

The B Company journal notes a road march of fifty-four miles on August 17. Although the direction was the same as that of the retreating Germans, there was no enemy activity along the route or in the new area. For about a week all companies remained in the same bivouacs. As was by now standard procedure in the 70th, no time was wasted. Tanks were cleaned and repaired, gunnery practice was held, and all personnel kept fit and alert with close-order drill and calisthenics.

Gunnery practice made good sense—good gunnery was the lifeblood of the 70th. Further, new men were arriving constantly with consequent reshuffling of tank crews. They needed the training together. Close-order drill and calisthenics were another matter, and combat veterans looked upon them as being "chickenshit."

A Long Road March

On August 23 orders came for the troops to move out. At 1900 the road march started. The last time one began at that hour, Mortain was the destination. This was different, however, with complete companies in convoys. The route was different, too. B Company, for example, passed through town after town, and in each the populace greeted us as liberators. These towns seemed relatively unscathed, unlike those in Normandy, which were devastated. We had seen few French people in Normandy. Bivouacs were seldom in a town, and towns were generally deserted or the people hidden.

In one town I saw the scars inflicted by war and occupation by a hated enemy. As the column moved down the main street, it turned left to avoid the center. At this juncture, an angry mob was chasing and screaming contemptuously at a young woman, barely clothed, her head shaved close to the scalp. I learned that this was the way women who had "slept" with the hated Boche were treated. The column moved on, with this scene of abject hatred seared into my memory.

Darkness fell, and in the morning road signs pointed toward Paris. That did not mean the B Company kitchen truck was going there. As usual, if anyone knew the destination, he was not sharing the information with lowly cooks peering out the back of their truck as it sped along. Still, everyone agreed that something important must be happening. Why else start out in a hurry at 1900 and travel all night?

The author as a private in 1942.

Colonel John C. Melborn, 70th Commander, March, 1942–August 1944.

70th Tank Battalion on parade in Baltimore, Memorial Day, 1942.
(U.S. Army)

Temporary quarters of the 70th in 1942 at Caserne Bideaux, Tlemcen, Algeria.

Blade of dozer tank provides a comfortable seat.

German "Little Goliath" remote controlled explosive device. Note amphibious carrier in rear. (U.S. Navy)

70th dozer tank in Normandy hedgerow country. (U.S. Army)

Evidence of the accuracy of German gunnery as 88mm shells penetrated a 70th Sherman tank.

German Mark V "Panther" tank.

Citizens of Paris greet
their liberators at Hotel
de Ville. (U.S. Army)

Parisians run from small-arm's fire in Paris Square. The barricades were likely put in place by Germans. (U.S. Army)

Photo taken from 70th vehicle passing in front of Notre Dame on liberation day.

A 70th Sherman tank, with 4th division infantrymen on board, passes through the Siegfied line. Note added armor plating on the tank over ammunition and gasoline storage areas. *(History of the 70th Tank Battalion)*

Confident 70th crewman pose beside their Sherman tank.

DD tank ready for launching with floatation screen fully raised and propellers engaged.

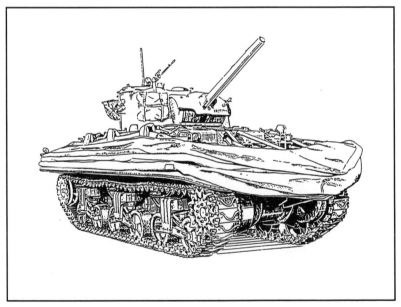

DD tank ready for battle with flotation screen lowered. Propellers at rear (not shown) disengaged.

9
The Glorious Liberation of Paris

I could not have been treated any better if I were a prince or a king.

—Raiford Blackstone,
B and C Company platoon leader

One old woman said, with tears in her eyes, "My stomach is empty, but my heart is full of happiness."

—Clarence Kleinhuizen
B Company tank driver

Excitement mounted in the back of the B Company kitchen truck when we passed the road sign "PARIS 50 KM," and even more when we reached the 30 Km sign. Someone said, "That's only eighteen miles! No wonder we left in the evening and traveled all night. We really are going into Paris!" The road march covered 156 miles, and many battalion tanks broke down. By noon the B Company column was moving through the suburbs, and throngs of people packed both sides of the streets. T-4 George Sharpless, always a jolly fellow, was becoming more jolly street by street as wine, flowers, and fruit were passed up by ecstatic citizens. The flowers and the fruit he passed back to others. Not for long. There was enough wine for all.

It was wonderful and had happened so suddenly, so spontaneously! People came out of nowhere, laughing, crying, eager to touch any available outstretched hand of anyone wearing an American uniform.

Around midafternoon, the column halted at Villejuif awaiting orders. As vehicles stayed in place, people emerged from a pharmacy with eyewash and cotton, and went from tank to tank tenderly washing dirt from the eyes of tankers. What a magnificent gesture!

Orders were not to enter Paris. The French 2d Armored Division was to be given the honor of being the first to enter their capital.

(French cadres trained by the 70th more than a year before in Tlemcen, Algeria, formed a basic core of the French 2d Armored Division. Along with supporting French infantry in Tunisia, the liberation of Normandy, and now of Paris, men of the 70th could well have said, "Lafayette, we are here again, and again.")

B Company spent the night in Villejuif, one or two kilometers from Paris city limits. Villejuif translates into "town of the Jews." Probably no one at the time, however, thought much about liberating a place with that name, nor was much time given to the fact that Paris was the first occupied Allied capital to be freed from German rule. Given the scene on the streets of Villejuif that night, pondering symbolisms were far from anyone's mind. GIs and citizens toasted one another with an endless supply of wine. "Vive la France!" "Vive les Américains!" American flags were waved side by side with the Tricolor. "La Marseillaise" was sung dozens of times. Every citizen had dressed for the occasion, especially the women. "Vive les Femmes!" For more than two months it had been death and destruction, fear and anxiety, grime and dirt. Suddenly everyone was a hero, tanker and cook alike.

I spotted an absolutely lovely young woman in a yellow dress with blue polka dots. Instantly I was in love with Jacqueline Bortnikoff, daughter of Russian Jewish émigrés living in Villejuif. Jacqueline spoke some English, and to a small-town lad from Minnesota everything she said, everything about her, was charming and beautiful.[1]

That night in Villejuif, I saw another young woman, dressed in a white blouse, crawl under a tank. When she emerged the next morning, her hair was disheveled and her blouse an off-white, with two prominently smudged areas. The smile on her face showed pleasure at having done her bit to welcome American liberators.

D Company Enters Paris

D and B Companies were attached to the 12th Infantry Regiment, which had a major role assisting in the capture of Paris. Early on the morning of August 25, Capt. Herman Finkelstein, D Company commander, was at regimental headquarters waiting for orders. Major General Barton of the 4th Division strode in demanding to know the disposition of the 12th's three battalions and 70th tanks, and what opposition they were encountering. Colonel Luckett, the regimental commander, gave his report, adding that the 3d Battalion had "just been swallowed up. They have disappeared without a trace; not even a runner has come back."

To this General Barton roared, "What the hell has happened, Luckett? You can't lose a battalion like that. You know damned well they are in town having a good time. I want to eat dinner in Paris tonight, and I want to know what has happened to that battalion, so get busy."[2]

Finkelstein returned to D Company and ordered the entire column, including kitchen and supply, to move to the city line. There a horde of newsmen and photographers rushed past them into Paris. Thinking this was a sure sign that everything was safe and wanting to get into the city himself, Finkelstein sent a reconnaissance party into Paris by jeep. As the party drove down the Avenue d'Orléans, thousands of people encircled them, the first Americans they had seen. The jubilation continued as they slowly made their way to the Palais du Luxembourg. There, a French 2d Armored tank was firing at the Palais, where some Germans had established a defensive position. In a short time the firing ceased. The party returned to report to Captain Finkelstein, who moved all of D Company into the heart of Paris.[3]

An A Company View

Both A and B Companies dispute the D Company claim to have had the first battalion tanks in the center of Paris. They probably never saw each other. Different routes into the center were used, and, once there, the companies were sited in different areas.

Lieutenant Franklin Anderson had a rather unique experience. As A Company executive officer, his job was to locate the company tanks that had moved into Paris. As his jeep, driven by Emory Drescher, reached the outskirts of the city, French 2d Armored tanks were lined up for two blocks. "People were swarming around them, and they couldn't get into Paris. Maybe others of their units got in, but these didn't."

They moved around and got back on the street going into the city. "It was early in the morning, and things were quiet. I told Drescher not to drive too fast, as we thought A Company tanks and the 4th Infantry were ahead of us. Pretty soon an FFI [Free French of the Interior, a resistance group] panel truck raced by, and then more FFI in their Renaults and Citroëns." Down the street a couple of shots were fired. "We kept going and got to a big open spot, and I saw an arch. I thought it was the Arc de Triomphe. (To this day I think it was, though I don't know for certain.) We drove to it, and I saw people carrying their morning baguettes. In my limited French, I asked them if they had seen any Americans. English? French? They hadn't, and told us we were the first Allied soldiers here!" Finally their tanks and 4th Division infantrymen were located. "They had been moving toward the Hôtel de Ville [Paris city hall]. I and Drescher had been alone in a different area. We could have been in trouble if Germans had been around, which fortunately they were not."

A Company moved to a bivouac in the Bois de Boulogne, where there had been fighting. Yet it didn't take long for jubilant Parisians to celebrate with the company, as Franklin Anderson recalls. "But it was nothing compared to the scene on the streets during the actual liberation."

D Company in the Center of Paris

D Company had the best location of all, the middle of Paris, where its light tanks were ideal for scooting around city streets, setting up roadblocks. German armor had been withdrawn along with most other units, so only delaying actions took place within the city.

Jack Lovell was a tank commander in D Company. "We had some fire the first night when Germans or German sympathizers tried to knock some of us off. But they didn't come out of the buildings and we kept away from the location of the fire."

A day would begin early in the morning when eager members of the FFI "drove up with a roar in a requisitioned automobile and demanded a few gallons of gasoline so they could annihilate the Boche. Later . . . the crowd would thicken until about noon—about chow time—there wasn't room to lay a mess kit in the whole area. However, the company for the most part was happy and the sight of some hardened soldier of the line sharing his mess with a dainty mademoiselle dressed in her best was enough to compensate for any discomfort." Several members of the FFI were detailed to aid in maintaining order among the civilians in the bivouac area. They were of great assistance, "saving the kitchen crew from being fleeced by a get-rich-quick gal who was starting up a small black market in bum liquor." [4]

The most important assignment occurred on the day of the big parade down the Champs Elysées. General de Gaulle, establishing his claim as the head of the French government, led the parade. He first went to the Hôtel de Ville to receive political legitimacy, then to Notre Dame for religious legitimacy. While at the cathedral an attempt was made on his life. The provost marshal of the 4th, acting as provost of Paris, came to D Company and asked for a platoon to patrol areas where sporadic firing was taking place. A provisional platoon was quickly formed by SSgt. Ray T. Hart. After showing their force for a few hours, and finding nothing, the platoon returned. [5] On August 28, D Company reluctantly left their vacant lot in the city center and moved to the Bois de Vincennes.

B Company Moves Into Paris

B Company tanks prepared to move in to guard bridges over the Seine. To my best recollection, this was around 1000 on August 25. I played a major role in the preparation. Tanks of the 1st Platoon were to leave first. I was in a jeep, tossing up K rations to tank crews. All engines had already started. Paul Gaul was driving the jeep and, if his usual proclivity prevailed, was eyeing a mademoiselle. Whatever the cause, he raced the engine and suddenly let out the clutch with a jerk. The jeep lurched forward. I went backward and was instantly rendered hors de combat on the main street of Villejuif. The French audience gasped at the sight of a fallen hero, and several came to render aid and comfort. I looked around to see if Jacqueline was rushing to my side. She wasn't. Brushed off, with a brave smile and a nonchalant wave, I resumed my duties. The tanks departed on their mission as scheduled.

Lieutenant Raiford Blackstone, who led the 1st Platoon, recalls entering Paris on a broad boulevard and passing the bombed-out remains of the Renault auto factory. Instructions from the infantry

battalion commander were to turn right upon reaching the River
Seine, and position tanks to guard four bridges. "In moving to the
center, we saw no French soldiers, no French tanks or other vehicles. This was right in the middle of the day on August 25. Unfortunately, there were so many civilians gathered around us that I mis-
judged when we reached the Seine and were actually on a bridge
before I realized my mistake." He led his tanks to the correct position. "We were now on the correct street, and I proceeded to set up
a tank guard on each of four bridges. I positioned my command
tank more or less in the middle, near the Pont d'Austerlitz. This I
remember, because my tank was at #1, Quay d'Austerlitz."

People were around the 1st Platoon tanks all afternoon and well
into the evening. "They seemed unconcerned about the possibility
of German action or overtrusted the usual mixture of information
and rumor that abounds at times like these. Nearby was a bakery that
supplied us with the best baked goods they had to offer. I engaged
in long conversations with a seventeen- or eighteen-year-old French
man by the name of Claude Manet and his girlfriend, Jacqueline
Beaulieu." Residents in an adjacent building tried to persuade them
to come inside to spend the night. "But since we knew there were
still Germans in parts of Paris, and fighting was still going on, we
elected to stay with our tanks, sleeping under them on the streets."

Several bridges away, the tank crew of one of Blackstone's platoon
took a slightly different approach. Ed Gossler was the gunner. "Our
tank was guarding a bridge, but to tell the truth, the Germans could
have strolled across and nobody would have known they were coming. We were parked next to an apartment building. Before long
French people came out with cognac and champagne. Hell, we all left
the tank, including our tank commander, Dewey Kendall, and went
up into an apartment." The party went on for quite a while, but luckily nothing happened. "When the lieutenant arrived at the tank the
next morning, our tank commander was asleep on the back deck."

A few hours after the 1st Platoon left Villejuif, the rest of B Company entered Paris. Our welcome must have rivaled the return of
any triumphant Roman legion. Thousands upon tens of thousands
of cheering people lined every foot of the route. Cameras clicked

away, recording on film the historic occasion. It was like the day before, multiplied hundreds of times. Flowers and crepe paper festooned every vehicle. Everyone in the back of the kitchen truck again enjoyed the libations of liberation. Everyone for the moment except Sharpless, who suffered from yesterday's excesses. Soon, however, he proved his stamina and began once more to bow and wave to an admiring multitude. "Vive les Américains" was called out time and again. Many tanks had nicknames stenciled on the side, so it was "vive" this, and "vive" that. The kitchen truck had "Prestone" stenciled on the radiator indicating the presence of antifreeze. Sure enough, an exuberant spectator honored the crew with "Vive Prestone."

The column passed by the west front of Notre Dame, the only building everyone recognized. From there, the route was down Rue de Rivoli to the Place de la Bastille, a name that also rang a bell. Proceeding down a broad boulevard, the company stopped in the Bois de Vincennes, where a bivouac was set up. By the time the column arrived, B Company was far more ready for love than for war. First Sergeant Hall, entirely cognizant of this state of military unreadiness, commanded in carefully measured cadence: "Alright, goddamnit, tear off the goddamn crepe paper. The goddamn circus is over."

Indeed it was. It was because the first sergeant said it was. Hall was a regular army soldier, and army regulations do not permit flowers and crepe paper on vehicles. The offensive colors were duly removed. All vehicles returned to their military state of olive drabness.

Beyond the first sergeant's control were the French, who milled freely about the company area, examining "les Américains" at extremely close quarters, treating us almost as objects of worshipful admiration. As Raiford Blackstone relates, "We could hardly eat, shave, change clothes, or do anything of a personal nature. We finally tied ropes to stakes and trees to delineate our area, and the crowd did respect it." At one point, Blackstone was trying to wash his hands and face when a middle-aged woman approached him. She persuaded Blackstone to go with her. They went some four or five blocks to an upper-middle-class house. "She took me up to the second floor and showed me the bathroom. There she said in English that if I wished to take a bath, I could. She retreated, and I did take a bath, the first tub bath since leaving the States. After I bathed, changed underclothes, and dressed, I thanked her and returned to the company. I have no idea why this woman selected me, and it has always escaped me how she was able to persuade me to go, because I was very bashful and always stuck to the army unit and to business."

Paul Gaul, on the other hand, was anything but shy and tended toward a rather loose interpretation of any army regulation he at any given time chose to follow. Four times he achieved the exalted rank of private first class. Four times the army failed to view his antics in a spirit of fun and tore that single stripe from his arm.

In Vincennes Forest, I pitched my first pup tent in Europe. In it I had an array of goodies—Calvados, kartoffel schnapps, cognac. We hadn't been there long when I decided to take a whore's bath and shave. I heated some water in my steel helmet and put it on the ground next to a tree where I had hung my mirror. I was standing in my shorts, humming a tune, when I glanced in the mirror and saw a whole circle of people watching me—women, kids, men. Well, I finished shaving, then took some Aqua Velva in my hands, patted my face, and went around the circle to let them smell my hands. "Ooh, ah, *bon, bon,*" they said. I dressed and started talking with some of the people. Bottles of wine and brandy quickly appeared, and some people sat down to share it with me. One was a very good-looking young woman who was there with her son, about four, and really cute. She had come to the Bois on her bicycle, which quite soon I tossed in the back seat of the jeep and took her and her son home. She lived in an apartment way up on maybe the fourteenth or fifteenth floor. I spent the night with her, and it was a very good thing that I did. That was the night Jerry bombed the area, and I was there to protect them, brave American soldier that I was. Though I know I shouldn't say more, I will say that she taught me a lot about love!

In the German bombing raid, bombs did fall in the bivouac area. Blackstone was away from his tank when the raid began, but he made his way back to his tank through some huge sewer pipes lying above the ground. "Obviously, a steel tank is the safest place, so I made a dash for it and got underneath, though by the time I did, the raid was about over. As the kitchen always did when in an area for a day or two, they had dug a hole in the ground for a garbage sump. When the bombing started, some of the cooks jumped in it. Bomb fragments took off limbs and branches of trees, which fell on top of the cooks in the sump. To my knowledge, none of them were hurt."

Blackstone is correct in that no one in the sump was hurt, but they were not all cooks. Clarence McNamee, a tanker, was among them. "I was with some FFI, young kids my age. They took some of us to their house nearby and pulled liquor out from under a staircase they had papered over. We drank their good champagne, though frankly at the time I didn't know if it was good or bad since I had never had it before. I started back around 2300 and about the time I arrived in the company area, 'Bed-check Charlie' flew over and dropped bombs. The bombs were 'walking-in' so I dove into the nearest trench, which turned out to be the kitchen sump. Five guys jumped in on top of me. You talk about nasty! Drunk and nasty we were!"

I also missed the bombing. At dusk, four or five buddies and I were walking down a residential street near the Bois de Vincennes looking for a bar. We happened upon a small group of FFI standing alongside their Citroën auto. These "Freedom Fighters" exuberantly told of their exploits against the Boche during the last two or three days. They demonstrated how a machine gun had been mounted on top of their Citroën, and how two men positioned themselves on the rear bumper and leaned forward to support themselves as one man fired the gun and the other handled the ammunition belt.

After the demonstration, we were invited to join a wild liberation party already well under way. An electric atmosphere supercharged a small apartment, overflowing with excited and animated young Parisian men and women all talking at once. The din drowned out all exterior noise, including the sound of exploding bombs a short distance away in the B Company bivouac area. To be sure, I grasped little of what was being said, or rather shouted, yet, I understood enough to get a picture of how various resistance groups and the Paris police had all but liberated the city before Allied troops

entered. Embellishments could be assumed, but that did not matter. It was an absolutely glorious, wonderful occasion.

Close to midnight we were escorted back to our bivouac, a good
thing, for otherwise we would surely have been hopelessly lost. My
mind was so hazy that I became aware of my location only when I
walked into the volleyball net erected near the kitchen truck. This
shocked me into the reality that I was to immediately replace Stimson on guard duty. Luckily, Stimson was standing next to a tree in
my path and was willing to lend me his carbine. Properly relieved,
Stimson vanished. Improperly, I leaned against the tree, slid down,
and was asleep before arriving in a sitting position. Two hours later,
Teglas awakened and relieved me. As far as I was concerned, the term
relief was never more exactly used. Sleeping on guard duty in a combat zone was a capital offense. Thanks to Teglas, no one was the wiser.
Fine fellow that he was, Teglas never mentioned the incident again.
I never forgot and never repeated my negligence.

B Company Remains in the Bois de Vincennes

B Company headquarters stayed in the same bivouac in the Bois
de Vincennes for four days, assigned to the 12th Infantry Regiment,
which had primary responsibility for Paris. Regimental headquarters
was also located in the vast confines of the Bois.

Among the most poignant of memories for me was the sight of
young Parisian women bicycling along a street through the Bois.
Their full calf-length skirts bellowed out in the breeze, and it was obvious from their perky smiles that they were well aware of the attention they commanded. What a magnificent expression of liberation!
Well groomed and coifed, these "mariannes," perhaps for the first
time ever, were behaving in public as women and feeling good about
it. Liberated in every sense of the word, their lives in freedom had a
fresh beginning.

One afternoon, some young people sitting on the grass near our
bivouac asked a few friends and me to join them. We hastily accepted,
particularly since several were attractive women. Again, the ambience
was cordial, and language differences led to much good-humored
laughter. The conversation was the kind of relaxed chitchat young

people enjoy. Everyone had several splendid hours showing each other photographs and having pictures taken of us together. One of the young ladies gave me a photograph of her in a swimsuit. On the reverse side was written: "Remember of Eva, *le premier jour de Paris libre*." Remember, Eva? How could anyone forget?

The 70th Pays a High Cost for Liberation

Sadly, for others in the battalion, particularly the tankers of A and C Companies, the return to war was quick and deadly. From August 27 to August 29, in pursuit of the retreating enemy, several costly engagements were fought. A Company operated in the vicinity of Montfermeil and C Company near Clichy-sous-Bois, whereas B and D Companies were between the other two, but met little resistance. All of the actions were in suburbs at the east-northeast perimeter. The battalion lost thirteen men killed, eight in C Company, and five in A. Ten men were wounded, seven seriously.[6] Although the battalion suffered no casualties in the liberation of Paris proper, the German defense of their retreat route to the north and east was far more determined.

These engagements are further evidence of the vulnerability of tanks in urban areas. A *panzerfaust* team might be behind every window, an antitank gun waiting around every corner. Infantry could and did help flush out the enemy, but their task was all the more difficult, for Germans did not fire until we were well within range. Everything had to be checked, making rapid progress virtually impossible.

One of those killed on August 27 was A Company sergeant George Dudley. He had been with the 70th from its earliest days, fought through the Tunisian and Sicilian campaigns, and from D day and on. He was well liked and respected throughout the battalion. George Brookstein has said of his A Company comrade, "He was a man I greatly admired. He didn't have to be in the war, as he was in his late thirties, but he volunteered." Because of his age, character, and experience, "Big Dudley" had been a steadying influence on men around him, going out of his way to help replacements as they came into the war, frightened and unsure.

B Company Moves North

As part of the move north out of Paris, Lt. Raiford Blackstone went to 12th Infantry headquarters to receive instructions. He was told to lead his 1st Platoon to the vicinity of Le Bourget airfield. Warned there were twenty dug-in German tanks on guard, Blackstone decided not to tell the tank crews what they might be facing. There would be time for that later. They proceeded to Le Bourget and saw no tanks, dug in or otherwise. Upon reaching the area, instead of going across the airfield, they went cross-country through open fields to the east, encountering little or no opposition. In this move, Blackstone captured his first German soldier. "He was an officer, and so well and cleanly dressed that I took him to be part of a German staff. I made him climb up the slope plate to the turret of the tank. As he did so, I saw that he had a holster at his waist. I ordered him to hand me the pistol, my first of a number of acquisitions. It turned out to be a Belgian-made Browning automatic. Needless to say, the crew of tank #1 was put out with me for getting the pistol, because they wanted the gun themselves."

The Entire Battalion Attacks

On August 29 an attack occurred that was memorable in the annals of the 70th Tank Battalion. For the second, and last time in World War II, the battalion fought as a complete unit. (The first was at Barrafranca, Sicily, on July 29, 1943.) The primary mission was to seize terrain 2,000 yards north of Tremblay-lès-Gonesse and hold it until relieved by the 22d RCT. Were this attack to be made today, it would seriously impair operations at Charles de Gaulle Airport. The objective would be in the middle of a runway.

As the medium tanks moved boldly across level terrain in a line, light tanks from D Company were positioned in a semicircle around the town, Roissy-en-France. They flushed a platoon of Jerries and called headquarters to pick them up. "The attack was then pressed by all elements of the battalion and the objective was seized rapidly. Approximately 300 prisoners of war, and one enemy tank were taken, and three AT guns knocked out. The battalion then assembled at LivryGargan."[7]

This successful attack was the final feather in the cap of Lt. Col. John C. Welborn as commander of the 70th. He assumed command of the 33d Armored Regiment in the 3d Armored Division, with promotion to full colonel.

Welborn led the 70th from its formative period and in the campaigns of Sicily and France. There can be little doubt that his imprint was firmly established on the 70th, and that he was instrumental in successes the unit had accomplished. Frank Gross, who served under Welborn since 1942, both as an enlisted man and as a warrant officer, believes the high esprit de corps of the 70th was due in large part to his leadership. It would be difficult to find anyone who would disagree.

Major Henry Davidson assumed command immediately. He had been Welborn's deputy before leaving the States. Despite having been in the battalion so long, few of lower ranks knew much about him and felt uneasy about the change. Yet, if there was any time to replace an admired and respected commander, it was now. The enemy was on the run, an attack involving all assault units had been successful, and, despite the loss of thirteen comrades on August 27 and 28, spirits remained high from the liberation of Paris.

The Meaning of the Liberation of Paris

On a personal level, for the men of the 70th, the liberation was one of those rare moments when each knew he was part of a triumphant historical event. Usually, the individual felt overwhelmed by what he was part of, and what he had to do was often brutal and ugly. Upon entering Paris he was welcomed as a hero by adoring throngs of people just like him and with whom he could identify. This gave him a renewed sense of worth, that what he was doing had to be done and it was the right thing to do.

Clarence Kleinhuizen's letter to his farm family was printed in the Willmar, Minnesota, newspaper. "It is a French custom to kiss each other on the cheek. Men and women, babies, nice-looking girls, all kissed me. They even kissed our dirty hands. One old woman said, with tears in her eyes, 'My stomach is empty, but my heart is full of happiness.'"

I wrote home: "Seldom in history has such an ovation been given to a group of men, and I had a ringside seat . . . It made me happy to see them so happy."

A poet has written, "Paris is a woman's town with flowers in her hair." She was on liberation day, and she was beautiful, and the flowers were fresh. What a time! Nothing, absolutely nothing can compare with it! Ask anyone who was there.

10
To the Siegfried Line

We chased the Germans all day, every day. At about sundown we would catch them, have a little firefight, gas up, get more ammo, have some food and some sleep, and start again in the morning. The Germans would have run all night and the next day until we caught them again at sundown and had another firefight.

—Clarence McNamee
B Company tanker

The 70th had been fortunate that the change in commanders occurred when it did. With the enemy in full retreat, Major Davidson (soon to become lieutenant colonel) had a breathing spell that enabled him to settle into his new position. It was also important for the men to see that the change would not affect them directly. The same junior officers and noncoms gave the orders, and the same men obeyed them.

On August 30, the battalion covered twenty-eight miles, and the next day another eighteen. This rapid movement kept spirits high. Jerry was hightailing it back to Germany.

Somewhere between Paris and St. Quentin, Lt. Raiford Blackstone witnessed what he calls the only atrocity he knew about from personal knowledge. "It was a bright, sunny day, and my platoon of tanks was advancing on a highway. The powers that be decided to place a couple of jeeps and at least one armored personnel carrier ahead of me as an advance." As they moved through the countryside, Blackstone saw two well-dressed German officers approaching from the opposite direction. "As the two officers reached us, our column stopped and a conversation ensued between them and a captain of infantry in the lead jeep. Some 300 to 400 feet farther along the road was a substantial French farmhouse, and a large Frenchman, probably in his middle to late fifties, came out and walked along the road to the

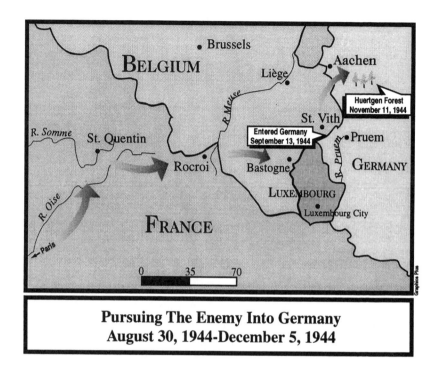

Pursuing The Enemy Into Germany
August 30, 1944-December 5, 1944

head of the column and stopped." Blackstone was standing in the
turret with a clear view of what happened, although because of the
noise of the tank engine, he could not hear what was being said. "After a few moments, the Frenchman pulled out a pistol and shot and
killed both of the German officers. Our column moved on almost
immediately and we passed right by the bodies of these two dead
men. I don't know if the Frenchman was turned over to higher au-
thorities, and I didn't see any of the infantry in the personnel carriers or in the jeeps make a move to arrest or detain the Frenchman.
We simply moved on, and I saw nothing else."

Blackstone is a precise, well-mannered man who chooses his
words carefully. He always played by the rules, which did not allow
for the shooting of unarmed men trying to surrender. The rules of
war did call for stopping a retreating enemy if possible and killing
him if necessary. An enemy who does not surrender today will try to

kill you tomorrow. A few days later Blackstone's platoon neared St. Quentin. "There were two parallel roads leading into the city from the southwest. We stopped on one of these roads and observed on the other road, to our right, that is, to the east, a retreating German column of vehicles, troops, and horse-drawn carts and wagons. They were perhaps 3,000 to 4,000 yards away, but in clear view. We opened fire with high-explosive 75mm shells and appeared to cause extensive damage to their vehicles and extensive casualties. We continued to fire until the column was out of range."

Germany had changed warfare with its *panzer*-led motorized columns in 1938 and 1940. Now they were in headlong retreat using horse-drawn carts and wagons.

The Liberation of St. Quentin

The German column was not pursued, because it was late in the day. Rather, Blackstone's 1st Platoon tanks were ordered to proceed to the objective, St. Quentin. "I received instructions to go forward and set up guards in the central section of the city, but, before I could execute these orders, they were countered and I was told to turn around. These orders then were changed again, in fact three or four times. Because of the darkness, I was turning my five tanks around by holding a handkerchief in my right hand and jiggling it so the drivers could see what to do." This was occurring in roughly the same place, with a large group of civilians watching. "A woman approached me and placed a whole, unfrosted cake in my hand. Though I always shared with the men in my tank and in my platoon, this time in my preoccupation of repeatedly turning these tanks around, I inadvertently ate the whole thing. To this day, no member of my platoon knows that I ate a whole cake and didn't share it with them!"

Carving Up Dead Horses

Eventually, whoever couldn't make up his mind, did. The 1st Platoon of B Company moved into central St. Quentin, the key to the sector, with a population in excess of 50,000. "When we got into the city to set up our guards," Blackstone relates, "we saw a number of dead horses around. They might have been maimed when we shot up that retreating column and later killed. One was near a water fountain at a street intersection about 125 feet from where our tanks were parked. When daylight came, all we found was the horse's head, and some French men and women were washing that off in the water fountain. Everything else was gone."

Cecil Nash and Tony Zampiello, both in C Company, and Clarence McNamee of the 2d Platoon of B Company all recall St. Quentin citizens carving up the dead horses. When McNamee and his wife visited St. Quentin some thirty years later, "I remembered almost everything about the city. I showed my wife where our tank was parked and, in fact, parked our car in the same place. I showed her the fountain where a dead horse had been carved up into pieces and shared by many people. She asked what they were going to do with it, and I said, 'Why, eat it, of course.'"

To the men of the 70th, the welcome they received in St. Quentin was special. In few other places did they see so closely the meaning of liberation. Perhaps the smaller scale of the setting made this possible. Perhaps the realization that people were carving up dead horses out of hunger made it more personal. Whatever the reasons, the outpouring of appreciation by common, ordinary citizens was genuine.

Clarence McNamee remembers: "We almost didn't even go to bed that first night in St. Quentin. The whole city was rocking with liberation parties." They were leaving the next day when the rest of the battalion moved in. Companies bivouacked in various places throughout the city, but none set up tents. This would be a short stay.

"All for One, and One for All!"

In the early evening, I went with four or five buddies to the central square. It was packed with people celebrating in unabashed joy. A number of bars had wine and beer available. Our group went from one to the other, toasting and being toasted, time and again. The increasingly convivial little group soon held a caucus and voted unanimously together to seek women engaging in the oldest profession. It was to be all for one, one for all, comrades in arms, so to speak.

But where to find the arms? Several bartenders were queried in pidgin French as to the location of a local pleasure palace. Either they didn't understand or didn't know. These attempts proving fruitless, one of the more cosmopolitan members of the group suggested that taxicab drivers always know. None were around. There wasn't room for a bicycle on the square, let alone a cab. Out of desperation, a gendarme was sheepishly approached and shown THE WORD in a pocket dictionary. He beamed with delight, said, *"Oui, mon amis,"* and pointed to a street leading off the square. He counted on his fingers the number of buildings from the square and waved to the left side of the street. There, it was understood, was a bar where would be found the unholy grail.

The jaunty little group moved up to the bar, ordered beers, and called the bartender's attention to THE WORD in the still open dictionary. With little more than a furtive glance at it, he jerked his head toward the rear of the room. Mounted on a staircase was a line of GIs, which the group hastily joined. Someone made a reconnaissance up the staircase and past the turning. He returned with a count. The bad news was that ten men were in line. The good news was that there were two ladies-in-waiting. I cleverly volunteered to go for more beer, mainly to position myself as the last of the group in the unlikely event the place was suddenly closed. This became less likely with the rapid turnover. One by one, GIs were coming back down the stairs, each with a different version of the same grin. In what seemed no time at all, it was my turn. I looked for an escape but was unable to move. The GI in back gave me a gentle shove, and stiff legged, like a toy soldier, I marched into the room. There, dressed in the flimsiest of garments, was a woman, otherwise naked as a jaybird. Although my discernment was marred by excitement bordering on terror, she appeared to be magnificent. Ample, but not overly so. Older than I, but that was good. At least one of the two people in the room would know what to do. Most important, she seemed willing and able to act as the handmaiden—if that is the correct word—to my rite of passage. My head was spinning, so I remember little else except how calm she remained throughout the brief encounter. How could she be so tranquil on such an important occasion? Yet, she was. When I was again semiconscious, I found myself descending the staircase, Duchamplike, only clothed. The line of GIs was now longer by half than when the group first came in. When I rejoined my buddies at the bar, I was a composed and knowing man of the world.

Heading East to Belgium

The 70th left St. Quentin on September 3, going northeast, then east. Movement continued to be so fast "it was not impossible to obtain a good bet that the war would be over within another thirty days . . . The V Corps, to which the 4th and the 70th were attached, pushed . . . toward the Meuse River, cutting off large forces of enemy troops and preventing escape to the Siegfried Line. The 70th crossed the Meuse in the vicinity of Rocroi."[1]

Since leaving Paris, the route had been through World War I country. I recall talking with someone about this and looking for evidence of trenches. Clarence McNamee remembers, "You could still see ripples across fields where trenches had been." World War I had ended just twenty-six brief years before. Fathers and uncles had been here then. Now it was sons and nephews.

For several weeks, the same pattern of chasing the Germans all day and engaging them at sundown continued. Firefights were now less frequent, as the enemy was moving faster. On September 5, a minor action took place. On September 6, the 2d Platoon of B Company ran into German tanks, which quickly moved off. This was after we had traveled another ninety-seven miles or in the case of a number of tanks, until they ran out of gas. Those were resupplied and caught up at the bivouac near La Mesnil, still in France on the Belgian border. From September 6 to 13, no further encounters took place.

Maintenance and the Installation of Flamethrowers

While on the Belgian border, the 70th halted for a five-day respite. Tank maintenance was sorely needed. They had been driven more than 300 miles since heading for Paris on August 23. Flamethrowers were now installed on at least one medium tank per company, and personnel were trained in their use. The Siegfried Line was near; flamethrowers would be devastating against pillboxes.

Clarence McNamee was one of the first to be trained. "They sent us back to Quartermaster as they had to rig up the tank for the flamethrower. I don't remember how I was conned into it, but I was. I think there was some soft soap that they needed someone smart enough to run it. Well it wasn't the easiest thing to operate, but it wasn't that complicated either. Nothing that you couldn't learn in two or three days."

By the time Robert McEvoy joined A Company in the Huertgen Forest about six weeks later, flamethrowers were apparently not thought to require even that much training. "The first day I got to the company they put me in a tank as an assistant driver and bow gunner. This tank had a flamethrower, so I had to learn how to operate it. It took a half hour or less to learn, though I didn't learn anything about the machine except how to activate it. There were three buttons. One was to spray the gasoline, one to ignite the gasoline, and the third was for the napalm. That's the way it worked, bang, bang, bang. Hit three buttons in the correct order. That's about all that I knew."

McNamee described the modifications made in the bow gun position. They made a crowded tank more cramped. "Just to the right of the bow gunner's seat was a small space where you could keep your little stove, some food, and personal papers and books. Well, that space was where they put the air tank." Behind the seat was placed a cylindrical tank full of napalm. "To throw the napalm flame seventy-five yards required 1,800 pounds of air pressure. Napalm, a jellied gasoline, was heavy, which is why so much air pressure was needed. You were sitting there in a potential fireplace. If your tank got hit, you were going to have fifty gallons of lighted napalm in your lap in seconds.

"The flamethrower replaced the .30-caliber bow gun, and the tube that extended out was roughly the same length. You could see the difference up close, but I doubt the Germans could distinguish a flamethrower tank from any other from a distance unless they got a lucky fix with binoculars. But in combat things happen so fast that this was not likely."

On German Soil and Against the Siegfried Line

After the respite, the battalion made several road marches across Belgium to the German border. On September 11, the B Company journal notes, "We traveled 63 miles, arriving at 1530 in the vicinity of St. Hubert. On this march we passed many bombed, wrecked towns caused by the enemy." The next day, B Company moved another thirty-four miles to a bivouac just five miles from the German border.

The milestone was reached September 13. B Company tanks had the distinction of being the first in the battalion to enter Germany, but the enemy gave ground grudgingly. One tank was destroyed by *panzerfaust* fire on September 13 without casualties. The journal entry for the next day notes that for the first time pillboxes and obstacles of the Siegfried Line were encountered. Now was the time to use the recently installed flamethrowers. Clarence McNamee affirms, "We did knock out pillboxes on the Siegfried Line like hell with them. We waited until one of our regular tanks got Jerry pinned down by blasting away with APs and HEs. Then we moved up and fired the napalm flame into the slots or anyplace else to get into the pillbox, and in seconds it would burn up the oxygen inside and set the whole thing ablaze. Whatever you hit, burned. A couple of times we fired it at troops lying flat against the ground, and they burned, too. Mostly, though, we used them against pillboxes."

McNamee's View on the Morality of Using Flamethrowers

As noted earlier, tank crews were told not to use phosphorus shells, as Germany had maintained they were gaseous and therefore in violation of the Geneva Convention. No one, however, has reported a complaint about the use of napalm, by far a more terrifying weapon.

Clarence McNamee has stated his personal view of the use of flamethrowers. "I never had any moral difficulties. I always thought what I was doing was right, that I was doing what I was supposed to do." In Luxembourg, right after Christmas Day during the Battle of the Bulge, he asked one of the chaplains how the Lord looked at the taking of lives in war. "I never got a good answer. He was very evasive on how the taking of lives in combat would be viewed on Judgment Day. Killing is killing, and as far as I know there never were any specifications laid down as to the difference in killing, be it by a flamethrower, an atomic bomb, machine gun, whatever." So on this issue, the chaplain was no help. "He said a soldier in combat pretty much walks alone. It was an individual matter. In those days we all took a chance on Judgment Day. I never got into the philosophy of it, or the theology, other than the personal theology on how it would be looked at later on. I didn't worry about anyone else, or how this conflict was to be judged."

Winter Begins in the Schnee and Schlausenbacher Forests

As good as it felt to have brought the war to the Germans in their own country, advances now were only 500 yards a day on three successive days. Everything about the area favored the defense. The Schnee and Schlausenbacher Forests were dense, and through them ran the Siegfried Line. Rain was incessant, making movement difficult. The Germans fought hard as they were defending their homeland now, and skillfully took advantage of the terrain and their long-prepared defensive positions. "Countless machine-gun nests hidden in the forests had to be cleaned out by the 4th Infantry and 70th tanks. The battalion suffered many casualties, although not nearly as many as the infantry. It was really nasty fighting . . . While in the forest, elements of the 70th were shelled constantly . . . As in most of the barrages the enemy threw at American troops, about one out of every five shells were duds . . . put together by a forced laborer in some German munitions factory."[2]

The Germans had mined all approaches to defensive positions. "Sometimes they would stack two or three antitank mines on top of one another," as Cecil Nash explains. "One C Company dozer tank hit one of these stacked mines and it almost blew the tank apart. One or two of the crew were killed, and the rest were injured. The tank couldn't be salvaged."

Once again fighting was in terrain and conditions ill suited for tanks. Again it was an infantry war with tanks jammed into the forests with them. George Brookstein saw this and the terrible casualty rate of the 4th when he went forward to find the exact location of an A Company platoon that hadn't returned when expected. "I remember climbing on a hill with a plateau slanting out from it. Our infantry were all around and had dug in for the night. It was very hot with continuous mortar fire. The platoon of tanks were there, but they had little room for maneuver because of trees, foxholes, and infantry. They couldn't have left anyway, as they needed to stay in place to support the infantry."

Just as Brookstein and his driver started back, he was hit with shrapnel over one eye and on his chin. "We went to an infantry aid station but the medics were so busy they couldn't spend much time with me. The place was filled with casualties, many far more seriously wounded than I. They patched me up, scribbled my name on a form, and we took off for the company. Actually, this wound does not appear on my records, which under the circumstances was understandable." This was the third wound he had suffered in three countries. Brookstein would get his fourth in four countries shortly before the end of the war.

The 70th stayed around this border area for about four weeks. Most company bivouacs were in Belgium, several near St. Vith. Although contact with the enemy was maintained, the only attack in the period occurred on October 7 and 8 in the vicinity of Losheuntfraken, Germany. All four line companies took part. A roadblock was set up by the Germans along the road through the forest. D Company moved to the edge of the woods and engaged enemy dug-in positions before an enemy barracks. "Under the cover of D Company, B Company moved up and passed through D Company to press the attack. The position was taken, the building burned and prisoners taken. The following day the attack was carried farther and another roadblock was destroyed. The enemy fled, leaving their weapons behind them."[3]

The fact that a permanent barracks was located in a heavily forested area was not surprising, because it was part of the Siegfried Line. Tony Zampiello went into a pillbox after an attack and found it to be "three stories deep. They had everything in there." George Brookstein saw a frontline dugout that "had everything, including latrines. On the lines, it seemed they lived as in garrison."

Cold rains that chilled to the marrow and the dark, brooding forests led me to reach out for home as never before. My sister, Carol, then a pretty sixteen, had sent a recent photograph. "I'll try to keep it with me, but it may be hard to carry it and keep it in good condition. You certainly have changed since I left. I hope you haven't changed too much!" It was my tone regarding the war that had changed. Shortly before, I had hoped it would end soon. Now, I wrote, "About this business of VE Day, I believe the people back home think the war is over. Well, it's far from it." In several letters I referred to the cold, rainy weather. "It's getting cold over here now . . . so it's hard to keep warm all of the time. I sure hope this war ends before winter or it will be rather unpleasant to live outside." Rather unpleasant to say the least. A few days later, on October 14, I wrote: "Germany is noted for its long winters, and I'm not looking forward to this one the least bit. I only hope we can end this thing before it sets in . . . but the weatherman is sure against us. The rain is slowing us up considerably, and this part of Germany is all forests, which makes it harder, too. We all know that we have Jerry licked. All that is left is to deliver the knockout punch."

This assessment was essentially correct, although Jerry still had a few blows to deliver. The knockout punch would not be thrown until months after the worst winter the men of the 70th would ever experience.

The Supply Shortage

A pause now became essential to build up stocks for large-scale operations in November.[4] In the rapid advance across northern France, Allied armies had outrun their supply lines. The tanks that ran out of gas on September 6 couldn't be resupplied until the following day. By late September, the problem was so acute that gasoline and other supplies were dropped by parachute in the 70th's zone.

There were instances when the fuel shortage could have put 70th tanks in precarious situations had the Germans been able to mount counterattacks in force. Of course, their condition was no better.

Rumors that abounded around the battalion blamed the "Red Ball Express" (transportation battalions) for refusing to bring supplies to the front. These were ugly, divisive rumors. Most of the truck drivers and helpers in the "Red Ball Express" were blacks. As with most rumors of this type, they had no substance in fact. These same men had consistently brought supplies to the front lines under far more dangerous circumstances than now prevailed.

Battalion supply sergeant Louis Rizzo recalls that at this time First Army Quartermaster was much farther back than the usual thirty miles. "Normally they advanced as we did, but now we had to drive more than forty or fifty miles to get what we wanted, and gas wasn't available for a while."

Support Troops in Combat

In a tank battalion, a larger number of men were in the support services and did not normally engage in combat. They were, however, vital to the operations of the battalion and in constant danger, particularly from artillery and mortar fire, air strikes, and mines. When tanks were committed, line company bivouacs were located about two miles behind the lines.

The company commander and his executive officer were seldom in the area during daylight. They were often leading or directing an action, at a meeting, or performing any number of duties. The first sergeant really ran the company and was usually in the bivouac.

Supply, clerks, medical aides, maintenance, and the kitchen all had vehicles and tents in the bivouac. The area had to be large enough for these services to function, plus space for seventeen tanks. Tanks were concealed, usually under trees. A bivouac had to be set up and dismantled quickly as a routine.

During campaigns, bivouacs were moved almost every day, sometimes twice a day. At each new one, tents would be set up, a kitchen sump dug, and then, individual soldiers would dig foxholes. In inclement weather, lower ranks erected a tent for two men made of two shelterhalves. Officers had the luxury of a private tent. Tankers didn't dig foxholes. Their tanks were more adequate for shelter. They usually tied shelter halves to the side of a tank for their tents.

Maintenance

In a tank unit, maintenance was obviously a high priority, with minor work done by line company crews. Anything major belonged to battalion maintenance in Service Company, which in Sicily also had the T-2 tank retrievers. Later all line companies had T-2s. Even in Service Company, overhauls of tanks and other vehicles were not usual. They, too, were always on the move, and parts were not available. "The only way we got spare parts," Walter Waszyn of B and later D

Company asserts, "was by stripping knocked-out tanks of the parts we thought might be useful. Ordnance, or whoever allotted parts for maintenance sections, sent us stuff we couldn't use, and the stuff we needed they didn't have." Waszyn has described company maintenance as "sledgehammer and crowbar mechanics." If a tank threw a track, it was put back together with a sledgehammer and crowbar. "We did more of this than anything else, aside from changing spark plugs."

Mechanics often had to go to or near the front to retrieve or repair a tank. They could then be in an unprotected and precarious situation, such as that which Francis Snyder describes: "I was driving the half-track when our crew went up to work on a tank. The Germans had a machine gun position on a hill overlooking the tank. As soon as we got out and started to work, they fired on us. We got in back of the tank for safety, and as soon as a burst ended I hightailed it to the half-track and got it started. After the next burst the rest of the crew made a dash and got in. We got away alright and went back to the tank later, when the Germans had left."

Walter Waszyn recalls an occasion when the B Company bivouac was close to the front lines. "We were in the hills, and I was working on a tank starter. This was at night, so I had to do it mostly by feel since we couldn't show a light. Some time after two in the morning I finished and was so tired that I just flopped down on the ground behind a tree and went to sleep. At daybreak about fifteen tanks started up and took off, and I was so tired I didn't even hear them. Nobody missed me, so when I finally woke up I was alone." Artillery shells were coming in across the road. "I had no food, no gun, no water, no nothin', and just stayed behind that tree for hours saying more prayers than I normally did. Finally someone did come for me, and we went to the new bivouac."

"During the day's action, the tank my friend Eckard was in got hit. Two guys got killed and Eckard was a mess. Well, I had been saving a bottle of Scotch for my twenty-first birthday, which was that same day. I opened it and handed the bottle to Eckard. He drained about half of it without coming up for a breath, that's how shook up he was. Anyway, that Scotch lasted only a few moments, but I celebrated being a man, scared to death, hungry, and thirsty."

Supply

Louis Rizzo worked his way up from company supply sergeant to the assistant in battalion, and eventually battalion supply sergeant. "Each company supply sergeant would list items they wanted me to requisition. Every item had a military order number. We had to go to division for a few things, but most came through army. Battalion supply took care of everything except food rations. Whether it was tanks, trucks, socks, machine guns, ammunition, you name it, we wrote the requisitions. If Quartermaster or Ordnance was out of an item, we would back-order."

Each man had his full allotment of clothing when he went overseas or arrived at a company. "Tankers might have their stuff shot up or lost when a tank was hit or destroyed." A good supply sergeant could make a difference. Rizzo didn't go by the book. "If I wanted something I would go after it. If I had to do something unethical, I did. I learned to chisel, connive, manipulate, fake requisitions, forge names, to do whatever was needed to get stuff for guys. Once I arrived at a supply dump with two trucks. The guard asked if we were a division. I said, 'No, the 70th Tank Battalion.' He said, 'Then you can't get anything, you have to be a division.'" Rizzo and his men drove away, then stopped out of sight a short distance away. "I started erasing and changing the form. I wrote 70th Armored Division. Captain Bushey became Colonel Bushey. Every item I multiplied by three. When we got back to the dump I made sure we went to a different guard. He waved us through and another guy directed us to the right place. He even said they would load us up, which they did. That's how we had to get supplies."

Most used items were supposed to be counted with a like number of replacements received. Rizzo knew from experience that some items such as socks and underwear were never counted at depots, so he inflated the number being turned in. "I had enough clothes to take care of the men three times over."

Inflating the number of tanks knocked out was something even the redoubtable Rizzo never attempted. "We would requisition them immediately from army Ordnance. They would get them from a replacement center or wherever they were kept. Usually a tank commander and a driver would go pick them up. It would take at least a day or two to get a replacement tank up to a company." Probably the item replaced most was machine-gun barrels. "They were always being burned up. We took the burned ones back to get replacements, perhaps because they wanted to know if they really were burned. They wouldn't count them, but in this case we were pretty honest. We never ran out.

"Ordnance and Quartermaster were always behind us about thirty miles moving up as we did. Battalion supply was about five miles behind the front." This was generally out of artillery range. Aircraft was another matter. Identification panels were put on vehicles so our airmen would know they were friendly. That was fine—unless the enemy was overhead. "On one occasion right after breakfast four planes came over and started to peel off. I was standing by the ammunition dump, of all places, and thought, Uh-oh, I'm done for. Captain Bushey was with me, and he started digging a hole with his bare hands. Some bombs were dropped, but they fell near some Germans in a prisoner compound about fifty yards from us."

The Field Kitchen

The kitchen crew consisted of the mess sergeant, four cooks, and usually two permanent KPs (kitchen police—helpers). Two-man teams of cooks worked shifts of twenty-four hours on duty, twenty-four hours off. Everyone helped at serving time. KPs worked every day, but by no means all day. They would dig the sump hole, wash pots and pans, and do other menial chores to help the cooks.

The kitchen truck was a standard two-and-a-half-ton vehicle pulling a two-wheel trailer. Both were jam-packed when in movement. The mess sergeant rode with the driver in the cab, the kitchen crew in the back. Two or three rows of boxed rations were packed forward in the back end, stacked from the floor board nearly to the canvas top. Most of these were emergency rations, which did not have to be unloaded at every bivouac. On top of the stacked boxes the barracks bags belonging to the crew were stashed. Usually a line of boxed rations was used for seats. Three field stoves were placed side by side near the end of the truck. They could be used for cooking in the truck, though normally they were lifted off and put into a pyramidal tent or, if fortunate during the winter, into a building of some sort.

The two-wheel trailer held a staggering amount of material, including the tent, pots and pans, various and sundry kitchen utensils, garbage cans, and cans to wash mess kits.

Shortly before serving time, KPs would fill three large galvanized cans with water, then attach and light gasoline burners. One can had soapy water, used by each man to wash his mess kit with a brush thoughtfully provided. The other two cans held rinse water. Purification tablets were added, since water did not always come from a known source.

How pure the water was after a number of men had used it was another matter. Each man was supposed to dump remaining food particles into the garbage can, and generally did. Even so, after 120 to 145 men had cleaned their mess kits, the last five or ten faced three cesspools. According to Lt. Raiford Blackstone, the last four or five men were often officers, because in the field U.S. Army policy was that the men were fed first. This was alright with him, but the problem was that officers then also cleaned their mess kits last. By the time they went through the line, the soapy water was cold, greasy, and full of the floating remains of the meal. The rinse waters were also cold, cloudy, and generally unsavory. Blackstone remembers that, as a rather fastidious person, he had to find other means to put the final touches on his mess kit with a clean handkerchief. Frequently in a bivouac situation, he admits, the company commander's orderly would serve company officers at a table. He did not state whether the orderly cleaned all the mess kits, or whether he would trust him to clean his.

Each company mess sergeant ordered rations according to the unit's strength. He could make a difference by getting more rations than allotted. Of the emergency rations, C had cans of meat and vegetables, such as beef stew, hash, or frankfurters and beans. In emergencies, cooks would open and heat canned products for a meal. Tanks always carried several cases of emergency rations. They might be C or 10 in 1 (one meal for ten men) or K, a small waterproofed package containing a meal for one man. In it were combinations including a can of concoctions similar to those in C rations, or egg and ham or bacon; packets of crackers, instant coffee, or lemonade; concentrated chocolate "energy" bars; rubbery cheese; and four cigarettes, always leading American brands. Most men carried a small can opener with his dog tags on a chain around the neck. Canned bacon was also available, cooked both by the kitchen crew and by men in the field. The mainstays, however, were coffee and cigarettes. Cigarettes were free in combat zones. Most men smoked, and neither tanks nor tents were designated "smoking sections" or "nonsmoking."

Everybody in the company put a dollar or two into a slush fund so when time in the same bivouac allowed it, the mess sergeant could buy a cow. Walter Waszyn describes an occasion when a cow was purchased. "Sabo was a big burly guy from the coal mining area of Pennsylvania. He hit the cow on the head with a sledgehammer. The cow said 'moo' and didn't budge. Sabo said, 'They ain't feeding me enough,' and hit it again." The T-2 tank retriever was used to hoist the carcass off the ground to dress the meat. Most often the cost would include dressing by the farmer.

Clerks

Frank Gross "enlisted in the army in 1939 to get away from a woman." He got into a "horse and mule company" and was in the infantry that formed the core of the 70th. Before leaving the States he was a sergeant in the battalion clerical section. In England, Gross was elevated to the rank of warrant officer in charge of all battalion clerks. It was his responsibility to see that all records were up to date. "Every man had a service record, posted with every facet of his military life. Every medical examination he got was posted, every shot, when he last heard the Articles of War. Everything was kept up to date. It was the personal diary of every GI. The most difficult and most traumatic job was to get all the information I could on casualties—who was wounded, killed, or a prisoner of war. I visited Grave Registration and cemeteries and interviewed soldiers who were present when the casualty occurred."

If there were any questions, Gross went to great lengths to seek the answers. "Once in Normandy several tanks had been knocked out and I went up to find out who was in them and the circumstances." There was a lot of artillery and small-arms fire. "I ran over and got into one of the tanks to search for dog tags or any information and pick up a few personal articles. I stuck my head out of the turret, and all hell broke loose. Captain Finkelstein was just sitting there, very calm, as if nothing was happening. I waited for the fire to subside, then ran over to my jeep and got the hell out. Finkelstein laughed."

Gross was in charge of making up the payroll. This was very complicated during a campaign, with constant changes in personnel occurring every day of the month.

Armies move not only on their stomachs, as Napoleon said, but also on pieces of paper. Joseph Nesbit, the C Company clerk in all campaigns, reminds us that everything had to be in writing. Included in the first sergeant's morning report was an accurate accounting of casualties, orders for replacements of casualties, and orders for rations, which were based on a daily number of men in a company. Commanders of all levels had to know exact information for appropriate decisions to be made. That is why clerks landed in Normandy about three or four days after D day, prior to kitchens and some other service functions. It was essential to keep personnel records current. Next of kin had to be notified in the event of death, and it was the company clerk who closed out a man's service record.

During the campaigns in Europe, Nesbit says, "We were back with Service Company as part of the personnel group. In the summer, our office was a large tent covered by a camouflage net." When autumn came, the maintenance section acquired a big flat-bed trailer. "They constructed a plywood cover that was blackout proof and we 'liberated' a gasoline generator for lights. This was pulled behind a two-and-a-half-ton truck. It was painted green, then white when snow fell. Our working conditions for maintaining payroll and other records were fairly comfortable. We even had a small woodstove when the weather turned cold."

Medics in the 70th

After basic training in 1941, James Feeney became a clerk in the medical section of the 70th. His only qualification was that he could use a typewriter. Later he became a medical aide and a good one. During combat, he reports, infantry took care of most casualties. "In theory, each company was assigned several aides and a medical half-track. Actually, this was impractical. With companies supporting different infantry regiments, our twenty or so medics would have been spread too thinly. Infantry medics were on the spot and better able to give immediate aid to frontline casualties, though we did take care of some.

There were occasions when 70th medics evacuated crews from knocked-out tanks. Once, Feeney and other medics were called upon to evacuate wounded in an area that U.S. engineers had mined. Only the medical half-track was allowed to go through a road-block. Shells were landing all around, but Feeney believes that the Red Cross was respected. "We were often near the front, but only officers could wear side arms. If we had, we could have been shot."

He says that in Africa and Sicily there was a lot of jaundice and malaria. Starting with Normandy and continuing, combat fatigue appeared frequently. "In the Huertgen Forest we had a problem with trench foot, but there wasn't much we could do except evacuate the men. Most soon returned." When the battalion was in a stable situation, aid men were sent to each company. They had to make sanitary reports, immunization reports, and monthly VD reports.

Feeney agrees that "Doc" Shechner was the medical officer most men remember. "He was with the 70th from the beginning to the end. Schechner was a good doctor, and a wonderful, kind, compassionate man. What you saw was what there was. He practiced and lived in a blue-collar section of Newark."

At full strength the battalion had two medical officers. For a time, Feeney says, there was also a dental officer. "About all he could do was pull teeth. He had a drill operated by a foot pedal, which was not very practical. Little was done in the way of preventive dentistry."

A Long Hiatus

The 70th penetrated into Germany only a few miles in late September and early October when operations were halted because of supply problems. For the better part of a month the battalion was located around the Belgian village of Hunningen. This was the longest stay in one place after D day. Companies were quartered in abandoned houses, barns, and assorted outbuildings. B Company even built a log cabin, used as a schoolroom and big enough to use as a shop for the maintenance crew.

It was an implausible situation approaching garrison duty, for most of the men most of the time. Close, but not quite. The 4th Infantry maintained outposts, and tanks were assigned to them.

The B Company journal notes band concerts, instructional classes, inspections, calisthenics, and one long hike that all but four men were able to complete. In one football game, the 3d Platoon ran roughshod over the 2d Platoon. Even PX rations were made available, consisting mainly of nonissued personal items such as aftershave lotion. Men such as Paul Gaul might need it in case he went on a trip to Liège on "official" business in the CO's jeep. Most surprising of all were barrels of American beer. The log cabin was opened with a company beer party.

All of this took place a few miles from the front. German V-1 "buzzbombs" droned overhead on a regular basis, heading for London, other British population centers, and European ports under Allied control. These were the bombs designed to fly a measured distance before plummeting to earth. They seemed to reach altitude right over the bivouac areas, indicating that the launch site was not far away. One malfunctioned and hit in an open field not more than a half mile from B Company. I was among the many who walked over to see the size hole it made. It was impressive.

B Company got a new mess sergeant. In one of the moves just before Hunningen, mess sergeant Baird and Sergeant Yeatts went on a spree and failed to show up when the convoy left. Baird was reduced to private and transferred to C Company. Sergeant Suranic, a tanker recently returned from the hospital, replaced him. Due more to the situation than to the new mess sergeant, cows and pigs were purchased three or four times. I remember the use made of at least one pig. Aside from cooking pork chops and roast pork, the fat was rendered to make lard. This was used for french fries, and I made a batch of apple pies. Also, some of the guys had chitterlings for the first time since leaving home.

Francis Songer was finally promoted to captain, the rank he deserved as B Company commander. The reasons for the long delay remain a mystery. Songer had commanded the company at least since Sicily excepting for the time spent in the hospital because of his second wound. Aside from wearing a second bar at Hunningen, carried $10,000, with my parents as beneficiaries. I also had monthly deductions for the purchase of war bonds to build up a nest egg.

Bartering went on, usually involving captured weapons or other war booty. Later, in Germany, looting happened despite orders against the practice. Official German marks began to be seen later as the war moved to Germany. These were mostly in the hands of combat soldiers who transferred the money from prisoners' pockets to theirs. Clarence McNamee states that his tank crew did better. Twice they blew bank vaults. "The sides of the buildings were already demolished, so in both cases we backed up a little and threw an AP into the safes. Money was everywhere. Johnny Detch and I had bales of the stuff. Though we couldn't use it at the time, I kept some and, after the war, found places where they still accepted these marks. It was the only money they had right after the war. Several nights I bought drinks for the guys."

A Rumor in St. Vith

Throughout this period in Belgium, Franklin Anderson was the A Company executive officer. "I would occasionally go into St. Vith, where I came to know a husband and wife who owned a soda bottling plant. We went there to get cases of orange soda. One day, passing through St. Vith I saw a crowd of people on the square, including this couple I knew. I told my driver to stop, and I asked my acquaintances the cause of all the commotion." The man told Anderson these people suspected and feared the worst. There were indications the Germans were going to come through here. "I asked, 'Why here?' The man said, 'The Boche always come through the Ardennes.' He went on to say that people don't mill around like this unless there are reasonable suspicions—noises they hear, things like that. I thought perhaps this was important enough to report, so when I got back to the company, I told Brodie, the CO. 'Well,' he said, 'you never know, it wouldn't hurt to report it.'" Anderson did report what he had seen and heard to battalion headquarters. "Here I was told to go back to 4th Division headquarters where some of our battalion officers were going to attend a meeting. Brodie and I did, and gave the information to a 4th Division staff officer. After that, I don't know what happened to my information. It was enough to stir me

Songer also donned a pair of freshly laundered long-handled s
drawers, formerly belonging to a German officer. More important
he was awarded the Distinguished Service Cross for an earlier actio

Passes to Paris were issued to a limited number of men, usually
those who had seen much combat. Many others were deserving, ho
ever, and although a few more went later in the war, most never ha
a chance.

A number of men returned to the battalion who had bee
wounded and hospitalized. Many new men also arrived, as the ba
talion got up to strength. One of the replacements was Virgil Wa
ner, who joined the mortar platoon. Since it had no specific dutie
at the time, Wagner was temporarily assigned to assist Headquarte
Company supply sergeant Bell. "I found out right away that I wa
among old-timers. Old-timers in the army, overseas, and in comba
Most of the mortar platoon had been in North Africa, Sicily, Nor
mandy, and all the way through. I was a bit awestruck, being a neo
phyte, but I apparently fitted in alright." Soon after his arrival, Wag
ner celebrated his twenty-first birthday. "Sergeant Bell and Firs
Sergeant Kosmalski scrounged up a birthday dinner for me. We had
corned beef hash, onions, and potatoes. Man, we had a dinner tha
wouldn't quit. I thought that was something else, a hot dinner in cel
ebration of my birthday, and me just new to the outfit!"

The Value of Money

With little to do in the evenings, and with companies together for
a change, poker games went on until the wee hours of the morning.
Despite moderate stakes, sizable sums were won and lost. With so
many games being played at Hunningen, most winners possessed
wealth only on a temporary basis before it changed hands. A few re
tained enough to buy available goodies in Luxembourg six weeks
later. I did and left Hunningen with at least $25 extra. All military
scrip was called "funny money" and was looked upon as little more
valuable than that in "Monopoly." The 70th was nearly always in the
field. Seldom was there opportunity to spend money. Most needed
items were issued, including cigarettes.

Most men had deductions taken from their meager pay and still
had enough to make do. Insurance was available at low cost. I

up, and Brodie as well, but I don't know if our intelligence used it."
Intelligence is a compilation of bits and pieces of evidence. "Yet it
was later said we didn't know the Germans were coming through the
Ardennes. Maybe if information like mine had been investigated, we
wouldn't have been so surprised."

Preparing to Leave Hunningen
During the 70th's stay at Hunningen, the Allies were building for
a winter push. Supply sergeants obtained sizes from all personnel.
Shortly, winter overcoats and gloves arrived and were issued. Electric telephones and outside hookups were installed on some tanks.
In future operations with these tanks, infantrymen would have direct
communication with tank commanders, an invaluable feature for coordination between the two components.

With constant training and maintenance of vehicles during the
weeks at Hunningen, everyone and everything was in a high state of
readiness. Commanders of V Corps units came for inspections, a tip-
off that a campaign was about to begin, and the 70th would be part
of it. Although no one knew where it would be, the direction could
be deduced, and it was what everyone wanted. The pay was military
scrip in German marks.

On November 5, the last vital detail was put in place. "Doc"
Shechner came to B Company to lecture on venereal diseases. Doc
must have hated this duty. He was a most humane individual, admired and trusted by all. The men hated what they called "Mickey
Mouse" lectures, but they were ordered by army regulation, and they
had to be attended. Every man *shall* hear the Articles of War read at
prescribed times, and *shall* hear how those twin German battle cruis-
ers, Syphilis and Gonorrhea, will take aim and destroy any wayward
individual. Although Doc certainly didn't go into it, it was implied
that a man's soul also was at stake.

As the men packed their gear, they heard radio broadcasts of the
reelection of Franklin Delano Roosevelt as president of the United
States. Those old enough to vote, including myself for the first time,
had cast their ballots some weeks before. I voted for FDR, as did most
of my comrades. Those not old enough to vote, and there were many,
jumped back in their tanks and tried to shoot before the enemy did.

I do not recall hearing anyone say, "If I'm old enough to fight, I'm old enough to vote," as was said decades later.

The Move to Hell

The road march began in snow and sleet at the ridiculous hour of 0015 on November 9, 1944—two years plus eighteen hours after the 70th hit the beaches in French North Africa.

It took ten and a half hours for all elements to cover fifty miles. All night, without sleep, tank drivers, assistant drivers, and tank commanders had to keep their hatches open to be able to follow the vehicles ahead along narrow, winding roads through the hilly and forested terrain of the Ardennes. Occasionally the column would halt, giving the men time to wipe the frost from their faces. Along the way, according to the B Company journal, "We saw many pillboxes and dragon's teeth." Although this was the best way to see the Siegfried Line, they were ominous indications as to the destination.

With good reason. The 70th had arrived in the Huertgen Forest.

11
The Battle of the Huertgen Forest

> Other battles in this war have been more dramatically decisive—
> Normandy, St. Lô, the Falaise Pocket—but none was tougher or
> bloodier than the battle for this Huertgen Forest.[1]
>
> —William Walton
> *Life* magazine

Men of the 70th were in all the World War II battles that *Life* corre-
spondent Walton mentions and are thus in a position to judge. They
would agree entirely. None was tougher or bloodier than the Huertgen Forest. It was a terrible battle, with conditions the worst of the
entire war.

On November 11, precisely at 1100, each artillery piece in the
American line fired one round into enemy positions. The armistice
ending World War I duly observed, the 70th spent the next five days
preparing and moving into place for battle.

The Battle Scene
The forest contained about fifty square miles of trees, most closely
ranked tall firs towering up to one hundred feet. It was a dark,
gloomy place, perfectly suited for a Wagnerian *Gotterdammerung*
with modern weapons. The weather was miserable, with incessant
cold rain continuing for days on end. German mortar and artillery
tree bursts came in without warning, anywhere and anytime. Mines
and booby traps were everywhere.

It was a natural area for defense, part of the Siegfried Line, with
plenty of time to prepare. The 9th Infantry Division, old comrades
from the States and French Morocco, was sent into the forest, where
two of three regiments were decimated. Then came the 28th Infantry
Division with similar results. Next the 4th and the attached 70th

Battalion were given the unenviable mission of battering through the middle of the forest to the plains beyond.

Once again, the 70th was operating in conditions decidedly unsuited for tank warfare, even worse than the hedgerow country of Normandy. It was so bad that heavier German tanks were not encountered in densely wooded areas. Even our lighter Shermans found movement difficult, as enemy artillery, antitank guns, mortars, *panzerfaust,* and antitank mines took their toll.

If it was terrible for tanks, the Huertgen was even worse for the 4th Division. Losses were appalling. Carl Rambo describes a typical scene. "We were in place about Thanksgiving. The infantry was fixin' to attack, and so were we. They brought in a whole bunch of brand new infantry; there must have been close to a battalion. One of the boys told me he was drafted on D day, and this was Thanksgiving! They got them over that quick. Directly, I said, 'My God, are the Germans coming in or something?' Pow! Pow! Shots were being fired. They were shooting themselves in the foot. They were really carrying them out!"

Yank, the official army magazine in the European theater of operations, assigned Mack Morris to cover the 4th (and therefore also the 70th) during the last stages of the battle. In an article titled "In the Huertgen Forest,"[2] Morris described the forest as having only a few narrow unsurfaced roads, firebreaks, and an occasional clearing. He wrote that, due to the rain,

> The roads and firebreaks became rivers of mud, which were mined and interdicted by machine-gun fire. In one break, there was a teller mine every eight paces for three miles; in another over 500 mines in a narrow break. One stretch of road held 300 teller mines, each one with a pull device in addition to the normal pressure detonator. There were 400 antitank mines in a three-mile area.
>
> Huertgen had its roads and they were blocked. The German did well by his barricades, his roadblocks of trees. Sometimes he felled 200 trees across a road, cutting them down so they interlocked when they fell. Then he mined them and booby-trapped them, and finally, he registered his artillery on them

and his mortars, and at the sounds of men clearing them he opened fire.

The log and earthen bunkers in the Huertgen section of the Siegfried Line were screened by barbed wire in concertina strands and were six feet underground. Paneled with wood and with neat bunks, they afforded reasonable comfort as well as protection.

The 4th Infantry went through the Huertgen at an average rate of 600 yards per day. Twenty-one days at an average gain of 600 yards per day. Thousands of nonmetallic "shoe" mines and box mines had to be cleared by probing on hands and knees or by rifle grenade, artillery and tanks, or "flail" tank fire. (Shermans with drums protruding in front with heavy chains that "flailed" the ground, exploding mines close to the surface.) Also there were "ointment box" mines, so called because that was what they resembled. While small, they could blow off a foot.

Close Support for Infantry

Seldom before had 70th tanks worked so closely with infantry. Sometimes the tanks led the way, exploding antipersonnel mines and enabling infantrymen to walk in the cleared path made by the tracks. This worked for antipersonnel mines, but if the tank hit an antitank mine, infantryman and tanker alike were endangered. Tanks were unable to go everywhere foot soldiers could, however. As Cecil Nash points out, a combat-loaded thirty-five-ton tank could knock down trees of substantial girth but had to be careful not to put the gun out of alignment or damage periscopes and the radio antenna. Tanks clearing paths through trees was generally not a good idea.

The closeness of tanks to infantry is illustrated by Robert McEvoy. (His story is of an unusual instance when a 70th man went into his first combat inadequately trained.)

I was at the 92d Replacement Depot, where Captain Brodie, A Company CO, picked me up. As soon as we got to the company in the Huertgen, I was assigned to Sergeant Yost's tank as bow gunner. Since this tank had a flamethrower, which replaced the .30-caliber bow gun, I had to learn to operate it. After a quick run-through, about a half hour, I was told, 'Mac, you'll do fine.' There were three buttons, one for spark, the second to spray lighted gasoline, and the third to release the napalm. If not fired in proper order, the ignition of the heavy napalm would not occur.

Orders came down that our tank was needed to help infantry get across a firebreak. Jake [Yost] informed us that our boys were on the right side, and only to fire to the left. Anything that moved there was the enemy. Well, I was petrified. This was my first combat. The krauts had the doughboys pinned down with machine-gun fire, so this gun was our objective. I had not yet seen a German soldier or a dead person, so my imagination and anxiety were beginning to build. In my dark little corner of the tank, visibility was limited to what the periscope would allow. Suddenly a figure appeared to my front, with his back toward me. Automatically, I began pressing buttons on the flamethrower—and pressed them wrong. I could see the jelly-like fluid splatter on the back of the soldier's jacket. He stripped it off, and it ignited as it hit the ground. I now realized it was a GI, and the next thing I saw were his boots going up past my periscope to the turret. I was thinking, I'm in trouble now! But maybe thirty seconds later the boots came back down and the GI headed into the trees on our right. He evidently pointed out the area of our objective to Jake. We were by then moving up the firebreak, all guns firing. We moved about seventy-five to one hundred feet and could see doughboys making it across.

As we started to back up, Jake's voice came over the intercom: 'Hey, Mac, get some practice. Set those piles of underbrush on fire over on the left side.' I did, and it worked perfectly. Smoke was now moving across the firebreak, and we could see doughs moving through it. That was an awful first experience, which could have been tragic. It was the last time I fired a flamethrower. Within a week our driver was killed and I replaced him.

Tanks could go no faster than the infantry. If the 4th made 600 yards a day, so did the tanks. Infantry, however, had to stay on the line all night, whereas tanks usually withdrew. Usually, but not always. Cecil Nash recalls "a stretch of about four days and five nights when we were engaged all the time and had lost communications. German artillery and mortars poured in with tree bursts, raining shrapnel down on us. We lived in the tanks. If you had to relieve yourself, you would get out, race around to the back of the tank, and squat for protection under where the hood of the engine comes out aways. The stuff we tied to the outside, like musette bags or sleeping bags, were peppered with shrapnel."

Tony Zampiello, like Nash in C Company, drove the company commander's tank. "We were at a crossroads all day long, and the Germans had us zeroed in. I had to relieve myself, so I got out, went to the back of the tank, lowered my fatigues, and squatted down. There was a lot of snow on the ground, and as I glanced down, I saw that I was partly standing on a dead German soldier. I'll tell you, I made fast work of that detail."

When he got back in the tank, the 88s started coming in. "The first shot hit short, and the second went long, right over the top of the tank. The third hit the sponson on the left side and set off the fire extinguishers. We all took off, leaving the motor running. After a while, we crawled back. The motor was still running. We found out after all that the tank wasn't badly damaged, so we got the hell out of there. That was a bad place, but then all of the Huertgen Forest was a bad place."

Rubbing Elbows With the Enemy

Germans and Americans were crammed into a confined space together. In one such case, two 4th Division battalion command posts 800 yards apart had been in operation for three days when they discovered thirteen Germans with two antitank guns between them the entire time. In another case, engineers bridged a creek, but before they finished their work they found twelve Germans sitting on a hill 200 yards away directing artillery fire on them.[3]

All company bivouacs were closer to the front than ever before, well within artillery range as usual, but also subjected to mortar and rocket fire. Tree bursts were constant dangers. (These were shells that exploded in the tops of trees, showering a sizable area with shrapnel.) These dangers along with cold rains presented a quandary in bivouac. A deep hole was necessary for protection, but it was impossible to keep it dry. Virgil Wagner was with the Headquarters Company mortar platoon. "We all dug foxholes, but they didn't do any good unless you wanted to go swimming."

Stimson, my tent mate, and I tried to dig a foxhole big enough to sleep in. We made a tent from two shelter halves placed over our spot before we began digging. It was no use; water poured in as fast as dirt came out. We slept under a tank at night and dug individual foxholes for protection during the day.

Virgil Wagner relates that if the mortar platoon had no firing assignments, they were given other tasks. "Every time we moved in the Huertgen, we had to log up a command post for Lieutenant Colonel Davidson. We cut down full-length trees, carried them in place, and built up a structure about six feet high. We did this at least three times."

Although Wagner and his mates built log structures for the battalion commander, they didn't for themselves. Instead, they erected a tent next to their half-track to crawl under for protection. It had a steel floorboard strong enough to ward off shrapnel. "Walt Larsen, the half-track driver, had scrounged up an old kitchen canvas big enough for us to make a squad tent for four guys. We could bunk in there. Walt made a stove out of fifteen-gallon oil drums, using tomato juice cans for stovepipe. Somebody would find some bread, which we toasted over the fire using sticks. We would take cheese out of K rations to make toasted cheese sandwiches, except the cheese wouldn't melt." Given the situation, they were relatively cozy and comfortable, which made for bull sessions most evenings. "One night, though, an artillery round came in. Being a rookie, I said, 'What the hell is that?' The old-timers said it was probably a portable artillery round, then kept talking. A second round came in, which I knew was closer, but I didn't say anything, and no one moved. When the third round came in, Frank Jensen said, 'That's close enough for me' and started for the tent opening, as did everyone else. I was sitting in the back of the tent, but I beat the three others out and under the half-track."

All of Clarence McNamee's tank crew except Gene Mayberry

would get out of their tank if conditions warranted. "We carried food to him, emptied his steel helmet all the time. He never left the tank in the Huertgen Forest. He slept in it, did everything in it. In the bivouac area at night, we would combine our shelter halves and tarps, tie them together and to the sides of our tank, which we parked parallel to the direction of German artillery. With tent pegs or trees, we made a tent big enough for all of us to unroll our bedrolls. That is, the four of us. Not Gene." Other tank crews did the same. This left room under the tanks for the cooks.

My most vivid reminder of how close bivouacs were to the front occurred early on the morning of November 23. We cooks were in the kitchen tent beginning to roast turkeys for the Thanksgiving meal.[4] The lieutenant in charge of the guard that night came in for a cup of coffee and to get warm. After shooting the breeze for a while, he started to leave and said as an aside, "Oh, by the way, fellows, I wouldn't make so much noise rattling the pots and pans if I were you. The Germans are about 200 or 300 yards away." There seemed no point in questioning the lieutenant's accuracy in yardage. According to the B Company journal entry of November 16, the kitchen stove was riddled with shrapnel.

Paul Gaul remembers taking me up "to serve chow to a platoon of tanks. Chow got served fast that time." I recall that it was a very scary ride. When we arrived, all five tanks were buttoned up, parked in a clearing close to the German line. Gaul pulled up a few feet from a tank, and we tried to get the tankers' attention without notifying the Germans that hot chow was available. Muffled yells not doing the job, I tapped on the tank's side with a can of food. The top hatch opened slightly and a head slowly appeared. "Got any canned fruit, Jensen?" I replied that I had some. "Well, toss it up." This was done quickly, and the hatch closed again. Gaul and I jumped back in the jeep and got out of there as fast as possible. If it was too dangerous for tankers to get out of their steel foxholes, it was sure as hell too dangerous in an open jeep.

Day-by-Day Fighting
Entries in the B Company journal are laconic but reveal the nature of the fighting in the Huertgen Forest.

November 17. The 2d Platoon and DT-6 at 1300 in support of 2d Bn, 12th Infantry. Engaged enemy. Enemy mortar fire and mines encountered. Private O'Leary lightly wounded by shrapnel but remained on duty. The terrain being tough on tanks caused DT-6 to bog down while #6 became disabled and the crew returned to bivouac safely.

November 18. The 1st Platoon . . . received mortar fire, harassing the crews and wounding T-5 Gamble by shrapnel. Tanks #2, #4, #12, and #14 went to direct fire on enemy positions . . . During the day's operations, tank #12 threw a track, later replaced, and #14 hit a mine, causing the crew to evacuate under infantry cover fire. At 1730 they returned to bivouac area less #14. Our T-2 is trying to retrieve #6 and #14 but at present not successful. [Note that #6 had been disabled the day before and still could not be retrieved.]

November 19. We learned that Staff Sergeant Whitaker's bedding roll was booby-trapped.

November 20. At 0730 the 1st Platoon moved out in support of the 2d Bn., 12th Infantry. Engaged enemy at 1100 vicinity of checkpoint 16. Encountered enemy mines and mortar fire. Tank #2 hit a mine, throwing off the right track and one bogie wheel. Disengaged enemy at 1630 and returned to bivouac. Tank #3 remained on outpost. Sergeant Whitaker and Corporal Newman took up that tank crew's bedding rolls. When Sergeant Kendall was receiving rolls, a barrage of heavy enemy gunfire came in. The second shell wounded him from shrapnel in the left leg, and the 4th Division medics evacuated him.

November 21. The bivouac area was roused by a rocket or a shell hitting maintenance and causing one injury.

November 22. At 1400 the company headquarters traveled four miles to rejoin tank platoons. [This was a new bivouac. With only a few hours more of daylight, everyone would have been busy digging foxholes and setting up camp. The kitchen crew set up the large kitchen tent. That was the night we roasted turkeys close to the enemy line.]

November 23. A rainy Thanksgiving. At 0730 the 3d Platoon left for an attack with the 2d Bn., 12th Infantry. Later in the day,

DT-6 had to go up front to remove roadblocks. We had turkey for our supper today.

November 24. The 3d Platoon still out. The 1st Platoon was alerted to move with the 3d Bn. 12th Infantry, but didn't. Today we learned that our own troops destroyed #14. During the day's operations DT-6 hit a mine and was retrieved to our bivouac area, which is around 700 yards from the front line.

Actually, Tank #14 had hit a mine on November 18 and was destroyed by our own troops to keep the guns from falling into enemy hands. This shows how little was the movement in that position. Germans and Americans must both have been right around that tank for days.

Booby Traps

As often happened in the Huertgen, at night the Germans would move into some of the terrain they had lost during the day. That probably happened when Staff Sergeant Whitaker's bedding roll was booby-trapped. The Germans knew what havoc would be created if it exploded and caused injury. Without exploding, it provided a great deal of consternation to many Americans. Accounts of the incident would be passed along.

I recall that everyone was warned frequently to be wary of anything that could be booby-trapped: a fallen tree limb, a helmet, a dead German soldier, an item on an abandoned vehicle. Injuries such as fingers or feet blown off were often more valuable to the enemy than soldiers killed. Wounded men must be cared for but replaced just the same. No one in B Company was injured by a booby trap, but the extra caution kept anxiety levels high.

C Company Is Badly Mauled

In all of the 70th, C Company fared the worst in the battle of the Huertgen Forest. Cecil Nash was now a platoon sergeant in the company and was called to a meeting at 22d Infantry regimental headquarters the evening of November 24. "It was long after dark, and we had to walk maybe a mile or two in the cold and the mud. The CP was in a large dug-out log bunker with dirt piled on top of the logs. There must have been thirty people in there, officers and non-coms. The smoke from the stove and from cigarettes was so thick you could hardly see." A colonel opened the meeting with a rousing talk about going all the way to Cologne after breaking out of the forest and into the Cologne Plain the next day. "You guys and we are going to do it. We're going all the way," he said. Then the colonel passed around a bottle of whiskey, and everybody had a swig. We were then given our assignments and maps. When I got back to my tank, my feet were so wet that I put on dry socks and tennis shoes. We had picked up our mail, and I read mine in the tank, where we spent the night. Artillery was so heavy we didn't dare leave it."

In the morning the platoon moved to the edge of the forest and waited for other assault elements to reach their positions. Nash searched the whole area with binoculars. "I could see Germans walking around in a patch of woods beyond the forest about 2,000 yards ahead and to our right. It had all the earmarks of a trap, of them trying to draw us out. In hindsight, we could have plastered that patch with phosphorus and smoked them out, but we didn't. We had been told not to use it, as Germans claimed it was gaseous and hence in violation of the Geneva Convention."

As the platoon moved single file into the clearing, the first tank was immediately hit. "Al Orner, my driver, stopped, but I told him to go around it. We did, and got about 100 yards into open country when they got us. There was a blinding flash, and my legs folded under me. Ralph Planck, my gunner, was hit in his rear end, and the loader, Al Kieltyka, in the back." All managed to get out, using their arms, as none could crawl. "Orner and the assistant driver were not wounded and helped us get to the ground and away from the burning tank before it exploded." Nash told them to stay low and run back to the forest to get help. "I told them to contact our people—the 70th—as they would know what to do. Besides, the infantry had their hands full. It was really hectic. As it happened, the rest of our platoon was also knocked out and needed help, and the same with the TDs who were with us." Nash counted fourteen vehicles burning. The three men started back. One couldn't make it. "I told him, 'wait here, and you'll be the first man out when help arrives.' He was." Finally a C Company tank came to the edge of the forest, and the crew got limbs of trees, wrapping blankets around them to make stretchers.

"By the time they got to us, we had been dragging ourselves by the arms for three hours. I don't know how many times the guys carrying us on the makeshift stretchers had to put us down and hit the dirt. The Germans were coming in with machine guns and mortars. Goddamn, they were really after us."

They finally reached a road where jeeps could get through to take them back. "The infantry medic who gave us aid said he couldn't do much, as he was out of supplies. It was that kind of day. I am so thankful there were no deaths in my crew. Seldom was a tank knocked out with a well-placed 88mm shot that all the crew lived."[5]

Note that again the high silhouette of the Sherman made the turret the easy target. The driver and the assistant driver/bow gunner were unscathed; the three in the turret were wounded.

Five C Company men were killed that day and eleven wounded, including Nash and two members of his crew. In a few days, C Company lost ten tanks of its seventeen. Captain Chester Peterson commanded until wounded on November 23, then Lt. Preston Yeoman commanded for only one day, and he was also wounded. Next came Capt. Lewis Taynton, the third company commander in three days.

Men from other companies, including Taynton, were transferred to C Company to provide balance between replacements and combat veterans. Lieutenant Raiford Blackstone was transferred from B Company. Blackstone said that C Company "had lost all officers except a newly arrived lieutenant named Giles Meinhart. I was chosen to give them an additional experienced officer."

Despite the heavy losses, Blackstone asserts, there were still vital objectives in the C Company sector that had to be taken. "Captain Taynton and I made various moves, and eventually did help to take the villages of Huertgen and Grosshau. Then we moved beyond the forest into open country. Here we were fired upon by German *panzerfaust*. As it happened, two of the projectiles hit my tank but apparently were fired at a lofty angle and struck while sharply descending. Both glanced off the tank, exploding on the ground, saving my tank and crew."

After the *panzerfaust* quit firing, things were quiet for a while. "Then a German sniper tried to pick me off. I was standing in the turret, with my head and shoulders above the hatch, as I did 99 percent of the time. Fortunately, the sniper missed with his first round, which I heard go by. I ducked down into the tank for a few minutes, then raised my head, and another round went by. This kept up for a while, with the sniper bouncing bullets off the open hatch covers." Both sides were open and locked at a forty-five-degree angle. "Our tanks had a very heavy coating of paint, which over time had hardened. The bullets apparently were soft, so when the sniper would fire into the inside of the hatch cover, there would be bullet and hardened paint splash."

Blackstone was wearing army gloves, with leather palms and woolen backs. "Despite the gloves, the backs of my hands became peppered with bullet and hardened paint splash. It punctured my skin but did no real damage to my hands. Also the back of my neck was similarly peppered. The only real damage was that one piece of bullet and paint splash entered the corner of one of my eyes, which filled with blood so I could not see with it."

Later, near nightfall, Blackstone was instructed to return through Huertgen and Grosshau to a clearing southwest of where the day's action had been. "I then received instructions to leave the platoon and return to company headquarters for medical attention. Lieutenant Giles Meinhart was sent up to relieve me." In the bivouac, mechanics had rigged up a light in the T-2. "Captain Isadore Shechner, our battalion medical officer, and several of his medics climbed into the T-2 with me, and with tweezers picked out the bullet and paint splash from the backs of my neck and hands. Captain Shechner also got the particle out of my eye and cleaned out the blood, instructing me to come back to the battalion medical tent the following morning."

After the treatment Blackstone was told to go forward to the platoon and relieve Lieutenant Meinhart. "I did so, then advised Meinhart to get some sleep. He crawled under a tank, and I remained on guard all night. When daylight came, Meinhart got up and took over the platoon so I could go back to the company and on to the battalion medical tent. 'Doc' Shechner treated me again, but as I was seeing double out of the wounded eye, he put a black patch over it."

Blackstone returned to the company CP. "When I did, I learned that Meinhart had been instructed to go through Huertgen and

Grosshau again, then back to the same position where the sniper had fired on me. I further learned that Lieutenant Meinhart had gotten out of his tank and had been shot dead by a sniper."

When this news reached the CO, he instructed Blackstone to go back up and take over the platoon. "I tossed aside the black eye patch and returned to the platoon. I had been relieved part of one day, and during that time my relief had been killed and I was spared. He had been killed almost exactly where the sniper had aimed at me."

What was left of C Company on December 1, became part of Task Force McKericher, named for the 70th executive officer in command. Other units were C Company, 709th Tank Battalion, and C Company, 803d Tank Destroyer Battalion, forming a task force that wielded considerable firepower. The attack, in an unforested area, was made in support of the 2d Battalion, 22d Infantry Regiment. "Five tanks from the 709th Tank Battalion crossed the open ground to the southeast of Grosshau under the cover of smoke and fire laid down by C Company, 70th Tank Battalion. This assault assisted the infantry to straighten the regimental line."[6]

"Punchy" Brown Clears a Road of Mines

Simultaneously with the Task Force McKericher operation, A Company attacked to support the 3d Battalion, 8th Infantry Regiment, near the village of Haf Hardt. "At 0900 enemy minefields and small-arms fire stopped the attack. The 'flail' tank led the attack and stayed on the hard-surfaced road. A hasty minefield had been placed on the highway. The flail exploded five mines, then became disabled itself in the explosion of a mine. Sergeant Brown came forward with maintenance men. He walked down the road and picked up mines as he went, hurling them into the ditch." The infantry looked on in amazement as Brown tossed one mine after another from the road in order that the T-2 might be brought forward to retrieve the disabled flail tank. "For this action, 'Punchy' Brown received a commendation and the Silver Star. When the tank attack stopped, the infantry could make no progress. The infantry took up defensive positions and the tanks were withdrawn."[7]

At the same time, B Company supported the 12th Infantry in the vicinity of Gey. The 1st Platoon stayed on line. Carl Rambo recalls,

We had been there two nights or more, and this was another place we couldn't sleep. I was up there with three or four tanks, working with the infantry. All I had was long-distance radio contact with the company. I would call them about every hour or two. Late one afternoon [December 4], an infantry captain had his troops dug in over the crest of a hill. The Germans had a gun in place over yonder several thousand yards, and they were laying them in there direct. I didn't have a lieutenant with me, and this [infantry] captain talked me into pulling my tank over the crest of the hill, which I did.

German infantry were coming up that hill, and, when they did, I was giving them canister shots. Man, that kept them back. But I told that captain, "I'm getting my tank out of here before dark; I'm not staying after dark." That's another time I should have used smoke [phosphorus]. I went over a firebreak and got into these bushes. They couldn't find me, but they knew I was in there for sure. When I went over the crest of that hill, backing out, that's another time I didn't tend to my own business, didn't keep my head straight. When I went over the crest of that hill, they got me. The first shell, I felt the tank shake, and the driver said, "We've been hit—jump!" I bailed out, and a shell came through the turret. The gunner bailed out, and another shell came through. Every time someone bailed out, a shell came in. They shot six holes clean through that damned tank. Three went through the turret, and the first one stopped between the driver's feet. We all bailed out and the tank sat there chugging. We had three inches on the turret, and one shell came through where I had been standing, went through the radio, and went through three more inches out the back of the turret—clean through six inches of armor.

When things quieted down and the tank was still running, I told my crew I was going to get that tank back. We had all our gear in it. I thought all I had to do was back up about 100 feet for better cover. Well, I did. I jumped into the driver's seat, and, while I was doing it, all our infantry broke and ran. I mean, that company of infantry went through the bushes like jackrabbits. Well, there was nothing for us to do but keep going back. I needed somebody else to ride with me, because our tank would only steer with one track; the left side was shot up. I'd pull right, go, straighten up—kept doing that for several hundred yards. Finally I got the tank back to a pretty safe place out on the roadway where our other tanks were sitting. Well, I got out to see what was going on, and about then our artillery got the word that the Germans had broken through and were attacking. I mean they really poured the artillery in there, and I was on the outside. I jumped into another tank, and this guy says, "You're bleedin' on me!" I looked down, and one finger was hanging down. I threw a band around it. We left our tank there and in the others set out for the bivouac. It was long after dark when we got there. I didn't bother about going to the aid station, just wrapped the finger. But it killed me that night. Somebody from battalion came up and said to go with him to infantry headquarters.

There was a full colonel in a big tent, and they quizzed me. "What happened up there when the Germans attacked?" I said they hadn't attacked. They had been trying to attack all day but I had been throwing them back with a canister. The colonel said, "What do you mean they didn't attack?" I said, "Your boys broke and ran." I told him that his captain had them dug in over the crest of that hill and they had been taking direct fire all day long and yesterday. When I moved that tank I didn't know what they thought was going on, but they broke and came running out of there like birds. The colonel said, "Are you saying there weren't any Germans attacking?" I said, "No, not that minute, they weren't hitting us." That's all they asked me, but I'll bet they got that captain. That was a stupid trick having them dug in over the crest of a hill.

The next morning they got me to a field hospital and worked on me. When I woke up they were putting me on a train going to Paris. [8]

The Assault Gun Platoon

Although part of Headquarters Company, the assault gun platoon was usually assigned to whatever infantry division the 70th supported.

Throughout the Huertgen Forest, this was the 29th Field Artillery Battalion of the 4th Infantry Division. With them was Francis Snyder, who previously had been a truck driver. "The thanks I got for doing a good job was being 'shanghaied' to the assault gun platoon on the Fourth of July." The platoon consisted of six 105mm howitzers, each mounted on a tank chassis. "We carried our own ammunition in a trailer that each 'tank' pulled," Snyder observes. "Mostly we fired HE but on rare occasions AP. We were used strictly to support artillery battalions. They usually gave us the targets.

Lieutenant Oakes was in command of the platoon, and Lieutenant Simpson was normally the forward observer. You had seven powder charges [sacks of powder]. If you wanted maximum range, all seven were used. For shorter ranges, you used less." Snyder was a gunner. "We would be given the range, elevation, and deflection, and I would fire three rounds, or whatever it took to get on target, then 'fire for effect'—fire at will. For interdictory fire—harassing—an area was targeted and we might fire a certain number of rounds per hour." The men in the platoon did their own cooking about half the time, and the other half were fed by the 29th. "At first they didn't want to feed us, then later they did and liked to see us around. When we moved up, they put our 'tanks' at the head of the column for protection."

In the Huertgen Forest, Snyder recalls, "We had to cut down quite a few trees to clear our line of fire." It was not necessary to change positions often, as all of the forest was within range.

During this battle, the assault gun platoon was given assignments requiring three times the personnel. "The men stayed with their guns and continuously threw the enemy forces off balance, firing more rounds in a given time than the ordinary full-strength artillery battery. For this accomplishment the platoon was cited by the commanding general of the 4th Infantry Division." [9]

"The Bloodiest Damn Ground in Europe"
Huertgen was an evil place. Even after being shed of the dreadful forest, its satanic grip was unbroken. The villages of Grosshau, Huertgen, and Gey lie just beyond the edge of the trees. After forcing Americans to pay dearly for every yard of mud in the forest, the Germans were waiting behind minefields as we came out, guns registered

on all likely routes of advance. Grosshau, as reported in the citation that follows, was made into a virtual fortress.

All elements of the 70th probed enemy defenses until December 5, making almost no headway. Tanks in B and C Companies were hit by *panzerfaust* fire, the tanks being abreast or ahead of infantry. Close-in fighting continued in open country.

In the *Life* magazine article quoted at the beginning of this chapter is a conversation between an infantry captain named Swede and Col. Buck Lanham, commander of the 22d Infantry Regiment. It took place during the fight for Grosshau, which C Company supported. The colonel said without looking up from a map: "You didn't know it was me on the phone last night, did you, Swede?" Swede replied, "No, sir, but Colonel, sir, I don't care if you break me for it. I meant what I said last night even if I didn't know it was you on the line. That little patch of woods we're fighting for ain't no good to anybody. No good to the Germans. No good to us. It's the bloodiest damn ground in all Europe and you make us keep fighting for it. That ain't right." Lanham was silent for a moment, then said, "There's nothing I'd like better than to tell you boys to call it off and go home. You know that, Swede. But it can't be done. The only way we can get this thing over is by killing krauts. To kill them you've got to get to them." [10]

Some forty-six years later, Clarence McNamee expressed sentiments similar to Swede's. "The Huertgen Forest was sheer, unadulterated misery, and as far as the forest is concerned, it was worthless. There was nothing there worthy of losing one man, much less hundreds and thousands."

Some published postwar critics agree with Clarence McNamee and Swede. Carlo D'Este has written that Bradley's "misguided attempt to take the Huertgen Forest resulted in a gruesome butcher's bill." [11] Misguided as it probably was, it was more than an attempt. The Huertgen was taken because that was where the krauts were, and the 4th and the 70th paid their share of the gruesome butcher's bill.

Most elements of the 70th left the Huertgen on December 8, 1944. Two days before, I wrote in a letter home from "somewhere in Germany" that "I am going to church now, in the church that God built, in the wide open spaces."

As the column climbed to the summit of a hill, the men of the 70th could look down on what man had done to God's church. It more closely resembled a surrealistic landscape. Hundreds upon hundreds of trees looked like giant toothpicks, their limbs violently shorn from them. Clearings were pockmarked by explosions and studded by hulks of burned vehicles. "Jesus," someone said in the back of the B Company kitchen truck, "we were right in the middle of it. What genius decided to fight a war in this awful place?"

Well-Deserved Battle Honors

For their gallantry in the Huertgen Forest, the 22d Infantry Regiment and attached units, including C and D Companies of the 70th, C Company of the 803rd Tank Destroyer Battalion, and C Company of the 4th Engineer Battalion, were awarded a unit citation. Since much of the description pertains to all of the 70th and is an apt summary of the whole battle, it is reproduced in its entirety.[12] The citation was dated April 19, 1946, and issued in the name of "the President of the United States as public evidence of deserved honor and distinction." The named units were cited for:

extraordinary heroism and outstanding performance of duty in its determined drive to overcome bitter opposition in the Huertgen Forest. On 16 November, the 22nd Infantry Regiment, with attachments, opened an offensive with the mission of clearing a portion of the Huertgen Forest of powerful enemy force and fighting its way to the Ruhr River and Cologne Plain. Throughout the campaign, the progress of the unit was seriously impeded by an unusual combination of inclement weather and difficult terrain. Unseasonable precipitation and damp, penetrating cold were a constant detriment to the health and well-being of the personnel. The terrain was characterized by densely forested hills, swollen streams, and deep, adhesive mud, which retarded all movement of troops and vehicles. Fully cognizant of the decided strategic advantages which this area afforded for effective defense, the enemy had prepared an elaborate system of mutually supporting fortifications. The effectiveness of enemy artillery and mortar fire was considerably enhanced by the frequency of tree bursts in this heavily timbered area. Inasmuch as natural conditions and rigid construction of enemy strongholds frequently precluded the effective employment of aerial and motorized support, the burden of neutralizing fanatically defended enemy fortifications fell heavily upon the shoulders of the infantrymen, as exemplified in the capture of Grosshau, a town in which concrete and steel reinforced basements rendered each house veritably impregnable to repeated artillery and aerial attacks. The town was ultimately captured by an assault in which the infantry closed with the enemy in hand-to-hand fighting. The 22nd Infantry Regiment with attachments cleared its portion of the Huertgen Forest and reached its objective on 4 December 1944, opening a gateway to the Cologne Plain and the ultimate rapid conclusion of the European conflict. The individual courage, valor, and tenacity displayed by the personnel of the 22nd Infantry Regiment with attachments, in the face of superior odds, unusually hazardous conditions and unfavorable weather were in keeping with the highest traditions of the armed forces.

BY ORDER OF THE SECRETARY OF WAR:

Dwight D. Eisenhower
Chief of Staff

OFFICIAL:

EDWARD F. WITSELL
Major General
The Adjutant General

12
The Battle of the Bulge

After the Huertgen Forest we had been sent to a quiet front, to refurbish ourselves and our tanks. It was quiet for a little over a week, then it was quiet no more.

—George Brookstein
A Company liaison corporal

Limping Into Luxembourg

The road march to Luxembourg was thankfully long, as all 147 miles were headed away from the Huertgen Forest. Aside from the tanks that had been destroyed, a number were in such disrepair that they could not begin the trip. Many others broke down en route. By the time the 70th arrived in and around Luxembourg City, only twenty-six out of seventy-nine tanks were operational.

It would take several days to bring the broken-down tanks to repair facilities. Battalion maintenance crews worked long, hard days, as did all line company maintenance platoons. Tanks not requiring overhaul were completely serviced. Tracks were replaced if needed, and bogie wheels thoroughly checked.

Lieutenant Raiford Blackstone was part of an advance party detailed to reconnoiter Luxembourg City and the surrounding area for bivouac and headquarters sites for C Company. "As was the custom, we approached the headquarters of the 4th Infantry Division, which had control of Luxembourg." Staff officers told Blackstone to examine a former army camp.

We went out there and found it was little more than a set of pigsties. This we reported to the 4th, who then told us to try Mondorf, a small city in southeastern Luxembourg. It turned out that Mondorf was a health spa with mineral baths, and the principal building was a hotel, called the Palace. It was about

**The Battle of the Bulge and the Campaign for Pruem
January 17, 1945-March 5, 1945**

ten stories, and I was bold enough to take over the entire place. When C Company moved in, we established everybody in hotel rooms, with beds and mattresses, though no sheets or pillowcases were available. We were very comfortable . . .

Now, Captain Taynton [company commander], being an enterprising, energetic person, did something hardly anyone else would think of doing. He located a chef and what materials he could find around town and from kitchen supplies and had the chef prepare pastry delicacies for late evening snacks. Among the delicacies were chocolate éclairs. It is hard to imagine that, in the midst of a war in an overrun country, anyone would have the initiative to find a chef and the materials to supply chocolate éclairs for the whole company! Twice!

After what C Company had gone through in the Huertgen Forest, sleeping on mattresses in a hotel and enjoying chocolate éclairs did wonders for morale. Such luxury did not last long, of course, but the next locations weren't bad either, according to Blackstone. "We were moved into the city of Luxembourg and quartered in residential homes. There was a lot of ice and snow, and it was bitterly cold. Our tanks were in a parklike area, where we painted them white, welded on chicken wire, and mounted evergreen branches to make a blend looking like a snowy scene in evergreen trees."

B Company was located in the village of Scheidgen, living in homes and barns. Compared with C Company, it wasn't much, but no one complained. Everyone was indoors at night and out of the Huertgen. Scheidgen was near the German border, close enough for German troops to hear tanks, as the few remaining were driven back and forth on the Luxembourg side of the Sauer River in a fruitless attempt to conceal weakness. German intelligence, as would soon be learned, was acutely aware of the strengths and disposition of Allied forces all along the line. They knew exactly where to start their counteroffensive.

A Company was in a commodious school in Dommeldange, a northern suburb of Luxembourg. Its most prominent feature was a large indoor swimming pool. A Company enjoyed it alone until December 20, when B Company headquarters moved in with them. Both companies shared facilities for about a week.

"The Krauts Have Broken Through"
On December 15, B Company was rewarded by being given quarters in a chateau also located in Dommeldange. Sleeping in aristocratic surroundings was wonderful. After noon chow had been

served the next day, some friends and I slipped out of the chateau and found a *gasthof* with beer and schnapps for sale. It was Sunday, a time to relax. Soon the group was in a frolicky mood and decided to visit other *gasthofs* located on a hill not too far away. It was bitterly cold, and the sharply inclined hill was a sheet of ice. In our inebriated state, none us could manage to get more than halfway up before slipping and sliding back down to the bottom. It quickly became fun, as grown men were sliding down backward singly or in tandem, cavorting and laughing like boys in a playground.

The *gasthof* was crowded with local people and GIs. It felt good to be out of the cold and in an atmosphere of good fellowship. The first beer was downed in a flash, but the second was really being enjoyed when in walked the familiar figure of Paul Gaul. For the first, and probably the last time in his life, Gaul interrupted someone in the middle of a drink. "Get back to the company," he announced, "the krauts have broken through."

As Gaul tells the story, Captain Songer had found him in the chateau and said briskly, "Gaul, go round up the guys. You know where they are. Tell them to get back here fast, the krauts are making a move." So Gaul got in his jeep and drove to the likely places. The only problem was, "After I rounded everybody up, I forgot to come back myself. I got drunk and tangled up with some woman. Boy, did I get into trouble. This time, 'the old man' finished me as his jeep driver and put me in a tank as assistant driver and bow gunner. I got to fight in the war a bit."

The German Counteroffensive

The Belgian people Franklin Anderson talked with in St. Vith were right. The Germans did come through the Ardennes, just as they had in 1940. On December 16, 1944, they struck with great force at the center of the American line, where only four divisions held a front of seventy-five miles.

Had the 70th stayed at Hunningen, they would have been directly in the path of one of the most powerful German thrusts. Instead, the 70th endured the hell of Huertgen and now were on the southern flank of the advance. The major task of the 4th Division and the 70th was to stop German attempts to take Luxembourg City, the major rail and road center for an extensive region and the location of General Bradley's headquarters. Roadblocks were established at key road junctions commanding the approaches to the city. In the first hours of the offensive, the Germans bypassed a number of them, surrounding 12th Infantry Regiment companies at Echternach, Berdorf, and Lauterborn.

A Scare at the Radio Station

When the Germans made their move, D Company was sent to guard the Luxembourg radio station, the most powerful in Europe. Maintenance sergeant Walter Waszyn was sergeant of the guard the first night. "We had been told this station was so important that Germans might drop paratroopers to take it. There were five or six towers and a central building surrounded by barbed wire and a main gate. We were changing the guard at about two in the morning, and it was pitch black." All of a sudden the whole sky lit up. "German voices came over really loud. We were absolutely frozen in our tracks, not knowing what the hell to do. Just as suddenly the voices stopped and it was pitch black again. I guess what had happened was that one of the transmitting wires had broken and shorted out. I have seldom been so scared. I just knew German paratroopers were landing."

D Company to the Rescue

D Company was quickly relieved at the Luxembourg radio transmitting station by B Company crews of disabled tanks and maintenance men, all serving as riflemen. 12th Regiment infantrymen were loaded on the backs of D Company light tanks. After brisk fighting on December 16 and 17, they were able to break through and rescue the infantrymen at Berdorf and Lauterborn. The force was insufficient to reach Echternach, however, which remained encircled.[1]

Surrounded at Dickweiler

Shortly after noon on December 16, B Company managed to get three medium tanks operational. With eleven 4th Division infantrymen riding with them, they moved northeast to Osweiler, where an infantry company was cut off and running low on ammunition. While at Osweiler, the small force was advised that two platoons of yet another company of infantry were surrounded at Dickweiler and in immediate danger of being overrun.

Ed Gossler was the gunner in one of the tanks. He reports they had no opposition getting to Dickweiler and were supposed to return to the company in Luxembourg later in the day. About the time they were ready to leave, an infantryman on the second floor of a house yelled down to them: "You guys got binoculars? I think they're sending us reinforcements!' We passed up a pair to him. He took a look and said, 'Hell no, those are Krauts coming in!"

They waited until the Germans were halfway down a bare hill, then pulled their tanks up to the edge of the building line. "The Germans heard our tanks, of course, and dropped to the ground and started setting up machine guns. They were too far away for *panzerfaust,* so we kind of had a field day. We had a pretty good defense. Besides the firepower from our three tanks, the infantry had a couple of mortars and a 57mm antitank gun." Gossler says the Germans didn't have a chance. "They had no protection, no place to hide, and were only a couple hundred yards away, so we had little trouble hitting them. The whole hillside was littered with dead Germans. We kept firing until those who were left surrendered." Thirty- six enlisted men and one officer were taken prisoner.[2]

However, as Gossler reports, "The Germans came from the direction of Osweiler, so we couldn't get back. Also, we lost all communications for several days. We were really cut off and on our own. As far as the battalion was concerned, we might have been lost. The Germans never tried another frontal assault, though, and even if they had tried we could probably have stopped them. It was foggy and damp. The fields were so wet that neither our tanks nor theirs could go cross-country. We had the only road into town zeroed in."

Americans couldn't get out, and Germans couldn't come in. This stalemate lasted from December 16 to 24 for these three B Company tank crews, a handful of infantry, and thirty-seven German prisoners. The enemy was not even able to bury their dead, and Gossler was horrified to see "pigs who must not have been fed for days went to that hillside and were rolling over dead Germans looking for food. It almost looked like they were eating the bodies, though I can't say for sure whether they were or not."

A couple of times German planes flew over and dropped leaflets. "They told us we were surrounded and couldn't get out, so all we had to do was go 300 to 400 yards to a wooded area and surrender. The leaflets said we would have it easy and be well treated and all that bullshit. Of course, nobody fell for that. Luckily, the 4th infantrymen had some provisions and we always carried some in our tanks. We butchered a couple of pigs and fried the meat for a few meals. Someone got honey from a beehive, which we put on K ration crackers." On Christmas Eve, the 5th Infantry came in to relieve them. "We were really happy to get out of that situation and back to Dommeldange. It was probably the best Christmas we had ever had. On Christmas Day we had a good dinner, were inside, and could even have a swim."

The German officer taken prisoner at Dickweiler revealed that the Germans planned to take Osweiler and Dickweiler on December 16, the first day of the operation. Panzers then were to move through to Luxembourg and continue south.[3] The panzers never had a chance to threaten Luxembourg City.

With C Company

Tony Zampiello drove the C Company command tank. "I was at mass with some of the guys that Sunday when the Germans broke through. When we got back to the company area, all our tanks were running and ready to go. The gunner of my tank was zeroing in the 76mm, as the tank had just returned from maintenance." A truck came by and hit the gun and stripped its gears. "We had to go up without any power and had to traverse the gun by hand. Captain Taynton was in command, and we were going back and forth between four or five little towns day and night without much rest. We had only seven tanks left in our company. One time an officer pointed to the palm of his hand and said we are here, the Germans are here and here—on both sides of us. We were really short of men and tanks and were lucky we made it."

C Company on December 18 moved to the town of Beck to support the 22d Infantry Regiment. "Upon arriving at the 22d CP, it was found that it was surrounded by enemy troops. Captain Taynton's tank was knocked out by bazooka fire. He mounted another and led an attack, which cleaned out the enemy. At 1700 the tanks escorted the CP personnel . . . through enemy lines to Herborn."[4]

With A Company

Rumors of German airdrops persisted, sending A Company tanks into action. Robert McEvoy drove a tank in the 2d Platoon. "On December 16 we were told the Germans had dropped in paratroopers. So out we went with a company of infantry and didn't get back until Christmas Eve. For a while we were cut off and nearly out of ammo—down to about six or seven rounds per tank. We held them off, but it was a tight situation."

The 1st and 2d Platoons of A Company served as a mobile reserve in the thinly held American sector along the German border. On December 17, a German force of regimental strength threatened Consdorf. "There was only a handful of cooks, stragglers, and MPs, and one medium tank (manned by only two men) in position to meet the attack. The tank with seven doughs moved into a ravine and formed a block. Later the enemy turned west, lessening the threat upon Consdorf."[5]

On December 19 the 3d Platoon of A Company was drawing back for maintenance when they were ambushed. Tanks #13, #14, and #15 were hit. Only #15 got back, and it had a hole through the turret. The #13 crew was captured, and #14 tank was knocked out, the crew fighting as foot soldiers. They did get back to their area with two men wounded.[6]

Reaction to the Malmédy Massacre

On December 17, German troops machine-gunned unarmed American soldiers who had surrendered near Malmédy, Belgium. The news of the massacre quickly came to the 70th, infuriating the men. Clarence McNamee recalls: "We were up, though the front was very fluid—really nonexistent. Our mail overran us, and the Germans had taken one of our mail trucks and killed all the men in it. We then engaged the same outfit and completely overran them. When we did, we saw that the Germans were eating our Christmas cookies. Several men went into a rage and started shooting Germans before they could fire back or surrender, whatever their intention. This was after we heard about Malmédy. It was a wild time during the Bulge." Ed Gossler also records that after Malmédy "We had orders to bring back some prisoners. They weren't getting any and wanted some for interrogation."

Chaos and Confusion

With so many tanks out of commission, crews were constantly being changed. The light tank that Jack Lovell commanded in D Company was out with engine failure. "Lieutenant Heist, our platoon leader, came to me and said: 'Jack, there are 200 krauts across this river, you want to go out and help push them back?' I told him I would, and we went out along with medium tanks from A Company. They were out in front of us as we went to a little town near the German border. In the town the krauts were in one building and 4th infantrymen in another across the street. We were supposed to help get the krauts out." A Company sent in a brand-new tank with a 76mm gun on it. "Well, this tank went into the town and its engine cut out. They couldn't get it restarted. We were sitting along a road waiting for orders. I guess they didn't want to push us too hard, as quite a few tanks were already lost. Krauts were all around so we didn't go in, and A Company couldn't get that tank out. They took the breech out of the gun and blew up that brand-new tank." They then fell back into some woods.

"Both our light tanks and some A Company mediums were in there. Of course the krauts knew exactly where we were. Starting about dark the krauts sent more damned HE artillery into those trees than you can imagine. We were buttoned up and fairly safe because the artillery shells were exploding in the trees. But it was coming right in on us, and the noise was terrible."

This wasn't Lovell's regular tank, so he had a new crew that day. "One of the guys, we called him 'Friday,' couldn't take all the explosions so close to us, and he went off his beam. He wanted out of the tank, and I had a hell of a time—nearly had to knock him out—keeping him in. He would have been a goner from all the shrapnel coming off those tree bursts. I finally quieted him down and called the medics on the radio. I told them we had a man who had to get out of here." They came to get him when the artillery stopped. "I helped get him out of the tank, and he was completely nuts by that time. During the Bulge we had put a lot of people in tanks who had never been in them before. People like cooks and clerks, who weren't trained or anything."

The next day they were able to move the enemy back and pushed them out of the town. "We kept going forward until we saw a bunch of Sherman tanks coming down a hill from the German side. I reported this, and so did others. They were our tanks, but Germans were in them. So we had to fall back again. Late that evening my tank and one more were with some 4th infantry platoons to give them support in case the Germans came in." They were at a farm, and Lovell was backing his driver in toward a barn where the tank wouldn't be exposed. "Well, there was a German standing in the doorway. I yelled at him to come out with his hands up. He didn't, so we shot him. Then all hell broke loose. Machine guns, 'shooting stars,' everything was being fired. We got out of there fast and went back into that same town." He reported where the Germans were, but no one seemed to know what to do. "Captain Finkelstein, our company CO, was there, and since it was nearly dark, he decided we would stay put. Some armored division, I think one of Patton's, was supposed to be sending us help. Early the next day [probably December 22] my tank and some infantry went back to that same area around the barn, but the Germans had left."

They went down a road with Lovell's tank following Lieutenant Heist's. There was fighting all around them. "We were supposed to take some high ground off on our right, which we could see about a mile away. There was a big building full of krauts up there, and we were on the road going to it. Krauts were hidden in trees next to the road and were firing on us. Lieutenant Heist got pretty far ahead of me, and I was firing HE and canister at the krauts. Our bow gunner was firing his .30-caliber machine gun as fast as he could." Lovell fired a canister shot, very effective against infantry. "But some slugs, kind of like big buckshot, must have stayed in the chamber. I wanted to throw some HE into these woods full of krauts, but we couldn't get the breech closed. About that time, Lieutenant Heist called me on the radio and said to come on down. Well, I was working with the gunner to get the chamber clean so we could fire, but I did tell the driver to move down, which he did. Just as I looked out of the turret I saw Lieutenant Heist, who had been standing up in his turret, slump down. A sharpshooter had put one right in his head." Heist's tank then came back and went past Lovell. "We turned around and followed them back into the town. Lieutenant Heist was dead. Killed instantly. He had made a mistake. The krauts were firing from above, and we should have cleaned them out before going down that road. Also, he shouldn't have been standing in the turret with all that firing coming in. But there wasn't a whole lot to say after he was dead. Lieutenant Heist was a fine officer and a good man."

The next day Lovell was ordered to go up that same road. "I don't know if they were trying me out or what, but just our tank was sent. We went all the way up to that high ground and to the building that had been loaded with krauts the day before." This time they made it without any trouble. "I got out of my tank to see if there were any krauts still in the building. While I was inside checking, artillery started coming in. They had the place zeroed in, and brother, they plain blasted us. I ran out and jumped back into the tank. Manross, my driver, was shaking like a leaf. I told him, 'Let's get the hell out of here,' and he did, fast."

A Defensive Line Is Established

The chaotic situation of the first three days was somewhat improved when three Headquarters Company half-tracks mounting SCR 528 and SC 508 radios were moved to positions near operational centers. Another half-track with a radio was located centrally to act as a relay station. Until then, many units had been unable to contact company or battalion headquarters (as reported by Ed Gossler).

On December 20, American forces abandoned Berdorf, Lauterborn, and Echternach and established a defensive line to the west of the Sauer River through Waldbillig, Consdorf, Osweiler, and Dickweiler.

Attached to Patton's Third Army

On December 21, 1944, the 4th Infantry and the 70th became part of the Third Army under General Patton. The 70th had been under

Patton before, in French North Africa and Sicily. For most, however, detachment from the First Army and attachment to the Third didn't mean much to the ordinary soldier. All I recall was that an order came down from Patton's headquarters ordering every enlisted man to shave once a day and every officer twice a day—whether in combat or not. Needless to say, we greeted this order with derision. Taken more seriously was a remark attributed to Patton to the effect that "I'll cross the Rhine if it takes a two-and-a-half-ton truck full of dog tags to do it!" Nonetheless, his tactical and leadership abilities were genuinely appreciated. He was a fighting general.

No change was noted in either the foggy weather or in the situation. That is, not until Patton's famous prayer was composed by his chaplain and solemnly uttered on December 22. It was sent to all attached units.

HEADQUARTERS
THIRD UNITED STATES ARMY
APO 403
U.S. Army

Prayer

Almighty and most merciful Father, we humbly beseech Thee, of thy great goodness, to restrain these immoderate rains with which we have had to contend. Grant us fair weather for battle. Graciously hearken to us as soldiers who call upon Thee that, armed with Thy power, we may advance from victory to victory, and crush the oppression and wickedness of our enemies, and establish Thy justice among men and nations.

Gen. George S. Patton

With that, the heavy fog lifted late on the day of December 22, so allied planes immediately began to provide tactical support and drop supplies.

A Company was one of the units most in need of ammunition, as Robert McEvoy has reported. He recalls that when the sky cleared, "Wall-to-wall American bombers and cargo planes came over. They dropped us supplies by parachute—red ones, green, yellow, white. Man, were they a welcome sight."

Frank Ciaravella, in B Company says: "The day the fog lifted a British Spitfire with British markings came over. For whatever reason our ack-ack started firing and shot it down. When it hit the ground, I could see the motor rolling down a big hill, turning into a ball of fire. Rumor had it that a kraut was flying it and had not properly identified himself as British."

The Mortar Platoon Fires for Effect

The mortar platoon knocked out a German company in a strategic valley on December 22. "We didn't know it when we were firing, of course, but that's what we did," Virgil Wagner remembers. "We were given a sector, as was usual for weapons like ours, and picked a spot where we could put the mortars on the ground in a little gully that offered some protection." It was too wet in the gully for the half-track to maneuver, so it was kept on top. "I was sitting in it with the door open while manning the radio and waiting for an order to fire from Sergeant Babick, who was up on the observation point. Suddenly I heard an 88 whistle in. I looked over the top of the half-track and saw it explode not too far away." Another came in even closer, and Wagner ducked. "I swore my legs were being sliced to pieces by shrapnel, as tree limbs and branches were being cut around me. I was sure I'd been hit and was searching both legs with my hand to find out where, when I heard someone calling 'Wagner, get your ass down here!' I said I couldn't because I had to wait for orders. It's funny how I didn't think about the danger because I had a job to do." Later he went down to the mortars and someone else handled the radio.

"We had about five targets we were zeroed in on, and then Sergeant Babick changed to another. He asked for a round, called for another one, and shortened the range. Then he shortened it again and came on the radio to say he still couldn't see where we were hitting and couldn't even hear them explode. So he shortened the range again. The fourth round even I heard. It hit in the trees above us. Babick now moved a bit and told us the reason he couldn't see or hear the other rounds was that they were landing in a river and not detonating." Now he knew what to do and gave new coordinates. "We got on target and fired for effect. The Germans had been bringing up reserves in trucks, and we wiped out damn near a whole company. It was always with a sense of gratitude when Lieutenant Jones or Sergeant Babick said we had done well. They did this time, and I wanted to see for myself what we had done."

Wagner got permission to go up to the observation point. "When I got there, some combat engineers had a water-cooled .50-caliber machine gun and were preparing to fire on the Germans who were visible. I told them, 'No, please don't fire. You'll give away our observation point,' and they didn't."

"This Was the Craziest Time of the War"

On December 20, B Company headquarters moved from the chateau to share the school in Dommeldange with A Company. Throughout the period from Decembar 16 to 24, all men in both companies not engaging the enemy could use the swimming pool after duty hours. Recalls George Brookstein: "This was the craziest time. I would go out as liaison corporal during the day and do whatever I was called upon to do, then come back in the evening and have a swim in the pool!"

During this most peculiar situation of the entire war, at no time were more than half the tanks operational, meaning that far more men than usual were around the area, and for many the duty was light. There was nothing they could do to aid their buddies in the field, so why not swim if given the opportunity?

When tankers returned, all of A and B Companies could swim. The pool area was absolutely jammed with men, many of whom had just hours before they faced death.

Celebrating Christmas Day Indoors

After December 22, the German counteroffensive collapsed in the southern sector. On Christmas Eve, all tank companies returned to their bivouacs in Luxembourg City and environs. Being off the line and indoors made it memorable. To make it even better, mail arrived after long delays, including packages from home.

B Company cooks prepared not one, but two good meals on

Christmas Day, and so, presumably, did those in all other companies. I noted the B Company menus in a letter home dated December 27, 1944.

> Christmas '44 is over. It was another day of war in Europe. But we did have a good dinner and were out of the cold. For breakfast we had fried eggs and hotcakes. For dinner we had roast turkey, mashed potatoes, dressing, giblet gravy, canned corn, pickle relish, cranberry jelly, apple pie, and coffee—and we had plenty of it . . .
>
> I wish you a Happy New Year, and may it bring much more happiness than 1944 . . . I hope the New Year sees me in St. Paul—permanently. My thoughts were with you on Christmas more than ever. I wished you all a Merry Christmas and then tried to imagine how you were spending the day . . .
>
> I am sending a letter with some Jerry stamps for you, Carol. Also a few pictures we had taken in Paris. The girls in the pictures sent them to me.

A Respite in Luxembourg

The assault gun platoon remained in a fighting position near Herborn until January 3. All other elements of the 70th were on alert and in reserve until New Year's Day. The enemy made no movement, so all was quiet on the southern front. The battalion could at last enjoy a period of rest and build up its strength.

Some B Company men returned from the hospital, including Bob Knoebel and George Hammersmith. Also, the journal states, five men returned after a two-month absence on special duty. With these men and recent replacements, B Company was above strength, so seven men were transferred to C Company, which had not recovered from its losses in the Huertgen Forest. Living conditions were as good as they ever got in a combat area. B Company had the school and pool in Dommeldange to themselves, as A Company moved to the center of the city. This was an opportunity to get to know the people of Luxembourg. George Brookstein made friends with whom he corresponded long after the end of the war. "The people seemed very friendly toward us, even though some had brothers, fathers, and uncles in the German army."

Although the front was quiet, we knew that the Germans were not far away. Rocket projectiles exploded in and around the city, causing many civilian casualties. Fragments indicated they were large and heavy rounds, with fins similar to those on a mortar shell. They started coming in on December 30, and continued as late as January 15, when, according to the B Company journal, "The area is alarmed from enemy rocket shells hitting near our CP." These rocket attacks as well as nightly bombing raids were obviously more of a nuisance than anything else and did little to interrupt the flow of activity.

Tinkering With the Sherman

The B Company journal notes that five new medium tanks arrived on January 5, and that the company now had its full complement. These new tanks were arriving with a full load of ammunition, equipped with a 76mm gun instead of the old 75mm.

Some tanks with 76mm guns reached other units as early as Normandy. When Eisenhower made an inspection of the Normandy battlefield, he was told that the new gun couldn't penetrate the armor of a Tiger or a Panther. He was appalled. "You mean our 76 won't knock out these Panthers? Why I thought it was going to be the wonder gun of the war!" Bradley told him it was better than the 75mm, but the change was too small. Eisenhower wondered, "Why is it I'm the last to hear about this stuff? Ordnance told me this 76 would take care of anything the Germans had. Now I find you can't knock out a damn thing with it." [7]

Because of the long delay in getting a bigger tank into production, Ordnance was forced to tinker with the Sherman. When more armor was added in addition to the larger gun, "The inevitable result was that during the fighting in France, Belgium, and Germany, the now badly overloaded Sherman was not only still out-gunned and out-armored but on too many occasions, particularly in mud, snow, and ice, outmaneuvered by the Panther." [8] Although a tank may look like a lumbering hulk, it is actually a complex and balanced vehicle. The Sherman had more than 25,000 separate parts with most of the weight in the armor and gun. Adding a larger gun and extra armor made it overloaded and less maneuverable. The tinkering included an attempt to increase traction in mud, snow, and ice by extenders that maintenance crews clipped onto tracks to widen them.

Criticism of American tanks continued both at home and on the front. Hanson Baldwin, an early critic, wrote in the *New York Times* on January 5, 1945: "Why at this late stage in the war are American tanks inferior to the enemy's? That they are inferior the fighting in Normandy showed, and the recent battles in the Ardennes have again emphatically demonstrated. This has been denied, explained away, and hushed up, but the men who are fighting our tanks against much heavier, better armored and more powerful German monsters know the truth . . . It is not that our tanks are bad, they are the best in the world—next to the Germans'."[9]

The new 76mm gun was high velocity and unquestionably superior to the old 75mm, but what was needed was the larger tank finally being built. The M-26 Pershing tank reached the battlefield in limited numbers with the 3d Armored Division in late February 1945. Firing a 90mm gun, this was the tank that could take on either Tigers or Panthers, but it was too late to affect the outcome of the war. The long delay constitutes a blunder of mammoth proportions, one that probably lengthened the war. The 70th, of course, never saw the M-26 until after the war in Europe, when training began for the Far East.

Priorities for which units were first to get innovations and upgrades remain a mystery. Perhaps supply sergeant Louis Rizzo is correct in stating that divisions had the weight to get items denied to battalions attached to divisions. If the 76mm was designed to enable Shermans to take on larger German tanks, then independent tank battalions such as the 70th needed them in Normandy. More to the point were telephone hookups outside tanks that enabled infantry to communicate with tankers in the midst of an action. Providing close support for infantry was exactly what the 70th did, but they did not get the device until late October. The 70th was also late getting flamethrowers on tanks.

I Solve a Problem

During this period of relative relaxation, B Company men were given passes to go into the city of Luxembourg with truck transportation provided. Side arms were required as the area was still a combat zone. I went in one day with a buddy and, not wanting to carry my carbine, borrowed a .45-caliber automatic from a friend. "But dammit, Jensen," he said, "I'm responsible for it, so never let it out of your sight."

The truck dropped us off at a square in a residential section not far from the city center. Everyone headed for the same bar just down the street. After a few beers most men drifted off, but my friend and I had something else in mind. Being a suave, cosmopolitan man of the world in these matters since St. Quentin, I approached the bartender for information. Asking for the location of "ladies of the night" didn't seem quite right in broad daylight, but luckily the bartender spoke English and obviously had been asked the question many times before. "Go three blocks down this street, turn left and go two blocks, then turn right for one block. On the corner is a house painted light brown with three steps leading to the front door."

The house was easily located, but anxiously rapping on the door were two U.S. Army lieutenants. Without any response, the two officers shrugged their shoulders and left. "Damn that bartender, he was just getting rid of us," I said. "Well, hell, we might as well try," my buddy commented dryly.

At our first rap, a male face appeared from behind a window curtain. The door opened and we were welcomed in. There stood the man, a middle-aged women, presumably his wife, and two younger women. This, however, was not a normal family scene. The man stated an amount of money, which was duly tendered. Following a perfunctory introduction, the two young women led us to the second floor. Each pair went into one of two bedrooms.

The woman assigned to me was ready for combat within seconds. It was easy for her. She was barely clothed to begin with and bore no responsibility for my friend's gun, which now became an embarrassment and a problem. My first thought quite naturally was to wear it during the performance. I quickly rejected that solution. It would be cumbersome and somehow didn't seem to fit the occasion. There was no bedstead on which to hang the weapon, and to place it on the floor would have put it out of view. Furthermore, the gun had to be within reach in case this was all a plot designed to make off with the valuable commodity. I tried to remember if the officers at the door had .45s strapped on. If they hadn't, maybe that was why they were rejected for me. The best solution was to hang the belt, holster, and gun on a high-backed wooden chair on which I now was sitting to take off my shoes. It was too far from the bed, so I nonchalantly inched the chair closer, again and again. Finally it was within arm's length and definitely in line of sight. The woman had a bewildered look on her face but said nothing.

The encounter took less time than it took to position the chair. Never did I take my eyes off the gun. I thought it moved once, but only for an instant.

"Jerry Bit Off More Than He Could Chew!"

On January 17, 1945, the 70th left the City of Luxembourg. Phase II of the Battle of the Bulge was about to begin. That would be to re-take the Grand Duchy of Luxembourg from the Germans. The 4th and the 70th remained under the command of General Patton and the Third Army.

The night before leaving Dommeldange, I wrote home: "The news is getting more sensational in the last few reports. I guess the Jerry counteroffensive sort of hit a stalemate, or as you used to say, Dad, he bit off more than he could chew. The Russians are driving on Berlin at a fast pace. This new drive should bring the end much closer."

Much hard fighting remained, nonetheless, and the movement north was slow, mainly due to icy conditions. The B Company journal records that on January 19, the company left Godbrange at 1300 and arrived at Larochette at 1515. It took two hours and fifteen minutes to move only five miles, without enemy opposition. On the same day, A Company tanks, in support of the 8th Infantry Regiment, had to cross the Sauer River out of the 4th Division's zone of action because road conditions and enemy action made it impossible for engineers to construct a support bridge.

In the B Company journal entry for January 21, company tanks took the town of Gongsdorf, tank #14 being credited with knocking out a German tank. Many buildings were "lowered" and numerous German infantry killed. One B Company tanker was wounded and another "took off." A later entry confirms that this soldier was in the hands of 4th Infantry medics, suffering from "combat exhaustion."

When this entirely understandable condition occurred, it was not talked about at company level.

We learned earlier that Paul Gaul was relieved of his duties as the CO's jeep driver and put into a tank as an assistant driver/bow gunner. The date of the transfer was January 3, so the action at Gongsdorf may have been his first in a tank. As Gaul tells the story, "We were backed into a farm and parked right alongside of a manure pile. It was cold, oh, was it cold! The krauts had white uniforms on and were sneaking up on us. Well, Trujillo had the GIs, so he got out and went back of the tank to do his job. We saw a kraut at the corner of a building fire at him. Trujillo dove headfirst into that manure pile. We gave him covering fire and he managed to get back in the tank. There was no question but that we had to let him in, but boy, did he stink!"

Worth mentioning in the B Company journal was that an Associated Press reporter interviewed Captain Songer and took pictures of company men. That day, January 22, another German tank was destroyed by B Company, and the following day two more at Fouhren. Entries do not indicate the size of these German tanks or the circumstances, but knocking out four in three days was exceptional.

The Fouhren engagement was sharp and highly successful. Captured were three multiple-barrel 20mm guns, one 88mm gun, and two 75mm antitank guns. Twenty-five of the enemy were killed, and only four prisoners were taken. One B Company tank was lost, with one man killed and three wounded.

Back Where We Were in September

An adjustment of American corps and army sectors now took place. As part of it, the 4th Division and the attached 70th moved seventy-two miles north, much of it along the same route Patton had used to relieve Bastogne. Franklin Anderson, A Company executive officer recalls: "Back in the Schnee-Eifel, we saw equipment from the 106th Infantry Division. Basketballs, volleyball nets, and the like were scattered all around. They thought they were there for R and R and the Germans came right through."

Though Patton's relief columns had fought their way to Bastogne several weeks before, destroyed American and German tanks and other vehicles were strewn about—ugly burned-out hulks disfiguring beds of white, freshly fallen snow.

The B Company convoy went through Bastogne but did not pause. Scarcely a building was standing. No one in the back of the kitchen truck said anything. It was a solemn occasion, as each man reflected on what had taken place here.

Soon a directional sign indicated that St.Vith was but a few miles away. "My God," someone said, "we're right back where we were in September." It was true. We had been here when first entering Germany and encountering the Siegfried Line. What a strange and sickening feeling it was to have to retake territory fought for before. It seemed almost as if the hell of the Huertgen was in vain. We had been on the offensive then, whereas during the Bulge we had not. We were ready to resume the offensive again, but it was back to square one— near St. Vith. Was there another Huertgen Forest ahead?

4th Division Commendations

For actions during the Bulge, the 1st and 2d Platoons of A Company received the following commendation[10] issued by the 4th Infantry Division on January 11, 1945:

During the period 17 December to 24 December 1944, the 2nd Battalion, 8th Infantry, with the 1st and 2nd Platoons of Company A, 70th Tank Battalion attached, was employed as a part of "Task Force Luckett" against the German offensive in LUXEMBOURG. On or about 19 December, the battalion was ordered to attack and seize two very steep hills overlooking the road through the village of MULLENTHAL in order that an armored column might break through the enemy position. The battalion was pinned down by very heavy artillery and mortar fire and by rifle and machine gun fire from a prepared enemy position on top of the battalion objective. It was impossible to assault the enemy position frontally because of a sheer cliff . . .

The 1st and 2nd Platoons of Company A, 70th Tank Battalion, without infantry protection because of the reduced strength of rifle companies, volunteered to make an attack around the left flank of the enemy position and strike it from the rear. With great skill, the . . . tanks of the platoon were maneuvered into position and placed heavy machine-gun and 76mm high-explosive fire on the enemy position causing great casualties as later determined from PW reports. Again on 20 December, the tanks were employed in support of the infantry and pressed the attack with great skill and determination, inflicting heavy casualties and causing great confusion in the ranks of the enemy.

The Division Commander wishes to commend each member of the 1st and 2nd Platoons, Company A, 70th Tank Battalion, for his courage, initiative and ceaseless devotion to duty. The success of the 2nd Battalion in holding the German attack was greatly dependent upon the initiative and tactical skill displayed by these two platoons of Company A, 70th Tank Battalion.

By command of Brigadier General BLAKELEY

A Letter of Commendation to C and D Companies.
In a letter addressed to Lt. Col. Henry Davidson, commanding officer of the 70th, and dated December 26, 1944, Col. R. H. Chance, commander of the 12th Infantry Regiment, wrote the following:

1. Throughout the period of 16 December to 24 December 1944, Companies C and D of the 70th Tank Battalion rendered invaluable tank support to the 12th Infantry in bringing to a standstill the German counteroffensive launched against this regiment in the Battle of Luxembourg. Your wise tactical recommendations for the strategic employment of your tanks resulted in the battalions and companies of the 12th Infantry receiving adequate tank support at all times whenever and wherever needed. During the fiercest fighting your tanks were ever foremost in the action providing strong fire support and inflicting very heavy casualties against the enemy. On occasion when units of the regiment were completely surrounded and cut off your tanks were ever ready to run the gauntlet of fire to deliver ammunition and food to the isolated troops. At times when our lines were thinly held and all available firepower was

needed at the front your tanks unhesitatingly remained in the front lines with the infantry troops, thereby bolstering the morale of the foot soldiers and strengthening our defensive positions.

2. The highest praise is deserved by you and other officers and enlisted men of the 70th Tank Battalion for the most outstanding tank support that this infantry regiment has ever witnessed.

13
The Battle for Pruem and On to the Rhine

We lost a lot of people in this area. I remember in one place there was a pine forest and a narrow road coming through. A grave registration unit was moving down that road in a jeep pulling a trailer full of frozen bodies of dead GIs. Their arms and legs were sticking out in all directions. I'll never forget it.

—Tony Zampiello
C Company tank driver

The next objective was the strongly fortified town of Pruem.[1] Whereas it was only about fifteen air miles from the location of most 70th bivouacs in the last days of January, the area of the Schnee-Eifel was hilly and heavily wooded, reaching an elevation of 700 feet. Winding its way through the approaches to Pruem was the Siegfried Line.

Although we had pierced the line in September, it was much tougher this time. During their counteroffensive, the Germans corrected many of the line's deficiencies and made it stronger throughout. Narrow, twisting roads linked numerous small towns and villages nestled in valleys. (Some twenty-nine were fought for before and shortly after Pruem.) Adding to the difficulties again was the weather. Road conditions continued to plague tank operations, and going cross-country was an invitation to disaster. Again, this was primarily an infantry show, with the 70th supporting the infantry in country ill suited for tanks. It took two weeks to capture Pruem, and two additional weeks to reach terrain more suitable for tanks. This became a major campaign, requiring several divisions. The 4th and the 90th Infantry Divisions bore the brunt of the attack, with the 90th on the 4th's northern flank.

A Devastating Death
George Hammersmith was again the B Company liaison corporal. Several weeks before, he had returned from a long stay in a hospital

recovering from wounds received back around Mortain. Hammer-smith and his close buddy, Sgt. Ed Provaznik, had led the company convoy to a new bivouac close to Burg-Reuland, Belgium, near the German border. On arrival Paul Gaul and I joined them and we walked four abreast down a logging road cut through trees, heading for a shed to be used as a command post. After only a few yards, a mortar shell came in without warning. All four hit the dirt, and George cried "I'm hit," but didn't get up. Pro, Gaul, and I carried George to the shed and placed him face down on a bench, as he was hit in the back. The bench was too short, so I cupped my hands on George's face to hold his head up. A medic arrived almost immedi-ately. He cut away clothing to reveal a tiny wound in the small of the back. The wound was cleaned and bandaged and a shot of morphine administered. "You'll be alright, George," the medic said. "It's a very small wound." George was inched back to allow him to rest his face on a rolled combat jacket. Shortly an ambulance arrived. Everyone wished him well in the belief he would be back with us soon. We were wrong. The B Company journal listed Hammersmith as "lightly wounded" on January 29, and his death on February 1.

George Hammersmith, from Maryland, was a soft-spoken, warm, intelligent, and unassuming man who always carried a picture of his lovely young wife with him. His death affected me deeply. It per-sonalized the war, sharpening its dreadful image in a way I've never forgotten. He was a good friend and a cut above most of his fellows. Hammersmith was the only man killed in my presence. It could have been Pro or Gaul or me. George was the unlucky one. A tiny piece of shrapnel, no larger than a fingernail, had lodged in exactly the wrong place. War is indiscriminate and indifferent. The good die next to the bad. George Hammersmith was one of the best. What a terrible, horrible waste.

The same day I heard of George's death, I sent a V mail letter to my grandparents, addressing them in the Danish for grandfather and grandmother.

Dearest Bestefar and Bestemor,
    Just a V mail to tell you I'm still OK. It's kinda cold over here, but I'll make out alright, just don't worry. Mother wrote me that

you and Janus [their son] had a special prayer for me in church. I can tell you truthfully that made me feel much better. I, too, am praying that everyone will be safe back home, safe so that I can come back to them and live the life I was meant to live.

I know God is on our side and so we cannot fail. I hope He will hasten the day so this killing will end before we are all uselessly killed. Your selection for my Christmas package is now coming in handy. I mean the wool stockings. They feel good about this time of the year.

A Very Tough Fight for Bleialf

Shortly after daybreak on February 2, the 1st and 3d Platoons of B Company moved out to support the 12th Infantry Regiment in an attack on Bleialf, just inside Germany near the Belgian border. The roads were so icy that infantry, working at night, used entrenching tools to cut grooves to assist 70th tanks in going up a hill for the attack the next morning. In another case, all five 3d Platoon tanks had to be chained together to help get them up a hill. What ensued was, according to Bob Knoebel, "a tough fight, the roughest I was ever in!" (Knoebel had been in a very rough one in Normandy. Knocked out of two tanks within minutes, he was wounded and taken prisoner.)

In this engagement, he reports: "There was a lot of shooting going on. The infantry was being hit hard in the town, so we were sent down a hill just to draw fire from them. I heard Lieutenant Green say, 'We can't go down that hill!' The next thing I heard on the radio was, 'You *will* go down that hill!' So Green said, 'OK, here we go!'"

There was ice and snow and a lot of antitank fire. "We started out with nine tanks and only two reached the bottom, and we hit a mine when we did. All the tanks weren't hit—I think some of them went off the road—but most of them got knocked out. The mine we hit must have been very big or stacked mines, judging from the damage done to the tank. It blew the suspension system along with the track. We bailed out and managed to get into a culvert." Each time they left the culvert, the Germans shelled again. Tank commander Clarence Jay went to the tank that was not hit. "He told them when they went back up that hill not to forget to pick us up. He wanted to ride back up, but I didn't." All five crewmen did get up the hill on foot, using the culvert. "We went back a few days later to get our stuff from the tank. The place was full of mines. They were visible. Either they had not been buried or they had been in snow that melted."

In that same action, the B Company journal relates, Cpl. Don Calderari was killed and two men were wounded. (See Chapter 7 for Clarence McNamee's account of how Calderari died.) Our tanks had been under enemy observation for more than seven hours. After dark, the remaining tanks were withdrawn. Two slid off the road and became mired in mud, and another overturned—a bad mauling. The 12th did not take Bleialf until the next day, when B Company tanks moved in to help hold the town.

Another Bivouac Shelled

When we were in a town or village, we found buildings to sleep in. When not, men slept on the ground in the bitter cold. After one such night, as breakfast was being served in our bivouac, an artillery shell exploded not more than twenty-five yards from the kitchen truck. Men close to the front of the chow line and we cooks dove under the kitchen truck. Shells kept coming in, each on target.

Panic stricken, I now made my most stupid mistake of the war. I made a dash for a tank about thirty to forty yards away, the instant after another shell landed. Running full tilt through the trees like a football halfback dodging tacklers, I covered the distance in Olympic record time, negotiating the last ten yards with an enormous headlong dive. Bouncing under the tank, I landed next to a tanker with blood running in rivulets from his forehead down his nose and both cheeks. He looked absolutely terrible. "Christ, I'll run for a medic," I said. "Naw," the tanker replied calmly, "I think it's only a scalp wound. We better stick it out here, Jensen." After the shelling stopped, we found a medic. The scalp wound was not enough for a trip to the hospital.

Knowledgeable veterans told me the shells were probably 155mm. Being under them was my single most terrifying experience of the war.

The Siegfried Line Again

Fighting was at close quarters. Coordination and cooperation between infantry and tankers were as always essential. On February 5, the 1st Platoon of A Company was operating with a battalion of the 12th Infantry Regiment in an attack on Schlausenbach. As the platoon moved up a trail through the woods, "It was fired on by a self-propelled gun that was firing by sound into the trees along the trail. The #2 tank was hit and T-5 Melvin Greenlaw, the driver, was wounded. A second tank was hit a moment later, wounding PFC Raymond Babush. The infantry deployed into the woods in an effort to locate the enemy position, with the tanks firing over their heads as they moved forward. As they approached the enemy gun, its crew destroyed the vehicle and surrendered."

Again at Brandschield Company B took up positions on a hill, "with the mission of firing into the town to assist the move of C Company in an attack . . . [which] carried through the town and on into the Siegfried Line some 2,000 yards northeast of . . . Brandschield. The attack was made with close teamwork on the part of the infantry, which moved up to the pillboxes under cover of fire from the tanks and placed satchel charges against the bunkers and exploded them." More than 280 prisoners were captured, with forty bunkers, one 75mm gun, and many vehicles destroyed. "During the night, many enemy troops infiltrated the town and occupied several of the pillboxes from which they had been driven the previous day. This force counterattacked at daybreak, and a lively fight ensued. The 1st Platoon, C Company, moved from the center of town to check this attack. The fighting was extremely bitter, with the enemy taking up positions in the rubble of destroyed buildings as well as in cellars and the bunkers themselves." By noon, however, the 1st Platoon had cleared the town again.[2]

Tony Zampiello drove the C Company command tank in this engagement. "First Sergeant Carman was bucking for a battlefield promotion and needed experience on the line. When those Germans infiltrated, he was really shitting his pants. He wasn't alone. I was scared too!" In a few days Zampiello was on his way home on a rotation furlough. He was on the line the day the good news came. "It was cold and raining. A lot of guys had frozen feet. At the end of the day this guy comes up and says, 'Zamp, I'm here to relieve you, you're going on a thirty-day furlough.' I didn't believe him, but Lieutenant McCaffrey said, 'Zamp, get your ass out of here.' So I went back to the forward CP and ran into Captain Taynton. He had mail for me and told me he had found out I was next on the rotation list. He pulled me out so nothing would happen to me—which was very thoughtful."

The Traumatic and Disquieting Time Continues

Frustration and anxiety were widely felt. Was this hellish war never going to end? It seemed over after Paris, but then came the bloody Huertgen Forest, followed by the Bulge. The Germans had gambled and lost. Surely they were finished. Yet, yesterday, today, and tomorrow it was the same thing: more woods, more ice and cold, more buddies killed or wounded for land barely beyond where others were killed or wounded five months before.

The 1st Platoon of C Company was led by Lt. Raiford Blackstone at Brandschield. He was instructed to aid infantry being attacked from a location between the two villages of Untermehlen and Niedermehlen. "We moved our tanks into an open area and could see the Germans moving down a distant hill toward us. So with our tremendous firepower of fifteen machine guns and five 76mm guns, we were able to stop them and at least partially wipe them out. Everything had quieted down when Joe Di Salas, my bow gunner, opened fire. I was standing in the turret and looked to see what he was doing. Joe told me then that a German soldier had stood up in the foxhole and aimed his rifle at me, but Joe killed him before he could pull the trigger. That was the only occasion that I am aware of that a specific person saved my life."

A number of other incidents happened in rapid succession, that, along with Brandschield and being in the sights of a German rifleman nearly drove Blackstone to a nervous breakdown. He states that platoon leaders had an agreement among themselves that whenever possible they would take turns leading attacks. "It was my good friend Lt. Clarence Hedrick's turn in an attack in the Niedermehlen area. I was waiting with my platoon on a road when Lieutenant Hedrick's tank came back. His face and head were covered with blood, and he was waving his arms and shouting something I didn't understand. The other tanks in his platoon followed, and I directed them to turn around, as the rear of a tank is most vulnerable and German artillery was coming in."

Blackstone's orders now changed—to go cross-country to Unter-mehlen. "To get there, we had to go over a ridge that I knew was too steep for my tanks to get back out. In Untermehlen my tank was parked by the town hall and next to a manure pile." Standing in the open turret, he saw a 4th Infantry captain walk by, a rolled army blanket under his arm. "A German artillery shell came right in on us, and I ducked down into the turret. When I came up again, the captain, what was left of him, and his blanket were sprawled all over the manure pile." Moments later, another shell came in. "This one killed four artillery observers as they stood in a doorway just a few yards from me."

They moved out as the Germans were mounting a counterattack. Both sides were close together as darkness fell. "I went alone on foot reconnaissance and found a way to avoid the ridge and get back on a road. By the time we got to the assembly area, it was far into the night." Blackstone reported in, and company commander Lt. Preston Yeoman arrived. "It seemed like so much had happened that I was in pretty bad shape. Lieutenant Yeoman took me back to company headquarters and had me lie down in his tent. He had someone bring me a pan of hot water and some food. After I washed, ate, and had a little sleep, I was able to go back up and take over the platoon again. It was the one time in the war that I had about reached my breaking point. Fortunately, before and after that I was able to stand whatever came about."

Uncertainty and mixed emotions were also apparent in my letters home. I wrote: "Well, the Reds are drawing closer to Berlin. I wonder if the war is nearly over, but I guess if Berlin falls, it doesn't necessarily mean it is. Only time will tell." Then, on February 13 came an outburst in which I blamed people at home for having the same hope I had. "I suppose the people back home are betting heavily on a quick ending to the war. This makes me disgusted. The quicker they realize that the home front is closely linked to the war front and that the war can't be won when one or the other becomes lax, the sooner they realize that, the sooner it will end."

In answer to a letter from my paternal grandparents in which Bestefar made reference to his father having fought the German invasion of Denmark in 1864, I wrote:

Yes, Bestefar, I remember well the stories you used to tell me of your father fighting the Tysklander [Danish for German]. It's too bad they can't soon wake up to the fact that the world cannot be controlled by one power. Germany could be a respected country if only they would discard their militaristic attitude. This is the worst beating they have ever taken, and the longer they continue the worse it will get. They cannot last much longer.

How is little Askov now? I'll bet it's quiet and peaceful. When I left it wasn't lively enough for me. But I now know how good a little peace and quiet is. Is it still as friendly as always? That is something I really have missed since I left Askov. There would be no more war if the world could be like that little village. [3]

Blackstone's Platoon Battles a Panther Tank

Pruem lay in a valley alongside the Pruem River, with high hills on all sides. The narrow roads that led down to the town were all blown out, making them difficult for tank use. Approaches were heavily defended by infantry, antitank guns, artillery, mortars, and in some sectors by trenches. Although battalion elements on February 9 held high ground overlooking Pruem, those last few miles were measured in yards.

On February 10, an infantry major ordered Lt. Raiford Blackstone to take his platoon and accompanying infantry to the top of a hill where they were to launch an attack. "The major told me he had two companies of infantry occupying a location he referred to as Five Points, where five roads came together on the high ground we were to take. There was an obvious problem to carrying out the major's orders. The way to the top of the hill was along a steep utility right-of-way that would be a challenge to the hill-climbing capability of Sherman tanks. The stated incline these tanks could navigate was twenty-seven degrees."

Nevertheless the infantry troops mounted the tanks and the platoon started up the hill. Near the top, German small-arms fire was aimed at infantrymen, who quickly dismounted and took cover behind the tanks. The fire was coming from a brick building, which Blackstone's tanks set ablaze with HE shells. This silenced the German small-arms fire until an infantryman was shot through the neck by a sniper's bullet. "The infantry lieutenant asked me to try to locate the sniper, so I moved my tank, #1, and also #2 tank forward to get better observation of the entire area. We could not locate any enemy and subsequently cut our engines."

All was briefly quiet. "Tank #2 was parallel and about fifteen feet to my left, in the direction of Five Points. Tanks #3, #4, and #5 were to our rear, below the crest of the hill and out of sight of any enemy at or near Five Points. Suddenly I heard a loud explosion. Glancing to my left, I saw that tank #2 was smoking and immediately knew it had been hit on the left side." Blackstone told his driver to start the engine and back up. As he did, tank #2 was hit a second time on its left side, sending debris flying. "Over the intercom I instructed the driver to back up faster and told the gunner to traverse the turret left. Looking in that direction, down a slight downward slope, through high weeds and a thick haze, I saw the shape of a German tank at Five Points, which I had been told was occupied by two companies of our infantry."

Blackstone ordered the gunner, Corporal Oldani, to commence firing at the German tank. "Since we always carried an HE round in the 76mm gun chamber, there was some confusion between my gunner and the loader. The loader knew we should fire the HVAP [high-velocity armor piercing, to be used only against enemy tanks], and momentarily tried to unload the HE round from the gun chamber. I was shouting into the intercom to 'fire, dammit, fire!' since that was the fastest way to empty the chamber."

Corporal Oldani fired the HE, which hit the ground just in front of the German tank. He elevated slightly and fired after the loader, Homer Cottrell, threw in an HVAP. "These rounds had tracers, so I could see it streak toward the enemy tank, strike it on the front slope plate, and careen hundreds of feet into the sky." They continued to fire as fast as possible, all rounds now striking the German tank. "Tank #4 moved over the crest of the hill and commenced firing. The German tank continued to fire at us, but their rounds fell short. Apparently we had damaged the gun barrel. By now the enemy tank was on fire, and some of its crew emerged and ran into the brick building. I ordered my tanks to stop firing."

After a few minutes the Germans were seen running back to their tank. It was no longer burning! "Without waiting for orders, my crew and that of #4 tank commenced firing. Joining our barrage now was a tank destroyer from a hilltop about a mile away. Their 90mm gun and our 76mms set the German tank on fire a second time and put what proved to be a Panther tank out of action."

Corporal John J. O'Brien, commander of tank #2, and T-5 Bernard Ykema, gunner, were killed. They along with John Gzeckowicz were the only men in Blackstone's command to die in battle, all within five days. "I have many memories of the fine men whom I served with in World War II, but the memories of these three who were lost under my command will not be forgotten so long as I can remember anything." Blackstone had seen as much combat as anyone else in the 70th since joining on August 10, 1944, at Mortain. He had been judicious in command, trying not to expose his men to needless risks. He also admits that he must have been damned lucky.

A Bad Decision by an Infantry Colonel

The question of authority for the use of tanks had seldom arisen because of the good relationship between the 4th Division and the 70th. Yet, fairly late in the war, probably the worst case arose. Franklin Anderson had assumed command of C Company during the battle for Pruem. "We were to mount an attack in support of the 22d Infantry down into a valley. The night before, I had made a foot reconnaissance and saw tank traps the Germans had made by digging holes we couldn't cross. They wanted to force us to go a way they probably had zeroed in. I had gone back to a meeting at infantry headquarters to plan the attack with the regimental commander." Anderson knew that this colonel had a reputation for being hard nosed. "In fact, one reason I had replaced the previous company commander was that he couldn't get along with this colonel. There was also a Lieutenant Colonel Ruggles I had gotten to know, and him I liked very much. After this meeting, Ruggles asked me some questions, then said, 'You look concerned!'" Anderson told him the reason. "'There is a large open valley, not very deep, with a high ridge on the other side. That is the area I would protect and defend if it were me,' I said. The ridge provided a remarkable point of observation of everything coming in that direction, and the Germans could certainly put firepower into the valley."

"But the regimental commander said he could visualize tanks barreling over the hill into the valley. Of course if we did that, we would be ahead of the infantry and exposed out in the open. Well, the colonel said that is what we would do, and that the attack would begin at 0800, and were there any questions? I said I had one suggestion. 'Wouldn't it be possible to leave at daybreak or just prior to it?' I asked. At that time, the Germans would have poor observation. There might be fog, early-morning mist, or semidarkness. "The earlier the better," I said. The colonel said, no, it would be at 0800. Period. That's all he said, and a colonel doesn't have to give a reason to a junior officer."

"The next morning I told Lt. John Dixon that his platoon would lead. They had only four tanks left, and I figured if they got hit it was better to use fewer rather than more. I was really apprehensive about the whole setup. I told John to get his tanks going full speed and to head for a clump of trees, maybe 200 yards ahead and left at about a forty-five-degree angle. The idea was for Dixon to get that far, which would give us advanced firepower for the main attack."

An infantry major called Dixon on the radio and ordered him to move out. Unfortunately, Anderson's suspicions were correct. Anderson recalls that "Dixon got his tanks going full speed, but about halfway down, all hell broke loose. Tanks 1,2,3, and 4—all four were hit. We couldn't see where the fire was coming from on the ridge, but it was a hell of a display of gunnery, and they had excellent guns, probably 88s."

Lieutenant Raiford Blackstone was a witness to the attack and reports that he and Lieutenant McCaffrey went down to the tanks to aid the stricken crewmen. "I wrote on white enamel in a tank: 6 killed, 14 survivors, March 6, 1945."

Anderson remembers that any further attack was promptly canceled. "In the late afternoon, one of the two armored divisions that had moved into the area took over the attack. They had so many tanks going into that valley that the Germans couldn't hope to hold them. At least one full company of tanks spread out abreast and blasted the hell out of that ridge as they advanced. The Germans didn't even try to fire. They must have abandoned their guns and taken off. Against that firepower it was the only sensible thing to do." In most situations, tank and junior infantry officers planned attacks on the spot. "We didn't go up the chain of command but dealt with each other." In this case, Anderson was given an order by a full colonel who was not about to listen to a lieutenant, even though he was very wrong.

Pruem Finally Falls

Pruem was taken on February 12, but it was far from secure. The enemy from the hills could observe all traffic in the city so that resupply had to be done at night. Sniper fire, artillery, and mortars continued to harass our troops. Fighting for two weeks was for control of a number of small towns and villages, each stoutly defended. In one day, March 3, the 70th lost seven tanks, with three men killed and twelve wounded. Most were with A and D Companies in the battle for Gondelsheim, which remained in German hands.

Robert McEvoy drove A Company #6 tank in the engagement. This was the 2d Platoon command tank and was in the lead. "We traveled up a winding dirt road with woods on both sides for about a mile and a half. Then we came upon an open field on our left. On the horizon we could see the ever-present church steeple, which usually concealed an artillery observer and therefore was always a prime target.

"As soon as our tanks were stretched out along this open field, we turned left into it and headed for the town of Gondelsheim." There was a patch of woods to the left. "We were moving slowly across the field, firing every gun we had. It didn't seem as though we were receiving much return fire, but we were about to be surprised. About two-thirds of the way across the field, it sounded like somebody hit the side of the tank with a sledgehammer. This was accompanied with a short blast of air in the side of the tank." McEvoy turned and looked up in the turret. "In the light coming through the open hatches, I could see the loader like a silhouette in the now-smoke-filled turret. I also noticed that the sheet metal battery cover was wrapped around the back of my driver's seat, which probably deflected shrapnel and possibly battery acid from hitting me. The shell had come in about eighteen inches behind my seat, right at the level where the battery was located." McEvoy was now remembering what old-timers had said many times. "Once your tank has been hit and you can't move out of the direct line of fire, get out *right now*, because they've got the range, and three or more rounds will follow in rapid succession."

McEvoy continues: "I looked over to my assistant driver, and to my surprise he was already gone. I knew I had to get out of this tank, and right now. Feeling that a German rifleman or machine gunner was waiting for me to expose myself, I threw open the hatch and dived out, rolling down the slope plate and landing on the ground." McEvoy picked himself up and ran to the back of the tank. "I was intent on putting the tank between me and the wooded area to the left. I saw others running to the rear and realized now that our tank wasn't the only one hit. I jumped into a depression in the field to rest up and get some wind. In a moment I ran again, as fast as I could, and reached safety. I remember thinking when I did that somebody up there likes me!"

The following day the 1st Platoon of A Company went straight down the road, firing at anything that might be an enemy stronghold. Tank destroyers with 90mm guns were also part of the attack, and the 3d Platoon of A Company and the 1st and 3d Platoons of D Company lent support. After what had happened the day before, 70th commanders were taking no chances. That was a massive amount of armored firepower, and this time Gondelsheim fell.[4]

In crossing the Pruem River on improvised steel-tread ramps, one gave way, toppling an A Company tank into the cold river. Lieutenant Darwin Purvis rescued two of the crew from drowning. The decoration he received for his action was added to his Distinguished Service Cross, croix de guerre, and Silver Star. Purvis was the most decorated man in the 70th.

The Rear Echelon Enters Pruem

Pruem was utterly demolished. American and German forces alike had shelled it, and American planes had bombed it. The great

Gothic abbey in the town square was a charred mass of brick and stone. (The monastery at Pruem once housed famous medieval manuscripts.) Dozer tanks had to shove debris aside before vehicles could enter the city.

The scene made a lasting impression on me. As the B Company convoy wound its way down a hill into Pruem, I felt sickened and uneasy. Standing next to the rubble of what had been their homes were old men, women, and children waving white flags of surrender. It was the first time I had seen this pathetic and bewildering sight. Among myriad impressions from the war, citizens waving white surrender flags in their devastated city remains significant.

For some men, paticularly those in combat, any sympathy for the people was quickly dispelled. George Brookstein, a kind and decent man, also recalled the white flags in Pruem. "I felt no sympathy for the people, because gunfire came from the same place where the white flags were waved. When sniping began, we threw in some shells, not knowing if civilians were present but knowing that fire came from there."

The Headquarters Company mortar platoon was again called upon to perform additional duties. Virgil Wagner was with those sent into Pruem to set up the battalion command post. "They gave us three days' rations, which was an ominous sign. All three squads went in. We picked out a building. It was one of the few left standing, and with good reason. The walls were about eighteen inches thick. It was two story with a slate roof. The building looked good, so we moved in. Larsen again made a stovepipe out of tomato juice cans, and soon we got a fire going in a potbellied stove." It was early March and very cold, with a slight rain that chilled to the bone. "No sooner had the smoke started to rise when we got a mortar barrage. We had been told that the area had been cleared for twenty-four hours, and it was. At least Pruem was. But Germans were still on a bluff close enough to observe and fire on us. From then on, for the next day or so, any movement brought in a barrage. Of course we pulled down Larsen's stovepipe immediately."

Later an infantry company headquarters moved in close to their location. "We saw them unloading a whole bunch of cartons. Some of us went over to shoot the bull with them and spotted cartons of shredded wheat, which we hadn't seen for quite a while. They gave us a case of the shredded wheat and some powdered milk. Larsen and I each ate a whole box at one sitting. I also had a box of goodies from my Mom that I hadn't opened, and that I now shared with the guys."

Wagner describes the first night as eerie, with artillery shells passing overhead from two directions. "Walt Larsen had picked up an air mattress right after the Battle of the Bulge. He blew it up and put it on the floor and fell asleep. About midnight a mortar barrage came in, and I heard Walt scrounging around in his duffel bag." Wagner asked Larsen what he was doing. "He said that he was putting away his air mattress. I asked him why, and he said he didn't want it to get punctured. I told him that he was probably the one who would get punctured and wouldn't have to worry about it. Walt said, 'Ahh, I don't want it to get busted.'"

Rifle fire was heard on the streets as Wagner went on guard duty in the early morning. "As I came around the corner of the building, I heard the bolt come back on a rifle and a voice saying 'Halt.' I identified myself to the guard, who was about the youngest-looking guy I had seen in a long time. He was clean shaven, and his uniform looked new. The kid was really nothing but a raw recruit." Wagner and the young replacement chatted briefly. "'God, I'm scared,' the guard said, and I told him I was too but that he shouldn't get trigger happy. Some time later I heard a rifle shot. I went back to the kid and asked him if he shot. He said yes, and I asked why. He said he saw a pair of eyes, and I asked him what he thought it was. He said, 'I don't know, but I shot.' The next morning here was a dead cat with a bullet right through its eyes. The kid was a helluva good shot."

Clear of Forests and the Siegfried Line at Last

By March 5, the high ground beyond Pruem was attained. At long last there were no dense forests and no Siegfried Line running through them. The traumatic and disquieting time seemed to vanish overnight. It was like going from darkness to light, from winter to spring. In fact, the weather did improve, with ice and snow no longer a major impediment.

The significance to the total war effort of reaching an assigned objective was probably not understood by the average soldier. No one in most ranks ever knew what was going on beyond his own small piece of the front. In this case, however, results of the successful campaign were immediately apparent to all. This was the time and place for a specially organized, highly mobile task force to thrust forward a considerable distance.

Task Force Rhino was formed on March 7 under the overall command of 4th Infantry Division's General Rodwell. It consisted of the 8th Infantry Regiment (mechanized), 70th Tank Battalion (less C Company which was with the 22d Combat Team), 29th Field Artillery Battalion, 4th Medical Battalion, A Company of the 4th Engineer Combat Battalion, 4th Reconnaissance Troop (mechanized), Battery C of the 377th AA Battalion, 4th Signal Company, and A Company of the 610th Tank Destroyer Battalion. This task force was self-contained and loaded with firepower.

Usually when tanks and infantry worked together in a slugging match, the tanks could go no faster than infantry. With Task Force Rhino, the infantry was mechanized and it was the tanks that set the pace.

Lieutenant Colonel Henry Davidson, commander of the 70th, headed the assault unit, which started the drive at 0800 on March 8. Leading the way was a platoon of the 4th Reconnaissance Troop, followed by the 1st Platoon of D Company, then B Company, of the 70th, and one platoon of tank destroyers. In the next group were the battalion staff tanks and A Company of the 70th, followed by another platoon of tank destroyers. Next in line was the 2d Platoon of D Company plus the third platoon of tank destroyers. The remainder of the task force left one hour later under the command of 4th Division Colonel McKee.

The Kyll River was crossed at 1100, with no enemy force encountered until the town of Kerpen, where a platoon of about thirty Germans was killed or captured. Later, in Uxheim, one enemy tank was destroyed. East of that town, an enemy antitank gun knocked out a D Company tank, killing two men and wounding another.

On the outskirts of Adenau, the Germans had blown a large crater in the roadway, apparently thinking this would delay the force until daylight. It didn't. The crater was quickly filled in, and at 0200 B Company tanks with infantry aboard captured two bridges intact and moved into the city. The move caught the enemy completely off guard. Many German troops were asleep in houses until rudely awakened by a GI flashlight in their eyes and an American gun in their ribs.

Adenau had been the objective of Rhino. The task force was consequently dissolved with all units returning to their respective commands. In the span of about twenty hours, Rhino had advanced twenty-five miles, taken 1541 prisoners, and had captured large amounts of enemy equipment, including much that was American, taken during the Bulge.[5]

The rest of B Company journeyed to Adenau on the morning of March 9. I recall the upbeat spirits as the kitchen truck moved what seemed a great distance, deeper into Germany. In Adenau all company personnel were quartered in civilian houses for a night or two. The householders had left in a hurry, giving we cooks our first opportunity to loot. While looting was against army regulations, I don't remember anyone having second thoughts about what he was doing, considering the practice as part of the fortunes of war.

Attachment to the 63d in a New Sector

On March 7, the day Task Force Rhino was formed, the U.S. 9th Armored Division captured a railroad bridge intact over the Rhine at Remagen. Soon four divisions were across, but the 4th was not among them, despite the fact that Adenau was but an easy twenty miles from Remagen and the Rhine.

Instead, rumor had it that the 4th was going to enjoy a period of rest and rehabilitation, and naturally so would the 70th. After all, the fighting had been rough for several months. A rest period was deserved.

Except it wasn't to be, at least for the 70th. Higher command again showed how well they knew the 70th and its fine record. On March 12, after two days of maintenance, the battalion left on a long road march. The men could scarcely believe their eyes as they passed through all too familiar places such as Pruem, Bleialf, and Luxembourg. In two days the columns traveled 185 miles, entering unfamiliar territory around Metz before finally coming to a halt at St. Jean Rohrbach. "My God, we're back in France!"

It was bewildering. The rumor mill went into overdrive. The 63d Infantry Division was to experience its baptism of fire and their attached tank battalion was delayed en route. As with most rumors, this one was not true. The 63d had been on the line for a limited time and, as was the case with infantry divisions coming in from the States, had no attached tank battalion. Tank battalions, whether independent or from armored divisions, were assigned as need and plans arose.

Nonetheless, there was cause for bewilderment. The 70th had been attached to the 4th since before D day, and an excellent working relationship had developed between them. Just how essential tank-infantry cooperation was had been learned in Normandy at considerable cost. Such cooperation could not be developed quickly or easily. The two elements should, through training and combat experience, learn how best to operate for maximum mutual advantage.

Cracking the Siegfried Line for the Fourth Time

What the men of the 70th did not know was how brief would be the attachment to the 63d. Only A and B Companies and the assault gun platoon saw action, and then only for three days. A Company worked with the 254th Regiment at Encheim, near Saarbrucken, Germany. The tanks fired into pillboxes and bunkers of the Siegfried Line, enabling infantry to drive the enemy out of their prepared fortifications. B Company and the 255th Infantry captured the town of Ormesheim. Some of the fighting here was after dark with the use of searchlights, again against positions on the Siegfried Line. The assault gun platoon shelled Saarbrucken day and night.

That was all. The 70th traveled great distances to work with the 63d for three days. For these relatively inexperienced infantrymen, it was no doubt a good thing to have an experienced tank unit help them at the beginning of a planned offensive.

When Pruem was taken such a short time before, there was a collective sigh of relief. Supposedly we were at long last beyond the Siegfried Line. Yet here we were facing it again. In doing so the 70th must have established a record. The Siegfried Line was first encountered on September 13 in the Schnee-Eifel and Schlausenbacher Forest. Next was in the Huertgen Forest in November. Then in February in the fight for Pruem. Now, here it was again more than 100 miles south of the first encounter. It seems doubtful that any other tank battalion or few if any other unit of any type could have been engaged on the Siegfried Line four times in such widely divergent sectors. Difficult tasks are given to the best units. The 70th was equal to them.

Casualties in the New Sector

Even though C Company was not committed, it suffered the only casualties due to enemy action. Five men were wounded when the Germans shelled their assembly area.

There was one more battalion casualty and a chance for at least one other, but they were not caused by the enemy and do not receive mention in official or unofficial journals. A B Company tanker had confiscated a German army motorcycle that had been around the area for several days. A number of the guys had joyrides on it, which awakened my interest. When my turn came, I admitted that this was my first time and had to be shown how to operate it. "Depress the clutch lever, accelerate slightly, let out the clutch evenly, and, incidentally, this is the brake." Believing in the dictum that if some is good, more is better, I accelerated a lot and let out the clutch rather too quickly. The damned thing leapt off the ground and bounded uncontrollably fifteen yards and into a foxhole. At least the front wheel did. The mindless machine stayed put, but I was hurled another ten feet before crashing to earth. Onlookers roared with delight and asked for a repeat performance. Although unhurt, I declined.

The real casualty had to do with a ride Paul Gaul took on that same nefarious contraption. "I don't remember who was driving, but we drove out of the bivouac area, found a saloon, and got all drunked up. I had confiscated a pair of those infantry shoe packs, and they were far too big for me. Well, we started back to the company area on that motorcycle. I was on the back, trying to keep those shoe packs on the rider bar, but they kept slipping off. I had bottles of booze in both hands, and away we went, down a steep hill." The driver at least had handlebars to hang onto, whereas Gaul had only his imagination. "Suddenly the guy says, 'Here I go, Gaul, I can't make this turn,' and the son of a bitch jumped off. There I was, protecting the booze and riding that damned thing clear to the bottom of the hill. I wound up in a field hospital. So, I was lying in this hospital, and here came Lieutenant Windaugh to get me. My ankle, hip, both knees swollen, not knowing what was broken and what wasn't, and Lieutenant Windaugh says, 'We're moving out, Gaul, and you're coming with us!'" He took Gaul, crutches and all. "When we got back to the company, he put me on the kitchen truck. I rode with you guys to the next area."

Irrespective of how, Gaul was in fact badly injured. Medics sent him to a hospital near Nancy. When he finally got back to B Company, he was transferred to C Company for the rest of the war.

Back With the 4th

Yet another tank battalion must have been attached to the 63d, which continued to operate in this sector. The 70th moved another 100 miles and lo and behold, there was the 4th in an area north of Strasbourg. We were now part of the Seventh Army and would be until days before the end of the war.

Here at last, the men of the 70th enjoyed some R and R, staying in one place for a whole week. Because of great distances traveled, many tanks were in need of maintenance, and a number were turned in for newer models. Other than that and the usual inspections, everyone was able to relax in warm, sunny weather. According to the B Company journal, a Red Cross clubmobile dispensed doughnuts and coffee, and PX rations were drawn, including real honest-to-goodness American beer. Concerts were performed by the 4th Division band.

Since we were still in France, it made sense to exchange all German, Belgian, and Luxembourg currency into French francs, which was done on March 24. The day after we were paid, also in French currency. One of the favorite GI expressions was that there were two ways of doing things—the right way and the army way. So, these financial transactions were an obvious preparation for a move back into Germany, where the money couldn't be spent. This occurred two days later. After another 104-mile road march, the battalion arrived at Wachenheim, Germany, around noon on March 28.

Wine and Champagne for All

Wachenheim was near Worms, where a pontoon bridge had been constructed over the Rhine. The 12th Armored Division as well as the 4th (and attached units) shared the same road network, and the same bridge. Traffic was so heavy that the 70th waited until March 30 to cross the great river.

B Company men didn't mind the wait. Their bivouac ranked as one of the best of the entire war, and maybe any war. It was close to a winery, with several layers of cellars with thousands of bottles of Rhine wine and champagne just waiting to be liberated. The great drunk that ensued was going along well, I recall, until one wildly inebriated tank sergeant began firing his .45-caliber into full bottles of wine. This so disgusted other men around him that they retired to more suitable surroundings where they could drink in peace. Robert Knoebel says, "Some of us were in the cellars looking at dates on the wine and champagne, and so help me, we were knocking the tops off, taking a swig, and throwing it away until we got the best stuff!"

A Company also stayed in a winery. "It was one of the most brilliant things I did," George Brookstein recalls. As liaison corporal, one of his tasks was to look for places to bivouac. "I saw this champagne winery with a big loading platform. There was enough room for the whole company in the complex. I went up to the office and knocked on the door with some authority. The caretaker answered and was shaking like a leaf. Using Yiddish to make myself understood, I told him our panzer unit was going to move in very soon."

Actually, the company was not to arrive for hours, so Brookstein hurried to grab a few cases of champagne and put them in a room for the guys. "Then, I thought, this was crazy! There were thousands of cases. The guys could have all they wanted when they arrived. The men were overjoyed to see where they would be staying. Before we left, case upon case were loaded into tanks, trucks, and half-tracks. There was enough for the whole company with plenty left over to share with the rest of the battalion. I understand it was used to celebrate the end of the war, though I was not there."

Crossing the Rhine Awash in Rhine Wine
All tanks and most other vehicles had loaded a supply of champagne in advance of the crossing. The crew of Robert Knoebel's tank "put cases of champagne outside on the back deck, but with the heat from the engine and all the jostling, they all popped or blew up. We

did put some inside, which was saved, but there was little room, which is why we tried the back. Some crews stored wine in the 76mm gun, though our crew didn't. You could tell which tanks did because they were going along with the big gun elevated, which is something we otherwise never did."

How much wine could be stored in a 75mm or 76mm gun remains a great unanswered question. Presumably, though not necessarily, these crews intended to drink the wine before firing the gun, which they figured would be in several days. As Clarence McNamee reports, "My mother saw a newsreel of tanks crossing the Rhine at Worms and wrote that she was sure we were spearheading [the division]. I told her when I got home that we were so far behind at that time we couldn't even telephone the front. Anytime they photographed you, there was no front even close." (This claim was McNamee's experience. Actually a number of photographers were killed on the line.)

B Company started across the Rhine at 0945 on March 30. Clarence McNamee recalls, "We were all in bad shape that day. Everybody in the tank was drinking a bottle, including me, and I was driving, sticks in both hands and balancing a bottle of wine on my lap. I damned near missed that pontoon bridge as I went down the ramp, but I don't think anybody in the tank gave a shit if I hit it or not!"

The B Company journal notes that the company traveled 496 miles in March, the same as the rest of the battalion. Nearly all of those miles came after the fall of Pruem and the drive for Adenau on March 7. Once the Siegfried Line and the forests were penetrated, the German front in that sector collapsed. Open country lay ahead. The battle for Pruem had been pivotal.

After trying times, morale in the 70th was high, the opposite of that of the Germans. The propaganda they had been told about impending victory was revealed as lies. A story told by Clarence Jay is an example. American confidence was demonstrated by granting a number of rotation leaves to the United States. Tony Zampiello was one; B Company Sergeant Jay another. He had been in the thick of things from the beginning, a much-admired stalwart with an impeccable record. Jay was told if he wished to stay, a battlefield commission was already in the works, but he was a civilian at heart and opted to go home in early March. On board the ship, he was assigned to guard 300 German prisoners. As they neared North America, the ship was ordered to land in New York. When the Germans heard this, they laughed and said, "That is impossible. New York is kaput. Our new weapons have completely destroyed it!" On their arrival, Jay reports, "We took them up on deck to show them that New York was very much intact."

The last great barrier to the heartland of Germany had been pierced. Allied forces were now ready to strike the final blow. Among them quite naturally would be the 4th Division and the 70th.

14
Fighting to the Bitter End

The biggest fear I had was that I would be the last man killed in World War II. After going through all the way, the thought came to mind as the end was in sight that some diehard Nazi would fire one last shot for the führer with me as his target.

—Clarence McNamee
B Company tanker

After crossing the Rhine, the 4th Division and the 70th headed east, advancing at will, with towns falling in rapid succession. This was not the time to relax one's guard, however. As Clarence McNamee says, SS troops were fighting to the death. Occasional firefights were reminders that fanatical Nazis were carrying the war past its conclusion.

Concerns and Misconceptions

In a letter home dated April 9, I expressed another concern that would be on many minds from then on. "The European war cannot last more than a few months, and then comes another sweat—whether I go to the Pacific or not. I read in the *Stars & Stripes* today that we will go to the Pacific without delay. But if we have to go, I guess it will be for the best. Perhaps we can finish the Japs off quickly and get home for good."

This bravado, of course, was for home consumption. I was not nearly so brave nor so willing to accept a tour of duty in the Far East. Later in the same letter, I noted that the B Company mess sergeant had returned from his furlough to the States. "He said Americans don't know there's a war going on over here. Some people asked him questions like, 'Do you fight on Sundays?'" The attitude Sergeant Suranic encountered at home convinced him he belonged back at the front. He could have stayed in the States but volunteered to return.

RHINE CROSSED
MARCH 30, 1945

Worms •

FRANCE

R. Rhine

R. Rhine

Würzburg •

R. Main

Rothenburg •

Crailsheim •

Stuttgart •

R. Neckar

Aalen •

Ulm •

R. Danube

GERMANY

• Ansbach

Munich •

THE WAR ENDS
MAY 8, 1945

Bad Tölz •

R. Isar

SWITZERLAND

AUSTRIA

0   30   60

Graphics Plus

**From the Rhine to the End of the War
March 30, 1945-May 8, 1945**

Getting Lost in Darkness and Daylight

American divisions were pouring across the Rhine into adjacent sectors so fast that confusion often resulted. Such was the situation in which Walter Waszyn found himself on one occasion. Waszyn was a sergeant in the D Company maintenance platoon. "We were traveling in a column at night. I was in a jeep leading the T-2 and our half-track. Everyone was following the blackout taillights of the vehicle ahead, but we got behind a little bit and I guess the column made a right turn in a town and we didn't. Out of the town we stopped to get our bearings and suddenly the field we were next to lit up with flares, and artillery started to come in." They got away from the area as fast as possible and came to a crossroad, where they turned away from the artillery. "The jeep driver glanced back and said, 'Look at that!' Someone in a half-track behind us had a light on. I walked back and yelled at them, 'Put that damned light out!' Then I saw it was a major, so I asked him if he knew where we were going. He said, 'Yeh, I'm following the leader.' I said, 'Yeh, and I'm the leader and I don't know where the hell we are!' He looked at a map, which didn't give him a clue. He wasn't from our outfit and was really lost." The major kept going straight ahead, but Waszyn turned the T-2, the half-track, and his jeep around and headed back into the town.

"By now it was at least midnight. I told the guys we were going to find someplace to sleep. Someone said we couldn't do that because this was Germany and we don't know what we'll run into. I said, 'It doesn't matter, we can't drive around lost all night, so we might as well try to get some sleep.' It was a small town and I went up to a house and woke the people up by pounding on the door. I told them we wanted a place to *schlaffen,* and they showed us to a big beer hall. We all went in there and told them we were going to *schlaffen* here." He got no argument, and when the people left, all of the group started to lie down on the floor. "Someone asked who was going to stand guard. I said if the Germans wanted that junk outside they could have it. I was too tired to care, and so was everybody else, so nobody stood guard."

During the night a U.S. infantry lieutenant came in. "He came to wake me up, as I was the leading noncom. He said he had a platoon of men who were lost and dead tired. Could they flop down here, he asked. I said, 'Well, tell them to flop down, and why did you wake me to ask me that?'" The next morning two German soldiers came out of the house next door and gave themselves up. "So now we had two prisoners, or rather the infantry lieutenant did. After all, he had the rank. We were able to figure out where we were and finally found the company. We had been lost all night, and nobody seemed to miss us, and nobody came looking for us!"

It was possible to get lost even in broad daylight and with an officer who had been trained to read the map he held in his lap. The B Company kitchen did not leave the old bivouac with the rest of the company and was being led to the new one by a new officer in his jeep. No one in the back of the kitchen truck gave much thought on seeing a platoon of B Company tanks going in the opposite direction in a field bordering the narrow road. As the last tank came abreast, the commander waved for the truck and jeep to stop. He yelled at the top of his lungs, "Where in the hell are you going? See that crossroads up ahead? That might be considered the front line!" The crossroad was no more than seventy-five to one hundred yards away. The kitchen crew sprang into action as if their very lives were at stake, which might have been an accurate appraisal. Each man had the strength of ten as the trailer was unhitched and manually pushed off the road. Meanwhile, kitchen truck driver Mohnshine jockeyed the truck back and forth, forth and back, up over the ditch on one side, then over the other. When the truck was facing the right direction, the trailer was rehitched and Mohnshine tromped on the accelerator. All the while, the officer sat in his jeep, turning the map around and around as he scratched his head in bewilderment.

Captured With H for Hebrew on Dog Tags
It was George Brookstein who said, "We were moving so fast that we ran off our maps." He had been the A Company liaison corporal through all campaigns from Tunisia and on. He knew his stuff.

I would try to get landmarks to help get back to the company in cases where maps were insufficient. About a week after we crossed the Rhine, my driver and I were on an errand that took us completely beyond our maps. We were on our way back to the company and passed landmarks similar to those I saw going in, but then we went through one of our roadblocks facing the direction we were headed. I thought this was strange. Why had they let us through? Why was it facing that direction? I thought perhaps it was a double precaution, so we went ahead. Then I saw a few dead GIs, and since we didn't leave our dead lying around, I knew we were in trouble. I told my driver to turn the jeep around and step on the gas to get back out. As we were passing a wooded area, we received a lot of fire. The jeep was hit, so we got out and tried to run for our lines, which were no more than 100 yards away. We didn't make it. I was shot through the leg and was bleeding profusely. German soldiers came and dragged me to the woods. I was really saying my prayers because they were SS. Despite all the pain, I was able to think quickly and took my dog tags with *H* for Hebrew on them[1] out of my pocket and managed to drop them unnoticed to the ground. I never wore them when I was anywhere close to Germans.

In the woods, the Germans gave me first aid. One of them showed me my tanker's jacket, which was shredded. They must have been shooting at us with burp guns. Anyway, I weighed about 120 pounds and had a jacket that was a size 44 or 46, so they shredded it. The shot that hit me was from a rifle. The German looked at me and shook his head as if to say, How were you not hit in the upper body? He gave me the jacket, but I was so disgusted at being taken prisoner that I threw it away. (I wish now I had kept it. It would have been quite a souvenir.)

The officer in charge was not SS. When they treated my wound, I passed out from the pain. The next thing I remember, they were carrying me on a stretcher to an ambulance. Before it left, this Wehrmacht officer interrogated me. He asked who I was, what my unit was, and where it was located. He knew all of this beforehand because I had all the maps in my jeep, so I don't know the reason for the questions—unless it was to set me up, because then he pulled out a picture of my fiancée, and she was wearing a Star of David. The officer asked if she was German, and I said, no, she was a woman I met in England. I thought this was the end and said a silent prayer. Then he gave back the picture, which made me feel more relieved, but it was a close call. I was taken to a hospital in Rothenburg.[2]

A Change in Direction

Since the Rhine, our direction of movement had been due east, but on April 14, the 4th Division and the 70th turned and headed south, moving rapidly. Generally, tank platoons or companies with infantry on the back deck would approach a town and encounter fire; after a short fight, the enemy would surrender or retreat into wooded areas. These delaying actions were usually of insufficient strength, disrupting the advance only a short time.

B Company supporting the 12th Infantry Regiment came to the outskirts of Rothenburg on April 17. Shortly before nightfall, German antitank fire delayed further action. The tanks and infantry held their ground throughout the night. The next day, Rothenburg was taken without opposition. (Brookstein was then liberated. Medieval Rothenburg was declared an "open city." After the war the 70th occupied the city. I remember that the only visible damage was one hole in the wall.)

Meanwhile, A Company was part of a task force assigned to capture Ansbach. On the way they destroyed an enemy horse-drawn supply train, another indication of the state of the German military. In or near Ansbach, four men were killed—Cohen, Grimes, Fitzgerald, and Saville—the last A Company men to die, so close to the end. C Company and accompanying infantry captured Crailsheim on April 20. Its fall, along with Rothenburg and Ansbach demonstrates the nature of operations at this juncture. Ansbach lies about twenty miles east-southeast of Rothenburg, and Crailsheim, thirty miles south-southwest. All three medium tank companies with infantry mounted were driving for key cities and towns, widely separated from one another.

Task Force Rodwell

Task Force Rodwell, named after the 4th Division deputy commander, was formed on April 21.[3] Lieutenant Colonel Davidson and Maj. Kenneth Krach of the 70th commanded the assault echelon and the assault companies, respectively. As with the earlier Task Force Rhino, this one was also self-contained, with 70th tanks, tank destroyers, field artillery, medics, reconnaissance, and, of course, mechanized infantry. Because German forces now were anything but cohesive and fighting only sporadic delaying actions, Rodwell had a rather ill-defined objective—something like "Go as far as possible."

This powerful force was formed because of intelligence that indicated some towns were being defended strongly by SS troops. At

Leinenfirst an SS unit fought briefly before retreating to the next town, Neuler. The town was shelled, but since nightfall was near, it was decided that infantry and tanks would attack early the next day, April 22.

The Last 70th Men Killed in Action

Alvin Woods recounts that he and Joe Trujillo were like brothers, inseparable through the entire war, starting in the States. "We almost always were in the same tank together. When you saw one, you saw two." Now they were in B Company tank #9, commanded by Sgt. Charles Gallow.

Gallow, Joe, and I were sitting together the night before, eating boiled potatoes that Gallow had found somewhere. For some reason, that night was not like other nights before an action. Usually we would sit around, joke, and just try to be lighthearted even though we knew we were going into combat the next day. There was something wrong that night, a feeling that wasn't there before. I have thought about this ever since. You might say that the war was over, or should have been. I can't put my finger on it, but there was an atmosphere of feeling as if we didn't have to go into this thing, to take that place. I know that Sergeant Gallow had never sat down before and discussed his family. He talked about Altoona, Pennsylvania, and the things he and his friends had done as youths. Then he said to me, "You will drive tomorrow, and Joe will gun—or either way." I said, "Joe, you're the best gunner in the outfit." Joe had this way of speaking in broken English. He said, "You drive right, I shoot right." So we both agreed that I would drive and he would gun. We sat up quite late. Finally Gallow said, "Let's get some sleep."

Normally the driver went to the tank first, to check the gas and see that everything was OK. But Joe was up first in the morning and after checking the ammo said, "Let's go." That was strange. Gallow was up too, so we ate some C rations and waited for the rest of the platoon.

After the assault gun platoon fired HE shells into Neuler, B Company moved in with infantry mounted on the back deck of the tanks.

Gallow's tank was in the lead. The infantry dismounted and engaged SS troops in hand-to-hand combat. The tanks moved down a narrow street, infantry on foot behind them. Clarence McNamee was in a tank behind #9. He recalls: "A German stuck a *panzerfaust* over a ledge in a house. He didn't even stick his head up but just fired." Woods remembers hearing machine-gun fire and Gallow telling Joe to start shooting.

Joe did, with the coaxial machine gun. Gallow called me on the intercom and told me to turn a little to the right because we were getting fire. Just as I did, a rocket hit our turret and the tank seemed to explode. A *panzerfaust* projectile has a Monroe-type effect so that the penetration of the hull is small, but when it gets inside it fairly well ricochets around. I'm sure this one hit the gas line or some ammunition or both.

My hatch was down but not locked. Veteran drivers drove with the hatch loose. Sometimes they were hard to open, and, if a tank was on fire, a locked hatch could delay escape. I pushed the hatch open and got out. I knew something was wrong with Joe. I heard him yell, so I started to crawl around to the turret to get him and the others out. Papucci came out of the bow gunner's hatch, and I remember telling him to start shooting at the doors of houses where Germans were coming out. I am pretty sure he did. I had a submachine gun and, with Mahaffey, was trying to get Joe and Gallow out. But Joe was dead—there were no two ways about that. Three Germans got up on the back deck to fire into the turret. I slid around and got those three. I shot them off for sure. A fourth German was coming up on the right sponson. He had a *panzerfaust* cradled in his arms. I recall thinking, why does he have it in his arms like that? He was going toward Gallow, and I shot him. It seems then that other Germans came. Mahaffey was hit and was on the ground. I told Papucci to shoot, and I got another magazine loaded. I was coming around by my hatch. A German fired a burst with his Schmeiser. He didn't hit me but hit the periscope and blew it apart. To show how you can think of things that don't even pertain to the event taking place, I thought, well doggone, they blew the periscope apart. It was one of those odd thoughts that didn't fit in.

We fought our way to the front of a house. I went into the house and quickly out the back. I started around the corner shooting at Germans who had run there. Gallow was by this time on the ground in back of the tank. A German came around the side of the tank and bayoneted Gallow, and I shot the German. Then I saw a German medic and don't know what happened to him. By that time one of our infantry sergeants was there, and so was our platoon leader, Willie Winters. They were saying, "Stop, Woods, it's all over." Winters grabbed me and repeated, "Stop, Woods, it's all over!" Our medics came up and we started to walk across toward the tank. Then I saw the German medic, and he was dead. To this day, I hope I didn't kill him. I saw him one time and he was alive. I assume he was dead, because he was just lying there.

For a while I was so excited I didn't even know I had been hit, but I had been bleeding and was pretty weak. My arm was pretty badly wounded. The medics doctored me up a little bit, gave me a shot, and put something under my arm and around the back of my neck. Before they put me in an ambulance, an infantry sergeant handed me a helmet, saying, "Here's a helmet off one of the Germans you shot. We counted seven over there on or near the tank." He seemed to think there was a total of fifteen dead Germans. I am not saying I killed fifteen, because Papucci was firing, and Mahaffey may have, even though he was on the ground. I kept yelling for Joe. All I could think about was that Joe Trujillo was dead. My God, we had been together all those years, and they had killed him. I probably went berserk knowing Joe was dead.

Gallow died on the way to a hospital. Papucci and Mahaffey were both wounded but survived. How many Germans were killed is unknown. Clarence McNamee recalls the anger of B Company tankers at what they thought was a senseless killing of their friends. Many saw the Germans climb up on the tank to fire machine guns into the turret to kill men already wounded or to make sure they were dead. One tanker was also a close buddy of Trujillo. McNamee saw him go absolutely berserk. "He was a high-strung individual anyway, and a bull of a man. He came with a Thompson submachine gun and fired at anyone wearing a German uniform whether their hands were raised or lowered."

Bob Knoebel was another eyewitness. "All the SS wanted to do was kill Americans. Even though the war was really over, they were trying to defend a town and kept shooting. That's alright, it was their job. But not to see how many they could kill and then run out and surrender. Yeah, I was there. Trujillo and Gallow were old 70th men and both favorites." Charles Gallow and Joe Trujillo were the last 70th men to be killed in the war.

As a footnote to the incident, Woods says that a wounded German was put into an ambulance with him. "We ended up in the same hospital. We were together until I was sent to a hospital in England. It was hard to get used to seeing him around after what had happened, but he was a patient just like I was, no different. By chance we even went to the latrine together a couple of times."[4]

Another Stiff Fight Against SS Troops

It took two more hours to clear Neuler. The task force moved on to Sulzdorf and to Wasseralfingen, where German civilians helped Americans clear a roadblock and also gave information that Aalen would be defended by approximately 1,000 SS.[5] Nightfall intervened, so the attack on Aalen was delayed until morning. Assault guns pounded the town and roads leading south. At 0600 on April 23 the attack began. For two hours good progress was made until hitting the main defensive line in the town center. At the intersection of two streets in Aalen, German antitank guns and several tanks were in position. Robert McEvoy drove the 2d Platoon leader's tank in A Company. "The doughs needed a tank to get them across the street. We just barely got our nose into the intersection and WHAM! The lieutenant told me, 'Back off, we've been hit.' I was able to back it off until we were around the corner and out of sight. But that was about all. The track on the right side fell off, and the shell had also gone right into the hull."

With A Company and accompanying infantry momentarily hung

up, C Company worked its way into the city center from the north. B Company was sent to the southern approaches to seal off the enemy. After several hours of fighting, Aalen fell, with all remaining enemy forces surrendering and much equipment captured.

Off the Maps Again

The advance continued. C Company commander Franklin Anderson states: "We were having a difficult time keeping our maps current. One day we actually didn't know where we were going. There were no road signs, and sometimes we were going cross-country. We arrived at the edge of a small city, and I could see high ground behind it. I had some of the tank destroyers with me who were part of the task force. I told them to keep an eye on the high ground and to fire their 90mm guns at anything that moved."

Figuring there was not too much to worry about in the small city, he decided to take it even though there were no specific orders to do so. "I called battalion to tell them and started in. We stopped to let the mounted infantry get off our tanks. Colonel Davidson got on the radio and asked, 'What's holding you up, Andy?'" About this time *panzerfaust* fire opened up. "One just missed my tank and hit the veranda of a house we were beside. Wood and brick fell all over my tank, and Davidson said, 'What's that?' I said a *panzerfaust* round just missed my tank and stuff fell on it. 'Oh,' he replied, 'Well, General Rodwell wants to know what you're doing up there.' I said, 'Tell him we're fighting a war up here!'"

Anderson heard another voice. "It was the general. He said, 'Henry, I heard that last response.' Well, we went in and took that city at about 2000 or 2100." Anderson posted guards and got everybody bedded down. Unexpectedly, Lieutenant Colonel Davidson, Major Krach, and Captain Taynton walked in. "I supposed I was in deep shit about the remark the general had heard. After some small talk, Davidson said, 'I understand your tactics weren't what they should have been!' Taynton and Krach thought he was serious, and so did I. Either Taynton or Krach then came to my defense, saying, 'Colonel, that was an excellent tactical procedure. He went according to the book.'" Finally Davidson reached into his pocket and presented Anderson with captain's bars and offered his congratulations.

"I think what had happened was that General Rodwell was so pleased with the capture of that city, which was thought to be a Nazi stronghold and which he hadn't expected to take at that late hour, that was in the next sector, that he had congratulated Davidson, who in turn congratulated me."

Both Anderson and Brookstein tell of running off maps, of operating in sectors not previously delineated. It happened again on April 25 when C Company as the lead element in the task force moved toward Gundelfingen, the next assigned objective. Before reaching the town, 70th commanders learned that the "12th Armored Division would be found in the area. Contact with the 12th was made and Task Force Rodwell was ordered into the town . . . where it was dissolved . . ."[6]

With light and sporadic resistance, the overlapping of divisions caused no difficulty. If a prolonged battle had taken place, the situation could have had serious consequences.

Tired of War

German civilians had helped American soldiers clear a roadblock and warned of the presence of large numbers of SS in Aalen on April 22. Two days later civilians were involved in a more dangerous act, pointing out and then assisting the clearing of a German minefield. These same people warned C Company that three German tanks were in the area of Unt-Kochen. In Brenz, villagers turned out to wave to American troops as they passed through.[7] Although conjecture regarding the motives of these people is beyond the scope of this narrative, I can say that they were tired of war and hoped destruction would not be visited upon them. Everyone except a few fanatics knew that further resistance was pointless.

Even the kitchen truck was at this stage often part of the B Company column. Once, when moving down a secondary road, it stopped for a "piss call." I dutifully had complied with the order and was standing nonchalantly surveying a nearby wood. From it emerged a lone German soldier, hands on his head. He walked straight to me, so I was honored at being chosen to accept his surrender. I began to frisk him, as I had seen in the movies. Almost immediately several kitchen crew buddies tried to horn in, which I resented. Still, it would have been unseemly to fight for possession, and besides, a military policeman came within minutes to take charge. My captive was promptly marched to a military police prisoner truck, also part of the column. He was middle-aged with a decidedly unmilitary bearing. Such was the German army near the end—old men, young boys, with a sprinkling of regular troops, all anxious to give up the fight, which they did, unless driven to useless endeavors by SS or other Nazis.

Liberating a Concentration Camp

Our kitchen truck moved slowly through a gate into a concentration camp surrounded by a high wire fence, with rows of buildings. At the sight of hundreds of people dressed in prison garb, everything else was inconsequential. These long-suffering prisoners pressed in close as we off-loaded cases of rations for them. Glassy eyes stared out of deep-set sockets as tightly drawn skin revealed the facial structure beneath. Heads were shaven, and arms and wrists looked like sticks, hanging loosely beside distended bellies. German guards had left no more than an hour or so before, but there were no cheers, no animated demonstrations of joy, only unabashed weeping and wide smiles by those alive enough to know that their ordeal was over.

I have forgotten the name of the camp, its location, and the date we arrived. I believe that it was a labor camp, but do not know. What I can never forget is what I saw—the skeleton-like victims of atrocity. It remains for me the most poignant recollection of why this war had to be fought.

Heading for the Tyrolean Redoubt

B Company bivouacked one night next to the Danube River. I recall my disappointment as the river was brown—not blue—and running fast due to the spring thaw.

The 70th now was driving to the west of Munich on an autobahn. Parked alongside in one area were sizable numbers of German fighter planes and fighter-bombers, including a few old Stukas. They had used the broad concrete highway as a runway but were now apparently out of fuel, incapable of being moved.

Somewhere in this sector B Company set up a bivouac late in the afternoon. Some friends and I began a poker game on a GI blanket in a field. It was a lovely, warm spring day. Running next to the field was a creek, with bushes covering both banks, a perfect setting for a relaxing game among friends. A number of hands had been played when someone shouted, "Jesus, look at that!" A Messerschmitt jet fighter zoomed over the field at low altitude. In an instant it was gone. We had heard about jets, but this was the first one any of us had seen. Every player but one ran for the bushes. The one who didn't took the time to gather his money. The pilot didn't return. He was looking for a bigger game.

Clarence McNamee tells of a more frightening experience. "Our tanks were going down the autobahn in a column somewhere south of Augsburg. One of those new jets came down the column spraying us with machine-gun bullets. He didn't cause any damage, although we weren't buttoned up and could have been hit. The jet was past us even before we knew he was overhead. The pilot swung up and started back for another pass. Just as he did, someone got him with a very lucky shot. That was the first and last time I was strafed." From D day on, we had air superiority, which was to McNamee an overriding factor. "German pilots seldom flew in daylight, and, when they did, they had to fly looking up, not knowing when our planes would come in and overwhelm them."

Juxtaposed in a war that was over yet wasn't were horse-drawn columns in retreat while jets flew over, Stukas sitting uselessly along an autobahn—what was and what might have been—the past and the future.

For some time, rumors persisted that the reason for our due south movement was that Nazis were planning a last-ditch stand in a mountainous redoubt in the Tyrolean Alps, and that the powers that be had again chosen the 70th to be in the vanguard of those sent to disrupt the attempt. In the vicinity of Starnberg, west and south of Munich, the Alps were visible. Their sighting seemed to give substance to the rumor.[8] Once again men in the 70th were saying, "We're too damned good. Every time there's a dirty job to do, they call on us." The very thought of fighting tank warfare in high mountains and against fanatics was too much. Too much or not, the drive continued to the south after Starnberg, closer and closer to the mountains.

The area south of Starnberg was scenic with lakes, trees, and the Alps as a backdrop. Leading Nazis used it for idyllic retreats. Himmler's summer home was there, and it was fitting and proper that one of the last actions involving B Company was its destruction. I was told at the time that even after the main house was burning, tankers continued to fire machine-gun bullets into it. Himmler had been the head of the SS, and it was the SS who killed Gallow and Trujillo.

The War Is Over! The War Is Over!

Bad Tölz was only a few miles from the Austrian border. Upon reaching it, few doubted that the supposed Tyrolean redoubt was not very far beyond and that this was the route to it. There was very little action, but as sick of the war as everybody was, there were some who hoped to meet up with diehards. Better to get at them on relatively level ground than in the Alps.

On May 2, the 4th Division and the 70th again became part of the Third Army. What this portended no one knew, but rumors were rife with possibilities. It was known that elements of the Third were rolling in the direction of Austria and Czechoslovakia.

On the morning of May 7, the 70th went on a road march. Much to the relief of every man, the direction was north, away from the mountains and the rumored redoubt. Somewhere south of Munich the B Company column halted. The shout first came from the company commander's lead jeep, then made its way to the last vehicle and back again. "THE WAR IS OVER! THE WAR IS OVER! THE WAR IS OVER!" Every officer and man hugged and danced a little jig with whoever was closest to him. Then, with broad smiles they climbed back in their vehicles as the convoy continued toward its destination.

The B Company journal entry for that day is noteworthy for its laconic treatment of the most glorious news anyone could ever expect to hear: "The company moved from Holzkirchen 1045, arrived at Steinsdorf 2030, traveled by motor convoy ninety-five miles. The highlights of the day were seeing Munich and the news that Germany had surrendered."

Was the end of the war secondary to seeing Munich? Hardly. Each 70th man remembers the moment as vividly as any other moment of his life, although it occurred in circumstances not permitting prolonged demonstration. The war officially ended at midnight the following day, May 8, 1945. By that time B Company was bivouacked at a farm north of Munich near Steinsdorf. The journal notation is again subdued. "We had the first wine and cognac party in quite a while, much to the delight of everyone in the company."

Clarence McNamee reports:

We celebrated the end of the war with a bunch of Russians somewhere back near Bad Tölz on the edge of Austria. We were going down a macadamized road, which because of spring thaws came out from under us. Our tank was buried almost up to the driver's hatch. They hooked up the rest of the platoon of tanks to try to pull us out but couldn't. The rest of the company then left on the road march and our crew stayed behind with the tank.

These Russians had been liberated, seventeen of them, including one woman, all in uniform.Well, there was a monastery nearby, but we Americans felt we couldn't and didn't go in it. It was like "King's X" to us, but not to the Russians. They went into the monastery, terrorized the inhabitants, and found that a liquor dealer had put his stock in there for safekeeping. The Russians grabbed all they could carry, and we had the biggest drinking party you can imagine. There was even Johnny Walker Red label, cases of it. We celebrated V-E Day right there, and it was quite an experience.

All company bivouacs were north of Munich, and each of course had a party. George Brookstein believes that the champagne and cognac he had discovered just after crossing the Rhine had been saved for victory celebrations.

Judging from the account of Paul Gaul, however, C Company may have had the biggest bash. Gaul, as we have seen, was with B Company until improprieties led to his transfer to C Company as a tanker.

Now, I want to tell you something, the guys in B Company were a nice bunch, but those guys in C Company—why I never saw so much booze, drinking, and carrying on. Man, did we ever celebrate the end of the war. But never in my life was there anything better to celebrate!

I had made it. The survivor. It hadn't been all bad. Iceland was boring, in England I learned to drink warm beer. The invasion scared the hell out of me—I was sure I was going to be killed. God knows I saw many of my buddies die, among them Calderari, Hammersmith, Gallow, Trujillo, Papke, and Record. Hell, most of them I didn't even know their first names, ain't that a bitch! All I do know, the guy who said "War is hell" must have been there. I was twenty-two years old going on fifty. The war had interrupted my education. I didn't even graduate from high school, enlisted at eighteen—what a dummy!

In the course of the war, the 70th had 184 killed in action, with 709 Purple Hearts issued and twenty-one prisoners of war, for a total of 914 battle casualties. Michael Varhol, a 70th staff officer from the beginning, has estimated that 95 percent of these casualties were tankers. Yet, with chances of being killed or wounded in a tank so high, brave men of the 70th Tank Battalion went on, many of them through eight major campaigns. That only a few of them broke is a marvel.

The 70th Tank Battalion was at the center of events. It was there when the first shots were fired in French Morocco on November 8, 1942, and when the last shots were fired on May 7, 1945. It had been a long, grueling war. The 70th had done all that was asked, and more. Time after time, the men of the 70th were called upon for dangerous and important assignments. They were proud of what they had accomplished. Now it was time to go home.

Epilogue

Clarence McNamee saw a shell take a buddy's head "right off his shoulders . . . You couldn't dwell on it for long, but it made you sick at the time."

Some men even now cannot deal with the memories of agony, of the terror, with the killing and the maiming of buddies they knew well. Several told me they still have nightmares when thinking or talking about the war, and they could not be interviewed for this book.

Dealing with the war is such an individual matter, just as was dealing with fear on the battlefield. Some of the men broke down during interviews while describing details of the horror, particularly with the death of comrades.

Yet, 70th veterans wished me well whether they could contribute or not. They believe we owe it to posterity to tell the story of the 70th. Their experiences are the stuff of history.

Fifty years after losing both legs on D day, John Ahearn said, "In retrospect, the war was the most exciting thing I have ever participated in. People ask, 'How can you say that?' Because it was. It was a unique experience. It was a historical experience, not that you thought much about that at the time."

This is not to glorify war—far from it. Certainly the men who have spoken here would not glorify such legalized mass violence. It is unlikely that they would speak of war at all in general terms. The war they speak of is the war they experienced, *their* war, not only what they did in it but what they learned from it.

The great majority of them were brought into it by a mix of motives: excitement; adventure; the stimulus of risk; the gamble with fate; the challenge of their yet untried strength, stamina, and courage; the obligation to serve their country in time of need. In action all these merged and were put to the test.

But through all the terrifying surprises, shocks, and fury of combat, where death was always present, they discovered one great sustaining value—self-transcendence, where the good of the individual is identified with the good of his comrades. Above all other motives and values, this mutual dedication of fellow soldiers firmed up their resolve and heightened their morale.

Bob Knoebel, after being liberated from a German hospital in Rennes, Brittany, was sent to a hospital in Scotland. His recuperation was in England. "I didn't have to go back. I could have stayed in England in some safe, cushy job. But who do you trust? You trust the guys you knew. So I wanted to go back with the 70th. I had been with them a year, and you develop a lot of trust and friendship in a year."

John Ahearn was awarded a Distinguished Service Cross and a Silver Star. Asked why men fight heroically, he responded:

Recently when people were getting up in Congress on the flag issue, saying that men died for the flag, for a symbolism, I said bullshit. First of all there were no flags around, there was no standard out there. Men didn't die for the flag, or even in the heat of combat for their country; they died for their companions. They did things for their companions. You don't know the broad picture, at least I didn't. I knew my particular assignment, my platoon's assignment, my company's assignment. They were my concern. All fighting men are concerned about their fellows.

Such loyalty has been a part of war for ages. Every young Athenian soldier in ancient Greece swore to an oath: "I will not leave my comrade wherever I am stationed on the battlefield."

To endure through eight major campaigns, each man had to summon all of his inner strength and courage. He also knew he could rely on the 70th. He knew there would be cohesion among all units, and that in the 70th was the discipline to prepare for battle down to the last detail. Esprit de corps is often what makes the difference in a unit, and in the 70th esprit de corps never wavered.

Albert Pachella of C Company recorded that, no matter the situation, "You never had to look back to see if you were being covered. If it was called for, you always were. The 70th men were dependable. They knew what was to be done and did it."

When Cecil Nash and two fellow crewmen lay seriously wounded in a field just beyond the Huertgen Forest, he sent the two remaining unwounded crewmen for help. "I told them to find our people and tell them we were in trouble. I said 'our people,' the 70th, because they would know what to do and would be loyal to us."

The quotation in the introduction to this book is from Oliver Wendell Holmes, Jr. "Don't call me Hero. I trust I did my duty as a soldier respectably, and did nothing remarkable."

It was his duty to be a soldier. His nation was in great danger, as it was for the men of the 70th in World War II. Nowhere in his writings does Holmes lament his being called upon to serve.

Neither do the men of the 70th. Like Holmes, they fought as free men in defense of that very freedom. Also like Holmes, they returned to peacetime pursuits, confident that the job they had done had been worth doing, and they had done it well, even if they had done "nothing remarkable."

Notes

Chapter 1

1. Varhol enlisted in the army in 1934, hoping for a rare West Point appointment. After serving his "hitch," he was discharged and appointed a second lieutenant in the army reserve. He reentered active duty with the 70th in September 1940. He served as battalion adjutant until ordered to the Command and General Staff College, Fort Leavenworth, Kansas, in February 1945. He retired a full colonel in 1972 from the top-secret Army Security Agency.

2. Constance Green, *The Ordnance Department, U.S. Army in World War II* (Washington, D.C.: Department of the Army, 1955), p. 282.

3. George Forty, *U.S. Tanks in World War II* (Poole, Dorset, England: Blandford, 1983), p. 11.

4. "History of the 70th Tank Battalion" (70th Tank Battalion Association, 1950), p. 19.

5. Ibid.

6. Ibid., p. 20.

Chapter 2

1. Winston Churchill, *The Hinge of Fate* (Boston: Houghton Mifflin, 1950), p. 130.

2. Material on the saga of *Stone* from S. E. Morison, *Operations in North African Waters* (New York: Little, Brown, 1947), pp. 210–211.

3. Martin Blumenson, *Patton Papers* (Boston: Houghton Mifflin, 1972–1974), p. 110.

4. S. E. Morison, pp. 124–125.

5. Carl Sandahl, the author's friend since childhood, was at Rabat and Port Lyautey about a year later as part of an ordnance group providing the French with equipment. He became friends with several French officers who had been at Port Lyautey during the landings. They had been assured that this was a German landing. How long this was believed Sandahl was not told.

6. Krumwiede lost a leg by amputation on board USS *John Penn.* After about three months at Moore General Hospital in Swannanoa, North Carolina, he was transferred closer to home at Percy Jones

General Hospital, Battle Creek, Michigan. Here a young army surgeon, Dr. West, managed to save his remaining leg. Unfortunately, West was transferred to Gardner General Hospital in Chicago long before the leg was out of danger of amputation. Krumwiede asked for a transfer but was denied. The doctor who took over his case was either malicious or incompetent, or both. On one occasion he endangered a bone graft, whereupon Krumwiede took a heavy hospital drinking glass in his hand and told the doctor the next time he entered the room the glass would be bounced off his noggin. Colonel Kirk, the hospital commandant, soon approved the transfer. Back in the hands of Dr. West at Gardner, Krumwiede made good progress. He did so well that he regularly appeared on radio shows and on platforms on war bond drives. Granted a year furlough with rations, Krumwiede went home to Cicero and took a job at a war manufacturing plant. After his discharge from the army, he began several careers, which lasted until he became 100 percent disabled in 1969. He now resides in Tucson.

7. Official Historical Records and After Action Reports, C Company.

8. Ibid.

9. George Howe, *Northwest Africa: U.S. Army in World War II* (Washington, D.C.: Department of the Army, 1957), p. 164.

10. 70th Tank Battalion Association, p. 26.

11. Ibid.

12. Ibid., p. 34.

13. Ibid.

14. Ibid., p.35.

Chapter 3

1. Dwight Eisenhower, *Crusade in Europe* (Garden City, New York: Doubleday, 1948), p. 125.

2. Official Historical Records and After Action Reports, A Company. This detachment was part of the 82d Airborne Division. On D day at Utah Beach, June 6, 1944, the intrepid Colonel Raff was again in the heat of action in the same place as the 70th.

3. Dwight Eisenhower, p. 125.

4. Official Historical Records and After Action Reports, A Company, January 5, 1943.

5. Dwight Eisenhower, p. 147.

6. Omar N. Bradley, *A Soldier's Story* (New York: Henry Holt, 1951), p. 40.

7. Constance Green, p. 286.

8. Omar N. Bradley, pp. 40–41.

9. Dwight Eisenhower, pp. 148–150.

10. 70th Tank Battalion Association, p. 27.

11. Time/Life, *The War in the Desert* (Alexandria, Va: Time/Life Books, 1978), p. 193.

Chapter 4

1. Winston Churchill, *Closing the Ring* (Boston: Houghton Mifflin, 1950), p. 27.

2. Carlo D'Este, *Bitter Victory* (New York: Harper Perennial Edition, 1991), p. 275.

3. German air activity over the landing area was constant. One German raid took place almost simultaneously with an airdrop of the 82d Airborne Division on the night of July 11, 1943. Mistaking U.S. C-47s for German bombers, gunners on U.S. ships and antiaircraft batteries on land opened fire on the low-flying transports. It was one of the greatest blunders of the war. Twenty-three planes were destroyed and thirty-seven were badly damaged; 229 U.S. paratroopers were killed. See Time/Life, *The Italian Campaign* (Alexandria, Va: Time/Life Books, 1978), p. 24–27.

4. *Official 70th Tank Battalion Unit Journal,* July 15, 1943.

5. 70th Tank Battalion Association, p. 42.

6. Ibid., pp. 41–42.

7. Ibid., pp. 47–48.

8. Frank Suleski was first moved to a transit prisoner-of-war camp near Naples called Capua. Next he was loaded onto a train with officers and other noncoms. It was a four-day trip, day and night, up through the Brenner Pass and all the way to Stalag 2B, Hammerstein, a few miles from the Baltic. Suleski and his mates were locked in a cattle car, the kind with slatted sides. "The car was so crowded no one could lie down. There were no toilets; excrement was just pushed out. We were given only a pail of water once or twice a day, and for food a couple of loaves of black bread a day."

An analysis by the Military Intelligence Service, War Department, described treatment at Stalag 2B as the worst in any German camp established for American prisoners-of-war before the Battle of the Bulge. Suleski was here for twenty-one months until Soviet artillery could be heard. On January 28, 1944, he and his fellow POWs began a forced march west under guard. They averaged about fourteen miles a day, six days a week, for nearly three months. It was bitterly cold in February and well into March. Ill with hepatitis, Suleski kept going, fearing the consequences of being abandoned. On April 13, after nearly 1,000 miles, the American line was so close that Suleski just walked to them. He weighed 118 pounds and was hospitalized until discharged with a disability on January 11, 1946. He lives in Utica, New York.

While visiting the castle in Heidelberg, Germany, in 1981, I conversed with a caretaker who as a soldier in the German army was taken prisoner by Americans while in North Africa. He was sent to southern California, where he picked fruit. Later he was assigned to pick fruit in Georgia. While there, he was once in a group that got to meet FDR in Warm Springs. Although this case and that of Suleski are not necessarily representative, the United States did treat its prisoners far better than did Germany.

9. 70th Tank Battalion Association, p. 44.

10. Ibid., pp. 44–45.

11. *Official 70th Tank Battalion Unit Journal,* July 25–26, 1943.

Chapter 5

1. 70th Tank Battalion Association, p. 8.

2. Omar N. Bradley, *A Soldier's Story,* p. 41.

3. George Forty, p. 14.

4. Warrant officer (WO) was a separate grade with most of the privileges of commissioned officers. Officers' clothing was worn, and the individual rated a salute from an enlisted man. Warrant officers were called "Mister" and were specialists in communications, clerical, and maintenance. They ran their sections, though with ultimate responsibility assigned to a commissioned staff officer.

5. Norman Longmate, *The GIs: The Americans in Britain, 1942–1945* (New York: Charles Scribner's Sons, 1975).

6. I asked Stella if Jews in Britain knew about what later was called

the "Holocaust" in Nazi Germany and in occupied countries. She answered, "As far as I knew, leaders in Jewish communities in London did know, as did leaders in America. When we were still living in London, I overheard my parents and aunts and uncles discussing the fact that in Germany Jews were being killed, taken away, or beaten, and businesses stolen without notice or provocation. My aunt said, 'If Hitler comes to England, all Jews will throw themselves into the Thames.' I can still remember how this struck terror in my young heart." (This was 1939 or 1940.)

7. Nigel Lewis, *Exercise Tiger* (New York: Prentice Hall, 1950), pp. 34–35.

8. Nigel Lewis, p. 21.

9. Five landing sites were chosen: three British and Canadian and two American (Utah and Omaha). American beaches were on the right, British and Canadian on the left, because the first American divisions to arrive were put in southwest England. To switch beaches would have meant a crisscross of transportation in England. See Carlo D'Este, *Decision in Normandy* (New York: Dutton, 1983), p. 72.

10. Nigel Lewis, pp.34–35; Paul Fussell, *Wartime* (New York, Oxford University Press, 1989); and Ken Small, *The Forgotten Dead* (London: Bloomsbury, 1988). Lewis has a thorough treatment of the affair. Fussell is highly critical. For an account of one Englishman's efforts at uncovering the story, see Ken Small.

11. 70th Tank Battalion Association, p. 34.

Chapter 6

1. B Company Daily Journal, June 6, 1944.

2. DDs were scheduled to lead infantry ashore at H hour at all five beaches. This required exact timing, which proved impossible to execute, because of water currents and swells. When and where to launch became a matter of estimate rather than precision. According to R. P. Hunnicutt [*Sherman, A History of the American Medium Tank* (Novato, Calif.: Presidio Press, 1994)], the U.S. 741st Tank Battalion lost twenty-seven DDs launched at great distance in heavy seas at Omaha Beach. The navy, noting the dangerous conditions, took the DDs of the U.S. 743d Tank Battalion all the way to shore. The same was done for two British units.

Hunnicutt goes on to say that the 70th, one British, and two Canadian units landed their DDs successfully, though they were launched at closer range than originally intended. In the confusion resulting from the change of plans, he writes, most of the DDs landed after the infantry was ashore.

The 70th successfully landed all twenty-eight DDs that were actually launched, but they arrived about fifteen minutes late. C Company regular tanks and dozers came in on LCTs and were on shore prior to the DDs.

Yet even this fact does not necessarily mean that the innovative DDs were of no use to the 70th at Utah. They were in place to go through the seawall as soon as the engineers blasted holes in it. Further, landing space on the beach was more limited for LCTs than for DDs. This was a very important factor. DDs could land in places where LCTs couldn't, and they could be in position immediately upon reaching shore.

George Forty, in *U.S. Tanks in World War II*, states that, "A complete brigade of Sherman DDs was used on D day in the British and Canadian sectors, and they were the only gun tanks that managed to get ashore to support the assault."

Confidence in DDs to lead assaults on beaches open to the sea was obviously misplaced. Rivers were another matter. Forty and Hunnicutt agree that the British used DDs in assault crossings over the Scheldt, Rhine, and Elbe. They were never used again by Americans. The existence of DD tanks was not made public until September 1945.

3. 70th Tank Battalion Association, p. 61.

4. Ahearn's smile was reassuring, a gesture of a superb leader at a critical time. Gavigan did not see Ahearn again for nearly fifty years. Through all the years his image of Ahearn was of that smile at a momentous moment of his life.

5. Stephen E. Ambrose, *D-Day, June 6, 1944: The Climactic Battle of World War II* (New York: Simon and Schuster, 1994), pp. 282–283, 293.

6. 70th Tank Battalion Association, p. 61.

7. Ibid., p. 63.

Chapter 7

1. Carlo D'Este, *Decision in Normandy*, p. 155. D'Este quotes a British postwar analysis concluding that the effects of Allied air attacks were reduced 75 percent.

2. Ibid., p. 291.

3. Ibid., pp. 87, 206.

4. Ibid., p. 153.

5. "I ended up in a German hospital where German surgeons operated on me several times. Each time they took out a handful of shrapnel. They were very short of medical supplies. For an example, they washed bandages and used them again. We got one meal a day. There was no harassment or threats or anything like that. At first I was in a ward with Germans." Knoebel was moved to several hospitals. "The first move was in a truck with Germans. We stopped and some French came out to give us milk. The Germans told the French I was an American, and one Frenchman winked at me. I'll never forget that; I guess he was telling me he was my friend." He also remembers taking a bus trip. "Again I was the only American, and this time we went to a hospital in Rennes. I was hit mainly in my leg, and after a long bus trip I couldn't even get off my seat. I was sitting next to a German paratrooper who was all banged up. He motioned to me to just sit there, and he got out of the bus and told someone to get a stretcher for me, which they did. So they treated me fairly."

On August 8, the U.S. 8th Division neared Rennes. "Before they captured the city, the Germans took everyone who could walk, and left the rest of us behind. As soon as I was in American hands, they flew me to Scotland. I had been a prisoner two months. All that time my wounds had been seeping, and they still were when I got to the hospital in Scotland. This was about the time that penicillin was first being used, and, as soon as they put it on my wounds, they cleared." He still had to go through rehabilitation for several months. "Everybody talks about the Red Cross, but I tell you, I swear by them. They treated us very well in the hospital and took us on trips to neighboring towns in Scotland. When I was fit for duty, I could easily have stayed in Scotland or England in some capacity, but I wanted to get back to my outfit, to my buddies, so I did."

6. Gavigan was operated on in a hospital in England. "The buzz bombs [German V-1] were coming in so often that they moved me from the Channel coast to Ayr, Scotland. My wound was in the hip and leg. The sciatic and other nerves were shattered. I was sent home, where they did all they could for me, but my hip was never the same. I used crutches for years. Now I am in a wheelchair."

7. 70th Tank Battalion Association, p. 64.

8. Ibid., p. 65.

9. B Company Daily Journal, June 25, 1944.

10. Russell F. Weigley, *Eisenhower's Lieutenants* (Bloomington, Ind.: University of Indiana Press, 1981), p. 105.

11. B Company Daily Journal, June 25, 1944.

Chapter 8

1. Carlo D'Este, *Decision in Normandy,* p. 341. Also quoted are other top Allied commanders who agree that in planning the campaign they underestimated the difficulties of the *bocage.*

2. Ibid., p. 341.

3. Russell F. Weigley, p. 129.

4. 70th Tank Battalion Association, p. 66.

5. Ibid., p. 68. Tank #1 would be the 1st Platoon leader's tank. Carl Hallstrom survived the war.

6. B Company Daily Journal, July 10, 1944.

7. Russell F. Weigley, p. 149.

8. Ibid., pp. 151–152.

9. Carlo D'Este, *Decision in Normandy,* p. 402.

10. 70th Tank Battalion Association, p. 75.

11. Omar N. Bradley, *General's Life* (New York: Simon and Schuster, 1983), p. 281.

12. 70th Tank Battalion Association, p. 76.

13. Ibid., p. 137.

14. Russell F. Weigley, p. 197.

15. B Company Daily Journal, August 11, 1944

16. 70th Tank Battalion Association, p. 77.

Chapter 9

1. I saw Jacqueline briefly the next morning. Letters were exchanged throughout the remainder of the war. On my way home af-

ter the war, I saw her again on a twelve-hour pass into Paris. Without question, these were among the most beautiful ten or so hours of my life. She has ever remained my Beatrix, a lovely eighteen-year-old woman in a yellow dress with blue polka dots.

2. 70th Tank Battalion Association, p. 78.

3. Ibid., p. 79.

4. Ibid.

5. Ibid.

6. Ibid., p. 80.

7. Ibid.

Chapter 10

1. 70th Tank Battalion Association, p. 85. This area had been fought over countless times before. In 1643, France defeated Spain in the battle of Rocroi, thereby establishing land supremacy in this part of Europe.

2. 70th Tank Battalion Association, p. 85.

3. Ibid., p. 86.

4. Winston Churchill, *Triumph and Tragedy* (Boston: Houghton Mifflin, 1953), pp. 204–205. Also, Dwight Eisenhower, *Crusade in Europe* (Garden City, N.Y.: Doubleday, 1948), p. 288.

Chapter 11

1. William Walton, "Battle of the Huertgen Forest," *Life* magazine (January 1, 1945), pp. 33–36. Hürtgen has been anglicized to Huertgen to eliminate the need for umlauts.

2. Mack Morris, *Yank* (January 14, 1945). *Yank* was the U.S. Army magazine in Europe.

3. Ibid.

4. These were fresh frozen turkeys all the way from the States—a marvelous feat for the time.

5. Nash was moved to a hospital in Liège. "The cast on my right leg was open faced and I could see my foot getting bluer every day. On the fifth day they amputated close to the hip. It had to be. It couldn't be any other way." His left leg was severely injured and nearly amputated. "They saved it, though the knee is permanently stiff and I can't bend it. Other than that, I was fortunate to get back alive after all those days, months, and years over there. I feel very lucky."

Nash convalesced at Bushwell General Hospital, Brigham City, Utah, until discharged with 80 percent disability on December 27, 1945. For twenty-two years Nash drove around rural Illinois selling insurance. "It was not easy during the winter, and I suffered several bad falls on the ice. Once I broke the bucket (or cup) on my artificial leg and had to drive thirty miles to get it serviced." Then he had to use crutches, but he continued to work, though it was getting harder as his left leg continued to cause him trouble.

Nash's old C Company buddy, George Bailey, was assistant director of the Illinois veteran's department. Bailey also lost a leg when his tank was hit in the turret. With his help, Nash received a 90 percent disability, and eventually 100 percent. He has been confined to a wheelchair for years.

"The wheelchair I use was given to me by a hospital buddy in 1989," says Nash. "He was also badly shot up, and by then couldn't even use his wheelchair." The government rarely buys disabled veterans a wheelchair. "They loan it to you. In 1989–1990 I applied to Medicare for a power wheelchair, which was declined. They said need for power wasn't proven. I had a prescription from both a cardiologist and an orthopedic doctor, and a certificate of need from them." After several more attempts, Medicare declined to answer his appeals. With the help of his congressman, Nash finally got a written, final denial. "I'm not complaining. My pension has been adequate, though getting it raised wasn't easy. Without George Bailey I don't think it would have been raised so that I could retire." (I've seen George Bailey dance at several reunions. Artificial leg and all, he does wonderfully well.)

6. 70th Tank Battalion Association, p. 91.

7. Ibid.

8. "I figured I'd have a ball in Paris, but I didn't even get a shower." Everyone with a compound fracture was sent to England. "In England I mostly sacked out. The only discouraging thing in that hospital ward was to find a bed that didn't have SIW on it—self-inflicted wound. The hospital was full of them." After three weeks with physical therapy, Rambo felt fit to leave. "The finger was in as good a shape as it is now. In January, a colonel doctor came through the ward, and I said, 'You might as well turn me out of here, I'm alright.' He looked at my chart and said, 'Looks like you've done enough for

a while.' So I said, 'If it suits you, it does me!' I stayed there until March. I missed the Battle of the Bulge. That's one thing I regret missing. The boys had a ball then. They were waitin' on them."

Rambo was sent to a replacement center. "You know who ran these centers? All officers from colonel on down who had been kicked out of the front line. They were all bastards, chicken as hell." He had corresponded with men in B Company and knew of his battlefield commission but had no evidence. Even as a staff sergeant, Rambo was put on guard. "Staff sergeants don't go on guard, but there is no rating at a replacement center." The 70th eventually found out where he was and sent someone to get him. When the lieutenant in charge was told Rambo was a lieutenant, he was very apologetic. "Why didn't you tell me you were a lieutenant?" Rambo told him he had no proof. "But he was the worst chicken li'l ole lieutenant I have ever witnessed. What a little bastard he was."

9. 70th Tank Battalion Association, p. 91.
10. William Walton, *Life,* pp. 33–36.
11. Carlo D'Este, *Decision in Normandy,* p. 141.
12. 70th Tank Battalion Association, p. 90.

Chapter 12

1. 70th Tank Battalion Association, p. 97.
2. Gossler, who now lives in Seattle, attended a 4th Infantry Division reunion in 1990. He talked with a veteran who after the Bulge was detailed to bury German dead from this battle. He said there were more than 200. The man had seen a memorial to these dead at Dickweiler.
3. 70th Tank Battalion Association, p. 99.
4. Ibid., p. 98.
5. Ibid., p. 97. (I had several good friends among the A Company cooks and well remember them serving as infantrymen. B Company cooks were not called upon. I narrowly missed the experience.)
6. 70th Tank Battalion Association, p. 98.
7. George Forty, p. 116.
8. Constance Green, p. 284.
9. Ibid., p. 278.
10. The two commendations are from 70th Tank Battalion Association, pp. 142–143.

Chapter 13

1. The anglicized spelling (Prüm).

2. 70th Tank Battalion Association, pp. 101–102.

3. Askov, Minnesota, was founded as a Danish community in 1906. The population in 1944 was about 325.

4. 70th Tank Battalion Association, p. 104.

5. Ibid., pp. 104–105.

Chapter 14

1. Stamping *H* for Hebrew on identification tags after learning of the Nazi murder of Jews seems in retrospect to border on criminal negligence, but, it would no doubt have been difficult if not impossible to change the practice in the middle of the war. Stamping religious preference apparently was done so the correct clergyman could perform the rites at burials—when burials were possible.

2. The Rothenburg hospital was civilian but staffed by German army doctors. "They never tortured me or anything like that, but psychologically they did one thing that scared the life out of me." He would be taken out of the hospital in an oversized carriage. "It was like a baby carriage. A German soldier would wheel me along, and civilians would stop and look at me, asking the soldier who he had in the carriage. He would wheel me underneath an archway and leave me at a door. I imagined they were going to gas me—kill me." This caused Brookstein to have nightmares for years. "He would just leave me there, return in an hour or so, then wheel me back. I don't know what the purpose was, but this was repeated three or four times. Of course this unnerved me. It was always the same soldier, and always the same door."

Brookstein had been in the hospital for about three weeks when there was a lot of activity. "The military doctors began kissing the nurses and civilian workers and left hurriedly with all other military persons. Within an hour, I saw 4th Division infantrymen enter the hospital. I had been liberated by my own division! What a great feeling this was."

He was transferred to an American hospital and remained there until the war was over. "I had enough points to go home, but I had unfinished business in England. Stella and I were married in Swindon and had a wonderful honeymoon."

Six months after the war, the U.S. government notified Stella that she could get passage on a ship to the United States. She reported to Southampton in early March 1946. Stella had all the necessary documentation, including a letter from her physician stating she did not have VD or TB. One day before the ship was to embark, all the wives were told to report to a gym, where they were told to take off all their clothing and put on a robe. "We expected to be ushered into a room with a doctor and a nurse, but that was not the case. Picture if you will, facing you were two tables near the back wall, lined with about eight GIs, not doctors or nurses. We were told to stand there, open our robes, and be checked with flashlights. Complete frontal nudity for these leering men to see. After the first few women exposed themselves, about fifty of us decided to walk out, refusing to be treated in such a humiliating manner." That evening a directive was sent to the wives, stating if they continued to refuse, they would not be allowed to join their husbands. "The next day we submitted to this horrendous treatment, feeling there was no way out. It was blackmail we had to pay. I get hot and cold today thinking of this forty-five years later. It was the epitome of sexual harassment, as we call it today."

3. 70th Tank Battalion Association, p. 113.

4. Woods's wounds were so severe that he didn't get home until 1946. He reenlisted and served a full thirty years. Woods and Trujillo had made a pact to visit each other's homes after the war. "He was to come to meet my parents in Mississippi, then I was to go to Belen, New Mexico, to meet his family." Through the years, Woods found it impossible to relive the death of his friend, as would have happened had he gone to see Joe's family. His interview with me was the first time he had talked about the incident. Yet, even now, "I would like to fulfill that pledge, though I don't know if I should reopen old wounds."

5. 70th Tank Battalion Association, p. 113.

6. Ibid., p. 114.

7. Ibid.

8. Russell F. Wiegley, p. 701. American intelligence first accepted the rumor of a redoubt, then doubted it but concluded they could not ignore the possibility.

Bibliography

I. PRIMARY SOURCES

Private Journals and Letters
John Ahearn (journal), Marvin G. Jensen (letters), Charles J. Myers (journal).

Official Historical Records and After Action Reports
A Company: November 8, 1942–December 21, 1944, Algeria; December 22, 1942–May 13, 1943, Tunisia.
C Company: November 8–13, 1942, Morocco; July 15–20, 1943, Sicily.
70th Tank Battalion: July 13–27, 1943, Sicily.

Unofficial Journal
B Company Daily Journal: July 15–September 21, 1943, in Sicily; December 1–20, 1943, in England; June 1, 1944–May 29, 1945, starting in England and ending in Bamberg, Germany.

Magazines
Life magazine, January 1, 1945.
Yank magazine, January 14, 1945.

II. ACCOUNTS OF VETERANS OF THE 70TH

Oral Interviews and Conversations
John Ahearn, Franklin Anderson, Raiford Blackstone, George Brookstein, Frank Ciaravella, James Feeney, Paul Gaul, Owen Gavigan, Edward Gossler, Frank Gross, Clarence Jay, Robert Knoebel, John Lovell, Robert McEvoy, Clarence McNamee, Cecil Nash, Albert Pachella, Carl Rambo, Louis Rizzo, Francis Ross, Francis Snyder, Francis Songer, Clarence Stodulka, Michael Varhol, Virgil Wagner, Atlee Wampler, Walter Waszyn, Floyd West, Alvin Woods, Anthony Zampiello.

Written Accounts
Raiford Blackstone, George Brookstein, Stella Brookstein, Robert J. Connors, Lawrence Krumwiede, Robert McEvoy, Joseph Nesbit, Frank Suleski, Michael Varhol.

III. SECONDARY SOURCES

Ambrose, Stephen E. *D-Day, June 6, 1944: The Climactic Battle of World War II*. New York: Simon and Schuster, 1994.

Blumenson, Martin. *Patton Papers*. Boston: Houghton Mifflin, 1972–1974.

Bradley, Omar N. *General's Life*. New York: Simon and Schuster, 1983.

————*A Soldier's Story*. New York: Henry Holt, 1951.

Churchill, Winston. *Closing the Ring*. Boston: Houghton Mifflin, 1950.

————*The Hinge of Fate*. Boston: Houghton Mifflin, 1950.

————*Triumph and Tragedy*. Boston: Houghton Mifflin, 1953.

D'Este, Carlo. *Bitter Victory*. New York: Harper Perennial Edition, 1991.

————*Decision in Normandy*. New York: Dutton, 1983.

Eisenhower, Dwight. *Crusade in Europe*. Garden City, N.Y.: Doubleday, 1948.

Forty, George. *U.S. Tanks in World War II*. Poole, Dorset: Blandford, 1983.

Fussell, Paul. *Wartime*. New York: Oxford University Press, 1989.

Green, Constance. *The Ordnance Department, U.S. Army in World War II*. Washington, D.C.: Department of the Army, 1955.

Hanson, Victor. *The Western Way of War: Infantry Battle in Classical Greece*. New York: Knopf, 1989.

Hart, B. H. Liddell. *The Rommel Papers*. New York: Harcourt, Brace, 1953.

Howe, George. *Northwest Africa: U.S. Army in World War II*. Washington, D.C.: Department of the Army, 1957.

Hunnicutt, R. P. *Sherman: A History of the American Medium Tank*. Novato, Calif.: Presidio Press, 1978.

Lewis, Nigel. *Exercise Tiger.* New York: Prentice Hall, 1990.

Longmate, Norman. *The GIs: The Americans in Britain, 1942–1945.* New York: Charles Scribner's Sons, 1975.

MacDonald, Charles. *European Theater of Operations, U.S. Army in World War II.* Washington, D.C.: Department of the Army, 1972.

Morison, S. E. *Operations in North African Waters.* New York: Little, Brown, 1947.

Small, Ken. *The Forgotten Dead.* London: Bloomsbury, 1988.

Stanton, Shelby. *Order of Battle: U.S. Army, World War II.* Novato, Calif.: Presidio Press, 1984.

Terkel, Studs. *The Good War.* New York: Pantheon, 1984.

Time/Life. The Battle of the Bulge.

———*The Italian Campaign.*

———*Liberation.*

———*The War in the Desert.* Alexandria, Va.: Time/Life Books, 1978.

"History of the 70th Tank Battalion." 70th Tank Battalion Association, 1950.

Weigley, Russell F. *Eisenhower's Lieutenants.* Bloomington, Ind.: University of Indiana Press, 1981.

Index